DRUPAL®: THE GUIDE TO PLANNING AND BUILDING WEBSITES

Drupal®

THE GUIDE TO PLANNING AND BUILDING WEBSITES

Cindy McCourt

Wiley Publishing, Inc.

Drupal®: The Guide to Planning and Building Websites

Published by
Wiley Publishing, Inc.
10475 Crosspoint Boulevard
Indianapolis, IN 46256
www.wiley.com

Copyright © 2011 by Cindy McCourt

Published by Wiley Publishing, Inc., Indianapolis, Indiana

Published simultaneously in Canada

ISBN: 978-1-118-06686-7
ISBN: 978-1-118-14983-6 (ebk)
ISBN: 978-1-118-14982-9 (ebk)
ISBN: 978-1-118-14981-2 (ebk)

Manufactured in the United States of America

10 9 8 7 6 5 4 3 2 1

For general information on our other products and services please contact our Customer Care Department within the United States at (877) 762-2974, outside the United States at (317) 572-3993 or fax (317) 572-4002.

Wiley also publishes its books in a variety of electronic formats and by print-on-demand. Some content that appears in standard print versions of this book may not be available in other formats. For more information about Wiley products, visit us at www.wiley.com.

Library of Congress Control Number: 2011930294

This book is dedicated to my family: to my husband, BJ, who encourages me to continuously learn; to my dad, Joe, who helped shape my understanding of the many aspects of management and business ethics; to my mother, Barbara, and brother, David, who are always there for me; and, finally, to Codi, who made sure to remind me when it was time for me to go for a walk.

— CINDY McCOURT

CREDITS

EXECUTIVE EDITOR
Carol Long

PROJECT EDITOR
John Sleeva

TECHNICAL EDITOR
Doug Vann

PRODUCTION EDITOR
Kathleen Wisor

COPY EDITOR
Paula Lowell

EDITORIAL DIRECTOR
Robyn B. Siesky

EDITORIAL MANAGER
Mary Beth Wakefield

FREELANCER EDITORIAL MANAGER
Rosemarie Graham

MARKETING MANAGER
Ashley Zurcher

PRODUCTION MANAGER
Tim Tate

VICE PRESIDENT AND EXECUTIVE GROUP PUBLISHER
Richard Swadley

VICE PRESIDENT AND EXECUTIVE PUBLISHER
Barry Pruett

ASSOCIATE PUBLISHER
Jim Minatel

PROJECT COORDINATOR, COVER
Katie Crocker

PROOFREADERS
Lynne Burke, Word One, New York
Paul Sagan, Word One, New York

INDEXER
Johnna VanHoose Dinse

COVER DESIGNER
Ryan Sneed

COVER IMAGE
© Martin Strmko / iStockPhoto

ABOUT THE AUTHOR

CINDY MCCOURT has been a freelance website planner and builder, instructional designer and instructor, project manager, and facilitator, and has taken part in planning and building numerous Drupal and non-Drupal websites and web-based systems over the past 14 years. In 2005, she built her first Drupal website using Drupal 4.6 and has been using Drupal on her website development projects ever since.

Over the past 20 years, Cindy has been designing, developing, and delivering workshops and courses on technology- and non-technology-based subjects for both corporate and higher education organizations. She has also written technical papers on many topics for governmental and private-sector clients. Cindy maintains a close relationship with the Drupal community through her blog (`http://idcminnovations.com`), by speaking at Drupal events, and by offering Drupal training. She has been described by some in the Drupal community as a professional cat herder (`http://rocktreesky.com/professional-cat-herder-win`).

Cindy started acquiring many of her skills in 1985, when she went to work for TRW. Her 12 years at this worldwide contractor provided her with significant insights into project management and the many tasks associated with the lifecycle of a project. She was also an early TQM facilitator and trainer, and has made process analyses, design, and improvement tools in her web development toolbox.

Cindy built her first website for George Mason University's Graduate School of Education in 1997 and maintained the site until she graduated in 2000 with a Masters degree in Education. She went to work for GMU in 1999 and continued to build her web development skills by developing several more department websites, as well as by designing and coordinating the development of the online Workshop and Events Management System (WEMS), which is still used today by GMU's Division of Instructional Technology. She has also taught Instructional Design, Project Management, and Web Design for GMU's Graduate School of Education, and provided technology workshops to GMU's faculty and staff.

Cindy's extensive project list can be found at `http://idcminnovations.com/projects/listall-projects`.

ABOUT THE TECHNICAL EDITOR

DOUG VANN is an independent Drupal Developer and Trainer.

Doug entered Geekdom as a fifth grader in 1983 with a Commodore 64 and a 300-baud connection to CompuServe. Twenty-eight years later, he leads the Indiana Drupal Users Group and is a full-time provider of Drupal Training and Drupal Development.

Doug believes in the power of Drupal to meet complex business needs in a rapid-deployment system. Catch his blog at www.dougvann.com. Google "Drupal Song," and you're likely to find a few videos of Doug, jamming on the guitar, unabashedly proclaiming his passion for Drupal!

His love for learning and experimenting in Drupal is overshadowed only by his love for teaching and evangelizing it. He has presented in Minneapolis, Toronto, Houston, Indianapolis, multiple LinuxFests, DoItWithDrupal, and DrupalCamps in Dallas, Madison, Atlanta, Chicago, Orlando, Nashville, Denver, Los Angeles, South Carolina, and DC. You can often find Doug on the FREENODE IRC Network in Drupal-support helping people get through the steep learning curve of Drupal.

Doug, his wife of 14 years, and their four children reside in Indianapolis.

ACKNOWLEDGMENTS

I WANT TO THANK BJ for being the most supportive husband one could ask for. Thank you for your patience and understanding over the past six months as I worked to finish the book. Thank you for taking care of all the things that would have been a significant distraction to me. I love you.

I want to thank everyone at Wrox for giving me this opportunity. Thank you to John Kennedy, for bringing my book to the attention of executive editor Carol Long; to Carol Long, for reaching out to me and for convincing Wrox to give me a chance; to project editor John Sleeva, copy editor Paula Lowell, and technical editor Doug Vann, for all your efforts editing the chapters and for helping me improve my writing and the book's content — your energy and enthusiasm were incredible; and to all the people in the graphics department, for your work on all the figures.

I also want to thank all my friends and colleagues who have been supportive throughout the writing process — for listening, answering questions, and being helpful. Special thanks go to Carla Briceno, for your positive thinking and feedback; to Konstantinos Ordoulidis and Evangelia Ordoulidou, for making your theme comps available for use in the book; and to Emma Jane Hogbin, for encouraging me to write the book in the first place.

Last but not least, thank you to Dries and the Drupal community for making Drupal possible and sharing your expertise. I have learned so much from you over the past five years — from your modules, themes, tutorials, and books. Thanks for providing help to me and to all those who reach out for assistance. You are so generous.

— CINDY McCOURT

CONTENTS

FOREWORD

This book is about directing diverse forces toward a unified goal: the completion of a web project. While the goal in this case is very specific — a Drupal website — in many ways, it outlines successful steps for completing *any* life project, including Drupal itself.

I started the Drupal project in my dorm room in 2001, with no expectation that it would ever become big outside my circle of friends. But it grew, leaving that circle to power KernelTrap.org (which still runs on Drupal) and then, famously, the website for Howard Dean's 2004 presidential campaign. Drupal's gone through three major updates since then, and each time the Drupal community learns more about how to apply project management techniques to its development.

But, as with many projects, planning for Drupal was often *ex post facto*. I wrote it for a small, specific purpose: when it escaped the confines of my expectations, the Drupal community had to refactor it, sometimes ripping out large sections. Partly such changes were necessary because we wanted to take advantage of new web technologies, such as RDF for Drupal 7 and HTML5 for Drupal 8. But, sometimes they were because we didn't have a systematic method to plan and build.

This book provides that systematic method — but for Drupal websites. Few are the web builders who haven't created a "quick and dirty" site at some point in their careers, and then regretted it later when they had to make changes. We know why we do it: we're in a rush and don't think the project is worth the extra time.

However, once you learn proper planning techniques, you'll find that they don't add time to your project, because they reduce the number of revisions and corrections needed later. That's why I'm excited about this book. It will help people build Drupal websites the right way. And the more Drupal sites that are built well from the beginning, the better people will feel about Drupal overall.

The proof that Ms. McCourt understands her subject is in your hands, for this book is an expression of her ability to direct diverse forces toward a unified goal. I hope that it helps you harness the forces affecting your own Drupal website project, and look forward to seeing the results.

— Dries Buytaert
Founder and Project Lead, Drupal (drupal.org)
Co-founder and CTO, Acquia (acquia.com)

INTRODUCTION

IN JUST MINUTES, you can install a basic Drupal site and start adding content. In a few more minutes, you can have a new feature at your fingertips, ready to use, by installing one or more of the many modules that come with Drupal or any of the thousands of modules contributed by the Drupal community.

With so many modules to choose from, it is sometimes hard to know which modules are the right ones and how to best configure them to achieve your goals. This is where planning helps. In a nutshell, you identify what your site needs to do, decide what it should look like, and identify who will use it. With that information in hand, you can decide which Drupal installation and modules will give you the site of your dreams.

Sounds simple, and in some cases it is. You can plan a site, its development, and its future growth on a napkin over drinks. But most the time, it will take a little more planning to leverage the power and flexibility of the Drupal framework.

If you have never worked with Drupal before, you might be wondering how you can plan a site built with Drupal. One option would be to work side-by-side with web designers and developers who have experience with Drupal. But if you don't have access to those who can help, that's okay. This book provides a series of analyses and tasks that will enable you to start thinking in Drupal and help you plan each phase of your site's lifecycle.

I hope you find this book helpful as you venture forward on your next Drupal project.

WHO THIS BOOK IS FOR

If you are involved in or responsible for collecting requirements, creating a design plan, planning development, coordinating implementation, and/or sustaining a site built with Drupal, this book is for you. You could be a site owner, project manager, requirements analyst, interface designer, and/or site developer. Note that the book is *not* intended for those looking for detailed instructions on how to install and configure Drupal.

WHAT THIS BOOK COVERS

The analyses and tasks provided in this book are not specific to Drupal, but they are presented from a Drupal perspective. The Drupal-specific notes provided throughout the chapters speak to Drupal 6 and Drupal 7, providing you with development insights as you move through the planning process. Chapter 9 plans a Drupal site and Chapter 10 offers a Drupal 6 and Drupal 7 module solution.

HOW THIS BOOK IS STRUCTURED

The order of the chapters reflects a site's lifecycle and the waterfall development methodology. However, the sequence of the chapters is not necessarily intended to promote the waterfall methodology. Analyses and tasks provided in the chapters can be performed in an order suitable to your project. If this is your first exposure to development, consider walking through the chapters in order so that you can make an informed decision about whether you want to adjust the sequencing on your own project.

➤ Part I: Planning Your Website

> ➤ Chapter 1, "Introduction to Drupal and Planning," provides a quick introduction to Drupal, an overview of a site's lifecycle, and where planning fits in.
>
> ➤ Chapter 2, "Managing Open Source Projects," provides insights into various development methodologies and management practices you might find useful on a Drupal project.
>
> ➤ Chapter 3, "Conducting a Needs Analysis," goes beyond asking the question "Do I need a site?" and identifies the purpose of your site and how your competitors might influence how you proceed.
>
> ➤ Chapter 4, "Collecting Requirements," offers a series of analyses designed to facilitate the identification and analysis of what your site needs to meet its purpose.
>
> ➤ Chapter 5, "Creating a Design Plan" provides a process for translating your requirements into a visual representation of your site.

➤ Part II: Building and Sustaining Your Website

> ➤ Chapter 6, "Planning Development," offers a process to identify a development solution that meets your specific requirements and design.
>
> ➤ Chapter 7, "Coordinating Implementation," covers site launch and more. It covers many of the non-development tasks that should be considered for a successful site launch.
>
> ➤ Chapter 8, "Sustaining the Site" explores both routine and planned maintenance for your Drupal site, as well as site-management tasks that support your site's users.

➤ Part III: An Example Site

> ➤ Chapter 9, "An Example Plan," puts into practice the analyses and tasks presented in Chapters 3 through 5.
>
> ➤ Chapter 10, "Example Build Recipes," creates a development plan and Drupal 6 and Drupal 7 module recipe that can be used to build the site defined in Chapter 9. It also describes how the site will be implemented and sustained.

WHAT YOU NEED TO USE THIS BOOK

There are references to Drupal settings, modules, and resources in notes throughout the book, so access to the Internet and a Drupal installation, while not required, might be useful. Analyses and tasks discussed in the book can be performed with pencil and paper, on a whiteboard, using various applications like Microsoft Word or Excel, or a with simple drawing tool. If you opt to perform these analyses and tasks, choose a strategy that works for you.

CONVENTIONS

To help you get the most from the text and keep track of what's happening, we've used a number of conventions throughout the book.

 The pencil icon indicates notes, tips, hints, tricks, and asides to the current discussion.

As for styles in the text:

➤ We *highlight* new terms and important words when we introduce them.

➤ We show keyboard strokes like this: Ctrl+A.

➤ We show file names, URLs, and code within the text like so: `persistence.properties`.

➤ We present code in two different ways:

```
We use a monofont type with no highlighting for most code examples.
We use bold to emphasize code that is particularly important in the present context
or to show changes from a previous code snippet.
```

ERRATA

We make every effort to ensure that there are no errors in the text or in the code. However, no one is perfect, and mistakes do occur. If you find an error in one of our books, like a spelling mistake or faulty piece of code, we would be very grateful for your feedback. By sending in errata, you may save another reader hours of frustration, and at the same time, you will be helping us provide even higher-quality information.

To find the errata page for this book, go to www.wrox.com and locate the title using the Search box or one of the title lists. Then, on the book details page, click the Book Errata link. On this page, you can view all errata that have been submitted for this book and posted by Wrox editors. A complete book list, including links to each book's errata, is also available at www.wrox.com/misc-pages/booklist.shtml.

If you don't spot "your" error on the Book Errata page, go to www.wrox.com/contact/techsupport.shtml and complete the form there to send us the error you have found. We'll check the information and, if appropriate, post a message to the Book Errata page and fix the problem in subsequent editions of the book.

P2P.WROX.COM

For author and peer discussion, join the P2P forums at p2p.wrox.com. The forums are a web-based system for you to post messages relating to Wrox books and related technologies and interact with other readers and technology users. The forums offer a subscription feature to email you topics of interest of your choosing when new posts are made to the forums. Wrox authors, editors, other industry experts, and your fellow readers are present on these forums.

At p2p.wrox.com, you will find a number of different forums that will help you, not only as you read this book, but also as you develop your own applications. To join the forums, just follow these steps:

1. Go to p2p.wrox.com and click the Register link.

2. Read the terms of use and click Agree.

3. Complete the required information to join, as well as any optional information you wish to provide, and click Submit.

4. You will receive an email with information describing how to verify your account and complete the joining process.

 You can read messages in the forums without joining P2P, but in order to post your own messages, you must join.

Once you join, you can post new messages and respond to messages other users post. You can read messages at any time on the Web. If you would like to have new messages from a particular forum emailed to you, click the Subscribe to this Forum icon by the forum name in the forum listing.

For more information about how to use the Wrox P2P, be sure to read the P2P FAQs for answers to questions about how the forum software works, as well as many common questions specific to P2P and Wrox books. To read the FAQs, click the FAQ link on any P2P page.

PART I
Planning Your Website

Introduction to Drupal Planning

The task of planning websites has fallen on the shoulders of project managers, graphic designers, software developers, requirements analysts, web strategists, user experience experts, and information architects, to name a few. All these roles have their own perspectives of how a site should look and come together. Their individual experiences and skills associated with planning sites influence what is included in the site, how it is built, and how it is maintained. Their planning processes will emphasize their strengths, and typically, there isn't anything wrong with that.

Unless the individuals filling these roles have some insight into what Drupal has to offer and how it gets the job done, the site plan could miss some features that could make the site even better than originally thought. It could also set expectations that Drupal does not support at the moment. With some insight into Drupal and how it works, any of the people in these roles can plan a Drupal site.

By the end of this book, you will have methods, tools, and techniques that can help you plan Drupal sites. By the end of this chapter, you should be able to recognize:

➤ The basics of how Drupal works

➤ Some basic Drupal-related terms

➤ How Drupal sites are different from HTML sites

➤ Phases of a Drupal site's lifecycle

EXPLORING DRUPAL

You likely know what Drupal is, but in case you do not, it is an open source content management system (CMS). It is used to build:

➤ Dynamically generated websites

➤ Web applications

➤ Document repositories

➤ E-commerce sites

➤ Learning sites

➤ And more

To plan a Drupal site, knowing a little about how Drupal works can help. Don't worry; you don't have to be a developer to understand some of the basics. The following is offered as insight and to help the team communicate. If you are going to be a builder, developer, or themer, this short introduction is a must-read.

THEMER

A *themer* is someone who develops the PHP, HTML, and CSS that define the page structure and appearance.

Drupal Components

You do not need to know how to build the site in order to plan what you want, but the more you know about what Drupal can do and how it does it, the better off you will be. Let's start by taking a high-level view of what makes up Drupal.

Drupal's insides can be broken into the following three categories:

➤ Data storage

➤ Modules (and all the other important code that makes Drupal run)

➤ Theme code

Data Storage

The content of your site and its configuration settings are stored in a database. By default, each website has its own database. You can configure multiple sites to share a database as well. So, if you are planning multiple sites that need to share the same data, this is possible.

On the topic of multiple sites sharing, you should also know that you can have multiple sites, each with its own database, sharing the same Drupal installation. For example, assume you provide Drupal training and host the training sites. You can run all the training sites from one installation of Drupal. Each training site would have its own database, but they would share the code that is Drupal.

Data in the database is only part of your storage needs. If you have any media files or documents that you want to upload to the site, Drupal stores those files, by default, in a directory on the server associated with the site. If you have sites sharing the Drupal installation, the files will be kept separate from each other unless the sites have been configured to do otherwise. The setting that tells Drupal where to save files is stored in the database for that site. This means a series of sites using the same installation of Drupal won't get their media and documents mixed up.

PUBLIC OR PRIVATE FILES

In Drupal 6, you have the option of making all your files either public or private. Drupal 7 provides support for both public and private files.

Modules

If you have talked to anyone about Drupal, you probably heard him or her say something like, "There is a module that will do that."

Drupal is made up of a series of scripts that work together to produce the features you see in your site via a browser. The most common scripts are referred to as *modules*. Modules are bundles of code that enable Drupal, you, and/or your site visitors to see or do something in your Drupal site.

Drupal modules can be categorized. Here are four categories often referred to in the Drupal community:

➤ **Core** — Core modules are required for Drupal to work. You can see these modules in the administrative module list, but you cannot disable them.

➤ **Core optional** — Optional modules provide functionality that you can add to your site. Some of the most commonly used modules will already be enabled for you by default, although you can disable them if you do not need them. Each new version of Drupal refines the number of core modules, making the enabling of commonly used features easier.

➤ **Contributed** — Contributed modules are pieces of code that you can add to enhance the functionality of your site. Contributed modules are developed and maintained by members of the community. Some contributed modules are now part of the core.

➤ **Custom** — Custom modules are pieces of code that you create to provide specific functionality for your site. Custom modules are maintained by you. You can contribute custom modules to the community, but unless someone wants to maintain the contribution for you, you will be responsible for its maintenance and support.

If you have a particular feature you want to include in your plan, searching `Drupal.org` for existing modules that might support that feature is sometimes helpful. Planning a feature whose module does not yet exist could impact how the site is developed, when it will be finished, and the skills you need on board to actually implement the site.

CORE MODULE ADDITIONS

Each time Drupal advances to another version, it increases (and sometimes decreases) the number of core modules. Drupal 7 is no exception. The most notable addition to Drupal 7 is the ability to add fields to content forms. This is supported in Drupal 5 and 6 by the Content Construction Kit (CCK) module. Now, CCK is part of Drupal 7. According to `Drupal.org`, more than 60 contributed modules were integrated into Drupal 7.

Themes

A Drupal *theme* refers to the bundle of code used to create what you see in the browser. In Drupal, that code is not restricted to the theme you install; you can also find theme code in:

➤   Drupal's core modules

➤   Contributed modules

➤   Custom modules

➤   The theme (or base theme)

➤   A subtheme (if a base theme is used)

When Drupal loads a page, it looks for instructions on how to display the content in a specific order. It starts with the subtheme (if used) and works its way back from there: subtheme, base theme, and then to various modules you have enabled, including Drupal's core modules. If you don't like what the theme code in a module does, you can override it in the theme itself.

If you are planning a site, why do you need to know about theming? There are costs associated with theme development that are not always easy to predict. The more features your site has, the higher the probability that your theme will need more than the basics you find in many free themes. Your Drupal themer will need your *comps*, your style guide, and wireframes to get started. To finish, your themer needs to know how the builder or developer will create the objects in the wireframes, and will need some access to the objects as they are added to the interface.

> **COMPS**
>
> A *comp*, short for *composition*, is a graphic depiction of a site page.

So, when you are planning your site development, keep in mind that unless you are going with the default theme settings in an off-the-shelf theme, your themer should be part of your development team to ensure collaboration is possible.

> **THEMES IN DRUPAL 7**
>
> Themes built for Drupal 6 will not work in Drupal 7. You must modify them. This is not a new scenario. Each time a new version of Drupal has come out, themes needed to be modified in order to run in the new version.
>
> Also, Drupal 7 ships with a new set of themes. The Bluemarine, Chameleon, and Pushbutton themes have been removed but still live on as contributed themes. Bartik is now the default user interface theme, and Seven is the default administration interface theme. Stark has been added to make analyzing Drupal's default HTML and CSS easier for themers.

Chapter 5, "Creating a Design Plan," provides additional information about how themes work and how to design your site with your theme in mind.

From Data to Site Structure

One of Drupal's components is data. It is important to understand how the data is used to create the site structure. Figure 1-1 illustrates the role data plays in the site.

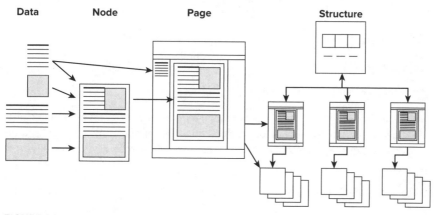

FIGURE 1-1

Imagine that you have a web form on the screen in front of you. You're going to use this form to create an article that will be on your site. You type the title in a field on the form; you go to the next field and type the article; maybe you assign the article to a menu and tag it with some predefined terms or add a few of your own terms.

The title, body, menu, and terms are data that get stored in the database. Other data get stored as well, such as the date when you created the article and your username. All these bits of data are associated with the article or node you just created.

Nodes are displayed in the main content area of a page and are the primary source for creating URLs. A series of pages linked together via some type of navigation forms the structure of the site.

While planning any site, you see the word *page* come up frequently. But what is a page in Drupal? You may see it referred to as:

➤ A content type (the online form used to collect your text and create a specific type of node)

➤ The web page you see in the browser

➤ The dynamic results of a database query (also known as a *view page*)

➤ The name of the theme template file that produces the web page you see in the browser

As you learn more about Drupal, the terminology will get easier to remember. To ensure positive and productive communication among the members of the site development team, remember that terms carry multiple meanings to people. This book helps you learn Drupal terminology that can help you communicate.

Drupal Terms

In addition to the concepts and terms introduced so far, Table 1-1 summarizes a few more terms that are helpful to know. Some of these terms may be foreign to you, and others may mean something completely different from what you are used to. If you are already familiar with the inner workings of Drupal and are simply reading this book to pick up some planning tips, feel free to skip this section.

TABLE 1-1: Common Drupal Terms

TERM	DESCRIPTION
Audience	Another word for user or site visitor.
Block	You can think of blocks as sticky notes, on a page, each note representing something you want to appear in a page. You can move them around and display them in different places in the page. Blocks are created from menu lists, manually, and by modules.
Contributed modules	Modules contributed by members of the community.
Core modules	Modules that come with Drupa.
Database	A series of tables made up of fields that contain data in the form of records or rows.
Drupal core	What you download from `Drupal.org` and install.
Fields	Spaces in a web form used to capture data. Fields are found in node forms as well as block forms and administrative forms. In Drupal, fields are provided by core and by other modules. You can use the fields to capture text, images, links, video, dates, and more.
Modules	Prepackaged bundle of code that adds functionality to or modifies Drupal's core.
Node	Commonly referred to as a "page" of content on a site. It is made up of data stored in fields and is associated with other descriptive data, such as author, date published, and taxonomy vocabulary terms.
Page	*Note: This term can be confusing.* A page in a Drupal site includes more than the node. It is made up of many components, such as header, footer, blocks, menus, and so on. "Page" represents the entire interface shown in the browser. Knowing the difference between a page and a node will be particularly important when communicating with themers, because you can theme a page and theme a node separately.

TERM	DESCRIPTION
Path	The URL of a node, or view, or term, etc. that appears in your browser's address bar.
Regions	Spaces in the page defined by the theme that can hold blocks. Not all themes have the same number of regions or region layout. Regions are planned during the design phase.
Roles	A bundle of permission settings that define what a user can do on the site. Default roles come with Drupal, but you can also create your own. There is one special "role" filled by the first user on the site. The first user on the site has permission to perform all tasks associated with the site. You cannot change the permissions of this user and its "role" because the "role" for this user is not defined the same as the other roles.
Tag	Another way of saying *term*.
Taxonomy	Taxonomy in Drupal is the feature that enables you to place content into categories, which you can use when organizing and describing your nodes.
Term	The words or phrases contained within a taxonomy vocabulary. Terms are used to categorize content. Terms are applied to nodes.
Theme	The feature in Drupal used to display a page and all its components. The theme is how you create the look and feel of the site. It defines the regions in which you can place blocks, a place where the node appears, and other components, such as Drupal's primary and secondary menus. You can't interact with Drupal unless you have a theme enabled. Garland is the Drupal 6 default theme. Bartik is the Drupal 7 default theme.
User	A term used to represent a person who "uses" the site.
Views	The term *Views* can refer to the module called Views or to a display generated by the Views module. The Views module is used to create database queries. Views can create blocks, pages (which act like nodes), RSS feeds, and more, depending on which modules you have installed and whether they integrate with Views. The Views module is the most common tool used to query the database and create displays of data that appear in a page. When you hear someone refer to a *view* in a Drupal site, it is likely they are referring to one of the displays the Views module produces.
Vocabulary	A vocabulary is the "container" in the site taxonomy used to collect terms that will be assigned to nodes. Vocabularies and their terms are used to organize, categorize, and describe the node.

GOING BEYOND HTML SITES

Now that you have some insight into how Drupal works, you have taken your first steps toward being able to think in Drupal. It might seem crazy, but it's true. When planning and building a Drupal site, you need to think differently than you may have done before, assuming you already have been exposed to web development. If you don't, you will likely limit what you can do on your site.

Traditional HTML website planning techniques fall short when used to plan a Drupal site. In an article comparing WordPress, Joomla!, Drupal, and Plone, Idealware said, "The flexibility of the [Drupal] system means it's important to think through the best way to accomplish what you want before diving in."[1]

Before systems like Drupal existed, sites often were created using HTML; later, CSS (Cascading Style Sheets) was added. Traditional planning techniques focused on designing a site from three perspectives:

➤ Designing the overall look and page layout

➤ The content that would be on each page

➤ Where each page falls in the site index

Flowcharts were used to represent every page on the site and how it related to other pages. Unless you were a savvy HTML developer, you would build one page at a time, linking the pages via a menu or some other embedded link on one or more pages. Not everyone who was responsible for content on the Web was willing or able to be an HTML developer.

As the number of pages in sites grew, the need for database-driven, code-based sites increased. These types of sites provided ways to automate menu updates and page development. It took skills to create database-driven, code-based sites. With systems like Drupal, the days of building a code-based site from ground up are over.

So, what changes when you go from the traditional HTML site development practices to using a CMS like Drupal? Table 1-2 provides a few differences for your consideration.

TABLE 1-2: HTML and Drupal

	HTML	DRUPAL
Page	HTML-coded file and other related files, such as images and CSS.	PHP program with multiple subprograms that dynamically create a page and all its components. The "page" that appears does not exist on the server as a file.
Layout	Beginners use tables for layouts. Advanced site developers use CSS for layouts. Can use templates or inserted library components to allow for fast updates across multiple pages.	Generated via a theme; the theme is made up of regions that allow various page configurations to appear given specific conditions.

[1] "2010 Comparing Open Source Content Management Systems: WordPress, Joomla, Drupal and Plone," Idealware, March 2009 (www.idealware.org/reports/comparing-open-source-content-management-systems-wordpress-joomla-drupal-and-plone)

	HTML	DRUPAL
Navigation	Anchor tags are embedded in the HTML file. Can be inserted anywhere in the page. Can be set as part of a template for easy updates.	Generated by one of the following modules: Menu, Views, Taxonomy, and more. The navigational data is stored in various tables in the database and called by the theme to appear in the page.
Content	Stored in its HTML file. Presented and formatted using HTML and CSS.	Stored in a database across multiple database tables. HTML sent to the browser is created dynamically with scripts.

If this comparison makes you nervous, don't be. You do not have to know how to code to make all this work. You just need to know that:

➤ The Drupal pages you see in a browser are not files on the web server.

➤ Much of what Drupal has to offer is accessed using its GUI (graphical user interface), much like other software applications.

➤ Drupal is a framework as much as it is a product, and therefore, you can shape it into what you want.

A WEBSITE'S LIFECYCLE

All websites have a lifecycle. Someone gets an idea and builds a site, the site is used, and the site goes away or becomes something different. This is probably obvious to you, so why bring it up?

The lifecycle of a site is a convenient way to illustrate the work that needs to be planned and performed. It addresses not only the site production but also what happens after the site is launched. If you know the path ahead, it is easier to anticipate and plan.

Figure 1-2 shows a simplified step-by-step process that represents what a site's lifecycle might be. The chapters in this book reflect this one-step-at-a-time approach because books are linear and, if this is your first exposure to the work performed to plan, build, and sustain a site, it is easier to experience it one step at a time.

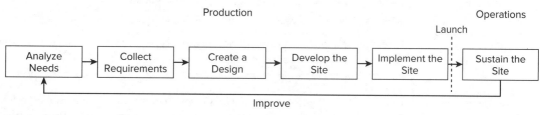

FIGURE 1-2

However, the work performed during production is seldom performed in this exact order. Figure 1-2 illustrates one extreme, whereas Figure 1-3 illustrates another. Figure 1-3 shows that production can be an iterative process — moving from requirements to design to development and back to requirements until all decisions have been made and all development has been completed. At the heart of the production process is the need for the site. Without that focus, your project scope can expand beyond its original intent.

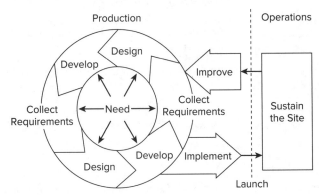

FIGURE 1-3

In reality, the production steps of a site during its lifecycle are something in between these two extremes. You can shape your production phase any way you want once you know the work that needs to be done. Chapter 2, "Managing Open Source Projects," explores different methods used to produce a site.

WHERE DOES PLANNING FIT IN?

The goal of those planning a Drupal website is the same as the goal that all roles have on a Drupal project: to help ensure the site is developed and delivered in such a way that it fulfills its purpose and meets the need. Table 1-3 describes planning tasks performed during the site's lifecycle.

TABLE 1-3: Planning in the Lifecycle

PHASE	DESCRIPTION
Analyze Needs	Identify why the site is needed and its purpose. Planning at this level helps to define the scope of the product and project.
Collect Requirements	Identify which features and functionality are required so that the site can meet its purpose. Planning upfront allows for different management, development, and implementation strategies to be considered before resources are expended.
Design the Site	Identify how the requirements will be delivered to the user. Planning the design before full development is underway gives the development team the opportunity to choose the appropriate tools to make the design possible.

PHASE	DESCRIPTION
Develop the Site	Work with the developers to evaluate technologies needed to support the requirements and design. Assess whether the development effort is worth the requirement or design strategy. Help decide where requirements and design can or should be changed to accommodate project management constraints. Help test the results to ensure they meet requirements and design expectations.
Implement the Site	Participate in or coordinate the transition from development to launch. Organize resources from the requirements, design, and development phases to ensure the site is populated with the appropriate content, that training (if necessary) is developed and delivered, and provide support where needed as the team prepares to launch the site.
Sustain the Site	After a site is live, it needs to be sustained. Depending on the site's purpose, plans need to be developed and executed so that services are provided, content is maintained and updated, the technology is maintained, and performance is managed.

SUMMARY

This chapter provided your first steps in being able to think in Drupal and start planning. Here are a few things to remember going forward:

➤   Drupal is more than a content management system; it is a data management system.

➤   Three components of Drupal are data, modules, and themes.

➤   In order to plan the work performed during a site's lifecycle, you need to know what work gets performed and in what order.

➤   Planning occurs at each step of the lifecycle.

The steps of the lifecycle don't just happen. They require someone to coordinate, facilitate, and, of course, manage them. Chapter 2 introduces different development methodologies that can be used for site production. It also provides some tips on how managing an open source project might differ from managing projects that use proprietary systems or create the system from scratch.

Managing Open Source Projects

Managing the production and operations of a CMS-based website has many facets. Managing a project that uses an open source CMS introduces some unique challenges that you might not have to consider otherwise. For instance, you don't have control over when updates are released for Drupal or its many contributed modules.

This chapter is not going to teach you how to be a project manager. Rather, it offers some insights into how using an open source CMS might require you to adjust the way you manage the production of your site. This chapter considers two perspectives of project management:

➤ Development methods

➤ The nine knowledge areas called out in the Project Management Institute's Project Management Body of Knowledge (PMBOK)

By the end of this chapter, you should be able to recognize:

➤ Different methods for managing the various tasks performed during the production process (needs analysis, requirements, design, development, and implementation)

➤ How open source technology can influence various project management tasks

DEVELOPMENT METHODOLOGIES

The benefits of using open source systems (with thousands of features you can simply turn on) can also be your biggest challenge when it comes to coordinating various aspects of a project. If you walk through the phases of a typical production lifecycle (analyze needs, collect requirements, create a design, develop, and implement) one at a time and do a good job carrying your documentation forward, you might not have many challenges when it comes to ensuring your requirements get implemented during development. But what happens if you use a method that is not perfectly linear like the one you saw in Figure 1-2?

Some people believe that unless you spend time collecting requirements and creating a big picture of what you want in the end, a non-linear approach to site production can give you solutions that can't support the big picture or might even create conflicts between site features.

> **PLANNING THE BIG PICTURE**
>
> Building a site is like building a house. You probably wouldn't design your living room and then build it without planning and building a foundation for the rest of the house at the same time. If you did, you would not have the foundation to support an entire house; you would just have the foundation for the living room. This example is a little extreme but not uncommon in a world with thousands of quick-fix solutions for the one problem you are facing at that moment.

Other people believe that you should dive into assembling your site's code as you decide what you want. Sure, why not? If you know the purpose of your site and a commonly used module recipe exists for that purpose, why not dive in and start with the obvious? This method is probably a little extreme as well, but it is not unheard of.

As with any set of extremes, something in between probably exists and makes more sense. The following descriptions provide brief introductions to some commonly used development methodologies that ultimately create your module recipe and produce a site. You will probably use aspects of a couple of methods to define how your site production will take place.

Waterfall Methodology

When using a traditional waterfall method, you perform one phase of the production lifecycle before moving on to the next. Figure 2-1 shows the same step-by-step process you saw in Figure 1-2, except it looks a little like a waterfall.

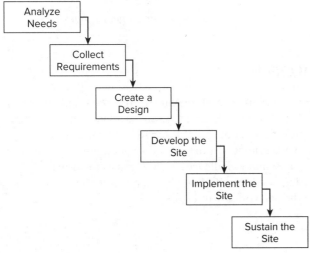

FIGURE 2-1

The names of the steps can vary. You can label the steps to be consistent with how your organization operates. The objectives are to complete one phase before moving on to the next and that the output from each task feeds into the next.

Following is a brief description of the type of work performed in each of these steps in this example waterfall.

➤ **Analyze needs** — Establish the site's purpose, identify how the site supports your goals, and determine if a site is your best course of action.

➤ **Collect requirements** — Based on the goals, gather, analyze, document, and evaluate your site requirements.

➤ **Create a design** — Based on the requirements, design your interfaces, workflow, interactions, information architecture, and various features you need developed.

➤ **Develop the site** — Based on the design and requirements, install, configure, organize, populate, develop, and test your site.

➤ **Implement the site** — Given the site and its purpose in your organization, manage the change the site will introduce in your organization, train your users, prepare your marketing campaign, and configure your site to go live.

➤ **Sustain the site** — Perform routine maintenance, planned maintenance, and site management tasks.

Advantages

An advantage to the waterfall method is that it creates an ordered project flow that you can schedule and manage step by step, making it easier to manage. Another advantage is that the outcome of the requirements and design phases gives you the basis for requesting a bid from a contractor, estimating schedules, and planning resources. If you do a thorough job with requirements and then design, project development has a greater chance of running smoothly.

Disadvantages

A potential disadvantage to the waterfall method is its perceived lack of flexibility. For instance, what happens if you need to change, delete, or add a requirement after development begins? This method implies that once the requirements are done, there aren't any changes. In reality, that is not the case, but the idea of waiting for all the requirements and design decisions to be made before the developers see them can introduce risks associated with requirements that are too costly to development or might extend the schedule.

Another potential disadvantage is the feeling that a lot of time is being spent talking and not doing: "It's been three months and we don't have a site." This does not necessarily mean you haven't been productive (or it might). If you have spent three months understanding what your site should do and building consensus among the project stakeholders, you increase your chances of receiving the funding and approvals you need to actually develop the site.

Others believe that you can't possibly know everything you need upfront, so why spend time planning a site that likely will change in the future? Although this is true to some extent, your not knowing the basics of what you want or need is unlikely. The fine details and specifications might be a little blurry upfront, but that should not stop you from scoping out the major functionality of the site.

In a perfect world, you can reduce these types of risks by involving designers and developers in the requirements and design phases. JAD (joint application design or joint application development) sessions bring stakeholders and responsible parties together in one room so that everyone can hear what is needed and why. Potential solutions are discussed and debated. By bringing together your best team members, you increase your chances of creating the best solution, as opposed to hearing about a great idea too late in the game.

 Chapter 4, "Collecting Requirements," briefly describes a JAD session and several other approaches you can use to facilitate collecting requirements.

Agile Methodologies

The Agile Manifesto is a set of principles that encourage collaborative interaction between the owner of the site and the development team. It promotes team development.

AGILE MANIFESTO'S 12 PRINCIPLES

The following principles can be found at `http://agilemanifesto.org/ principles.html`:

➤ Customer satisfaction by rapid delivery of useful software.

➤ Welcome changing requirements, even late in development.

➤ Working software is delivered frequently (weeks rather than months).

➤ Working software is the principal measure of progress.

➤ Sustainable development, able to maintain a constant pace.

➤ Close, daily cooperation between business people and developers.

➤ Face-to-face conversation is the best form of communication (co-location).

➤ Projects are built around motivated individuals, who should be trusted.

➤ Continuous attention to technical excellence and good design.

➤ Simplicity.

➤ Self-organizing teams.

➤ Regular adaptation to changing circumstances.

The principles recognize the weaknesses of the waterfall methodology by promoting iterative and incremental development as a means of delivering features of the site when they are done, versus when the entire site is done. Iterations are short production sessions where the software team works through requirements, design, development, and testing for each feature in the site. If the feature does not pass user acceptance testing or if the feature demonstrates the requirements need to be changed, another iteration of development is performed. Each time a feature goes through an iteration, the site is closer to being complete. As each feature is completed, another is started, thus incrementally completing the development process.

Figure 2-2 provides a detailed illustration of the agile concept of software development.

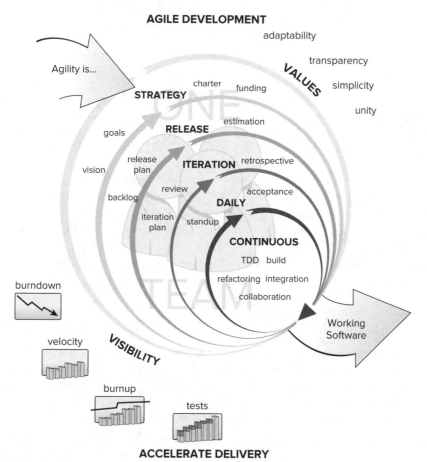

FIGURE 2-2

There are several methodologies that support agile software development. For instance, the Drupal community often uses *Scrum*, an iterative and incremental methodology for managing software development. Figure 2-3 illustrates the workflow of the Scrum methodology.

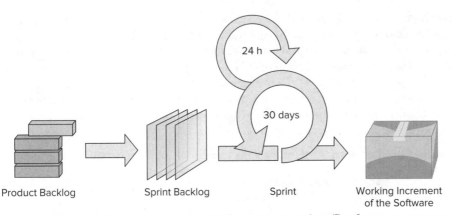

Product Backlog   Sprint Backlog   Sprint   Working Increment
                                                                  of the Software

WIKIMEDIA COMMONS IMAGE FROM HTTP://EN.WIKIPEDIA.ORG/WIKI/FILE:SCRUM _ PROCESS.SVG

FIGURE 2-3

One practice of the scrum process is the sprint. A *sprint* is a short block of time (up to 30 days) during which specific functionality of the site is developed. Sprints are a collaborative time when development is planned and executed. The objective is to complete the functionality in the given time. The completed functionality can potentially be implemented, depending on where it fits into the site.

 For more information about Scrum, visit www.scrum.org *and download the Scrum guide or learn about Scrum training opportunities.*

Extreme Programming is an evolving agile software development methodology. It focuses on frequent releases in short development cycles while being responsive to changing customer requirements.

Advantages

An advantage of using an agile approach for the production of a site is the ability to see the site come to life sooner rather than later. You can assess whether the original requirements are going to work as hoped before the whole site is done. The agile approach also supports site development projects in which requirements are more in the form of a vision or goal statement and need to be discussed to hone in on the details of what that vision or goal feature needs to do.

One of the biggest arguments for agile is faster delivery of code (site features) because you reduce the upfront time planning (requirements and design). Instead, you perform a series of mini planning or development sessions. The number of the sessions often is driven by the list of features you want in the site, as well as the availability of the decision-makers.

Disadvantages

If you have a fixed budget and need to hire a vendor to build your site, a fixed-price agreement with the vendor can be appealing. If you want to use an agile approach to collaboratively define requirements and identify solutions with your vendor, it might be difficult for the vendor to offer a fixed-price proposal until the requirements are better known.

If the vendor does offer a fixed-price proposal, ask that they include the assumptions they are making regarding the effort they are estimating. For instance, does their bid include a custom theme or custom modules? A list of what is included in the bid can decrease the chance of statements like "that is out of scope."

REQUIREMENTS DETAILS

Chapter 4 suggests four levels of detail when defining requirements: purpose, simple use case, specifications, and configuration.

Another disadvantage to incremental planning is the addition of a requirement that changes strategies already in place, thereby causing work already performed to be undone and redone. This can cause schedule delays and increase costs.

DISADVANTAGE SCENARIO

Assume that you have created three sections for your site (About, Services, and Projects), and a development decision was made to use the same input form for each section. You are on a tight schedule, so you want content developers to start creating content while other features in the site are being set up. They are cranking away and have created a lot of content or nodes.

Everything looks great but you realize you forgot something: "I want only the teaser for projects to be available to the general public. And I want authorized users to see the full project." Because you used the same input form for all the content, you might have a problem. That one input form was designed to behave one way. If you change the behavior of that form, you affect the other pages using that same form. You should have used a different input form so that this unique behavior could be applied more easily to the one type of content.

What do you do? This scenario can be fixed. You could explore using a module such as Node Convert. The bottom line is that additional effort is required, which can mean additional cost and time.

You might not run into these issues on your project, but knowing ahead of time that it is possible is good. To reduce the risks associated with change, consider shifting more of your planning upfront — not totally, as you would with the waterfall method, but enough to help you identify important attributes associated with your features.

RAD Methodology

RAD (rapid application development) methodology uses minimal planning in favor of rapid prototyping. A RAD method utilizes structured techniques (for example, modeling) and prototyping to define requirements. In other words, you can use a RAD methodology to fold the requirements, design, and, potentially, the development processes together. This sounds similar to what an agile method would do. The difference is the use of prototyping.

Figure 2-4 illustrates how the work performed during production might flow when using RAD. Notice the addition of "demonstrate" and "refine" to the process. This is the prototype.

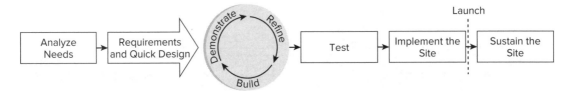

FIGURE 2-4

Advantages

Prototypes are not necessarily built with the same process that will be used to create the actual product. With Drupal, however, because the code already exists (via a module or set of modules) in many instances, "prototyping" features in a sandbox (sample) site to see what the existing modules do and determine whether that is what you want is often easy.

For example, if a requirement is to give each user a blog, you can enable the blog in the sandbox site and set up a blogger role that will be assigned to each approved user. You can play around with the feature as-is and fine-tune your requirements if the existing feature is not everything you want.

The objective of prototyping is to explore your options to see whether they work. Sometimes, planning before you develop is best. Sometimes, jumping into prototype development shows opportunities and issues you otherwise might have missed but can now accommodate in the plan.

Disadvantages

You might have noticed that RAD and agile are similar. With that similarity come similar disadvantages, such as the expenditure of repeating efforts and the potential for schedule delays. The nature of prototyping means you will likely have to undo or redo work until you get the prototype where you need it. But seeing it come to life might be worth the effort.

Spiral Methodology

In short, the spiral methodology provides an iterative and progressive approach to defining the requirements and design of your site using prototyping. Once an operational prototype is reached, the development phase of production starts and you proceed using a waterfall approach.

In 1988, Barry W. Boehm published an article presenting the spiral model as one candidate for improving the software development process. The spiral methodology uses iterative prototyping to define the system to be developed. Boehm states, "The major distinguishing feature of the spiral model is that it creates a risk-driven approach to the software process rather than a primarily document-driven or code-driven process."[1]

---

[1] Barry W. Boehm, "A Spiral Model of Software Development and Enhancement," IEEE Computer 21, 5 (1988): 61–72.

Figure 2-5 is a rendering of Boehm's original spiral model published in his 1988 article.

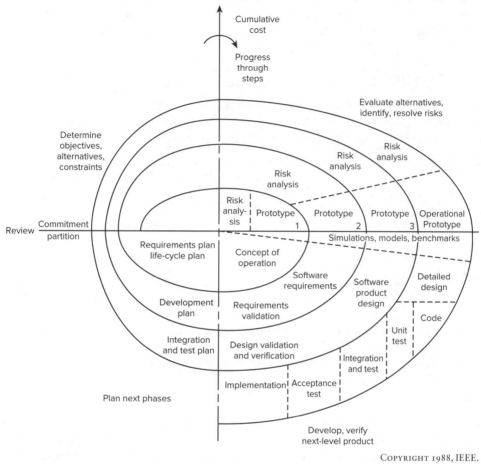

FIGURE 2-5

The spiral model suggests that a series of four steps be performed before coding begins. The following briefly describes the activities in each pass of the spiral, starting in the center of the spiral.

1. Determine your objectives, your alternatives for meeting your objectives, and any constraints that must be met.

2. Evaluate each alternative and identify its associated risks. Resolve the risks and create a prototype that reflects the alternative chosen. In the first pass, you create a rough prototype. Each pass through step 2 yields a more robust prototype based on evaluations from previous prototype evaluations.

3. Evaluate the prototype, make suggestions, and identify issues to be resolved. With each pass through the three, more detailed requirements and designs are created based on each prototype.

4. Plan and commit to the next set of four steps based on the output of step 3.

The number of prototypes depends on the site. The width of the spiral represents the cumulative cost of the project. When an operational prototype has been created, the project is completed following the last steps of the waterfall: development of the site, integration into your organization or other systems, and then site launch.

SPIRAL TUTORIAL

The Department of Computer Science at Virginia Tech has created Online Interactive Modules for Teaching Computer Science a resource that provides animations designed to assist learning key computer science topics.

The short tutorial on the spiral model located at `http://courses.cs.vt.edu/csonline/SE/Lessons/Spiral` puts the spiral into motion by walking through each of the four phases, providing an easy-to-follow explanation of how the process flows.

Advantages

When you are about to undertake a large project and there are several unknowns regarding if or how to proceed, the spiral method offers a way to manage your progress while limiting or avoiding risks. In addition to risk management, the spiral model also provides a clear definition of what your system should do and look like. The detailed requirements and design documentation that are created as a result of prototyping provide development with clear direction.

Disadvantages

The time it takes to go from a defined need to development might be longer than you like. Similar to the waterfall methodology, you spend time planning your system in detail before proceeding to development. Although the progression of prototypes demonstrates progress, the prototype typically isn't something you can use.

Another disadvantage is its potential cost. Depending on the prototyping approach you use, the cost to prototype a system could be more than the risk associated with diving into development using another method. Spiral typically is not cost-beneficial for small projects.

With that said, given the modularity of Drupal, you could create a prototype step by step with minimal investment. In each step, make note of how the prototype approach would need to be modified to meet your requirements.

Phased Methodology

The objective of a phased approach to development is to break your site into individual components or features that can stand on their own. You start with a needs analysis, identifying the purpose of your site. For instance, assume your site will be a combination of an e-commerce site, library site, community site, and a product brochure site. You can proceed one of two ways.

➤ Collect requirements and create a design for the entire system (all parts) and then develop each part one phase at a time (see Figure 2-6).

➤ Collect requirements, create a design, then develop and implement each part of the site (see Figure 2-7).

Once you have your phases decided, you can use whatever development methodology you feel fits for your project. You could use RAD for phase 1 and Scrum for phase 2 and then create your own strategy for phase 3.

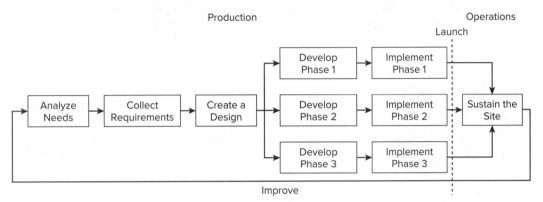

FIGURE 2-6

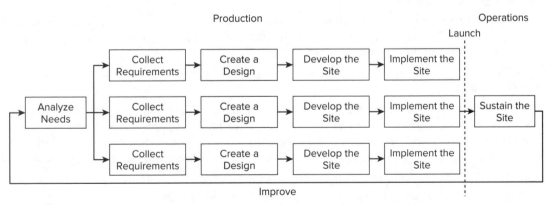

FIGURE 2-7

In order for the phased approach to work, the requirements and design steps need to recognize that there are several parts to the site that will likely need some form of integration. In the first option (Figure 2-6), the requirements and design are created before development begins. With this approach, the development team can create a development plan for each phase that takes into consideration the phases yet to come.

With the second option (Figure 2-7), lessons learned and decisions made during each phase get carried forward to the next phase. That is, phase 2 will need to fit into the decisions made in phase 1; or components implemented in phase 1 will need to be changed to accommodate components in phase 2. The same condition repeats for each subsequent phase.

ONLINE TEAM COLLABORATION TOOL

Drupal is a framework that supports the development of many types of sites. Sometimes, these sites are turned into ready-to-use Drupal distributions that you can download and install. Open Atrium is one such distribution. "Open Atrium is an intranet in a box that has group spaces to allow different teams to have their own conversations. It comes with six features — a blog, a wiki, a calendar, a to-do list, a shoutbox, and a dashboard to manage it all."[2] If you have a local or distributed team, having a collaborative space where ideas can be exchanged and documented for later use is helpful. To learn more, visit `http://openatrium.com`.

SHOUTBOX

A *shoutbox* is a chat-like feature that allows visitors to post short statements to a page on the site. It is typically an asynchronous feature, similar to an online bulletin board.

Advantage

The phased approach enables you to make incremental investments in your site, to launch the site one phase at a time. This is advantageous if you have a vision for something grand but don't have the funds to do it all in one effort.

Disadvantage

A drawback to the phased approach is the risk of building the first component in such a way that it prevents the subsequent components from being implemented appropriately or without restructuring a feature from a previous phase. This method requires you to spend some time during each phase thinking about the next phase and how your decisions today affect what you need for tomorrow.

MANAGING INTEGRATION

Project integration management refers to the process of integrating and coordinating all project plans to create one consistent plan, executing the plan, and coordinating changes to the plan. This is not unique to open source or Drupal. However, there are aspects of "integration" management from a technical perspective that are worth noting. Drupal's module approach to development introduces both module and system integration considerations to project and development management.

---

[2] Open Atrium: `http://openatrium.com/features`

Module Integration

Mixing (or integrating) modules is one challenge with regard to integration management and open source systems such as Drupal. You need to choose the right mix of modules so that you end up with the features you want. You often need to mix multiple modules to get one feature to work the way you want. The advantage of modularity is flexibility in how you shape your features.

While you are off mixing modules to create feature #1, others on your team might be mixing other modules to create feature #2. Add to this the coders on your team who are developing a custom module so that you can make an existing feature do more, and you increase the potential for bugs. Have you created three solutions that will work with each other? Has your team used modules for each feature that will play nicely with the others? Modules sometimes conflict. These conflicts are where integration management comes in handy.

The community development of contributed modules is not controlled in such a way as to ensure that every module plays nicely with every other module. The community has volunteers who work to ensure module issues are identified and resolved, and the community tries to let you know if one module conflicts with another; however, not every possible combination of modules can be tested prior to a module's release. Trying the module in your site configuration and then reporting any issues is up to you.

Systems Integration

On top of module integration, you might also be faced with systems integration — integrating your site with another system. For instance, instead of using Drupal's default user accounts feature, you might need to integrate your site into an environment that already has user accounts. Or you might need to integrate your site into an existing e-commerce, inventory tracking, and/or client relationship management system.

Integration of an open source system with other systems is not necessarily unique, unless you are using a contributed module to enable the integration and that module needs enhancements or further debugging.

> **LDAP INTEGRATION**
>
> LDAP (Lightweight Directory Access Protocol) allows users to authenticate against an existing user directory system, versus having to create a new user account and password on the Drupal site. For information about LDAP integration and Drupal, visit http://drupal.org/documentation/modules/ldap_integration.

There is no single way to deal with the challenges of integration. Integration success depends on many factors, including:

➤ The development method you choose

➤ The production and operations team you have

➤ The complexity of your site

➤ Your experience and management style

➤ Your expectations or your clients' expectations

➤ Who will maintain and sustain the site after launch

Anyone who has built a system from scratch already knows about these issues and should be aware that just because most (if not all) of the features you want potentially exist, you still face potential integration challenges depending on which modules and systems you are mixing. The point is to take advantage of Drupal's ready-to-go features and flexibility, but don't let that freedom keep you from planning, documenting, and validating as you build.

DETERMINING SCOPE

The term *scope* can refer to product scope (the website), project scope (the work to produce the product), or operational scope (the work done after the website launches).

One of the most common issues that arise in projects is *scope creep*, the incremental addition of requirements that fall outside what was originally planned for the site. The comment "that is out of scope" can come up a lot in projects where products are being designed and developed.

Consider the following scenario: you define your product scope to be a site with x number of features, and you define your project scope to include the assembly of pre-existing modules. What happens when you cannot implement one or more of your product requirements within the boundaries of the project scope? That is, what happens if custom coding is required? Is that custom code outside your project scope even though your product scope includes that feature?

The need to define the scope of a project is not unique to open source systems. Any system that has prepackaged features you can install and enable is vulnerable to assumptions regarding what those features can do. Manage expectations by communicating the scope of the project in clear terms. The following sections provide additional insight into scope issues.

Avoiding Product Scope Creep

All projects are vulnerable to scope creep. One way to avoid scope creep is to recognize what might cause it. Consider two scenarios that can cause scope creep.

Drupal has the potential to enable you to add hundreds of functions and features to your site. That much flexibility can be overwhelming and hard to ignore. However, if you don't focus on what you actually need versus what is possible, scope creep can result. It can happen very quickly, so before adding a module that is not part of the plan, ask yourself, "Is this module cool to add or is it needed to meet the requirements already agreed upon?" As your project progresses, if you start to explore Drupal.org and see the many features Drupal contributed modules have to offer, you can get caught up requesting that additional features be added after the scope has been defined.

Another scenario that could allow for scope creep is iterative and incremental planning. Depending on the development method you choose and how you implement that method, you could find yourself defining feature specifications that were not originally anticipated or priced out by your vendor.

Avoiding Project and Operational Scope Creep

Content management systems that make creating your own custom modules easy can lead you down the path of needing to maintain one or more custom modules. As the system goes through updates, you will need to test and potentially update your custom modules to update or upgrade the system. This affects the project scope when system updates occur during site production. It also affects operational scope, in regard to maintaining the site in the future. Do you have the resources to sustain development support after the site is launched? The point is to keep your eye on the target. Try not to get distracted with functions and features that seem cool but that can carry a price later.

BUDGETING FOR COSTS

You might be thinking to yourself, but doesn't open source mean "free"? Yes, it generally means free; however, not all licensing is created equally, so be sure to visit http://creativecommons.org/ to see which license is in use. The idea of open source can leave people with the impression that using open source won't cost much, if anything. For instance, some CMS communities allow you to build add-ons or modules and charge for their use.

With Drupal, you might run across someone trying to sell a service that is supported by a Drupal module but the module itself is free. Sometimes, module developers and maintainers post the option to donate to keep the module going, but that does not necessarily mean they are selling the module.

Even though Drupal is free, costs are associated with developing a web presence. In the open source arena, the old saying, "You get what you pay for," takes on a new meaning. You pay nothing but you get an incredible application that allows you to create a dynamic and exciting site. But you get what the community gives or donates. You don't necessarily get everything you need.

The following sections discuss the various costs you should consider planning for when building and maintaining your own Drupal site.

Software

You might incur software expenses from several sources, depending on what you are trying to build:

➤ **Content development software** — This category includes applications that help you create web-friendly content that will be placed in your CMS (images, video, HTML layouts, and more).

➤ **Code development software** — If you are creating any custom modules, you will likely want to use a software development application to help you with the coding and testing process. Some applications are open source and, therefore, free, whereas others are not.

➤ **Third-party applications** — If you want to add a feature to your site that requires a specific plug-in, that plug-in might not be free. For example, you might want to add a plug-in that performs a calculation for your visitors. You might have to pay a fee for the plug-in.

➤ **Server applications** — If you plan on being your own service provider, you might incur costs associated with the software needed to run the server. Of course, Drupal is made to run on LAMP (Linux, Apache, MySQL, and PHP), which is open source, so a big cost for server applications might not apply if you don't need Oracle or SQL Server.

SERVER SOFTWARE

Four types of software are needed to create the server environment Drupal needs: operating system, web server application, PHP, and a database. LAMP (Linux, Apache, MySQL, and PHP) is a popular open source configuration used with Drupal. MySQL, however, has its limitations. Drupal 7 comes with a vendor-agnostic abstraction layer for accessing database servers. It is designed to preserve the syntax and power of SQL as much as possible, but also:

➤ "to support multiple database servers easily

➤ to allow developers to leverage more complex functionality, such as transactions

➤ to provide a structured interface for the dynamic construction of queries

➤ to enforce security checks and other good practices

➤ to provide modules with a clean interface for intercepting and modifying a site's queries"[3]

Hardware

At the risk of stating the obvious, to build a website, you need a computer. If you are responsible for a team of developers, they will each need a computer. If you have chosen a development methodology that encourages collaborative development, where multiple developers are working together, you might need laptops versus desktop computers to ensure mobility in the team. If you are creating video or animated media to go on your site, you might need a computer with enhanced processing power to handle the development of the media.

The next potential hardware expense is associated with self-hosting. This includes the various peripheral equipment needed to make your server available securely on the Internet. Non-hardware costs are associated with managing your own server environment, such as the labor to manage the server(s). If you use open source applications to run your server, software costs will be minimal.

Labor

Labor costs are the next most obvious expense, especially if you plan to hire someone to build your site. Depending on the purpose of your site, other labor-related expenses might include, but are not limited to, the following:

➤ Content authors

➤ Editors

---

[3] Drupal API: http://drupal.org/node/310069

➤ User experience (UX) person

➤ Graphic artist to create the comps for the theme

➤ Themer to turn the comp into a Drupal theme

➤ Developers to create custom modules

➤ Trainers to train your content managers

➤ Server administrator

➤ Site administrator

➤ Customer support

Some of the labor costs can be purchased and some might be associated with employees (which add even more expense).

Materials

Open source is great, but not everyone is giving away their materials for free. For instance, unless you have a graphic artist or professional photographer on staff, you likely will have the costs associated with purchasing graphics-related materials. If you think you can buy an inexpensive photo or graphic and use it on your site, you might be mistaken. Locate the policy that describes how you can use the graphic and photos. Restrictions apply when you use low-cost materials commercially.

While you are planning your site and identifying content, flag content requirements that you might need to purchase so you can plan your budget accordingly.

Support

Support is typically just another labor-related expense, but it is worth mentioning. Support services often come in the form of maintenance agreements. After your site is built, who will maintain the site code? You can't have a computer and not know that every day, people are trying to find ways to invade your privacy, crash your computer, or worse. Your site might be fine today but tomorrow, someone might invent a new technology that can make your site vulnerable. Nothing can prevent this. However, you can monitor the community and patch the code in your site if an issue arises.

Another example is server-related services. If you have your own server, you likely have the skills to support that server; however, if you are using a hosting plan, what level of support does that service offer? Will it help troubleshoot issues, update applications, or install new servers without an extra fee?

SERVICES

Go to `http://drupal.org` and click Marketplace. You will land on the Services tab, but you will also see a Hosting tab and a Training tab. The services listed are not the only ones available, but they are good starting points.

Training

Will you need training? Depending on what is required of you, your team, or your visitors, you might need training. For your visitors, you might offer an online chat or email support to coach them. As for you and your team, you might need help learning how to post and troubleshoot formatted content. Or your team might need training on how to maintain various features on the site.

Either way, there is a cost is associated with developing, delivering, and attending training. Will you pay your vendor for the training? Will you require training materials?

Marketing

If you want your site to get visitors, you might need to consider investing in marketing strategies, which aren't typically free. You might find that print materials are needed for conferences or you might need to pay for online ads. Remember, just because you build it, that doesn't mean they will come. Depending on what your goal is, you might even need to hire a professional marketing and branding firm to help ensure that your site gets the attention you desire.

SETTING A SCHEDULE

Creating and maintaining a site-production schedule can be a challenge. Many factors go into creating a production schedule and many are not unique to open source. But some schedule challenges are associated with open source.

When you consider the unpredictability and lack of control often experienced with open source, your ability to predict a schedule and deliver a fixed set of features becomes a juggling act. Add to the mix potential learning curves, and you can have a scheduling challenge, especially if you promised that certain features on the site would be available at certain time.

The following sections offer some insights into scheduling a Drupal project.

Effects of a Development Methodology

Assume for a moment that you have chosen a waterfall approach. You have planned all your activities and it looks like it will be 12 weeks before the site will be ready to launch. Unfortunately, you need a web presence six weeks from now because you are presenting at a conference and want to promote your site. Assuming you don't have any other factors (such as approval cycles and funding availability) influencing your decision to use a waterfall approach, you might consider a different method.

You might choose a phased approach with an agile method such as Scrum to get the ball rolling quickly. You might not get all the features you need at your conference, but you will have a web presence that you can point to while the rest of your site is completed.

Ensuring Module Availability

Because open source systems are created and updated on a volunteer basis, predicting when a module will be available is hard. If you need some influence over when a feature is available, you have some options.

Developing Modules In-House

One way to get a feature is to develop, test, and maintain the modules you need in-house. Sometimes, though, this method is not worth the effort in the long run. For example, suppose that during site production, you decide you need a feature that is not available from the community. Your developers say they can create the feature for you in a custom module. You pay for the service and are very happy.

Then, the time comes to update Drupal's core or one of its modules, and your custom module breaks. Something in the module was coded to accommodate how the core or contributed modules used to work before the update. Do you hire your developer to come back and update your custom module? Was the feature worth this expense in the long run? A cost-benefit analysis can help with this decision process.

Developing Modules Collaboratively

If someone in the community is already developing the function you need, consider working with him or her to complete the module. Maybe you are a coder or you are willing to hire a coder to help with the community module.

Working collaboratively helps reduce duplication and helps the community get a new or updated module in a timely manner. Then, over time, as the core modules and contributed modules get updated, you are more likely to learn about updates that are needed and are more likely to have a solution in a timely manner.

Paying for Development

Another way to support module development is to be a sponsor of the module you need. Pay the developer or maintainer of a community module to either speed up the development or make an enhancement. In this scenario, payment is not procurement in the sense that you own the code or module; it is a contribution.

Remember, Drupal modules are often built and contributed to the community on a volunteer basis. Sometimes, a monetary incentive can help move a project up the developer's to-do list. You get what you need, the community gets an update, and the developer gets compensated.

Adjusting Site Requirements

One way to stay on schedule is to modify the site requirements or requirement priorities. If they are your requirements, understand that code development doesn't happen overnight. If you have a tight deadline and you want quality work, you might need to be flexible.

If you are the developer, changing requirements can be a delicate negotiation with your client, but if you explain upfront how Drupal and its contributed module development work, a conversation to adjust expectations shouldn't come as too much of a surprise, assuming you didn't make any promises without doing your homework.

So, the decision might be to change or delete a requirement until the feature is available (not the best option, but at times realistic). Or it might be to create a custom solution, but again, that could take time. Every time you add a requirement that is not currently supported by an existing module, you must allow time for development versus simply allotting time for module installation and configuration.

Considering Other Schedule Challenges

The following challenges are not unique to open source systems but they do exist, and warrant a mention.

Taking a Learning Curve into Account

Each CMS (open source or not) is different and some may appear to be easier to use than others. Some people say that Drupal has a steep learning curve if you do not have the appropriate web development background. If the learning curve for the CMS that you need is steep (given your experience), allow time in your schedule to come up to speed. But what if you don't have time to climb the learning curve? This could present a challenge.

However, just because a CMS is quick and easy to install and configure doesn't mean the CMS will actually meet your requirements in the long run. This, in turn, means you might have to start over again, which can negatively affect the project's schedule and costs.

Bottom line: choose the CMS that meets your requirements and choose a development approach that supports your needs.

Estimating Project Duration

If you have little or no experience estimating schedules, estimating project duration can be a challenge. *Duration* refers to the time that elapses between starting an effort and ending an effort.

You might hear that it will take 40 hours to build your site. Your first thought might be, Great, so I will have it next week, right? Not necessarily. Your time, your team's time, and your contractor's availability are factors in determining the duration of your project. In other words, you might need 40 hours of work to be done, but those 40 hours could get spent over a course of months.

Estimating project duration is not unique to projects using open source, but it can be magnified if you are working with Drupal community volunteers. Because volunteers often don't work on a schedule, you might need to wait a while before getting the feature you need or even a bid from a module developer.

MANAGING RESOURCES

There are at least two types of resources to consider when managing the production of a website: content and staff. The following sections provide a few insights, nothing earth-shattering, to help you manage the resources on your project.

Content

What is a site without content? One of your biggest challenges can be the creation or acquisition of quality content for your site. Depending on the site you want, building your site may be easier than creating the quality content that will be present on the site. Maybe this is hard to imagine, but it is true.

Before you had content management systems that were ready to go upon install, you had to build the system from the ground up. Web production projects could divide and conquer, one team building the system and another creating the content. And near the end, the two would meet. But given that Drupal can be installed and ready to publish in a matter of hours, you can find that your project is more about managing the development of content versus the system development.

> ### RAPID CONTENT PUBLISHING
>
> "Open Publish is an open source platform designed specifically for the online news industry. Content creation and delivery is easy and intuitive, while robust features maximize site engagement and monetization."[4]

The topic of content is covered in greater detail in Chapters 4, 5, 6, and 8, but you should consider a few items now from a management perspective. Following are some tips and insights on managing content resources.

Managing Text

What will the text do? Will it inform? Will it sell? Writing for the Web is different from writing a white paper or a report or even a book. Add to these considerations different writing styles (casual, formal), the audience's interest and attention span, and the authors' availability, and you have your work cut out for you. Choosing your site's content is just as much a planning task as deciding your site's color scheme and menu layout.

Managing Media

Media can be considered content, and you can include several types of media in your site. Three common media types are images, video, and animation:

➤ **Images** can be photos or graphics that you created, or they can be images that you purchase. Be sure to read the fine print in the image license. Those "free" or cheap images you find on the Web might not be "free" or cheap if you misuse them and get caught.

➤ **Video** can be short snippets that you made using a tool such as CamStudio, Captivate, or RoboDemo, or it can be captured the old-fashioned way, with a video camera. In each instance, you should plan who will create your video, format it for the Web, and upload it to your site. Depending on your approach, you might need to configure your site to handle video, so be sure to include that in your requirements.

➤ **Flash animation** can be used to define the look and feel of your site, or you can look to Flash to help you create interactive tutorials. In each case, think about who will do this task, how much time it will take, and how much it will cost (initial development and maintenance). Drupal can accommodate Flash in the theme and in the site. You just need to choose the right modules for what you want to do, and you will likely need a theme developer if you want Flash integrated into your theme (if theming is not your skill).

---

[4] Open Publish: http://openpublishapp.com/

The time you used to need to create your content has been drastically reduced with ready-to-go content management systems like Drupal. The way content is stored has also changed. Plan on spending some time analyzing your content requirements and designing a solution that will help you manage text and media efficiently.

People and Roles

Who will be doing what during site production, and who will be doing what after the site is launched? Involving the right skills at the right time can help you manage your budget and limit waste.

For example, if you can do all the work yourself, except for a custom theme, you can keep your budget reasonably low by bringing in a themer after you have a handle on your requirements and design. But if you aren't building the site yourself, you need to decide whether one person or five people will meet your needs. Your requirements can help you make this decision.

Sample Roles and Responsibilities

Saying you need help is one thing; knowing what kind of help is appropriate for the task at hand is another. Table 2-1 provides sample roles you might need for your website production and operations. Your organization might use different titles for these roles and you might combine some into one role. The objective of the list is to get you thinking about all the tasks that might need to be performed so that you can ensure someone performs the tasks.

TABLE 2-1: Sample Project Roles

ROLE	PRODUCTION	OPERATIONS
Audience (site user)	Inspiration for personas. Can test usability, accessibility, and applicability of the site and its content.	Use and interact with the site. Provide feedback, request help, and/or make inquiries.
Content authors	Identify types of content to be authored. Identify content relationships and keywords. Evaluate legacy content, develop new content, and publish to your site.	Develop and post content using the appropriate workflow and business practices.
Document maintainer	Record and track project progress and decisions.	Record and track operations issues and decisions.
Drupal site architect (maker of the site blueprints)	Collect and refine audience, process, task, content, and structure requirements. Design site workflows. Create the wireframes that meet requirements for data/content relationships, data fields, taxonomies, site organization, content flow, workflow, views, menu structures, and data access. Test the wireframes.	Provide architectural planning for site enhancements, expansion, and upgrades.

ROLE	PRODUCTION	OPERATIONS
Drupal site builder	Identify and analyze hosting environments. Assess legacy site functions and configuration. Create a plan to transition from legacy site to new site. Work with site architect to map legacy content to new architecture. Define a module recipe that will support the requirements and design. Install and configure Drupal and Drupal modules to meet the requirements and design.	Use the development version of the current site to test and build each new version of or enhancement to the site.
Drupal developer	Design and develop custom modules to meet requirements that are not currently supported by an existing Drupal module. Troubleshoot coding conflicts and identify solutions.	Upgrade (design, develop, test) custom modules in preparation for Drupal and/or site upgrade. Troubleshoot coding conflicts and identify solutions.
Drupal themer	Create the PHP, XHTML, and CSS used to bring the design to life.	Upgrade (design, develop, test) custom theme in preparation for Drupal and/or site upgrade.
Graphics designer/ developer	Draft and develop branding, layout, and content graphics to meet requirements and chosen theme layout.	Design and develop content-related graphics, as needed. Update graphics, as needed.
Media developer	Plan and develop Flash and video components that will run in the theme and content.	Design and develop content-related flash and video components. Update media, as needed.
Performance analyst	Identify site performance questions. Identify measures, metrics, intervals, and indicators to answer performance questions. Identify tools required to collect the metrics to be monitored.	Gather data on a regular basis. Assemble, display, and evaluate data patterns to answer performance questions. Make recommendations based on findings.
Project facilitator	Facilitate meetings to collect requirements, consider design options, and manage testing procedures.	Facilitate meetings to evaluate site performance. Identify new features. Plan upgrades.

continues

TABLE 2-1 *(continued)*

ROLE	PRODUCTION	OPERATIONS
Project operations manager	Project manager: plan project efforts and ensure all tasks are completed successfully. Interface with the end-user group (internal or external) to facilitate appropriate transitions.	Operations manager: plan and ensure the execution of routine operational tasks. Evaluate site performance and make recommendations for improvement. Interface with the end users and content authors to ensure consistent service.
Site administrator	Work with site builder/developer to transition legacy data to new site. Turn off legacy site.	Monitor performance, perform updates, and maintain backups. Manage accounts, messages, and permissions. Coordinate future upgrade procedures (from old to new).
Site content facilitator	Identify and design content publishing procedures (workflow). Identify community building and support requirements (if applicable). Test workflow.	Monitor content publishing. Monitor community interactions. Foster contributions. Provide assistance to the user community.
Site policy enforcer	Identify business processes, procedures, and policies that ensure quality. Identify how the site needs to support quality efforts. Test policy-oriented features.	Use processes and procedures to evaluate and monitor site quality and correct quality issues.
Support services	Identify tools required to provide help, collect service request information, and track services rendered.	Provide help and track services rendered. Provide help to users and authors.
System/server administrator	Configure server to meet site and Drupal requirements.	Maintain server and its applications. Upgrade systems upon request of site administrator.
Trainer	Identify training requirements for users and staff. Design, develop, and deliver training experiences to meet the requirements.	Provide training services. Update training to reflect system upgrades or updates.

Filling Your Roles

The site production roles and the site operations roles can be filled by the same people or by two separate groups — the decision is up to you. When looking for people to fill roles, conveying to the potential employees or contractors which roles they will fill and where the site is in its lifecycle is helpful. If you don't know this information, you might be committing to employee(s) that could be over- or underwhelmed after they are on board. Recognizing the different roles can help you make decisions regarding schedule, budget, workload, and risk.

A tendency can exist to throw more resources at a project to speed things up. However, if your project requirements collection process is too slow, you don't necessarily need Drupal coders. If your design process is too slow, the reason might be that you don't have the right people in the room listening, making suggestions, and making decisions. Too many chefs trying to cook in the same pot can cause more problems than they solve. The number of chefs isn't as important as the skills they have.

ENSURING QUALITY

Quality management includes the processes required to ensure that the project will satisfy the needs for which it was undertaken.[5] Quality also refers to the general standard or grade of something.[6]

Some argue that you can't get quality if you go open source. In some instances, they would be right; however, over time, systems like Drupal have been tested and re-tested to help ensure they are quality applications. Before you assume that quality must be something that is purchased, consider all the proprietary software applications and operating systems out there. How many have never needed a patch or update to correct an issue? Of those few that remain patchless, how long did it take for that application to come to market? How long did it take for that application to have new features added? Balance your expectations with your needs.

To assist the process of defining a quality project and then going forward to implement it, consider the following perspectives.

Satisfying Requirements

The power of an open source application like Drupal is defined by the many features it has to offer. If you assess Drupal based on its ability to ensure that the project will satisfy the needs, you have a greater chance of delivering a quality product with Drupal than you do with a system that has limited features. Okay, that states the obvious. But what's important to note is that Drupal is designed so that you can add custom features, change the existing features, and use the system as you see fit, helping to ensure that the project will or can satisfy your needs.

One other point: remember scope creep? You might feel that the more cool functions and features you add to your site, the better the quality. The objective measure of quality is to ensure that all the required needs are met. Of course, if your measure of quality is the number of functions and features that add value to your site, then you will want to define your project as such and incorporate plans to accommodate value-added functions and features.

---

[5] Project Management Body of Knowledge (PMBOK), Project Management Institute

[6] http://encarta.msn.com/dictionary_/quality.html

But can you assess quality simply by the number of features an application can help you deliver? No, of course not. But from a project management perspective, identifying which features will make the project a quality one is an important step.

Meeting Standards

Another side of the quality coin is often the need to meet a set of standards. Standards can be divided into the following three categories:

➤ **Industry standards** — You might need your site to be 508-compliant. In Drupal, your first step would be to ensure your theme produces 508-compliant pages. Next, you would look to the modules to ensure their output is compliant.

➤ **Professional standards** — You might decide you need magazine-quality images and layouts for your site to be considered a quality site. You could be selling graphic design services, so you would need your site to convey your expertise. The quality of what your potential clients see could make all the difference. Or you could have a site that provides free training. In that case, professional writing standards would probably be high on your list of requirements.

➤ **Personal standards** — These are subjective measures you can use to assess the quality of your site. For instance, you may feel that the use of photos versus icons or green versus blue is going to create a quality site. If photos and the color green have nothing to do with the purpose of the site, such standards might be considered personal. Personal or not, if that is what you want, then that is what you should plan.

The bottom line: whichever standards you aim for, be sure to include them in the requirements.

> **SECTION 508**
>
> Section 508 requires that federal agencies' electronic and information technologies be accessible to people with disabilities. If your site is 508-compliant, it meets this federal requirement.

Using Best Practices

More than one way exists to write code, build user interfaces, and assemble modules for a site. Depending on who you ask, you will find people who say "The best way to do that is... ."

With most applications, you don't have control over how the code is developed or documented. But with open source, you can change the code to meet your needs and your standards. Of course, you need to determine whether the results are worth the effort and any compatibility issues you will probably have down the road if you do change the code.

For example, suppose you really think the code that is core to Drupal needs to be changed and you change it. You have probably just created a situation where, if you update to the next version of the open source core code, your site might not function as you originally designed it to. You might also find that contributed modules that are important to your site might also stop functioning properly. Just think about the domino effect before making changes to existing and tested code.

> ## BEST CODING PRACTICES
>
> Drupal has been designed to support best coding practices. For more information, see the chapter "Writing Secure Code" in the book *Pro Drupal Development, Second Edition*, by John K. VanDyk, Apress, 2008.

The bottom line: quality is what you define it to be. With open source applications, you deal with the quality of work performed by hundreds (or thousands) of community members. At the same time, however, you have thousands of users checking and validating the core and its modules, so maybe code quality isn't going to be high on your list of concerns.

COMMUNICATING WITH THE COMMUNITY

If you were using a proprietary system, you could likely call a phone number to get service or help when you need it. Drupal doesn't have an official or formal help desk you can contact. If you need help and cannot remedy your need in-house, you will likely need to reach out to the community. You can do this passively by searching the Internet and sites like `Drupal.org`. Or you can actively engage the community by posting questions and helping others.

Communicating with members of an open source community requires patience and the understanding as you might not hear back from everyone you reach out to. When reaching out to the community, try to use the appropriate channels and methods set up by the community, such as forums, issue queues, and Drupal's Internet Relay Chat (IRC). To learn more about these options, visit "Talk with the community" at `http://drupal.org/node/314178`.

> *When you reach out to the community for help, provide details. This might be a challenge in a chat, but if you are posting to Drupal.org or Groups.drupal.org, don't assume that others will catch on to the context in which you commenting or requesting help. Set the stage, take your time, and complete your thoughts. You improve your chances of someone being able to help.*

From a management perspective, unless you have hired someone in the community, being able to count on consistent communication between you and the members of the community is unlikely. You might not hear back regarding a question you have, or you might get an immediate response. You might want to reach out to someone in the community directly but perhaps he has chosen to disable his contact form. If you don't have either the time or skills to work a problem on your own, you might need to pay for services.

ASSESSING RISKS

Risk is part of every project. Risk can be associated with product quality, cost overruns, and schedule slips, to name a few. You don't have to be using an open source application like Drupal to experience these risks. But if you are going to manage your project in such a way as to mitigate risk, you should be aware of a few aspects of open source applications that can introduce risk to your project.

Following are examples of potential risks for which you might want to create mitigation plans. When reviewing these risks, consider the probability of the risk actually occurring and what avoiding the risk in the first place would take. You might find that the effort to avoid risks costs more than the risk itself.

Getting Site Support

Unlike with proprietary applications, "support" in an open source community is not someone sitting at a virtual help desk waiting for your chat call or email. Even when you choose to request paid support from a vendor, you might not get what you need.

What do you do when you can't find a knowledgeable volunteer from the community to help you? Following are some options to consider when mitigating support risk:

➤ Increase your own skill base so that you don't have to rely on others for the small stuff.

➤ Offer to pay for support so that you don't have to wait on a volunteer.

➤ Partner with an experienced Drupal services business for development and maintenance support.

Application Redesign

If you were a user of Microsoft Office 2003 and are now using 2007 or 2010, you have seen application redesign. The navigation changed so much it was like having to learn a new way of thinking. Then, there are the compatibility issues to deal with when trying to open files created in the 2007 format in a 2003 application.

The same risk applies to open source applications. What happens if the community makes a significant change in the way the system works? A chance always exists that this will happen. The level of investment many of the community leaders have in the application will limit the probability of this happening overnight. Given Drupal's success, the community does not benefit from radical change that would prevent someone from upgrading.

DRUPAL 7 CHANGES

Each time Drupal has launched a new version, it has made improvements to the interface and the functionality. Drupal 7 has made many improvements and, as such, has positioned Drupal for significant forward movement. The ability to run Drupal on Oracle and other enterprise database systems is a significant change. But this change does not mean Drupal isn't what it used to be. This is an improvement. The community didn't start all over again with Drupal 7.

To mitigate an application redesign risk, try becoming involved in the community. Watch discussions on Drupal.org and follow Dries Buytaert's blog (http://buytaert.net/), where he talks about Drupal and addresses concerns regarding the direction Drupal might go from one version to the next. If you have a concern, post your comments and make your case, as many have done.

Open Source Application Cancellation

What if Drupal goes away? Drupal launched in 2001 and has been growing steadily ever since. In my humble opinion, the probability that the community would walk away from Drupal after its wide acceptance around the world is very low.

> **WHITEHOUSE.GOV ON DRUPAL**
>
> The number of government agencies adopting Drupal is growing. Many users of Drupal were convinced of its stability as a product before the White House used it to launch WhiteHouse.gov. To learn more about who is using Drupal, visit the Drupal showcase page at http://drupal.org/forum/25.

Just as with any application (open source, proprietary, or homegrown), you run the risk that someday, the people who made the application will go away and you will be stuck with an application that has no support and no updates in the future. This is simply a risk that you can't assume won't happen, but the probability is minimal with Drupal. Usage and growth trends indicate Drupal will be around for a while.

How do you avoid this issue? Technically, you can't; it's there all the time in every application you use. You just have to look at the situation and judge whether you feel enough interest and investment exists to sustain the community for the time you will have a need for the community.

Ensuring Site Security

Security in software applications will always be an issue. Some fear that open source applications are less safe than proprietary applications. In other words, they have a greater risk of having security issues. In some cases, this is true. The Drupal community, however, has good security monitoring and updating practices.

To mitigate security-related risks, consider the following options:

➤ Ensure that your installation of Drupal is connected to the community and your site is always monitoring the community for code and security updates.

➤ Apply security updates for Drupal's core and any contributed modules when they become available.

➤ Investigate a contributed module before using it. See whether anyone has found any issues and whether a resolution is available.

➤ If a security issue surfaces, assess its applicability to your use to determine your level of risk.

➤ Work with the module project developer to patch the security issue.

Chapters 4, 6, and 7 provide additional security-related insights.

Remember, no code is perfect. The number of code hackers out there today trying to cause damage continues to grow. Even if you build your site from scratch, you have the risk of unanticipated security holes. Assess your risk tolerance and proceed appropriately.

Missing Delivery Dates

Another potential risk is associated with scheduling. With open source, you run the risk of missing a delivery date if you did not take into consideration that one or more features are not currently available before you promised to deliver that functionality. Or the features are available but have not been fully tested, creating potential issues in the site.

Schedules are difficult to predict on web development projects. Unless you have your own coding team and resources, you might consider breaking your project into phases. Collect the requirements for the site and assess how much can be done with existing modules versus custom work, and then create your schedule. How many clients want to go through this process? Some will be willing and some won't, but it is an option.

Not Meeting Site Requirements

An incomplete deliverable is always a risk. Of course, incomplete deliverables might be a matter of opinion. What clients have in mind and what they ask for might be two different things. If you are the developer, digging past the "I want a blog" statements from clients to learn more about what they are trying to do is in your best interest. If you are the site owner and decision maker, be as descriptive as possible. Don't assume that your understanding of something is the same as your developer's.

To help mitigate the risk of incomplete deliverables, consider the following recommendations:

➤ Describe the process or task you want supported in the site.

➤ Avoid using terms like *blog* and *wiki* as your only description of what you want.

➤ Quickly assess the probability that a requirement requires custom work and plan accordingly.

➤ Select vendors that have prior experience building what you want.

Working with Vendors

If you hire vendors to help you build your site, you run the risks that they won't deliver as promised, that you will be out the money you have paid them, *and* that you won't have the site you wanted.

The demand for more sophisticated sites is increasing. An increasing number of want-to-be Drupal developers are making promises they can't keep. To mitigate your risk, consider the following:

➤ Ask for and check references. Vendor issues are not unique to open source applications, but checking references can help reveal the obvious issues.

➤ Establish a relationship with vendors such that you are an integrated team, thus allowing you to be aware of what they are doing and how well they are proceeding.

➤ Make an effort to learn as much about configuring Drupal as you can. Numerous videos, books, and training courses are available to help you learn enough to know whether a vendor is trying to pull the wool over your eyes.

➤ Hire a consultant to go between you and the vendor. Let that person be the learned colleague who can advise you on how the vendor is doing.

➤ Don't use a vendor. Hire your own development team and create your own web department.

➤ Don't be vague when communicating what you want. Even the best vendor is likely to misunderstand what you want when you are vague.

The more informed you are about Drupal and the vendor, the more active you are in the process. The more you communicate and document what you want, the more likely you are to have a successful vendor experience.

Identifying Future Maintenance Costs

If you focus primarily on getting your site to be exactly what you want, you run the risk of creating a site that cannot be updated later without significant time or cost.

Each time you deviate from how Drupal and its contributed modules are designed, you run the risk that your deviations will have to be redone each time you update the core system and/or its contributed modules. As long as you are aware of risks like these, you can plan accordingly. Remember — document, document, document. How quickly coding decisions are forgotten is amazing. Don't pay for someone to relearn what was done on your site by fishing through the code and configurations of the site.

Also, for each requirement, identify the maintenance associated with the requirement, if one exists. For each process, task, and type of content, plan how you will maintain it.

RISK MITIGATION VIA DOCUMENTATION

Documenting is one way to reduce your risk of having to spend time and money evaluating your site to determine how something was done. One way to support documentation is to use a documentation module. The Site Documentation module is one example currently available in Drupal 6. As of May 2011, a Drupal 7 version had not been started.

If you have ever managed a software application development project, the preceding risks are not news to you. A few open source–specific issues get thrown into the mix, but for the most part, you can encounter these risks (and others) if you are using a proprietary application or your own home-grown solution. The key to success is to keep these risks in mind so that as you make decisions about your project, you know whether you are introducing a risk that you can manage.

FACILITATING PROCUREMENT

Procurement is the process of acquiring goods and services. With regard to Drupal, the procurement process is simple:

1. Download the installation package.
2. Install it.
3. Use it.

As you have seen, however, building a website isn't just about the CMS you use.

What Gets Procured?

Procurement processes associated with open source systems are often associated with services. These services aren't any different than if you were using a proprietary system. They include:

➤ Vendor services used for site and theme production

➤ Hosting services procured to host your site

➤ Search engine services, such as those provided by Acquia Search (`http://acquia.com`)

➤ Merchant services associated with e-commerce processes

This list is not exhaustive, of course, but it is a start. A chance exists that you won't have the complete list of services that you need until you start collecting your requirements or planning your development.

Procurement Challenges

Your procurement challenges center on a still-maturing market (many of those offering services have not been in business long) and quality control (you might not get what you paid for).

Even though Drupal has been around since 2001, it appears that the Drupal community and its service providers didn't start maturing until after Drupal 4.4 was released between 2004 and 2005. A review of a Drupal Release Timeline (`http://drupal.org/files/issues/ Drupal%20Release%20Timeline.png`) shows an increase in level of activity, with Drupal core updates becoming more frequent. This is likely a reflection of new development and an interest in making Drupal what the community needs. As with any technology, not everyone can be an expert overnight. Add to this challenge that Drupal is continuously growing and improving, and keeping up can be a challenge.

Not everyone can transition his or her skills to the Drupal way of doing things quickly enough to meet the needs of clients. Too many vendors assume they can meet the clients' requirements just because they have developed other systems. Do your homework; find out how many Drupal projects the vendor has successfully completed versus how many CMS projects they have completed. Just because vendors know PHP doesn't necessarily mean they can develop in Drupal using the same techniques and strategies they have used on other projects.

My recommendation when it comes to procurement practices is to use the same practices you would use if you were acquiring a proprietary application and its applicable services. For instance, if you are with the government, you already know that you have regulations that govern how you procure services. If you are not sure, ask questions. Consult with those who have gone before you. What did they do and what did they learn in the process?

SUMMARY

This chapter provided insights into development methodologies and managing open source projects. Here are a few things to remember when planning the management aspects of your Drupal project.

➤ Choose a development methodology that fits the way you do business.

➤ If you choose an agile approach to development, commit to its structure.

➤ Don't skimp on your statement of work. Think about what you need and expect.

➤ There are costs associated with open source, even though Drupal and its contributed modules are free.

➤ Drupal is an open source system developed and maintained by volunteers in the community. Your schedule might be impacted if you don't have your own resources to fill in the gaps.

➤ Managing development resources includes managing your content and personnel resources as well.

➤ If you need to meet certain standards, be sure to include that information when requesting a bid for services.

➤ Be friendly and courteous to members of the community. Complaining is likely to get you ignored.

➤ There are risks in all software projects. The Drupal community has expended significant efforts to build a secure system for everyone.

➤ If you are hiring a vendor or an employee, ask about the methodology they like to use and determine beforehand if their way will meld with your organization.

Chapter 3 starts the production of your site by helping you identify the purpose of your site, potential alternatives, and your competition.

3

Conducting a Needs Analysis

Do you need a site? What do you need that site to do? Are there alternatives to building a site? For instance, if you need to sell products online, you could build your own site and work to bring your customers to you. Or you can sell your products on an existing site and potentially reach the customers that are already there.

Assuming you still want to build your site after considering your alternatives, will you have any competition? Continuing with the e-commerce scenario, are your products unique or do others sell something similar enough to create competition?

If you have competition, who is setting the benchmark that you need to reach or rise above? Does the benchmark suggest you need to offer more than you originally thought?

During a needs analysis, you identify the purpose of your site and whether there are any alternatives, and assess if/how a competitor might influence what you offer on your site. The needs analysis is the first step in defining the scope of your site and the scope of work required to develop and maintain it.

By the end of this chapter, you should be able to:

➤ Recognize common types of sites

➤ Recognize that a site is not the only way to reach a goal

➤ Recognize how the purpose of your site might influence how you proceed with the production of your site

➤ Describe how a competitor analysis might influence the purpose of your site

IDENTIFYING YOUR SITE'S PURPOSE

One way to define your site's purpose is to put your site into one or more categories. Categories not only convey the purpose of the site, but also start the process of identifying site features.

Examples of categories include:

➤ Marketing

➤ E-commerce

➤ Learning management

➤ Collaborative community

➤ Media hosting

➤ Media broadcasting

➤ Informative dissemination

➤ Business management

➤ Online applications

You can categorize sites any way you want to. This list is simply a place to start. The following sections provide brief descriptions of these categories, with the intent that they will prompt some ideas or help you communicate to others what you are trying to accomplish.

Marketing Brochure Sites

In the printed world, brochures come in many shapes and sizes. Brochures tend to:

➤ Have graphics and precisely placed print

➤ Include information about a product or service that a business offers

➤ Include the benefits of what that product or service has to offer

➤ Be written with a personal tone, as if the reader were the only one reading it

The objective of the brochure is to convince a person to become a customer or client. On the Web, brochures can contain the same content as a printed, multi-page brochure. The trick is the presentation of the printed word in conjunction with the images. During the requirements and design phases, ask yourself the following questions:

➤ Will the site mimic the printed version exactly?

➤ Will the site include additional details that did not fit in the printed brochure?

➤ Will the brochure pages integrate with other functions on the site, such as a shopping cart?

The effort required to produce a marketing site varies, depending on what you want the site to look like and whether you have other site purposes that you need integrated. If your site is strictly a brochure site, you might not need or want to use a CMS. There might not be that much content that needs to be managed. If you want your site to support more than one purpose, however, a CMS can be a good choice.

DRUPAL OUT-OF-THE-BOX

Out of the box, Drupal 7 does a better job at accommodating a basic brochure site than Drupal 6. Drupal 6 does not provide a way to upload an image to a page by default, whereas Drupal 7 does. If you don't add any modules to Drupal 6, you can include images on your pages using traditional HTML techniques.

E-Commerce Sites

Buying and selling online has become quite popular. If you are thinking about an e-commerce site, the first questions you should ask yourself are "What am I selling?" and "Do I benefit by hosting my own site?"

Consider the first question, "What am I selling?" Are you selling tangible goods that must be inventoried and shipped? Or are you selling a service? Don't forget the desire to sell site access fees, often called *online subscriptions*. Each type of selling uses different strategies and potentially different technologies.

Whether you are online or in a brick-and-mortar establishment, you need your customers and clients to see what you are selling and then buy. One strategy is to bring your products to the customers. Go where they already shop, such as eBay. Another is to create marketing strategies that help your clients find you.

Needing something and being able to afford it can often work against each other. Ask yourself, "Is what I want going to yield success at a price that I can afford?" Before diving into building your own shopping cart site, think about what you can afford and the time you have to manage the site after it is built. For example, you could choose an existing CMS to house all the information about your products; then, you can add on a shopping cart feature that is integrated with a service like PayPal; add to this any special customer interactions that are unique to your products (such as a demo), and you have a solution.

Remember, e-commerce sites facilitate financial transactions. When venturing forward with e-commerce, be sure that you understand your requirements as a business to protect the identity of your customers and the information they provide. Many services are available to partner with to make this part of your e-commerce business easier to manage. Before assuming you have to create all the pieces yourself, look at what services are already available.

E-COMMERCE IN DRUPAL

Several Drupal modules support e-commerce. With more than 20,000 reported installs, the Ubercart module is probably the most popular e-commerce module available for Drupal 6. Other examples include the e-Commerce module and the LM_PayPal module.

When this book was written, Ubercart had been ported to Drupal 7, a Drupal 7 version of e-Commerce was planned, and LM_PayPal had a Drupal 7 patch.

In addition to modules being ported, the Drupal Commerce module is available for Drupal 7.

Learning Management Sites

The instructional purists out there might state that a learning management site is just another way of saying learning management system (LMS). You might be asking yourself, why would I create my own LMS when so many exist to choose from already? Good question. The answer is that it depends on what you are really trying to do. Are you trying to manage a formal learning process or offer informal learning opportunities?

➤ **Formal learning management sites** — These sites offer structured learning experiences, often tied to scheduled courses offered by an organization or institution. Systems used to support this type of environment include Moodle, WebCT, and Blackboard, to name a few. These systems support requirements such as course spaces, grade books, quizzes, content restrictions, student performance tracking, and so on. These systems tend to be organized around a course session (for example, Math 101, Fall Semester).

➤ **Informal learning management sites** — Although structured learning can be offered informally, informal learning tends to be less organizationally structured. One doesn't receive a certificate or degree at the end of the experience. Informal learning happens all the time, each time someone researches something on the Web or views a how-to video. Informal learning tends not to require learning validation, such as completion recognition and assessments.

Before diving into developing a learning management site (and potentially reinventing the wheel), ask yourself what you really need to do. Do you need a system like Moodle or some other LMS, or is the learning process you want to promote and enable less formal?

COMMUNITY GROUPS

Drupal's community site (`groups.drupal.org`) hosts several learning management groups. LMS Learning Management System, Drupal for K–12 Schools, Scorm, and SoC 2006: Gradebook. Each considers LMS in its mission. Participants in these groups discuss using Drupal to create learning sites. Some participants focus on formal learning management, whereas others are more informal.

Collaborative Community Sites

Social networking has taken on a whole new meaning. Before the Internet and Web 2.0, social networking sometimes meant attending a business cocktail party to meet potential clients or employers. With today's social media technology, you can meet and greet people in your social and professional communities without stepping outside your front door.

The idea of shared knowledge and collaborative projects is reaching new heights with forums, blogs, and wikis. But what do you want to do? Do you want to build a:

➤ Social networking site like Facebook.com

➤ Video sharing site like YouTube.com

➤ Group site like groups.google.com

➤ Wiki site like pbwiki.com

➤ B2B or professional networking site like LinkedIn.com

➤ Photo site like Flickr.com

➤ Social bookmarking site like Digg.com

➤ Micro-blogging site like Twitter.com

➤ Podcast site like Podcast.com

Or do you want to build a site that has select features from more than one type of social media site?

As you can imagine, these are only a few samples. You can see a more comprehensive list on the Overdrive Interactive Social Media Map, at `www.ovrdrv.com/social-media-map/index.asp`. Because each of the preceding sites and those on the social media map tend to focus on providing one type of social media interaction, you will need to do some planning if you want to integrate multiple services.

> **COLLABORATION AND DRUPAL**
>
> Drupal originally was built to be a message board. The Organic Groups module takes Drupal's core collaboration features like comments and forums to another level. Organic Groups for Drupal 7 is ready.

Media Sites

Any type of site can offer media as part of its content, so what is a media site? You can group media sites into two categories:

➤ Hosting

➤ Broadcasting

Sites such as Flickr.com, YouTube.com, and Blip.tv provide hosting services. They allow you to upload your media and share it with others. Other sites, like CBS.com, focus on broadcasting their own media. Some sites use the hosting services of Flickr.com and YouTube.com but use their own site to display the media and put them into context.

What category does your need fall into? Are you focused on hosting media from multiple users, or is your site about putting media into context and broadcasting it? For example, maybe you want to build a family-history site where you store family photo albums and family videos. Or maybe you want to share how-to screencasts so that people can learn how to use a tool or perform a process.

When planning a site whose content is primarily media, you need to consider a few things:

➤ **Space** — Unlike text, media files can be quite large, so you will need enough space on your server to store them.

➤ **Upload process** — Some media are made up of multiple files that work together to create the media. On top of this, some of the files are organized into directories. The default upload process is to upload files one at a time. A common practice for uploading file packages is to use SFTP. This affects who can create content that includes this media.

➤ **Speed** — This refers to the rate at which your media is delivered to a browser. In some instances, you won't load the media until your visitor makes a request. But for those times when you need the media to arrive with the rest of the page, you should plan accordingly. For instance, if you have large images, send thumbnail versions that link to the larger versions. If you are sharing video, consider ensuring that it doesn't start playing until your visitor clicks Play.

➤ **Capacity** — Do you anticipate heavy traffic on the site? If so, can your server handle pushing large media requests to hundreds if not thousands of visitors at once?

The preceding are only a few of the things you need to think about when you decide that you want a media site. Remember, if you want the illusion of a media site, you can host your media on sites like YouTube.com and Flickr.com and then pull the files into your site.

DRUPAL MEDIA

Drupal supports media upload, aggregation, and broadcast. Drupal contributed modules enable you to play files such as MP3, MP4, PNG, JPG, SWF, and more.

Information Dissemination Sites

Most sites have some type of information, so what makes a dissemination site different? Sites whose purpose is to disseminate information tend to have a lot to share, and the information tends to increase and be updated regularly.

Examples of such sites tend to offer news, newsletters, articles, blogs, research, case studies, documents, and so on. An information site can also include how-to procedures and books whose pages are presented online using the previous-next navigation strategy.

The content on information dissemination sites can come from multiple sources, but the sources and the content are often vetted for quality and accuracy. The process to help ensure quality and accuracy varies, and these variances will most likely drive decisions regarding which technology to use for your site. Examples of information-rich sites include:

➤ WashingtonPost.com

➤ About.com

➤ Wikipedia.org

The process used to create information can vary. For example, Wikipedia.org is built on technology specifically designed for collaborative writing, where multiple authors add and edit the content on the page. The other two examples (WashingtonPost.com and About.com) are more about presenting a finished product. The authoring process is likely performed offline or in some moderated online environment and made public only after the content has been vetted and edited.

If you want an information dissemination site, part of your requirements process is to identify how information is created, edited, validated, and then made public. For instance, will you create, edit, and validate content online, or will you perform this process offline? In either case, part of your analysis should consider who does what. That way, if you do perform the process online, you have information regarding the roles you will need to configure.

Another aspect of information dissemination is its storage. Will you capture all your information in the body field or will you divide your content into parts and capture it in different fields?

 Chapter 4, "Collecting Requirements," provides additional planning insights into content storage and fields.

Information dissemination sites are often combined with other purposes such as e-commerce and media broadcasting. In such cases, one planning task is to determine how the information will map (or not) to the other functionality in the site.

Business Management Sites

Business management is a broad description for a site. Basically, it is a site that you use to run or manage some or all of your business processes. It can be an Internet site or an intranet site.

Drupal can help you manage multiple types of business processes. For instance, you could create a site that helps you manage your projects, or you could create a site that coordinates events and their registration from start to finish.

An online business management site empowers your employees to stay connected when they can't be in the office. You can create a virtual office environment where employees submit weekly task reports, timesheets, documents, and more.

MANAGEMENT IN DRUPAL

Several management-oriented modules are available for Drupal 6. For a comparison of project management and ticketing modules, visit `http://groups.drupal.org/node/17948`. When this book was written, the Support module has a development version available for Drupal 7. Support provides basic ticketing and helpdesk features. The Drupal distribution Open Atrium (`http://openatrium.com`) is another option for helping you manage your business online.

Online Applications

What is an online application? Some people would argue that all the site types previously described are online applications. The assumption for this type of site is that an online application provides a unique tool or set of tools designed to support a specific task. For instance, you could develop a site whose purpose is to manage athlete training and performance. In order to do that, your online application might need to offer the following features:

➤ Workout repository

➤ Athlete accounts

➤ Athlete calendars with links to either custom or pre-packaged workout plans

➤ A place where workout results are entered and tracked so that progress could be monitored

➤ A communication space for athletes and coaches to communicate and share files

➤ A way for athletes to upload power-training files

➤ A service that applies default training sessions given a specific goal or power output

➤ Charts or graphs that reflect performance changes and trends

The list of features could go on. The application would be specific to the task of tracking, monitoring, and supporting an athlete's training activities.

Another example is a site whose purpose is to manage student information. The application might have the following features:

➤ Course registration

➤ Attendance tracking

➤ Grade tracking

➤ Grade point average

➤ Percent complete for courses

➤ Dynamically generated transcripts

Many features could go into an online application designed to help manage students. The point is that if you need to manage data or generate data from data, you need an application or tool to help you do that.

MULTIPURPOSE SITES

Many websites have more than one purpose and fit into more than one category. For example, some sites exist both to market and sell products online, so they feature a brochure site combined with an e-commerce feature. Another example is an information dissemination site combined with a marketing site and an e-commerce feature.

Other combinations might include:

➤ Marketing + information dissemination

➤ Marketing + information dissemination + e-commerce

➤ Training + media

➤ Information dissemination + media

➤ Community + information dissemination + media

➤ Marketing + media

➤ Business management + online application + information dissemination

By choosing a CMS like Drupal and planning well, you afford yourself the opportunity to support each purpose with one site.

Identifying the purpose(s) of your site is a key contributing factor when planning how to configure your site. For example, the technology needed for a media site is not necessarily the same as the technology needed for an e-commerce site. By simply knowing the purpose of your site, you have narrowed down the features and functionality your site might need.

DOING IT ALL WITH DRUPAL

Out of the box, Drupal offers some features commonly used to create information- and community-oriented sites. Drupal's framework, however, offers the ability to support many other types of sites.

You can add modules that provide additional services and features and turn your site into an information and media dissemination site or an information and e-commerce site. Building a site is like an assembly process, adding on features and services until you have what you need.

 Chapter 6, "Planning Development," offers suggestions for evaluating modules. Chapter 10, "Sample Build Recipes," An Example Build Recipe and Post-Launch Plan provides module suggestions for building a multipurpose site.

When you have a multipurpose site, the requirements process might seem a little overwhelming. Depending on what you are trying to accomplish, you might want to take a phased approach to production and implement one purpose of your site at a time. For instance, a site for a business selling products in a store and online might have a site that has a:

➤ Brochure section that describes the products and services offered

➤ Information dissemination section that offers user guides and maintenance information for the products

➤ Community section so that customers can share their experiences using the products and make suggestions for product enhancements

➤ E-commerce component that allows customers to see and buy products online

In a phased approach, you could start with the brochure and information dissemination sections of the site, basically focusing on pushing content to existing and potential customers. The next phase might be to add a community: start inviting the customers to talk about their experiences and let potential customers ask questions while they are making their decision to buy. The community section generates customer interaction online. The last phase would be to add the e-commerce section.

In this example, to maximize the user experience (how they use the site), you would want to identify how each section is related to each other and offer a convenient way for the site visitors to experience the site as a whole versus only one section at a time. For instance, if a potential customer were reviewing a product, providing her direct access to the user guide, manual, and a list of the latest community posts from the product page would give her a unified experience.

A goal is to create solutions that can be integrated with one another as they are developed, thus reducing the chance that redevelopment is required. In the preceding example, you might choose to collect most of the requirements and create a design that reflects all the sections of the site. Then, for each development phase, use an agile approach (maybe the Scrum method) to refine the requirements for each section, build the section, and implement it.

CONSIDERING SITE ALTERNATIVES

Do you need a site to meet your professional or personal goals? Everyone seems to be doing it — why not you? Websites are an investment, and if you don't really need one, your time, money, and effort might be better spent on meeting your professional or personal goals via some other web-based service.

Table 3-1 includes some samples to get you thinking about your options when considering whether to create a personal or professional site. Please don't feel like these examples are provided as a way to convince you not to build your own site. You should, however, weigh your options against the resources you have.

TABLE 3-1: Assessing Your Need for a Site

PURPOSE OR GOAL	HOW WILL THE SITE HELP?	ARE THERE ANY ALTERNATIVES?
Advertise my business	If I had a site, I could post information about my business.	I could post business ads in various sites that I know my customers frequent. Or I could blog about my business on existing blog sites.
Create a community	If I had a site, I could create a place where people with similar skills and expertise could share ideas and consult with each other.	I could use existing networking sites such as Facebook or LinkedIn to create a community space and take advantage of existing networks and resources.
Post my resume	If I had my own site, I could ask potential employers or clients to visit my site to see all the great work I have done.	I could purchase "pre-built" site space that is designed to let me build a small site and upload some documents.
Sell my products	If I had a site, I could put my products online and let my customers purchase them without having to come to my store.	I could place my products on a site (such as eBay) that already has a large customer base and infrastructure in place to manage the buying and selling of goods.

After you have considered your goals and how a site would help you meet them, you will be better equipped to define your site requirements. However, just because you build doesn't mean visitors will come. Your intended audience might be busy on another site that offers the same or similar opportunities. You know what your goal is and have decided that you need your own site, but what about your competition?

CONDUCTING A COMPETITOR ANALYSIS

A competitor analysis focuses on finding out what the other guy is doing. In other words, you want to determine whether someone is already doing what you want to do and how to position your efforts to share the market. If you are lucky enough to be the first on the scene, another reason to do a competitor analysis is to discover different technological approaches for accomplishing the same or similar strategies needed to support the purpose of your site. Of course, this second option would require looking at sites that are similar but not your competition.

In the first scenario, assume you are trying to enter a business market where you need to compete with "the guy next door." You want to identify how you are better, faster, cheaper, whatever. You want to make sure your site is just as good as (if not better than) your competition. For example, you and your competition sell product A. Your competition sends the customer off its site to PayPal to complete the purchase. If you could match the price but make the purchasing process easier, you might gain an advantage.

In the second case, for example, if the purpose of your site is to post your resume, ask yourself, "How are others doing this?" Other people who put their resumes online aren't necessarily your competition for a specific job; they are fellow job seekers. What strategies are they using? How do those strategies fit your needs? This type of analysis is not only for non-competitive scenarios; you can use it to help determine how to compete with others offering what you are offering.

Performing a competitor analysis is one way to identify:

➤ Benchmarks for performance and service you need to reach or exceed

➤ How you can differentiate yourself from others

➤ Potential partners for your venture

➤ Products and services that aren't being offered that you can offer

➤ Opportunities to complete a product or service, not by reinventing the wheel, but by simply offering something that improves on what is already available

SUMMARY

The activities described in this chapter focused on defining the scope of your site production project. Here are a few things to remember when analyzing your needs:

➤ Determining a site's purpose is the first step toward defining the scope of your site.

➤ Your site can fulfill more than one purpose.

➤ Drupal can accommodate many site purposes.

➤ There are alternatives to building a site or a site that meets all purposes.

➤ You don't have to meet all your needs at once, but you should consider planning the big picture so that all the parts will integrate nicely when they are developed.

➤ Identify a benchmark for what your site should do by analyzing your potential competition.

Chapter 4 walks you through a series of analyses whose objectives are to help you think through what you need to meet your need. By defining the purpose of your site, you provide a context in which to collect requirements and create a design plan.

Collecting Requirements

When you start collecting site requirements, you should know the purpose of your site. Are you creating a learning management site, brochure site, community site, e-commerce site, or something else? The purpose of the site provides focus as you move forward into collecting requirements.

Another influence on the requirements-collection process is the development method you are going to use. Chapter 2, "Managing Open Source Projects," describes some commonly used development methods. Each method supports requirements collection. When you should collect the requirements and at what level of detail will vary.

Requirements, coupled with your design plan, help you to:

➤ Confirm that Drupal is the right solution for you

➤ Create a basis for a request for proposal from Drupal vendors

➤ Establish and maintain clear expectations with your team

➤ Select a development method, if you have not already done so

➤ Minimize the risk that the site won't be what you need it to be

At the end of this chapter, you should be able to:

➤ Recognize that requirements can be written at various levels of detail

➤ Describe multiple analyses that provide detailed insight into what your site needs

➤ Recognize how the decisions made while collecting requirements can influence your design and/or development decisions

➤ Describe what features are required to satisfy the purpose of the site

WHERE ARE THE WIREFRAMES?

Now that you know the purpose of your site, you can start making decisions about what you want the site to include. For some, this means imagining what it will look like. One way to illustrate what your site will include is to create wireframes for the pages. Wireframes are line drawings that represent the layout and components on a web page.

Wireframes are powerful tools that can help you capture and communicate requirements, designs, and development plans via a visual interpretation of the site. However, requirements are more than what you see on the page.

The analyses presented in this chapter provide a way for you to think beyond what is on the web page. For instance, requirements can help you identify workflow, content relationships, and user roles, which are not easily conveyed in a wireframe. A picture of a page is a great start, but it can also limit your vision into what is possible, both now and in the future.

See Chapter 5, "Creating a Design Plan," for information on creating wireframes for Drupal sites.

WHY DO REQUIREMENTS MATTER?

Understanding why you need to collect requirements might be easier if you can see how a site comes to life in Drupal. Figure 4-1 illustrates a simplified process by which content, which is made up of data, is entered into the database and displayed via a node, which is included in one of many pages that make up the structure of the site.

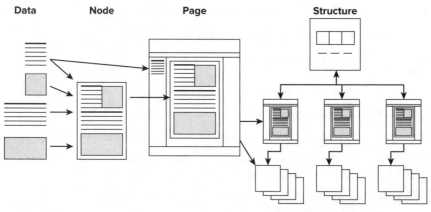

FIGURE 4-1

Figure 4-1 illustrates only one perspective. For instance, some data, which is collected and stored in the database, is not associated with nodes. There are several methods, other than nodes, that can be used to display data. What you see in the browser is more than a page; it is an interface that your site visitors can use to interact with the site and communicate with its members.

Figure 4-2, an N-squared chart, provides an additional perspective on the relationships between data, content (sometimes displayed via a node), interfaces (often called pages), and site structure.

Structure	Structure helps define navigation, which influences interface layout.	Structure organizes the various types of content.	Structure strategies influence data storage strategies.
Interface limits can influence the site structure.	Interface	Interface provides the way to collect and present content.	Interface provides the way to collect and present data.
Content types, topics, and purpose provide structural options.	Content influences the interface layout and interactions.	Content	Content evaluation reveals its data.
Data can be used to define site structure.	Data's form influences the layout of the interface.	Data can be assembled and reused to create multiple content pages.	Data

FIGURE 4-2

N-SQUARED CHARTS

An N-squared chart is "an implementation tool and methodology for the tabulation, definition, analysis and description of functional and physical interactions and interfaces."[1]

Drupal offers several options for bringing your data to the site interface. The requirements-collection process covered in this chapter (as well as the design plan) helps you identify the information you need to know so that you can choose the options that best fit your needs.

HOW MUCH DETAIL IS NEEDED?

Requirements are written statements that describe what features your site needs. How detailed should those statements be? To answer this question, consider the four levels of detail described in the following sections. You can use them when deciding how much you want to document. They

---

[1] System Engineering Methodologies: `http://systemengineering-lanomethodologies.com/cart/index.php?main_page=product_info&products_id=8`

aren't necessarily industry standards, just a way to help you establish an understanding with your team. This book assumes you will eventually reach the specification level before going into development, where the configuration level of detail will be determined.

Purpose

A statement or phrase describing the purpose of the site provides minimal description of what is needed and can carry with it many assumptions. For instance, the requirement is to build a community site. This level of detail is okay if you, the site owner, are buying a prepackaged site development product, where it is understood what you will get. On the flip side, the lack of detail can bring a site-development project to a halt.

Simple Use Cases

You can add some detail to your purpose by creating one or more simple *use cases*. "The use case technique is used to capture a system's behavioral requirements by detailing scenario-driven threads through the functional requirements."[2]

For instance, the requirement could be to build a community site where members of the site can add community content and comment on community content. In a system where these two tasks can only be performed one way, one could argue this simple statement is a use case. With Drupal, simply installing it accomplishes the requirement. But what if your requirement is not a default feature of Drupal? You would need more detailed use cases.

Specifications

You've seen specs before. When you buy a computer, you look at its specs — memory, processor, storage, and so on. Computer specs are details of what you are getting. For instance, an Intel Core 2 Quad Q9550 processor is just that, nothing more. Requirements at the spec level should leave little room for misunderstanding. At the least, they should provide enough information to allow for design and development discussion and decisions.

For example, if your requirement is to build a community site, the specs might state that an authenticated user will be able to:

➤ Create nodes using three types of content (page, story, and blog)

➤ Categorize the nodes created with each type of content using two specific sets of vocabulary terms (topic and section)

➤ Create links to establish relationships between each node

➤ Comment on the story and blog nodes but not on page nodes

➤ Show the page nodes on the site's front page

You can provide even more details in the specifications if need be. Specifications like these are helpful; when combined with the site purpose and use cases, the requirements become even clearer.

---

[2] Wikipedia.org: http://en.wikipedia.org/wiki/Use_case

Configuration

You can take specifications to the next level of detail by spelling out which technology should be used to meet a requirement. If you are the type to explore Drupal.org and read up on the modules that are available, you might find yourself tempted to explain to the developer how you think a requirement should be satisfied. You might go as far as to say, "The requirement is to create a community site and use the Organic Groups module." Saying something like this is not always a good idea unless you are a Drupal developer and know what you are doing. Why?

Often, more than one way exists to satisfy a requirement, and you might not know which other modules will be needed and whether the module(s) you select will conflict with other features on your site. A good developer waits and sees the requirements and considers all the modules that can satisfy the requirements before committing to any one module combination.

WHERE TO START?

This chapter provides the following analyses to facilitate the collection and documentation of site requirements:

➤ **Audience analysis** — Who will visit and use your site? What are they like? How does the purpose of your site support their needs?

➤ **Process analysis** — What are the processes being supported by your site?

➤ **Task analysis** — Which process tasks will your audience perform on the site? What are the use cases?

➤ **Content analysis** — What is the content needed to support the purpose of the site and the tasks that will be performed? How will the content be organized, structured, and configured?

➤ **Communication analysis** — Will there be ways for visitors and users to interact with each other? Will actions trigger site communications to its members? If yes, when?

➤ **Search/Browse analysis** — Will you provide features that help your audience find content and users on your site?

➤ **Feature analysis** — In addition to content, communication, and search features, what other features will your site offer your audience? What tools are needed in order for your audience to perform their tasks?

➤ **Role analysis** — How will your site recognize your audience? What permissions do they need to interact with content, use features, and perform their tasks?

➤ **Performance analysis** — How busy do you expect your site to be? How much traffic will it need to handle? Do you want to track your audience's interactions with your site? Is your site usable?

➤ **Security analysis** — How secure does your site need to be? Do you have requirements over and beyond what Drupal offers out of the box?

➤ **Collection strategies** — How will you collect requirements?

You might be wondering where to start. The short answer is, start where you want to start. Your starting point depends on the purpose of the site and simply where your thoughts are focused.

No matter where you start, you will either touch on or dig deep into each analysis described in this chapter. Skip one or more analyses and you increase your chances of adding missed requirements later. This can cause you to redo work or a cause a vendor to say, " ... but that is out of scope." If you skip an analysis, you run the risk of scope creep or not getting all the functionality your site needs.

There are three common starting points:

➤ Audience analysis

➤ Content analysis

➤ Site design

To help illustrate that you do not have to perform these analyses in the order they are presented, consider the following scenarios.

Audience Analysis First

You can start collecting requirements by first understanding your audience. Based on your site's purpose, identify your target audience. Get to know them and what they want from your site. Whether your site's purpose is to show your stuff or to foster interaction (buying, sharing), you need to consider your audience.

For example, assume your site's purpose is to disseminate information in the form of hundreds of articles. If you want your audience to read them, it helps to know which articles your audience will want to see and organize your site so that visitors can find what they want. If you bore or distract your audience with irrelevant articles, you might lose your audience altogether.

If you start with the audience analysis, you most likely are putting the audience's needs before the needs of the site owner. The example assumes that the owner of the articles will post only those articles that his or her audience wants to see, or the owner will create a site design that allows the audience to filter the content and see only what they want to see.

After you know who will be on your site, determine what they will do and how they will do it. Identify the processes and tasks your audience will perform and the content they will see and/or create. Then, identify the features your site needs to support the tasks your audience will perform and content they will view or create. Determine what site permissions they will need when they perform their tasks. Finish your analyses by identifying performance and security requirements. With your requirements in hand, move on to creating a design that makes your site come to life.

If you start with the audience analysis and let its outcomes influence the other analyses, you increase the chances that your site will be about your audience needs. But sometimes, a site is about what you, the site owner, need. Consider the next scenario.

Content Analysis First

In many cases, starting with an audience analysis makes sense, but just as many cases exist where starting with the content analysis makes sense. For instance, marketing brochure sites and/or personal sites (blogs or resumes) are about what you want to communicate — your message or your content. In this scenario, the audience analysis becomes a tool for determining how to present your content or your message, as opposed to being the driver for what the content actually is.

Instead of asking, "What does my audience want from me?" the question becomes, "Given all my stuff I want to put online, how will my audience need or want to see it presented?" In other words, the idea is to start with the content analysis and then identify who will use it and who will create it. Continue collecting requirements by identifying processes, tasks, and features needed to support the content and the audience. Next, identify how the site will recognize your audience (roles). Wrap up with the performance and security requirements. With these requirements in hand, design your site.

Design First

There are times when the design (the site structure, interface, and interactions presented on the screen) of the site will be a driving force in how the site comes together. Following are a couple of examples of when design might come first:

➤   The site is a copy of its print counterpart.

➤   The site is a virtual tour.

➤   The site is used to present an animated assessment that is changed based on user interactions with the animation. The content or data associated with the site is presented only in context with the assessment and under predefined conditions.

Each example considers the audience and the content, but it is not necessarily the audience or content that shapes the design. Nothing is wrong with having a vision of what your site might look like and how it might be structured before you know the details about your content and features or who will be visiting your site.

In the first two scenarios, there were reasons for design to come after requirements were collected. Imagine that you are designing a house. Unless you know how many bedrooms and bathrooms are needed, what type of kitchen is needed, whether the people living there will have any special needs, and so on, your efforts to create an appropriate design can be hindered.

Reality

You probably won't be able to perform any one analysis completely until you have taken a stab at each. Collecting requirements can be an iterative and incremental process. When you start creating a design that meets your requirements, you might identify other requirements you missed. Don't be discouraged; this is not unusual. Developers often find that their clients can't identify all the details up front, so they use an incremental approach to development.

As you move through the analyses, each one will make you think about your site from a new perspective and trigger you to say things like, "I forgot to include such and such in the other analysis." No problem; go back and add it. Then ask yourself whether this new information influences any decisions you have already made.

The requirements process is not perfectly linear. In fact, sometimes you may think you want a feature, but until you see it in action and understand what it takes to implement it, you might not be ready to say it is a requirement. These situations are where development methodologies like RAD (refer to Chapter 2) can help by prototyping features and options so that requirements decisions can be made.

Also, not everyone understands "requirements" to mean the same thing. The level of detail (purpose, simple use case, specifications, and configuration) can be a useful tool when planning requirements-collection activities. Most issues arise when two parties don't share the same expectations.

AUDIENCE ANALYSIS

The reason people build sites is so that they can communicate and interact with others and so that others can communicate and interact with them. So, with all this human-to-human inter-action going on, would it be reasonable to say that you must understand with whom you are communicating — your audience?

In the audience analysis, you get to know your audience, to understand how their needs, interests, and ways of interacting with sites should influence how you build your site. If you completed a competitor analysis (refer to Chapter 3, "Conducting a Needs Analysis"), you probably have a good understanding of who your target audience is and what they need. This audience analysis expands on what you know and starts your requirements-documentation process.

An audience analysis can be broken into two phases: audience segments and personas.

 Chapter 9, "An Example Plan," provides a sample audience analysis with segments and personas.

Audience Segments

Audience segments are groups of people. You can segment groups of people into many differ-ent categories, such as geographic location, type of organization, profession, hobbies, and so on. Individuals in your audience can be part of many segments, but you are interested in the segments that you want visiting and interacting with your site.

For example, if your site's purpose is to disseminate free K–12 lesson plans, one of your segments would be teachers in K–12, and knowing what K–12 teachers need can help you decide on your con-tent in general. But are all teachers created the same? Do they all have the same needs, skills, and interests? This is where the second phase, personas (discussed later in this section), comes in handy.

Another way to segment your audience is by roles. The most basic roles (from a Drupal perspective) are anonymous, authenticated, and admin. Visitors to your site who don't log in to your site are con-sidered anonymous users. Visitors to your site who log in to your site are, by default, authenticated users. Administrators tend to manage different aspects of the site.

You can break each type of segment (role-based and non–role-based) into smaller segments until you have the level of detail that helps you identify your primary and secondary audience segments. For example, you could break a non–role-based segment that is based on an organization into departments. You can break a role-based segment, such as authenticated user, into users who can also blog. The following sections explore different types of segments further.

Non-System Role-Based Segments

Identifying your audience segments can be like organizing playing cards. The first segment is the deck of cards; the next segment might be the colors; the next segment, the suits on the cards. Within the suits, you can further segment the cards into number cards and face cards. Each sub-segment is related to the other but is also different. The same process applies to analyzing your actual audience segments.

For instance, assume the audience for your site is people who cook. There are different groups of people who cook, as you can imagine. The following sample segments present different opportunities for the site. The members of each segment will vary but still have cooking in common.

➤ **Cook to survive** — If this group doesn't go out to eat or order in, they are simply trying to eat without poisoning themselves. They lack the skills, time, patience, or interest to do a lot in the kitchen. They are likely interested in quick and easy meal solutions.

➤ **Cook to entertain** — This group wants to make their guests happy, maybe giving them the "wow" factor with a special dish. They probably have some cooking skills and are willing to learn more. They will be careful not to select something complicated or extreme because they want to please multiple guests. They might be interested in recipes that can be prepared in advance and then quickly finished at the time of the party.

➤ **Cook professionally** — This group gets paid to cook and has been trained to cook. They probably have their own recipes, but every now and then, they need inspiration to create something new. Or they might be looking for unique recipes for a common dish. They might also be willing to share recipes or cooking advice.

Each of the example segments can be broken down further if necessary. For instance, the professional cooks segment could be broken into sub-segments based on type of establishment — for example, restaurant, hospital, fast food, and caterer.

Now that you have your segments, you can start thinking about the individuals in the segments. What do they have in common? What are their differences? Why will they come to your site? Answers to questions like these can help you create personas that represent the individuals in the audience segment.

At this time, you can move on to creating personas. But before jumping into personas, you should know a little about system roles. Having some insight into system roles can help you fine-tune your segments and personas. This insight can help you pick alternatives to segment groups and persona representations. The roles analysis discussed later in this chapter provides details on role-configuration strategies.

System Role-Based Segments

You have a lot of decisions and analyses to perform before you can lock in on all your system roles, but brainstorming a little if you are just starting to collect requirements is a good idea. You use system roles to manage access to content (among other things). Make some notes now if you have some ideas regarding which segment will have what type of access. You can use this information when you get to your roles analysis.

Anonymous

Your first inclination might be to focus solely on your site visitors (the customers of your information, services, and products), which would be an appropriate place to start. People who just come to look and not contribute in some way will get assigned to the anonymous segment.

In the previous cooking example, each segment would include individuals in the anonymous segment. But what about segmenting anonymous visitors from a technology perspective? You could group your cooks by the browser they use (Firefox, Safari, Chrome, and so on) or by device (mobile or not-mobile). Of course, these categories also apply to other segments, but they are worth considering, as they can influence your design.

Knowing the device they are using can influence your design and development strategies. If the majority of your users will be on small mobile devices, you might want to build that version of your site first.

Authenticated

Authenticated users can take on many roles in a site. An authenticated user has a site account, which typically means he or she can contribute or change something in your site. Your authenticated users can be those who simply comment on your posts. They can be people who post content such as articles, blogs, announcements, events, and so on. They can be the customers who come to buy your products. You could also have customers with special privileges, such as the ability to post discount ads or products.

Depending on the purpose of your site, you might have several types of authenticated users (also known as "roles"), each with different levels of site access assigned to their account.

DRUPAL'S AUTHENTICATED USERS

When Drupal 6 and Drupal 7 users are logged in, they have the permissions assigned to the authenticated role, by default. The permissions for the authenticated user should apply to all who have an account.

Administrators

Don't forget about the administrators. Different types or levels of administration go on behind the scenes of a Drupal site's interface. You could have a group of editors responsible for editing content and publishing it, as well as an account administrator responsible for managing user accounts.

Administrators often are those who interact with the administrative interfaces in Drupal. They are the people who will be working in your site to sustain its content, troubleshoot processes, approve posts, and monitor performance (staff, community members).

> **DRUPAL ADMIN ROLES**
>
> The first user in a Drupal 6 and Drupal 7 site can perform all tasks managed by the site. Drupal 7 comes with an administer role that you can assign to subsequent users. In Drupal 6, you can add the administrator role by installing the Admin role module.

Now that you know some different ways to segment your audience, ..., you can more easily identify the individuals who will fill each segment. The segment they represent is the main reason why they interact with your site. So, the next step is to create personas.

Personas

A *persona* is a detailed description of a character that represents an individual in your audience segment(s). Personas offer a way of viewing your site from multiple perspectives. Therefore, you might want to consider creating one or more personas for each audience segment you identified.

Consider the earlier K–12 example. A teacher might come to the site because she is a teacher, but she might not need the lesson plans you are offering. She might be there to see how she can contribute her lesson plans, or she might be more interested in sample test questions on a certain topic. The following sections explore a process for persona development.

Meeting Your Audience

You might be wondering, "Does my persona need to represent real audience segment members?" Yes, in a perfect world, the persona should represent your real audience. Of course, getting to know your real audience might be a challenge, but you do have options. To get to know your audience, you can:

➤   Conduct surveys

➤   Interview people

➤   Research existing statistics

➤   Procure marketing reports

Worst case, you use personas to define the audience you *assume* to be there or the audience you *want* to create. You can use your imagination and create your audience just as a novelist imagines and creates characters.

Risks are associated with inventing personas. The most obvious is that you could be wrong; however, the odds are in your favor if you are or once were the type of person you would find in your audience. If you can relate to your audience through past experience, you can pull from those experiences and the experiences of your friends and colleagues to define your audience.

Describing Your Audience

When you meet your audience, your goal is to get to know enough about them to predict what they would want or need from your site, why and how they would come to your site, stay in your site, and return to your site.

As you are getting to know your audience, ask questions that reveal their:

- ➤ Characteristics
- ➤ Behaviors
- ➤ Demographics
- ➤ Skills
- ➤ Interests
- ➤ Needs
- ➤ Activities
- ➤ Responsibilities

Defining Your Personas

You have done your research; you have met members of your audience segments and you know a little about them. Your next step is to create one or more personas that will act as audience segment representatives. There isn't an exact science to this process. Your goal is to paint a detailed-enough picture such that you and your site team can safely assume what your audience wants or needs.

If you collected information directly from your audience or obtained information about them indirectly, you could at this time look for patterns in the data. For instance, did everyone list the same needs or interests? Did they all have the same skill level? The differences are going to be the key in recognizing where different personas might need to be defined.

For example, assume you asked your audience whether they shopped online, and half said "yes" and half said "no." You might need a persona that represents online shoppers and one that represents potential online shoppers. Look at the data. What does it tell you? Do the online shoppers work during the day and don't have time to go to the store? Do the ones that don't shop online not have a computer? Or is their behavior simply personal preference? After you can define your persona, write it down.

Documenting Your Personas

If you do a search on personas, you will see that most of the explanations describe personas as narratives. They are one or two paragraphs that tell the story of the persona (the representation of a person is a segment) and provide enough insight to gauge what that persona wants or needs from your site.

SAMPLE PERSONA NARRATIVE

Carman, a 25-year-old accountant, gets up early every day to beat rush hour. She estimates that if she stops to prepare and eat a good breakfast, she either needs to get up a half hour earlier or add 45 minutes to her commute. She needs a healthy breakfast option that takes 5 minutes to prepare and can be eaten at a stoplight. Prepackaged food is no longer appealing to her, so she is willing to spend some time in the evening prepping her breakfast.

Another format is to create a bulleted list that describes key characteristics and site behaviors of the persona. The list can be the answers to a set of questions or it can be a free-form brainstorm list. If you create your list based on a set of questions, you could put your personas into a table so that you can compare your personas and understand how they are different.

SAMPLE BULLETED LIST PERSONA

➤   Carman is a 25-year-old accountant.

➤   She has little time to cook in the morning.

➤   She needs a breakfast option that she can prepare the night before and take with her in the morning.

Some of you will find the narrative more helpful, whereas others will prefer the bulleted list approach. Don't worry about which method you use. Your goal is to think beyond what you feel is needed and to put yourself (and your team) into the shoes of your audience.

Documenting the persona also helps everyone remember the persona. As project team members come and go, documented personas can help maintain a consistent understanding of whom the site is being created for. The personas are also helpful when you are:

➤   Identifying requirements

➤   Designing your interfaces

➤   Testing the site to see whether it works

➤   Defining training requirements

The personas also help you design a marketing campaign that will get your audience's attention, entice them to come to your site, and get them to come back regularly.

DOCUMENT WITH DRUPAL

A handy way to collect requirements and comments on requirements is to use a Drupal site. You can create separate content types to distinguish between requirement categories, or you can use a vocabulary with an existing content type.

PROCESS ANALYSIS

Some sites are built to help get a job done or support a process — a series of actions (tasks, steps, activities) that yield one or more results. But what does it mean to support a process or get a job done?

Consider a site that will have an events page. Will the page simply list events or will it do more? In other words, will the management of events be completed offline or will you:

➤ Build in a form that holds all the details about the event?

➤ Include a sign-up form so that people can register for the event online?

➤ Allow people to pay for the event online?

➤ Create reports that show who registered?

➤ Host online event activities such as discussions?

➤ Send notices about the event to members of your site or to those registered?

Many tasks are associated with the events process. Will your site play a role in one or more tasks associated with events? A process analysis can help you identify all the potential tasks you want your site users (visitors and staff) to be able to do.

Types of Processes

If you have never really thought about processes, you might be asking, "Where do I begin? How do I know if I have a process that my site can support?"

One way to kick-start your analysis is to group processes into two categories: life's processes and business processes. After you identify the processes your site will support, you need to consider how these processes are supported before and after site launch.

Life's Processes

If people are visiting your site, they have a reason for doing so. Something in their life is happening and they need to be on your site. The reason could be that someone's birthday is coming up and the site visitor is ordering gifts. Or someone might need to submit workout metrics, so she is uploading a file to her portfolio on the training site. Maybe the reason is that someone is your friend and wants to read the article you posted on your site. Whatever the reason, visitors are on your site as a means of continuing or finishing their task. In each of these examples, what does the process look like?

Consider the birthday gift example. What other tasks are performed by your audience in context with a birthday gift? The tasks associated with a gift-buying process might include the following:

➤ Remembering the gift

➤ Coming up with a gift idea

➤ Finding the gift

➤ Finding a card

➤ Purchasing the gift

➤ Purchasing the card

➤ Wrapping the gift

➤ Shipping the gift and card

➤ Tracking the shipment

➤ Calling the gift recipient to wish him or her well

Each task is related to the next. Where does your site fit into the process? Should your site do more than sell gifts? When in the process does your audience need to know about your site?

An e-commerce example is fairly easy to follow. Consider the workout file example. The tasks associated with the workout process might include the following:

➤ Getting a physical

➤ Identifying ways to improve your health

➤ Creating a nutrition plan

➤ Identifying an exercise program

➤ Signing up for a service that provides an exercise program

➤ Buying equipment that helps track exercise performance

➤ Uploading exercise performance data

➤ Analyzing exercise progress

➤ Making adjustments to the program

➤ Sustaining a healthy lifestyle

The same questions apply. Where does your site fit into the process? Should your site do more? When in the process does your audience need to know about your site?

Understanding what your audience is experiencing with respect to the task(s) they are performing on your site provides opportunities for you to enable your site to fit their needs and to reach them when they need you.

DRUPAL'S FLEXIBILITY

You can use Drupal as an intranet site for your business. You can also integrate your site into a Facebook feature with the Facebook for Drupal module. Drupal also comes with several e-commerce modules. The project leads for each of these features are preparing for Drupal 7.

Life's processes, the reasons that bring your audience to your site, play an important role in defining your requirements, creating your design plan, and planning your implementation.

Requirements

Identifying and understanding the life's processes your site supports can influence what requirements you need to collect. For instance, the process analysis reveals the tasks performed by your audience that therefore need to be analyzed. By exploring the reasons people come to your site, you can better identify the:

➤ Features your site will need

➤ Content your audience will need

➤ Types of audience-to-site interactions your site needs to support

Design

Life's processes can influence the design of your site. For instance, if your audience comes to your site for fast solutions or quick services, you want to design a site whose interface gives them what they want in the fewest clicks possible. You don't want to slow them down with flashy, cool stuff that does not add value to their experience.

If you are providing a site for people who want to explore and learn, you still might want a design that minimizes clicks, but maybe you want to create a virtual-reality site where the screen looks and feels like a library or a school. Your audience can imagine themselves in a place and can explore the place in context.

Whatever your design solution, it should be influenced by why your audience comes to your site.

Implementation

Just because you build it doesn't mean they will come. Implementation is not just about putting your site on a server and hooking up your URL. It is also about implementing your strategy for reaching out to your audience and letting them know your site is open for business. By understanding where your site fits into your audience's life processes, you have a better chance of knowing where to find them.

For instance, you might use a simple strategy, such as business cards at a conference, or go as far as to create a television ad. Have you seen the ads for websites like Ancestor.com and Match.com, two services that appeal to potential processes in your life: finding your ancestors or finding a match, respectively? Ads for these sites reach people at times when they might be receptive to hearing about a resource that could help them.

Business Processes

Business processes can focus on running your business or they can support processes you need to perform in your volunteer work. They could even refer to your job as the family events coordinator. Consider the following list of processes.

- ➤ Event management

- ➤ Project management

- ➤ Content publishing

- ➤ Service delivery

- ➤ Sales promotion

- ➤ Staff coordination

- ➤ Account access tracking

- ➤ Invoicing

- ➤ Community facilitation

- ➤ Meeting facilitation

A difference between business processes and life's processes is process execution. Typically, you have a say in how content is published on your site but have limited control over how someone shops for a birthday gift. And with business processes, you typically have a captive audience.

Your motivation to understand your business processes also varies. For instance, to understand your audience's life processes could mean additional revenue for your business, whereas understanding your business processes might mean improved customer service and/or a reduction in your cost of operations.

Consider the event management example at the beginning of the process analysis discussion. After answering the questions posed in that example, your event-management process might look like this:

- ➤ Make a decision to hold an event.

- ➤ Upload event details into your site.

- ➤ Create an ad page on your site for the event.

- ➤ Send out an announcement to past event participants.

- ➤ Provide a registration and payment option on your site.

- ➤ Track enrollment via online forms.

- ➤ Send reminder notices.

- ➤ Provide an app that connects your audience's smartphone to the event proceedings.

- ➤ Provide an event attendee list for event participants.

- ➤ Post follow-up activities and reports associated with the event.

In this scenario, each task might be performed offline or via another online service. Can your site do more than post an event? Should it? A process analysis can help you make that decision.

> **MANAGING EVENTS IN DRUPAL**
>
> In Drupal 6, if you combine the Calendar module, the Views module, and a custom content type with a Date field, you are on your way to managing events. Add the Signup module, and your users can sign up for events, as well. As of April 2011, the Calendar and Signup modules had Drupal 7 development versions and the Views and Date modules had a recommended Drupal 7 version.

Requirements

When defining your requirements, what you want your site to do, a business-process analysis can reveal how a task on your site is actually part of a larger process. For instance, consider the events page example. If this page is a list of events put on by your clients and you have nothing to do with managing them, then you probably don't want to have a sign-up feature or a way to track participants. But what if your agreement with your client states that users must be able to sort events? You might need to then organize events by location, date, or purpose. This makes your list a little more complicated, so the requirements for your site might be a little more than just a page where someone typed in a list of events.

Development

Different ways exist to meet requirements. If requirements are not complete or not understood, the development phase could yield undesired results. A business-process analysis can reveal features that need to be included in your site during development.

For instance, suppose you are building a gossip column site with several columnists. Your current process might be for your:

1. Columnists to email their columns as Word documents

2. Editors to edit columns and then pass the Word documents to your site content manager

3. Content manager to copy the content into your site, do a few formatting tasks, and click Publish

Assume you want this business process brought online. Your online process could be for your:

1. Columnists to compose online

2. Editors to edit online

3. Content manager to review and approve online

Development would go from providing a content type that holds the column and the role of content manager to something more. Development would need roles for the columnists and editors. There would need to be a workflow that manages column versions. You might need a method to send notices when revisions have been made.

> **CONTENT MODERATION IN DRUPAL**
>
> By default, you can set content types not to publish upon saving. A reviewer with the appropriate permissions can go to the default content list and list all unpublished nodes. From the list, the reviewer can publish the nodes before or after reviewing them. The Revisioning module offers a more sophisticated way to moderate content in Drupal 6 and Drupal 7.
>
> Chapter 5, "Creating a Design Plan," touches briefly on node revisions.

Implementation

How does understanding your business processes influence site implementation? If you understand how a process is performed before the site is launched and then how it will change after launch, you can manage that change as part of implementation.

For instance, a new or revised site can trigger change. It could be change from doing nothing online to doing something online. It could be change from performing one task online to performing a full process online. In either situation, you will need to manage that change. You might need a strategy that convinces your team and clients that moving your process tasks online is a good thing. Managing change (especially if you encounter resistance) can be a process unto itself.

Training is used to help facilitate change and is often part of implementation. If you have a new or revised business process being supported on your site, you might need training sessions to show your team and clients how to perform their tasks online.

Pre- and Post-Launch Processes

After you know the reasons your audience will come to your site and the processes your site will support, you need to consider how these processes look before and after site launch. Many changes can occur between production and operations, including your relationship with your developer (if you have one). So, plan now for what you should be able to do after launch and how you should be able to do it.

How Development Differs from Production

Life's processes that bring your audience to your site and the business processes that ensure that your site has what your audience needs are accommodated differently during the site's development than they are after the site launches. During site development, your goal is to develop your site and launch it with the appropriate content. After your site launches, your goal is to ensure that your site is successful. A measure of success might be the regular addition of new content.

When identifying and analyzing your processes, consider how tasks are performed pre-launch and post-launch. A common process that changes after launch is content development.

Pre-Launch Content Development

You might find that the people who post content to your site during development are not the same people who will post content after site launch. The skills and site permissions of those who post content before launch might be different from those posting content after launch. For instance, your content might have been posted using accounts with administrative privileges, including being able to load files to the server and changing the page layouts. Post-launch content developers might be allowed to change the page layout, or they might not know how.

To accomplish pre-launch processes and tasks, you might have received training or perhaps paid a developer to create your pages after you provided the content and applicable files. Depending on the purpose of your site, maybe you paid someone to create the content and then gave it to the developer to enter into your site.

As you can see, during site development, the focus is on getting the site ready for launch. What happens to your processes after the site launch?

Post-Launch Content Development

The processes you use to post to or configure content on your site before launch are not necessarily the processes you will use post-launch. For instance, site section landing pages are created and configured as the site is developed. Assuming you don't plan on changing the structure of your site on a regular basis, creating and configuring section landing pages might not be a process you need post-launch.

Assuming you do plan to add typical content pages to your site on a regular basis post-launch, how will you do that?

➤ Will you use the same resources and processes you used during site development?

➤ Will you be on your own to duplicate the efforts of the professionals you hired for development?

➤ Will you be adding new content developers who will be limited in the way they can add content to your site?

Same Resources as Before

If you answered "yes" to "Will you use the same resources and processes you used during site development?" you might not have an issue transitioning from pre- to post-launch. You can continue to produce content on the site just as you have done before — no real issues here.

If you answered "no," does one of the next scenarios describe your situation?

You Are on Your Own

If you answered "yes" to "Will you be on your own to duplicate the efforts of the professionals you hired for development?" you need to learn how to do what your hired help was doing. If you planned well, you configured a site that supports your skill level.

For instance, before launch, you might have hired a professional content developer and editor to work offline in an HTML-editing application to produce the formatted content that was published on the site using the appropriate form when it was ready. After the site launches, content will be typed directly into the same forms by people who don't know how to format with HTML. The pre-launch process doesn't need an HTML editor to be included in the form, but the post-launch process does. Also, pre-launch content was reviewed and approved before posting to the site. The post-launch process needs a content-moderation process.

New Content Contributors

What if you answered "yes" to "Will you be adding new content developers who will be limited in the way they can add content to your site?" Depending on how many new content developers you will have and what they will be contributing, you might not want them performing the same content loading tasks that you can perform.

For example, do you want the members of your open community site to be able to upload files to your site? When you created the initial content, maybe you uploaded images to the server and embedded links to the images included in the stories you wanted to tell. Now that your site is open to your community, should you allow your users to upload images for their stories?

Questions like, "Will I have enough server space to accommodate the images they want to upload?" might come to mind. Ways exist to restrict file uploads, but you still need to determine how images or files can be stored on your server. Adding images and files is just one example of what you can do on your site that you might not want your other content contributors to do.

If you are adding just a few content authors that you have a relationship with, maybe concerns about files being uploaded aren't a big deal. Whatever the situation, you might want to think about how you are going to accommodate the different skill levels of your content contributors.

Why Processes Matter

Part of the requirements phase is identifying the tasks performed by your audience or users. Tasks make up processes. If you don't understand the context of the task, you might overlook information that will help you design it. You also might miss opportunities for providing additional features that could help you distinguish your site from others like it.

Table 4-1 summarizes the pre- and post-launch processes. You might face many possible scenarios while identifying your requirements. This chart gives you some pointers on what to analyze as you go forward.

TABLE 4-1: Process Decision Matrix

	PRE-LAUNCH	POST-LAUNCH
Life's Processes	Why is your audience going to come to your site? What will you do to bring them to your site?	Why is your audience going to return to your site? What will you do to ensure your site continues to offer what it takes to bring them back?
Business Processes	What will your site do to support the tasks in your processes? How will you load the initial content of your site? Will processes exist in pre-launch that are not planned for post-launch?	How will you ensure that the pre-launch processes that need to be repeated post-launch will be accommodated? Will processes exist in post-launch that were not part of pre-launch?

TASK ANALYSIS

If you just finished the process analysis, you are well on your way to knowing what tasks your audience or users will perform on your site. Tasks are typically made up of a set of steps or activities and end with a specific output. A series of tasks defines a process.

Processes and tasks are obviously closely related. The process analysis focuses on the big picture when it comes to tasks and whether or how your site supports tasks. Now, it is time to get into the details of those tasks.

Task analysis helps you identify:

➤ The technology (site features) your users need in order to perform the tasks

➤ Content required for your site and the context in which it needs to be presented

➤ Workflow requirements so that content developed on the site is produced using the appropriate reviews

➤ Interface and node sequences required to support multi-step, ordered tasks

➤ Who will need to be able to do what — in other words, roles and permissions

When you move on to the design phase, you will find that you are designing interactions and interfaces that support specific tasks. The findings in the task analysis can play a major role in the design phase. The following sections provide techniques for identifying, analyzing, and documenting tasks that you want supported on your site.

Organizing Your Tasks

You can choose to organize your tasks any way you want. Following are some task-organization strategies that you can use as-is or as a starting point for creating your own way to organize tasks.

Process Task List

If you performed a process analysis, a good chance exists that you already have this list started or even completed. If not, go ahead now and list the processes you identified and their tasks. Flag the tasks that you will support on your site. A simple list can help your development team ask appropriate questions and define an appropriate solution. You saw a couple examples of process task lists when reviewing the process analysis.

Persona Task Matrix

Another way to organize your tasks is to create a persona task matrix. The objective is to identify as many of the tasks as possible (start with the tasks from the process list) and determine whether one persona will want to perform the tasks differently from another, thus creating multiple ways your site should support a task. After you have this information, you can get more detailed by creating use cases, which are discussed later in this chapter. Table 4-2 provides a generic version of what a persona task matrix might look like.

TABLE 4-2: Sample Persona Task Matrix

TASKS	PERSONA 1	PERSONA 2
Task 1	Performs this task but starts by logging in	Performs this task but waits to log in after the resource is found
Task 2	Does not perform this task	Performs this task only after receiving an email notification
Task 3	Performs this task by using a search feature	Performs this task by using menus

Role Task Matrix

Sometimes, distinguishing between how different roles perform a task can be helpful. If you already have some insight into the specific roles your site needs, you could organize your tasks against those roles as well. After completing your roles analysis, you will likely return to this list and adjust it accordingly.

Distinguishing between tasks that are process-specific and those that are not necessarily process-specific is also helpful. Table 4-3 is a sample matrix with some common Drupal tasks and potential process-specific tasks. Common Drupal tasks can be customized to be process-specific.

TABLE 4-3: Sample Role Task Matrix

	ANONYMOUS	AUTHENTICATED	ADMINISTRATOR
Common Non–Process-Specific Tasks	View content Search site content Create an account Log in	Comment on a node Create site-specific content Join a group Email the page Share the page on a social networking site	Manage content types Manage views Manage blocks
Tasks That Might be Process-Specific	Use a mortgage calculator Sign up for a newsletter Complete a survey	Submit a job or mortgage application Make a payment on a loan	Download survey results collected in your site Manually configure objects to appear on a page

By organizing your site tasks, you assess where tasks are similar and where they are not. Knowing this information can help you work through the next step, development of use cases, more efficiently. Use cases are the details associated with tasks.

From Task to Use Case

When someone performs a task, he or she typically executes a sequenced set of actions (steps) that produce an outcome. The way and order in which the actions are performed can be controlled. At times, specific tools are needed to support the action being performed.

A use case focuses on actions or steps performed on the site. If you have a task that needs to be performed on your site and it is important that it be performed in a specific way, it will be important to document the specific steps in the task.

Creating a use case can:

➤ Provide insight into the technology you might need on your site

➤ Influence the design of the interface

➤ Help identify different roles and what they can do on the site

Use cases aren't just for describing (to the designer and developer) what you want your users to be able to do on your site. If you do them with enough detail, you can also use them as testing procedures, site user guides, and training tools.

Testing procedures are often overlooked when most of the tasks are performed using default features and configurations. In other words, quite often, site behavior is assumed. So, if you want to test whether your site is performing as it should, you can start by creating use cases and then testing whether you can do what your use cases say you should be able to do.

If your users require training and your use cases describe what they should be able to do, you can turn around and use the use cases for step-by-step procedures in your site manual or training. You might change some of the verb tenses, but you get the idea.

Not everyone will perform each task the same way unless the task is designed to constrain their actions. With multiple personas and roles, you can identify how different personas (with different permissions) might want to perform similar tasks. Different methods might mean you need an interface that provides more than one way to accomplish the task. Whether you want to accommodate multiple methods is up to you.

Documenting Use Cases

You can use different techniques to document use cases — for example, a narrative, flowchart, table, or the Structured Analysis and Design Technique (SADT).

SADT is a method used to illustrate various aspects (inputs, outputs, controls, and mechanisms) of a task or a series of related steps. It is similar to a flowchart. The visual aspect of this method can come in handy during a brainstorming session when requirements are being discussed. You might recognize SADT if you are familiar with IDef (Integration Definition for Function Modeling).

The following sections introduce you to SADT, as well as other ways to capture information about your use cases.

Single-Step Use Cases

It is not likely that you will perform a single step or action on a site independent of other steps or actions, but there are two reasons to bring the idea of single-step use cases to your attention.

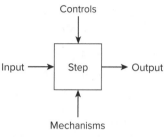

First, single-step use cases can be used to document a single deviation to a default task. For instance, assume your site has multiple types of content. Each time content is created, the same default steps are performed, except one. You can choose to document the default steps and the one step that is different, or you can document the deviation.

FIGURE 4-3

Second, it is easier to explain the SADT method when one step or action is being defined.

Figure 4-3 illustrates a single step in a task.

Step

The step is the action being performed by your audience or user. If you are using personas, the step is what your site's persona will perform. The challenge with identifying a step is to know how granular you need to get. For example, which of the following is a step?

➤ Click the Submit button

➤ Create an event

➤ Upload an image

The first step example might be too small to document unless it is a step that is uncommon to the task or if the submit process needs to execute more than your typical submit command.

The second step is more in line with the task to create an event. What does it take to create an event? The steps might include create a new node, complete the event form, upload the event brochure, upload an image, insert an image, and enable a view listing related nodes.

The last example, upload an image, can be accomplished using different features in Drupal. By isolating this action as a step, you can describe the way you want the image to be uploaded, where you want the image to be stored, who can see the image, and so on.

Input

Input is the data needed to perform the step. Input can be a word or term to be searched; it can be personal data used to create an account or place an order; it can also be the information needed to complete a web form. The objective is to identify what data, if any, is needed to complete the step and to identify its source.

Input can have several sources. For instance, it can come from the output of the previous step or be provided by the user(s) performing the step. In systems like Drupal, the source of the data can come from objects or elements that are loaded when the page is loaded (node ID, field names, term IDs, and more).

It is helpful to note the source of the data used as input. For instance, assume that you are filling out an application online and it is a multistep task:

➤ You complete part one of the application by filling in the form fields.

➤ You click Next and data from part one pre-populates some fields in part two of the application.

➤ In the third part of the application, you need to fill in some fields that want data that is on a statement you have. Although you are entering the data, the source of the data is the statement.

Knowing it comes from a statement may or may not matter. If the data from the statement were data stored someplace else in your system, there might be an opportunity to integrate with that system and pull the data for the applicable instead of entering it twice.

Not all steps require data as described above. For example, the step to create a node might require a decision regarding which type of content to create. A complete statement of the step can help clarify what is expected of the user completing the step as well as the developers responsible for creating the user experience.

By knowing what the input is, you can ensure that users have that input available to them when they go to execute the step.

Output

Output is the result of the step. You might require multiple actions to occur as the output of the step. For example, you might want a message to appear on the screen and an email to be sent. The output from one step can be the input for another step.

For instance, have you ever been on a site that allowed you to sign a guest register or create an account? When you submitted the form, did you get any feedback on the screen, like "Thank you for submitting your information"? Did the feedback screen give you the option to continue browsing the site, which might be the input to the next step? Recognizing that a step produces output helps you plan what needs to be done with that output: show it to the user, use it in the next step as input, store it, or maybe all three.

Controls

Controls are conditions that influence or govern how users perform the step. Controls can be enforced by the site technology. For example, controls can be implemented via a sequenced form that prevents the user from moving on to the next page until the form is complete. Other technology-controlled options include user roles and the associated permissions. Unless the user is assigned to a role and that role has the right permission, the user can't perform a step (such as viewing a form or accessing a page).

Controls can also be business policies that the user follows. Although a risk exists that the user will not adhere to the control policy, it might be a risk whose cost does not outweigh the expense of programming a technology solution.

The objective of identifying controls is to identify whether or when Drupal needs to validate conditions. For instance, does the user have permission, did the page load in a smartphone or a tablet, and so on.

Mechanisms

Mechanisms can be tools on the screen or functions that run in the background (back end). The screen mechanisms can include, but are not limited to, how-to pop-ups, calendar functions, calculators, fields, buttons, and/or forms the user needs in order to complete the step. Back-end functions might require Drupal to compare the dates selected with the dates in another field on the form to ensure the two dates don't contradict each other.

Mechanisms can also include tools that are not included in the site. Even if you aren't going to provide the tool, you might need to offer advanced notice that a tool is required or you might offer a link to another site where the tool can be used. For example, will you be providing download-able PDFs? You might need to tell your audience where they can get the PDF reader required for the download. The objective is to identify the functions and features that will be needed to complete the step.

Multistep Use Cases

Documenting one step is not very realistic when you are trying to document a task that is made up of several steps. When you connect a series of steps, you get a flowchart. Figure 4-4 illustrates that the output of one step becomes the input to the next. Note that not all output must be input to the next step.

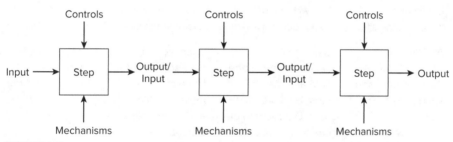

FIGURE 4-4

Task Versions

Unless you have implemented controls on your steps so that all users must do the same steps the same way each time, you might need multiple task flowcharts for the same task. By repeating the task analysis for different personas or different conditions, you validate the steps you have identified. If a different persona performs the task with different steps, you have validated the need for multiple paths through your site.

Sometimes, you won't be able to predict what the steps are for the task — for example, if the task is to find a page on your site that discusses a specific topic. Depending on your site architecture, you might have three ways a person can find a page (search, menu item, and vocabulary term link). Each option has a different set of steps whose inputs, outputs, controls, and mechanisms vary, while at the same time enabling the user to find the page.

Scenarios such as find a page are good candidates for usability testing to see if the design of the site provides an intuitive way for your audience to accomplish the task of finding a specific page.

Flowchart Alternative

A flowchart with boxes and arrows is a great visual, but if you have many tasks to document and don't have time to create flowcharts for linear processes, you could use a table. The example content in Table 4-4 is one way to document the task of creating an event node.

TABLE 4-4: Sample Table Task Analysis

STEP	INPUT	CONTROLS	MECHANISMS	OUTPUT
Access the event form.	An event needs to be created.	User must have permission to access this specific content type.	User accesses the Create Content link from the navigation menu.	The Create Node form appears.
Complete the event form.	Data comes from information submitted via a web form on the site.	User must have access to web form content.	User types data into the form fields.	The form's fields contain typed information.
Upload the event brochure.	A PDF file provided by the user is uploaded via the upload field in the event form and submitted on the site.	User must have access to the upload field and the file must be stored in a directory with the user ID as the directory name.	User clicks the Browse button to locate the file on a local drive, and then clicks an Upload button to upload to the site.	The upload field has the PDF loaded and ready for submittal.
Upload an image.	A PNG, JPG, or GIF uploaded via the web form and submitted on the site.	User must have access to the image field and the file must be stored in the user ID directory; the image field should be hidden in teaser and full view.	User clicks the Browse to Hard Drive button to locate the file, and then clicks an Upload button to upload to the site.	The image is uploaded in the image field ready to be inserted into the text.
Insert an image.	The image uploaded in the image field and a content field.	User must have permission to insert an image into the content field.	User uses an Image Insert feature to insert image into the field that holds the event description. User uses a WYSIWYG image editor to size and position the image.	The image shows in a content field with text.
Save the node to the site.	A completed form with a Save button.	User is restricted from publishing the node to the site audience. Node must be reviewed and published by the site admin.	User uses the Save button to save an unpublished event node in the database and trigger an action to send a template-based message to the site admin.	The new node shows in unpublished view mode and an email is sent to the site admin advising of the new post ready for review.

Narrative Alternative

Although a flowchart offers a great visual of how the steps flow together, a table provides a convenient alternative to document your requirements. Another alternative would be to create a narrative. The narrative might not include all these details, but if the task is relatively simple and you want to use system default settings and configuration, a short narrative might be all that is needed.

For instance, the narrative for creating an event node might be, "A user with the appropriate permissions has a link to the create event form. Clicking the link opens the form, where the user can fill in the form, and upload an image and PDF file. The user can embed the image in the event description, resize it, and position it. When the node is saved, it is unpublished and an email is sent to the site administrator indicating the node is ready for review."

Whichever method you choose, remember that the objective is to convey to the designer and developer what you want to happen. If you don't know what to ask for or don't know the ramifications of your request, your designer or developer should be able to advise you. Determining requirements is an iterative process, so be patient.

DRUPAL NODE TEASERS

Don't confuse a marketing teaser statement with a Drupal teaser. A Drupal node is used to post content to a Drupal site. A simple blog node includes a field for the title and a field for the body of the blog. A Drupal teaser is the first x number of characters in the node body. You can set the length of the teaser.

You can override the default teaser. In Drupal 6, you can manually insert a teaser break in the body and override this default teaser length for that node. In Drupal 7, you can manually create a teaser that is separate from the body.

Multistep Use Cases with Decisions

If this, then do that or do this other thing. The steps in a task are not always sequential and sometimes conditions need to be evaluated, decisions made, or choices offered.

For instance, assume you have a web form that requires specific fields to be filled in before the user can submit the form successfully. Figure 4-5 shows what this use case might look like using SADT. The diagram illustrates the relationship between the steps the system needs to support and also provides the inputs, outputs, controls, and mechanisms for each step.

When documenting the tasks you want your users to be able to perform on your site, don't assume one form of documentation will be all you need. In Figure 4-5, the SADT diagram does not document the details associated with the steps. For example, it does not indicate what the message should say when the form is returned to the user for completion. Additional narrative might be required to explain, in this case, that the message should list the fields that were not completed.

Another example of a task with decisions is a purchasing task. If you are building an e-commerce site, you need to spend some time on the different ways your customer might shop. The following example documents the task flow using a bulleted list of steps to describe one path through the task of buying an item online:

➤ Customer places an item in the shopping cart.

➤ Customer decides to check the status of the shopping cart versus searching for more products.

➤ From the shopping cart, customer decides to continue shopping versus checking out or changing his order.

➤ From the shopping area, customer decides to return to the shopping cart versus searching for more products.

➤ While in the shopping cart, customer decides to check out versus changing his order.

➤ From the checkout screen, customer chooses the guest checkout versus creating an account first.

➤ Customer completes the guest checkout form and submits order.

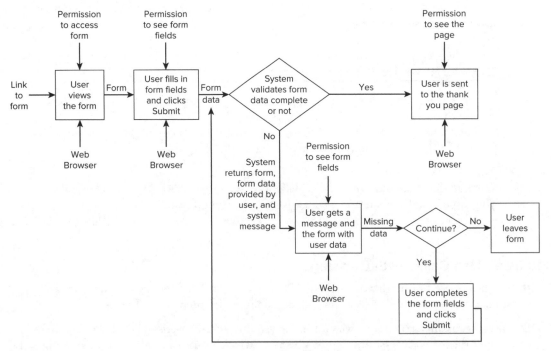

FIGURE 4-5

Can you see how these steps could be different? What if the customer never checked his cart? What if the customer chose the option to create an account during checkout? To answer these questions, you would need to create a series of bulleted steps until each scenario was addressed.

Like the SADT example illustrated in Figure 4-5, the bulleted list approach will need additional information if you are documenting requirements. For instance, you might need to explain that the shopping cart needs a way to temporarily store the items that have been placed in it so that when the customer looks into the cart and then leaves the cart to continue shopping, his items remain in the cart until he takes them out, checks out, or closes his browser.

Note that use cases are often used to present what the user will be doing on your site. What if the task is something your site needs to perform? You can use the techniques discussed here to document a specific functionality you want for your site.

CONTENT ANALYSIS

Content is the reason your audience comes to your site. Add to this the fact that you have chosen a CMS to develop your site, and you have two pretty big factors encouraging you to understand your content needs fully. The content analysis is an in-depth look at your content needs.

Making Content Decisions

Content influences several design decisions. It also influences the site structure (how the site is organized), the interface (how the content is laid out), and some user interactions (how the content is loaded to the site). Table 4-5 provides a brief introduction to the various content-related analyses discussed in the pages that follow. Each decision in the table can affect content decisions you need to make later.

TABLE 4-5: Content Analyses

ANALYSIS	DECISIONS
Types of content	Identify all the types of content your site needs
	Ultimately determine the best strategy for distinguishing between one type of content and another
Content purpose	Identify the purpose of the content
User-content relationships	Determine whether/how the content and/or its data relates to your audience
Content data	Identify what data makes up each type of content
Content sources	Identify where your content or data will come from
Data reuse	Determine how content data will be used outside the node to which it was originally assigned
Content categories	Determine whether your content should be categorized
	Decide whether you want your categories to be links
	Decide whether you want predefined terms or user-defined terms
Category terms	Identify which terms you need for each category
Content relationships	Determine how those types of content relate to each other
Content metadata	Determine whether the data needs metadata

continues

TABLE 4-5 *(continued)*

ANALYSIS	DECISIONS
Content language	Determine whether your site needs to accommodate multiple languages
Content access	Determine whether you want to control who can view, create, edit, and delete your content
User content	Determine whether you want to capture content about your users
	Determine whether you want your users to be considered content

When you get to the design phase, you will visit content again by considering how it is organized in the site, how it is arranged in the site interface, and how it is displayed, to name a few considerations.

Identifying Types of Content

In this part of the analysis, the objective is to identify all the types of content your site needs. During your needs analysis, audience analysis, process analysis, and task analysis, you identified types of content and may not have realized it. For instance, an event is often a type of content and an article is a type of content.

Decisions made during this analysis can influence:

➤ How you manage permissions associated with viewing, creating, editing, and deleting content

➤ Content theming strategies

➤ Which vocabularies (categories) to apply when creating content

> ### DRUPAL CONTENT TYPES
>
> A Drupal content type is an input form used to create a node. Drupal 6 comes with the Page and Story content types enabled. Drupal 7 changes the name of Story to Article. You can create custom content types, as well. For example, you can have an event content type with event-related fields, such as Date and Location.

You can distinguish one type of content from another in different ways. You don't need a separate content type (the Drupal form used to create a node) for each type of content. Following are three strategies to consider.

➤ **Content types** — For each type of content (e.g., article, event, project, and so on), use a different predefined form to collect the data that defines that content.

➤ **Vocabulary terms** — For each type of content (e.g., article, news, report, commentary, and so on), use one predefined content type to collect the content and use a vocabulary term to distinguish between the different types of content.

➤ **Content type field terms** — For each type of content (e.g., article, news, report, commentary, and so on), use one predefined content type to collect the content and use a value assigned to a field to distinguish between the different types of content.

At this stage of the analysis, you might have enough information about your content to discern the best strategy, or you can start to list content you anticipate needing.

If this is your first time contemplating types of content for a Drupal site, getting a handle on what is meant by *types of content* might be hard. One way to help you make decisions about types of content is to use examples. Table 4-6 provides some types of content you might find in particular types of sites.

TABLE 4-6: Sample Types of Content

INFORMATION SITE	LEARNING SITE	E-COMMERCE SITE	COMMUNITY SITES
Articles	Lesson plans	Product	Member profiles
Journal posts	Student profiles	User manuals	Experts
Case studies	Lesson pages	Training guides	Leaders
Reports	Course summaries	Sample uses	Business ads
White papers		Testimonials	Group posts
Project status			Events
Sponsors			Announcements
Blogs			
Videos			

Notice that each sample type of content describes what the content is, not what the content is about. Content can be about many topics, such as cars, fruit, countries, and so on.

After completing your content analysis, you will have the information you need to decide which strategy (e.g., content type, vocabulary term, content type field term) you want to use. For example, you might decide to:

➤ Use a Drupal content type to define a node as an article and a taxonomy vocabulary to organize the articles into topics

➤ Use a default content type plus a taxonomy vocabulary term to define the node as an article, and then use another vocabulary to organize the articles into topics

Factors that can influence your decision on the use of content types include the following:

➤ The fields needed to capture and organize the content in the node

➤ Whether there are taxonomy vocabularies that are unique to the type of content

➤ The level of control you need regarding which role can view, create, edit, or delete the type of content

Don't worry if the list of types of content you define for your site isn't perfect. As you proceed through defining your requirements, you can return to the list and update it. Just remember to update all the other aspects of the content analysis as well.

Assigning Purpose to Content

In this part of the analysis, you are assigning a purpose to each type of content. Decisions made during this analysis can influence:

➤ Theming decisions

➤ The type of data you want to include in each content type

➤ Category terms used to reinforce purpose

Defining Purpose

You may recall that your site's purpose was defined during the needs analysis. Now, it's time to apply purpose to content. Even if your site has one purpose, each type of content might not share that purpose. For example, the purpose of the *About* page is not the same as the purpose of the *Events* page.

If you have a list of the types of content you need on your site, next to each type of content, state the purpose of the content. Some types of content are obvious, but consider the examples in Table 4-7.

TABLE 4-7: Sample Content Purposes

TYPE OF CONTENT	PURPOSE(S)
Story	To inform the site audience of newsworthy events
Event	To promote an event, convey event logistics, and accept event sign-up
Document	To present metadata about an attached PDF document
Media	To show movie clips on the page
Lesson	To provide instruction that meets a learning objective
Book	To tell an entertaining story via a series of sequential pages
Page	To introduce the content being presented in a site section (such as landing pages)

In some of these instances, the type of content has more than one purpose and the purpose appears obvious based on the type of content. With others, the purpose is not obvious. For example, one of the most overlooked pages on a site is the site section landing page. When your users click on a menu link, where are they going? Are they going to a page with an article or are they going to a page that introduces all the articles on the site?

Why Purpose Matters

Purpose can affect theming decisions, data requirements, and the vocabulary terms you use to categorize your content. For instance, assume the media content mentioned above is spooky movie clips:

➤ **Purpose** — The purpose might be to present spooky movie clips.

➤ **Theme** — A theme setting with a black background might present the right atmosphere to show your spooky movie clips.

➤ **Data** — Data comes in many shapes, including movie clips. If you are going to store the clips on your site's server, you might use a field to upload and display your movie clips.

➤ **Vocabulary terms** — You might want to help your visitors find different types of spooky clips, so adding a vocabulary with terms such as crazed killers, ghosts, the supernatural, and so on might be useful.

As you can see from this example, if you know the purpose of the content, you might see a need to present the content in a specific context or you might need to connect your content in a specific order so that your content can fulfill its purpose.

Stating the purpose of the content enables your site designers to take the purpose into consideration and present a design that supports the content appropriately. Another example is content whose purpose is to mimic a book. How should a book be presented or designed?

➤ Should each page of a multipage resource be made available in a page list or just the first page?

➤ Should a background image make the pages look like they are pages in a book? If so, how will this affect the pages that aren't in a book?

➤ Should "previous" and "next" be included at the top and bottom of the content?

➤ Should a table of contents be provided in a sidebar to enable the audience to go to the page of interest at any time?

By identifying the purpose of your content, you help facilitate agreement regarding what the type of content will represent. Identifying the purpose is not intended to be a big deal, but if you don't take a moment and consider the content purpose, you might miss a data requirement or an opportunity to present your content in a meaningful way.

Determining User-Content Relationships

In a user-content relationship analysis, the objective is to determine how the content relates to your users. Decisions made during this analysis can influence:

➤ How you implement access controls

➤ Your decisions regarding workflow

➤ Which publishing status you want to use

➤ Why you create content types

You can relate content to users in different ways. Two common ways are based on persona and role, as discussed in the following sections. This analysis isn't complicated, and for simple sites or sites with one purpose, this analysis could be one you do on scratch paper or combine with another analysis.

Persona-Content Relationships

From the persona's perspective, the relationship is typically about whether and how the persona will use the content. Will you have one set of content for one persona and another set of content for another persona? This might be hard to imagine, so consider an example.

Suppose you have a site that sells a product. Your site includes information about the product, in the hope that users will buy it. The other information on your site is instructional; it teaches users how to use the product after they have purchased it.

Here are two examples of why you would want to know how the content relates to your site personas:

➤ **Content access** — When the persona is in a buyer role, he or she can see the sales information and buy the product. But to get instruction on how to use the product, the buyer might need to be in a different role with different permissions. This different role could be one based on a special agreement the buyer purchased or some other criteria.

➤ **Writing context** — Assume the products you are selling are appliances. You will need content that sells the appliance and explains how to use the appliance and, potentially, how to repair the appliance. Each type of content could speak to three different personas: the decision-maker, the user, and the repair person. Each persona might have a different skill set, different motivation, and different set of tasks to perform in context with that appliance.

Role-Content Relationships

From a role perspective, you consider not only view access (whether the user can see the content while in their role) but also the ability to create and edit. If you have multiple types of content, which role will create, edit, delete, and/or publish the content? Will you restrict the view by content type? The answers to these questions will influence design and development.

> **CONTENT TYPE VIEW ACCESS**
>
> In Drupal 6 and Drupal 7, you can set a role to view all content types or not. You can control which role can create, edit, and delete individual content types. If you want to control which role can view a specific content type, you need a contributed module. The Content Access module has been used frequently in Drupal 6 to accommodate content-type access control. As of April 2011, there was a -dev version for Drupal 7.

Consider the two ways to relate users to content and see whether you can map the types of content you have listed to the personas and roles you have drafted so far. Do you see overlaps or inconsistencies? Do you see any conflicts? You can manage content access in Drupal using different approaches. Just remember that you should plan them *before* you start creating nodes.

Identifying Content Data

In the identifying content data part of the analysis, the objective is to identify which data will make up each type of content. Forget for a moment that your content will appear on your screen surrounded by other elements, such as the header, menus, sidebars, and footer. Picture your content as it is standing alone, unencumbered by its surroundings. What is the data that makes up your content?

Decisions made during this analysis can influence:

➤ Whether or how you can reuse pieces of data that make up your content

➤ Whether fields will be used to label or categorize the content

➤ How you will apply theming

➤ Which roles can see which pieces of data

To identify which data makes up each type of content, consider the fields and their form, as discussed in the following sections.

Data Fields

Data fields are fields that hold different types of data. The content you enter into your node form to create your page gets stored in fields. Only one field is required to create a node: the Title field. You don't have to display the Title field, but you do need to include it as part of the content type. By examining what data makes up each type of content that you have identified, you can determine how many fields you need and what they might be.

Other data is associated with a node, including (but not limited to) the node's author, publish date, update date, path, ID, and menu. Combining this other node-related data with the fields can give you a lot of power to filter, locate, and reuse node-related data.

FIELDS IN DRUPAL

In Drupal 6, content types come with two fields: Title and Body. The Content Construction Kit (CCK) module enables you to add various types of fields to a content type.

In Drupal 7, the ability to add fields comes already installed; you don't need to add CCK. The ability to add fields has also been extended beyond just content types. You can now add them to user accounts, comments, and taxonomy vocabulary terms.

Potential Fields

Table 4-8 provides four sample types of content: article, report, project, and event. Listed under each sample is data that is likely to be included in that type of content. In each instance, you could enter the data into one Body field or you could add additional fields to help organize your content and provide data that you can reuse in other places on your site.

For each type of content, identify the data that makes up the type of content. Start by looking for patterns. For example, if you have a stack of reports that you want to present on your site and the table of contents varies from report to report, you might decide to store all the text in the report the default Body field. However, if you see a pattern (for example, all the reports have the same sections), you can list those sections as data.

How granular do you need your content to be? *Level of granularity* refers to how many fields you are going to use to collect and store your content. Consider the content type called *article* referenced in Table 4-8. In this sample, the Article body field contains all the information that is the article (introduction, story, conclusion, references). The level of granularity used to store the article is low.

TABLE 4-8: Sample Types of Content

ARTICLE	REPORT	PROJECT	EVENT
Title	Title	Project name	Name
Article body	Written by	Start date	Description
	Executive summary	End date	Location
	Background	Client	Start date
	Methods	Statement of work	End date
	Findings	Schedule	Start time
	Conclusions	Status	End time
	References		Cost
			Directions
			Agenda

Now consider the report example. You could store the executive summary, background, methods, findings, conclusions, and references in one field (lower granularity) or you could break your content into six separate fields (higher granularity).

Your decision regarding level of granularity will be influenced by:

➤ How much control you want to have over your content developers

➤ How much control you want when displaying the data

➤ Whether you want to capture and reuse the data in the fields

DRUPAL TEASER TIPS

A Drupal teaser is the first x number of characters in the node's default Body field. The teaser is displayed on the home page and other pages that list nodes, such as a page that lists all nodes that have a specific vocabulary term.

In Drupal 7, you can remove the default Body field and then add it back later. Warning: by design, if you delete the default Body field from a Drupal 7 content type and then add it back, the teaser will not show on the home page or other pages that show the Drupal teaser by default. The Body field gets treated like any other text field.

Drupal's default teaser is available only from the default Body field. If you break up your content into separate fields and want a default teaser, be sure to use the default Body field. In Drupal 6, use the default Body field to hold the content that will make up the default teaser. In Drupal 7, do the same or use the summary feature, which is part of the default Body, to create your teaser manually.

Why Fields Matter

You might be wondering, why all this fuss? Why does it matter what data is included in my content? Technically, you don't have to break down your content into separate fields, but if you want to maximize the results Drupal can offer, giving the idea of fields some thought is worth it. If you plan your content's data, Drupal will enable you to:

- ➤ Dynamically generate new pages from existing content (as shown in Figure 4-6)
- ➤ Organize your content into different groups based on the value of the data in one or more fields (e.g., grouped by role, grouped by client, grouped by strategy)
- ➤ Create multiple content entry points for your audience (see all content for role X, from client Y, or using strategy Z)
- ➤ Ensure that your content is consistent from one page to the next

In the world of HTML sites, the type of content reuse and organization options described above are not the norm and, in some cases, not possible without going beyond HTML. When transitioning from planning HTML sites to planning and building sites with Drupal, you need to think differently to maximize the power of Drupal. Of course, you can use Drupal to mimic your HTML practices (to a certain extent); that is your choice.

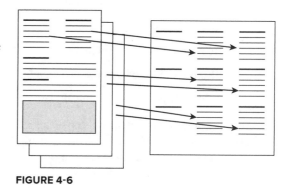

FIGURE 4-6

Layout Considerations

Content layout is a design consideration, but it is worth mentioning now so that you can plan ahead a little. In Drupal, if you divide your content into fields, the fields appear on the screen in the same order that they appear in create/edit mode. You can choose to hide or show the labels for custom content fields. You can control how some fields display their data (e.g., show the image or show the file name for the image).

If you do not like how the content "stacks up" on the page when you view the node, you will need to set aside time during the design and development phases to choose a strategy for making the content more pleasant to look at and easy to use.

FIELD LAYOUT STRATEGIES

Several options are available for configuring the layout of your fields and other data items. Some options don't require any coding, whereas others require some coding. For example, in Drupal 6 and Drupal 7, you can use the Panels module to organize your fields. In Drupal 6, the Composite Layout module is also an option. As for the coding options, you can use the Contemplate module in Drupal 6 and Drupal 7, or you can create a theme page designed specifically for that content type.

Even if you aren't adding any new fields, continue reading to learn about data form and what you need to consider when identifying the type of data you will include in your node.

Data Form

Data is not created equal. You have numbers, text, images, links, dates, sounds, video, animation, PDFs, and so on. You can capture data many ways. For instance, you can type it into a form, select it from a drop-down box, or select it with a check box or radio button. Because data comes in different forms, the way it is displayed, stored, and viewed varies. The amount of space data takes up also varies. All these conditions influence the design and development of your site. They also affect the processes and tasks you use to sustain your site.

Assume you have identified a type of content and have determined the content for that type can be broken into the following fields:

➤ **Title** — The default Title field

➤ **Goal** — A text field that holds a goal statement

➤ **Client** — A select field listing all your clients

➤ **Status** — Radio buttons with a choice of status milestones

➤ **Description** — The default Body field relabeled

The next question is, what will those fields contain? As mentioned earlier, data can include numbers, text, images, sound, video, animation, PDFs, and so on. The form of your data influences several aspects of your site, including:

➤ Type of field

➤ Data entry strategy

➤ Data storage

➤ Data visibility

➤ Screen real estate

Type of Field

Because not all data is the same, the fields that hold the data probably won't be the same. Numerous modules allow you to add different types of data to your node. For example, you can add text fields, numeric fields, image fields, link fields, date fields, and so on.

The types of fields don't have to be limited to what you enter on the screen. You can add fields to your content types that:

➤ Perform calculations

➤ Create relationships between nodes

➤ Create relationships between a node and a user

➤ Display the results of a database query

➤ And so on

In order to know which type of field to use, you need to know the form of the data.

Data Entry

Typing numbers and text into forms on the screen is one thing, but including files such as images, sounds, video, animation, and PDF is another. Assuming your site's server space is large enough to hold the various media you want to present in your site, what process do you want your users to use when uploading and displaying media in your pages? Depending on what your users need to be able to do with the images after they have been uploaded, you have several options to choose from.

At this point of your analysis, try to include decisions regarding the following:

> **Upload via online form or SFTP** — Will the file format be usable after it's uploaded via a field or will SFTP be required to get the files on the server? For example, will your users be uploading a SWF file along with its associated folders and files? You won't be able to do this via a field and still have the SWF play correctly. You need SFTP access.

> **File type restrictions** — To avoid giving someone the ability to upload an executable file that can do serious harm to your server and site, you need to limit what types of files users can upload. Drupal provides default options that avoid security issues, but if you need to change what users can upload, don't include file extensions that can be harmful.

> **Media file to be displayed in a query display** — Files uploaded via a WYSIWYG editor are not typically seen by the Views modules (the module used to create database queries). If you want a file that can be included in a dynamically generated list, you need a field.

> **File width requirements** — How wide must the media be in order for it to be shown as desired? Some media won't shrink or expand to fit and still look presentable.

Other considerations, such as file storage, are addressed next.

IMAGE FIELDS

Drupal 6 comes with the Upload module. This creates the file attachment feature that is associated with each content type. You can enable or disable the attachment feature on a content-type-by-content-type basis. You don't have to use the Upload module; you can use one of many file-management modules available, including the FileField module. The Upload module is not part of Drupal 7. Drupal 7 enables you to add a file field, if you want to attach files to a node, by using the File module that comes with Drupal 7.

Data Storage

Not all data is created equal. Text and numbers are stored in the database, whereas web-friendly files, such as images, sounds, video, animation, and PDFs, are stored on the server in a directory (similar to HTML sites). The database also stores information about the files (filename and page reference information).

Different upload features store data in different locations on your server. Some upload features allow you to designate a default directory of your choice for each type of upload; others do not. Will you require specific storage locations for each type of file or media uploaded? If so, where?

DATA STORAGE

In Drupal 6 and Drupal 7, data collected in fields is stored in the database. In Drupal 6, the Title and Body fields are stored in the node_revision table and the custom fields are stored in content tables generated by the Content Construction Kit (in conjunction with the specific field module) and labeled content_*fieldname*. In Drupal 7, the structure is similar; however, the Body field is just like any other field you can add, and the data is stored in tables labeled field_data_field_*fieldname* and field_revision_field_*fieldname*.

Data Visibility

Data that is entered directly into a form field, such as text or numbers, is easy to display in a node. The process used to display non-text data, images, video, audio, and other types of files is different. In short, you need to store the non-text data item on a web server and establish a link between the node in which it will be displayed and its storage location. Once the link is established, you can display the non-text data using the HTML command that applies to the type of data or via a method provided by a module. The HTML command is often provided by the module you use.

By identifying the forms of data and how you want your audience to see them, you can make sure your design has the screen real estate and your development strategy has the necessary technology to accommodate your requirements.

DATA VISIBILITY OPTIONS

In Drupal 6, the display of fields created with the Content Construction Kit is managed via CCK's Display Manager. The display of Title and Body fields is not managed by the Display Manager, as they are not CCK fields. In Drupal 7, the Display Manager works with all fields.

Screen Real Estate

Screen real estate refers to the amount of space available to show your content. Your content space competes with the space taken up by the header, menus, sidebars, regions, and footer. Different forms of data take up different amounts of space. Some data, such as text and numbers, can flex within their environment; other forms of data, such as images and video, have a fixed size and shape when displayed in a page.

Why do your requirements need to convey the form? To answer, let's jump ahead for a moment to screen layouts. The size and shape of your data can influence whether you have sidebars and, if so, how many.

Figure 4-7 shows three sample layouts. From left to right, the area that holds the core of your content gets larger, allowing larger forms of data to be presented. Depending on the width of your content display, you might not be able to have the sidebars you want. Data tables, images, and other media often need more space than just text.

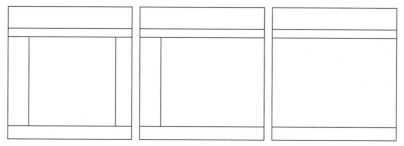

FIGURE 4-7

Maybe you are thinking, okay, when I add a table or image to my page, I will simply turn off one or more sidebars when I need more space. Well, in the world of HTML and possibly other content management systems, this thinking would be fine (assuming you want to ignore the topic of usability, as well). In Drupal, the goal is to plan well so that content in your sidebars will appear based on a condition being true versus your manually adding a block to every new page that gets created. For example, a condition could be, "if the URL path includes a term from a specific taxonomy vocabulary, show a specific menu block."

Imagine a site for which multiple content authors add pages of content. Would you want them adding, removing, or changing the content in the sidebars as they create content? Probably not. For one thing, that would be a pain. Second, you would have to grant them access to administer blocks, which is not a good idea. Third, you could create a usability issue with menus and other relevant content appearing and disappearing based on a content developer's wishes or needs.

> **MANAGING BLOCKS IN DRUPAL**
>
> In Drupal 6, the default block administration interface lets you control whether blocks are displayed by user role, URL path, and/or a PHP conditional statement. In Drupal 7, the options are role, path, and content type. The Context module provides additional conditions that can be used to govern when and where a block appears. Context is available in Drupal 6 and Drupal 7.

You need to plan ahead. Know the form of the content you want to include in your pages, and create a set of parameters that your designer and developer can use when creating your layouts.

 Chapter 5 presents more about planning content layout and Drupal themes.

Identifying Content Sources

In this part of the analysis, your objective is to identify where your content or data will come from. Content can be considered internal or external to your site. That is, the content is either stored in your site or it's stored external to your site and pulled into your site interface using various methods.

Decisions made during this analysis can influence:

➤ How you implement your input filters

➤ What type of fields you need

➤ Copyright practices for your site

➤ How you display your content

The following sections consider the content sources for text, media, attachments, and other content.

Internal Text

Internal text, the text you type into your content type forms, is stored in your site database. It is likely that most, if not all, of your site's content will be text written by you, your team, volunteers, site members, or even hired authors.

The text might be composed by typing straight into the content type forms, or it might be composed offline in a desktop application and then copied and pasted into your site's content type forms. Your text might need to be formatted with bold or italics, bulleted or number lists, sub-headers, and so on.

Internal text might imply that your text is an original work, but that might not be the case. If you obtain permission to post copyrighted works from authors who are external to your team, are they considered external? From an organizational perspective, they probably are. But from a technology perspective, if you enter them into your site's database, they are internal to the site.

Continuing with the topic of copyright, if you open your site for others to post their text, who owns the copyright to the text entered by your site members? Do you need to protect the text or does it become yours to reuse on your site? As you can see, planning your internal text is more than deciding a field strategy (as discussed in the previous analysis).

Much about internal text on a site has to do with processes, tasks, and policies. The process and task analyses were presented earlier in this chapter. In addition to text ownership and reuse policies, decisions made regarding how you will enter text and who will enter text into your site can influence the:

➤ Site roles

➤ Permission for each role

➤ Forms and features needed to capture and format the text

➤ Need (or not) for instructions and guidelines on the screen during data entry

External Text

External text refers to showing content on your site that is created and stored on another site. One of the most common practices today is to use RSS (Really Simple Syndication) feeds to show data from one or more resources on a site. Another practice involves merging data from one or more sources and presenting it in a new way, resulting in what is referred to as a *mashup*.

With the success of Web 2.0 technologies and social media, more and more systems are making it possible to send and receive data between systems. For example, you don't have to be logged in to Twitter or Facebook to make a post to Twitter or Facebook. You can "Digg" a blog article on one site, and your Digg gets reflected on another site. Drupal offers many ways for you to include text from external resources. Figure 4-8 shows three screen shots and how you can display text from another site (using an RSS feed) and Twitter posts on your site.

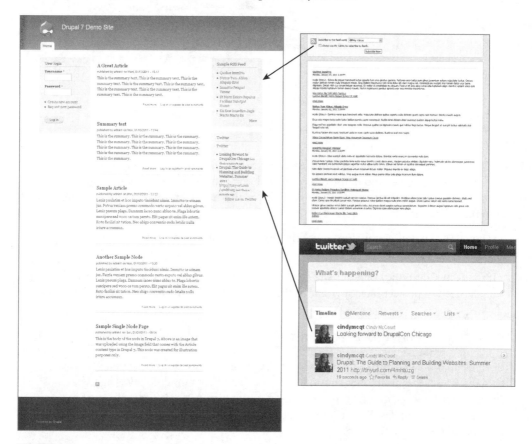

FIGURE 4-8

In addition to showing data from other sources on your site, you can send data to other sources. Figure 4-9 shows that by installing Facebook applications on a Drupal site, the Facebook comment generated on your Drupal site can be sent to your Facebook wall.

Planning where your content is coming from is important for design and development. If your requirements say to show a list of articles on the XYZ topic, the developer needs to know where the articles are coming from. Is it a list of articles you have on your site, or is it a list of articles on another site?

You also need to plan for copyright issues. Any time you pull content from one site into another, you need to be sure that you are allowed to do so. The scope of this book does not include providing legal advice regarding the practice of showing the work of others on your site. You can learn more about U.S. copyright law at www.copyright.gov/title17. If it isn't yours, get permission by asking or following the copyright policy posted at the source.

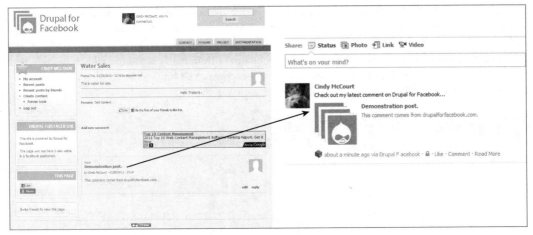

FIGURE 4-9

After you have permission and start pulling external text into your site, will it be managed by the processes, tasks, and policies you defined for internal text? In some instances, it might. If you are pulling full written works from another site into yours, the text is internal. Consideration needs to be given to the following:

➤ If you have limited permission to use the text, you will need to govern if or how you and others reuse the text.

➤ If the copyright policy on your site conflicts with the permissions you have been given, you might need to protect the copyright of the works you pulling into your site.

COPYING CONTENT INTO YOUR SITE

Both Drupal 6 and Drupal 7 come with the Aggregator module, which enables you to show RSS feeds from other sites on your site. The Feeds module takes aggregation to another level, allowing you to import content from other sites into your site's database as nodes. If you want to merge multiple sites into one site, the Feeds module might be a useful approach.

Internal Media

Users of the Internet have come to expect sites to offer more than text; they want media (images, video, animations, and audio). When you're considering sources of internal media (media uploaded and stored within your site), the same concepts apply as with internal text. You need to consider the:

➤ Process used to upload the media to the site

➤ Source of the media and media ownership

Another consideration in regard to internal media is how you will present the media to your site visitors. Will you use a field or will you place the media on the server prior to creating the node and use an HTML tag to reference and display the media? In traditional HTML site-building practices, you manually upload images, video, and other media to the server via SFTP. This method creates some challenges when you want or need multiple authors to post content on your site. With Drupal, you can use SFTP and manually embedded links to the media in the body of your content, following the same practices used in traditional HTML sites, if you really want to. However, this is not a process that is convenient to sustain. Devising a plan for managing on-site media is likely to be more convenient.

External Media

As with the external text options discussed previously, you can pull media that is stored in different locations. With some planning, you can configure Drupal to enable you to show videos and images from sources such as YouTube.com and Flickr.com.

Figure 4-10 shows an image from a video that is housed on YouTube.com being displayed in a Drupal site.

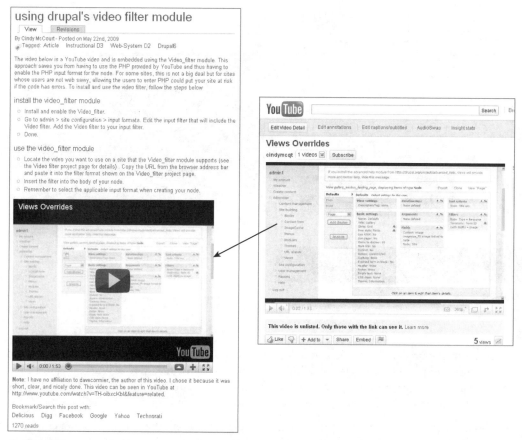

FIGURE 4-10

Figure 4-11 demonstrates that you can show images from Flickr.com in your Drupal site.

MEDIA FILTERS

The Flickr module provides a filter that you can use to display images that are stored on a Flickr account. The Video Filter module uses a filter technique, as well. It allows you to use a filter to embed numerous types of video in the body of your node. The Flickr module is available for Drupal 6 and, as of April 2011, there is a -dev version for Drupal 7. The Video Filter module is available for Drupal 6 and Drupal 7.

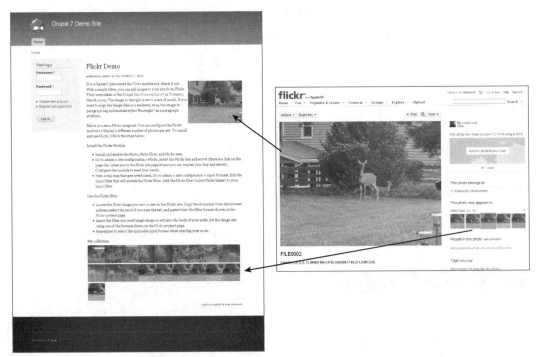

FIGURE 4-11

Files

Files are another source of data. You can upload PDF documents, Microsoft Word and Excel files, and other files and provide your visitors a link to open or save the file. Where will these files come from and where will they be stored? If your content authors are uploading files to be stored internally on your site, you will likely follow similar practices to those you use when uploading media.

What about external files? Will you provide links to files stored on other sites? This is a common practice, linking to resources on other sites. The challenge regarding links to other sites is, what if the other site removes the page or file to which you are linking? Suddenly, you have a broken link on your site. If you do need to link to other sites, consider setting up a maintenance task to check for broken links on your site.

On the topic of external files, what if you don't want to simply provide a link that opens a file? What if you want to display a file in the page? With services like Scribd, you can load your files to Scribd .com, convert them to iPaper, and then display them on your site. This is similar to the technique of loading video to YouTube.com and then showing the video on your site.

IPAPER IN DRUPAL

A contributed module called iPaper is available in Drupal 6. As of April 2011, posts on the iPaper project issue queue suggest a merger of this project with the Scribd field module; however, neither module has a Drupal 7 version, yet. If you need this feature, maybe you will be the one who ports it to Drupal 7.

Other Content

So far, the discussion of content sources has focused on separate pieces of content. However, you can join pieces of content together. You can display a video with a story or an image with a story. You can combine the items from multiple feeds into one list. You can also combine content from multiple sites into one site. The number of combinations seems endless.

But what if you had content that was an integral part of a feature? Sometimes, features need multiple pieces of content from multiple sources coming together to form what appears to be one piece of content. A perfect example is maps.

Have you been to a site that displays an image of a map with a lot of dots on it? Where did the map come from and what do the dots represent? Providing a map can be as simple as embedding a link to Google Maps, or you can integrate map tilesets into your site and overlay geo-sensitive statistics on the map. For example, Figure 4-12 shows a map from the data section of the World Bank site (http://data.worldbank.org/).

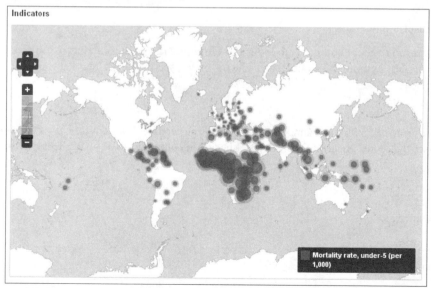

FIGURE 4-12

MAPS IN DRUPAL

The strategies for integrating maps into Drupal sites vary significantly, but there are modules to help you. Starting with the basics, the GMap module provides an interface to the Google Maps API. If Google has a map and you have a location, this module is handy.

Another popular option is the OpenLayers module, which enables you to combine maps from different providers with data from various fields and queries. If maps and data visualization interest you, keep your eye on Development Seed, which, as of April 2011, had 115 blog posts on mapping (`http://developmentseed.org/tags/mapping`).

The power of mashups adds a new dimension to your content planning. Using data and resources from other sites might be a new idea for you, or it might be just what you have been waiting for. Either way, when you consider the data that makes up the types of content you will have on your site, consider where that data is stored and how it will be shared on your pages or interface.

Reusing Content Data

In this part of the analysis, the objective is to determine whether and how content data can or will be used outside the node to which it was originally assigned. A flexible CMS like Drupal enables you to capture content once and then reuse it.

Decisions made during this analysis can influence:

➤ How you capture data

➤ How you upload data

➤ How you store data

➤ How you display data

The most obvious reason to reuse content is to reduce or eliminate the need to maintain the same content (text, media, files) in more than one place. The following sections offer reuse strategies for your consideration.

New Pages

Assume that you are creating an online course made up of multiple lessons. Your course has multiple lesson content pages (see the center image in Figure 4-13). The lesson content is made up of the following:

➤ Lesson title

➤ Lesson objectives

➤ Lesson resources

➤ Lesson narration

➤ Lesson image

The plan is to show participants a list of lessons, the objectives, and resources when they log in to the course. At the end of the course, the participants will see a lesson recap that shows the lesson objectives and the image. How do you accomplish this task and not type content twice? You guessed it — fields (and a module called Views).

If you store each part of the lesson in its own field, you can reuse them to create other pages. The images on the left and right in Figure 4-13 represent the pages that you can create by reusing lesson content that has been stored in fields.

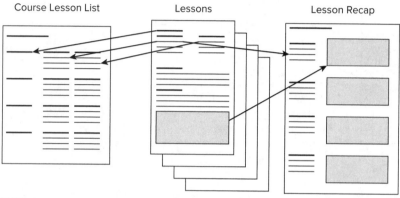

FIGURE 4-13

DYNAMICALLY GENERATED DISPLAYS

Drupal 6 and Drupal 7 have a contributed module called Views. The Views module helps you reuse data in your site. You can create blocks and pages that display data you have stored in your site database. It helps you query Drupal's database and then display the results of the query on your site. To learn more about Views and how they work, check out the book *Drupal's Building Blocks* (Addison-Wesley, 2011), by Earl and Lynette Miles, with Emma Jane Hogbin and Karen Stevenson. Earl developed the Views module.

Dynamic Navigation

Navigation on a site is more than the predefined menu you often see across the top of the site or down the side of a page. Sites whose content grows on a regular basis might want a way to provide navigation to the new pages without having to manually update a menu each time a new node (article, project, report, etc.) is added to the site. The simplest solution is to reuse the title of the node and make the title a link to the node. The list of titles can be displayed in a field, block, and/or a page.

The simple wireframe on the left in Figure 4-14 illustrates a block with a list of article names in one screen. The wireframe on the right illustrates the full list of articles on a page.

Latest Posts

If you have an active site and multiple users posting content, you want your content lists to be updated dynamically when the content is added. If you reuse the node title, teaser, author, and post date, you can create a list that updates automatically when nodes are added.

But the list can show other content as well. If you added fields to your content types to increase the granularity of your data, you can show more than just the title, teaser, author, and post date. For instance, you might have an event date and location field in your event content type that you want to include in a list of latest events added to the site. Because you chose not to type the date information into the body of the node, you can use the Date field as part of the data being displayed from the query.

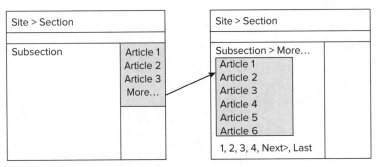

FIGURE 4-14

Featured Posts

Have you ever been on a site's home page and seen an image and some teaser text letting you know there is a new article on the site? That article is being featured or highlighted.

Featured or highlighted posts are similar to the idea of latest posts but with a twist. Assume that you want to show part of a node in a block on your home page. You want to include the title of the node and a marketing statement, something catchy to convince your audience this information is worth looking at. This method is similar to what you might hear on a commercial for the news: "Cat rescued from tree. News at 11."

You can show part of a node in several ways. One way would be to rewrite the content manually into a block and then display the block on a page. Or you could create a block that reuses one of your node fields in your news post. For instance, you can add a field called Advertisement Blurb to your content type; when you're selecting the fields you want to show in your block, choose the Title and the advertisement field. If you load your images using a field, you can also show a thumbnail version of the image in the advertisement.

The preceding might seem like a lot of work for one ad, but seldom will you have just one featured post or ad. But what if you added a check box field to your node and called it "Featured"? With the right configuration, you could build the block once and configure the block to show nodes that have the Featured field checked. Just uncheck the node when it is no longer featured and check a new one to feature.

Advertisements

Assume you are hosting nodes that are advertisements for your clients. Assume the advertisement node contains the following:

➤ Ad image

➤ Ad promotion ("Get 20% off when you … ")

➤ Name and location of the business

➤ Expiration date of the promotion

This much information might not fit on other related pages, so perhaps you create a block with just the ad image and link it to the ad.

If you upload the image into a field, you can create a query on the database to find the node in question and show only the image. You could use a module to automatically resize the image in the block so that you don't have to create multiple versions of the ad image. If you choose to use traditional HTML practices to embed the image into the body of the node versus using an image field, you won't be able to reuse the image in the ad block.

IMAGE RESIZING WITH IMAGECACHE

In Drupal 6, the ImageCache module allows you to set up presets for image processing. This means you can upload the image once and then show the image (with different presets applied) on different locations on your site. The presets typically involve changing the size of the image using various techniques. ImageCache is part of Drupal 7's core.

Reuse Considerations

When reusing data associated with one or more nodes, size can matter. Data that fits well in one part of your page might not fit well in another. However, you do have options. You just need to think about how, when, and where your data is used.

Recall how the titles of nodes were used as navigation in Figure 4-14. If you use this strategy, you need to consider the length of your titles and how they will display in the block. Because a block can be narrower than the main content area of a page, your titles might not fit well. Unless you limit the number of characters that are displayed, the title will wrap and create a multiline link. Multiple multiline links make the block longer, which takes up space on the screen. If this is going to be a concern, you might want to consider a business policy that titles are only so long, or your design strategy might be to only show the first X number of characters in the title.

Another example of size matters was illustrated in Figure 4-13. The lesson includes a wide image directly under the lesson narrative. What happens if you place the lesson objectives next to the image? The width of your page increases. In order to create the Lesson Recap page, you might need to display the image with a smaller preset.

Don't forget about permissions. If part of your web strategy is to entice people to buy a membership to your site, you might want to feature some of your best articles on your home page. If a visitor needs to be a member of your site to view your content, how will an anonymous visitor to your site see some of the same content? The answer might be to manage your content permissions at the field level versus the content type or node level.

To sum up the discussion on reuse, the question to ask is, "When I create a node, is there any data in the node that I would want to use again someplace else?" Figuring out what data you might reuse might be hard at first if you haven't done it before, but the preceding examples should offer some inspiration to your planning endeavors.

Categorizing Content

This is not the first time content categorization has been discussed as part of the content analysis. When you were deciding how you would distinguish between different types of content, you were planning content categorization. In the categorization part of the content analysis, you are refining your content categorization strategy by making three decisions:

➤ Whether your content needs to be categorized further

➤ Whether your categories are presented as a vocabulary or a field

➤ Whether the categories should be predefined or user-defined

Decisions made during this analysis can influence the following:

➤ How you define your content types

➤ Supplemental navigation strategies

➤ Faceted search capabilities (if you need them)

➤ How database queries are created and maintained

➤ Theming decisions

Before you can make a decision about whether you want category terms to be predefined by the site administrator or generated by your users, you need to decide first whether you even want your content to be categorized.

CATEGORIES IN DRUPAL

Drupal 6 and Drupal 7 come with the Taxonomy module. In Drupal, taxonomy is made up of vocabularies, and vocabularies are made up of terms. Vocabularies and their terms are used to categorize your content. Terms can be associated with nodes by using the Taxonomy module's default feature. You also use the Content Taxonomy module to manage the term association via a field. As of April 2011, Content Taxonomy had a -dev version for Drupal 7.

To Categorize or Not To Categorize?

Some people consider the type of content to be enough categorization. Quite often, however, content can be organized into at least one more category. Table 4-9 shows four example content types and how the nodes (pages) created with those content types might be categorized.

The example categories in Table 4-9 focus on organizing types of nodes (project nodes, expert nodes, etc.) within one content type. You are not limited to organizing within each content type.

You can create categories that create a relationship between different types of nodes. For instance, you could organize each type of content by topic. The result would allow your audience to find all project, expert, article, and product nodes associated with one topic.

TABLE 4-9: Sample Content Categories

CONTENT TYPE	CATEGORIES ORGANIZED BY
Project	Type of contract
	Type of client
	Project team
	Type of service
Experts	Areas of expertise
Articles	Topic area
	Publication
Product	Product use

A common method to categorize content on a Drupal site is to use Drupal's taxonomy. A Drupal taxonomy is made up of vocabularies; vocabularies contain terms (aka, tags). When you categorize content, you create a relationship between the nodes that are placed in the category. Nodes can belong to many different categories at once, but they cannot belong to more than one content type. Sometimes, terms are predefined and, sometimes, you are allowed to create your own terms to describe the content.

Later in this chapter, a search/browse analysis is described. If you find that you want or need to provide a faceted search feature or a predefined way to browse content, you will likely need to categorize your content.

> **METADATA AND DRUPAL**
>
> Metadata is data about data. Two types of metadata worth mentioning are structural metadata and descriptive metadata. In Drupal, content types provide structural metadata about your content — how the various digital objects are related and stored. Vocabulary terms provide descriptive metadata — what the content is and what it is about.

Vocabulary or Field?

When you categorize content and store that category information in the site database, you can use that information later to help describe or filter your content. You can categorize content using a vocabulary term and/or terms in a select field.

In Drupal, taxonomy vocabulary terms are typically links that can appear above or below your content. Providing a vocabulary term is a way to let your visitors know that there might be other pages on the same topic. When users click on the term link, they get a default teaser list of pages that all share that term.

Figure 4-15 shows a sample node with three tags (noted with the arrow under the image).

FIGURE 4-15

Figure 4-16 shows the screen you get if you click on the tag *Trees*. In this example, you see what can be referred to as a *teaser list of nodes* that have been tagged with the term *Trees*.

Another way to categorize content is by using a predefined field. In Drupal, you can create a text field in the form of a select list that offers terms or phrases that you can assign to the node. You can create predefined select list fields in different ways. Two options include:

> **Field** — Create a text field select list and include the options you want to be able to select. When you select a term or phrase in the list, that value is stored in the database. If you change the values in the select list, the value stored for the node does not update automatically.

> **Vocabulary field** — Create a vocabulary field and use the terms from one vocabulary as the select options. The vocabulary term's ID is stored (versus the actual term). If the vocabulary term changes, the node will display the updated term.

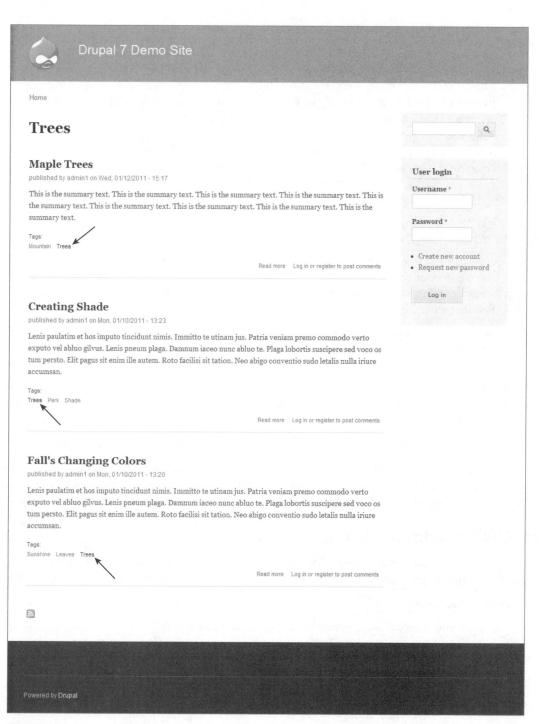

FIGURE 4-16

You will select the best method when you plan your development strategy.

DRUPAL CONTENT TAXONOMY

In both Drupal 6 and Drupal 7, the Content Taxonomy module provides a way to create a field using terms listed in a vocabulary. By using the Content Taxonomy field, you can dynamically update the values in the field and have those changes automatically reflected in the nodes using those terms. In the case of a traditional select field, the changes made to the select list are not automatically reflected in the node.

Predefined or User-Defined Terms?

You can predefine the terms in the vocabularies that create your term links (a practice often referred to as a *taxonomy*), or your content developers can add terms when they create content (a practice sometimes referred to as a *folksonomy* or *free tagging*). Each approach has pros and cons, so you might find that a combination is warranted.

Predefined terms refer to terms that you, as the site administrator, have created and made available in a vocabulary. The advantage to using predefined terms is predictability. If you know which terms your users will use, you can consistently query the database and use those terms as filters.

The disadvantage to using predefined terms is associated with sites whose content topics can vary and grow. You can't always predict all the categories you will need to provide, and adding new terms might not be convenient.

The advantage of user-defined terms is flexibility. Your users can categorize content the way they see fit.

The disadvantage is inconsistency and lack of predictability. Free tagging can cause duplicate terms to be added to the term list, and combining terms to "clean them up" is not an automated process. Also, you cannot consistently predict the term you want to use in your queries when filtering your content.

Identifying Categories and Terms

In the previous analysis, you decided whether to categorize your content and considered different strategies for managing your categories. Now, it is time to identify which categories and terms you need.

Decisions made during this analysis can influence:

➤ How you ensure content appears in an interface (or not)

➤ Which vocabularies apply when creating content

➤ Your content's content — what topics it covers

Even if you have identified your categories, the following common categorization strategies might give you some ideas.

Topic

Topic is probably the most common category of terms. What subject matter does your content address? For example, if you have a site that hosts blogs, your blog topics could be about cars, web design, or houses. Or, if your site is about people, the topic could be their areas of expertise or their interests.

Type

Assume the type of content is resource. Pretty vague, right? So, maybe you have types of resources, such as articles, reports, white papers, video, and so on. By creating a type category, you can use one content type to create different types of content. Options like this can be overwhelming at times, but that is why you are taking a hard look at your content.

Purpose

What is your content doing for your audience? Is your content supposed to entertain your audience or teach your audience? Think about a newspaper site such as WashingtonPost.com. It has many types of content, and some might say the sole purpose of all of it is to inform the reader. But doesn't it also have content whose purpose is to persuade the reader to do something, such as advertisements?

You might not present your audience with the purpose of your content, but purpose might be what influences how you present the content. For instance, flagging a node as a promotion might trigger an email to be sent to all the members of your site. If your content is flagged as being used to solicit information, you might configure blocks to appear that include tips for submitting information.

Structure

The preceding three categorization strategies focus on describing what the node (page) is or what it is about. This next strategy considers the *structure* of the node, or what makes up the node content.

For example, your site visitors might want to view all content that contains a video reference. In other words, you are organizing your content by the different types of data that make up the content. Another example might be to show all content that has a PDF file attachment.

No one solution to categorizing content exists, as you can see, but identifying ways to describe your content so that you can create different ways for your audience to find it is important. Category terms (whether created in a vocabulary or a field) are great for finding and organizing content.

TRIGGERS AND ACTIONS

The idea of "if this, then do that" is very common in development. The categorization discussion has actually been about "if this, then do that." When a site visitor clicks on a term link, they trigger Drupal to perform an action. In other words, if the term is X, then show a teaser list of nodes that have been tagged with X.

Drupal offers a way to create your own triggers and actions ("if this, then do that" scenarios) through the use of the Triggers module, although the options offered by the Triggers module in both Drupal 6 and Drupal 7 are fairly limited.

The Rules module is an alternative to the Triggers module and offers more flexibility and options. Many modules (see a list at `http://groups.drupal.org/rules/rules-modules`) integrate with Rules, providing Rules with additional conditionally executed actions you can use when creating a rule. The Rules module is available in Drupal 6 and Drupal 7.

Establishing Content Relationships

When you analyzed your need to categorize your content, you considered ways to organize the nodes created with different types of content. You also considered creating relationships between different types of content using categories. In the establishing content relationships part of the content analysis, you consider content relationships from two more perspectives.

The objective is to determine how types of content relate to each other. Many ways exist to establish a relationship between content. Two commonly used methods are:

➤ Parent-child relationships

➤ Referenced relationships

Each method has implementation options. For now, however, you just focus on determining whether a relationship exists.

Decisions made during this analysis can influence:

➤ Your use of vocabularies

➤ The fields needed

➤ Which modules you need to install

➤ How you configure database queries

➤ Content navigation options

➤ URL configurations

Parent-Child Relationships

Instead of trying to describe what parent-child relationships might mean to your content analysis, take a look at some examples. Table 4-10 shows four types of content (course, project, product, and event) and the types of content to which they relate.

For instance, the Course content node in the table has two types of child nodes: Syllabus and Unit. The Unit page has child nodes as well: Lessons, Assignments, and Quizzes.

TABLE 4-10: Sample Parent-Child Relationships

COURSE	PROJECT	PRODUCT	EVENT
Syllabus	Status reports	Description	Agenda
Units	Schedules	Specifications	Information
- Lessons	Budgets	Requirements	Handouts
- Assignments	Deliverables	User guide	
- Quizzes			

You can create a parent-child relationship between nodes in different ways. You won't decide which technique is best until the design and development phases. You need more information than what is shown here to make that decision, such as:

➤ How you want the relationship between nodes to be displayed

➤ Whether a child node will belong to more than one parent node

➤ The type of navigation that should be in place to reinforce the relationship

---

PARENT-CHILD RELATIONSHIP MODULES

There are several modules that let you create a parent-child relationship between nodes. The outline feature, which comes with the Book module, is part of Drupal 6 and Drupal 7 by default and allows you to create parent-child relationships between different nodes. You do not have to create a Book node in order to create the parent-child relationship. The Node Hierarchy module, available for Drupal 6 and in development for Drupal 7, allows you to create a tree-like hierarchy of nodes. The Forum module, which comes in Drupal 6 and Drupal 7, uses nodes to create topics and subtopics (parents and children).

Referenced Relationships

What does it mean when one node references another? Different ways exist to answer this question. Of course, you have the traditional reference in a text narrative or in a footnote. In Drupal, however, modules are available that enable you to create a relationship between two nodes manually. References are more like siblings versus parent-child; each node can have many siblings.

An advantage of referenced relationships is that you can use them to automatically generate lists of related nodes that appear on the node in question. For example, if visitors land on a page whose node has been related to other nodes, you can set up a block that displays those related nodes. As related nodes are added, the block updates automatically. If no referenced relationships exist, the block doesn't appear.

> **REFERENCES**
>
> In Drupal 6, the CCK (Content Construction Kit) module comes with a Node Reference field. It creates a one-way relationship between the node with the field and the nodes it references. You can use the Reverse Node Reference module in conjunction with Node Reference to create a two-way reference.
>
> In Drupal 7, the Node Reference module did not get included in Drupal when the CCK module was integrated into Drupal's core. You need the References module to create this type of relationship. As of April 2011, there was a Drupal 7 -dev version for References, but a version of Reverse Node Reference was not available, yet. But that doesn't mean you can't create the two-way relationship manually.

Determining the Need for Metadata

"Today, the most valuable feature [meta tags] offer the web site owner is the ability to control to some degree how their web pages are described by some search engines."[3] In this analysis, you are determining whether your pages need metadata. Decisions made during this analysis can affect:

> ➤ Your search engine optimization (SEO) strategy

> ➤ Who you want to have entering content on your site

Metadata is data about data. You might be wondering, "What data about what data?" There are different types of metadata. Structural and descriptive metadata were mentioned in a note previously in this chapter. This part of the analysis is focused on descriptive metadata.

Assume you've written an article about a baseball game that you want to post online. The article is data. A short description of the article might be, "A play-by-play account of the baseball game between the Giants and the Padres on July 10, 2009." In this scenario, the short description could be the metadata about the article. (Jonathan Sanchez of the Giants pitched a no-hitter, by the way.)

Sometimes, the data in the node is the metadata about something else in the node or attached to the node. For instance, assume you have a site dedicated to hosting baseball videos. The videos are the data to be described. You use the node to show the video and include the metadata about the video in the node as well ("A video of the home run that won the game between the Giants and the Padres on July 10, 2009.")

---

[3] How to Use HTML Meta Tags: http://searchenginewatch.com/2167931

Meta Tag

At this point, you may be thinking, okay, I get it; metadata is data about data. What does this have to do with my content analysis? Ever hear of the meta tag? Or maybe you recognize the meta elements such as description or keyword.

The short description in the preceding section about the baseball article is a description about the article. You can add it in your node to provide search engines with additional information about the node or page that holds the node. If you have never created an HTML page, you might be asking yourself, "But where do I stick it?"

This is where the meta tag and its elements come in. The meta tag is placed between the <HEAD> tags in an HTML page. Where's the <HEAD> tag, you ask? If you view the source of a web page, you might see where. Look for code such as the following near the top of the source code:

```
<HEAD>
<TITLE>Giants No-Hit Padres</TITLE>
<META name ="description" content = "A play-by-play account of the baseball
    game between the Giants and the Padres on July 10th, 2009." />
<META name = "keyword" content = "baseball, Giants, Padres" />
</HEAD>
```

This example shows a description of the node and three keywords that also describe the content of the node. The description might be straightforward, but what about the keywords? What is the difference between the keywords listed in the meta tag and the vocabulary terms you used to categorize or describe your nodes?

➤ **Meta keyword** — The meta tag keyword was intended to provide search engines with terms that describe the content on the page. Today, it might be read by a search engine, but it is highly unlikely that it makes a difference in your search engine rankings.

➤ **Vocabulary term** — The vocabulary term helps you organize your content, and helps your visitors find content while on your site. In Drupal 7, however, the term is getting more attention through the use of RDF and RDFa.

RDF/RDFA IN DRUPAL

"RDF/RDFa is major new functionality in Drupal 7 which describes Drupal entities (nodes, user, comments, terms) and their relationship in a format machines can understand."[4]

RDF stands for "Resource Description Framework." RDFa stands for "Resource Description Framework attributes" and "provides a set of XHTML attributes to augment visual data with machine-readable hints."[5]

For an introduction to RDFa, visit http://groups.drupal.org/node/22231.

---

[4] Drupal.org: http://drupal.org/node/574624
[5] W3C: www.w3.org/TR/xhtml-rdfa-primer

By default, Drupal provides the `<TITLE>` tag in the pages that get sent to the browser. If you want to add the `meta` tag elements manually, such as `description` or `keyword`, you need to plan for them so that your developers can install the appropriate modules and allow you access to enter this type of metadata when you start creating your nodes. This brings up the topic of who is creating your nodes and whether you want your content authors creating this type of metadata. Keep this in mind when defining your content development workflows and permissions.

ADDING META TAG ELEMENTS

In Drupal 6, the Nodewords module allows you to manually add `meta` tag data such as `description` and `keyword`. As of April 2011, the Nodewords module will not migrate to Drupal 7 but is being replaced by a new module called Metatags. As of April 2011, the Metatags module has a -dev version.

RDF and Semantic Metadata

By definition, semantics is "the branch of linguistics that deals with the study of meaning, changes in meaning, and the principles that govern the relationship between sentences or words and their meanings"[6] As humans, when we see content, we add meaning to what we see. The organization of the content on the page and the context in which a word or phrase is presented are used to interpret meaning as well as the definition of the words. But what if the machine you are using could also interpret what is on the page? What if your browser understood that the `<H1>` header tag meant the title of the article? And what if it knew that `<H2>` was the article's author? Would this change how search engines and other programs interpret and present data? It most likely would.

Semantic metadata is made possible by Resource Description Framework attributes (RDFa) in XHTML. "The essence of RDFa is to provide a set of attributes that can be used to carry metadata in an XML language (hence the *a* in RDFa)."[7] Did your eyes just glaze over? Maybe the following will help.

You might recall the screen shot provided in Figure 4-15, which showed the vocabulary terms associated with the node created on a Drupal 7 site. The source code for the tags on that page is shown here:

```
<h3 class="field-label">Tags: </h3>
  <ul class="links">
    <li class="taxonomy-term-reference-0" rel="dc:subject">
      <a href="/tags/sunshine" typeof="skos:Concept"
        property="rdfs:label skos:prefLabel">Sunshine</a>
    </li>
    <li class="taxonomy-term-reference-1" rel="dc:subject">
      <a href="/tags/leaves" typeof="skos:Concept"
        property="rdfs:label skos:prefLabel">Leaves</a>
    </li>
```

---

[6] Dictionary.com: `http://dictionary.reference.com/browse/semantics`
[7] Wikipedia.org: `http://en.wikipedia.org/wiki/RDFa`

```
          <li class="taxonomy-term-reference-2" rel="dc:subject">
            <a href="/tags/trees" typeof="skos:Concept"
              property="rdfs:label skos:prefLabel">Trees</a>
          </li>
        </ul>
```

Notice the `typeof` and `property` attributes assigned to the anchor (<a>) tag. They provide the RDF attributes to search engines so that they know what to do with your terms.

On a Drupal 6 site, the source code for a set of tags might look like the following code. Notice the difference?

```
<div class="terms">
  <ul class="taxonomy">
    <li class="vocab-term">
      <a href="/category/phases/needs-analysis" rel="tag" title="">Needs Analysis</a>
    </li>
      <li class="vocab-term">
        <a href="/category/phases/management" rel="tag" title="">Management</a>
      </li>
      <li class="vocab-term">
        <a href="/category/phases/development" rel="tag" title="">Development</a>
      </li>
    </li>
  </ul>
</div>
```

Too much information for you? The point is, vocabulary terms and other Drupal entities are playing a new role when it comes to making search engines understand what is on your page. Do you want to include this type of semantic metadata in your content pages? Probably yes. "As semantic web technology begins to have a real-world effect on search engine rankings, those who don't start learning about and implementing semantic metadata in their content stand to be left in the dust."[8]

SEMANTIC METADATA OPTION

The Calais module connects your site with the Calais web service. The service automatically creates rich semantic metadata for the content you submit. For an introduction to Calais, visit `www.lullabot.com/articles/introduction-calais`. To learn more about the service, visit `www.opencalais.com`.

Accommodating Multiple Languages

Have you ever been to a site where you click on a flag from another country and suddenly the site appears in another language? That's very cool, in my opinion. How do they do that? They might be using Drupal. Now, don't get excited that you, too, can have a site with multiple languages simply by clicking a button. It takes planning.

---

[8] McCall, Logan, What is Semantic Metadata?: `www.associatedcontent.com/article/1766486/what_is_semantic_metadata.html?cat=15`

As its name implies, in the language accommodation part of the content analysis, you determine whether your site needs to accommodate multiple languages. Decisions made during this analysis can influence:

➤ The language you choose for your initial Drupal installation (your default language)

➤ Content development processes

➤ Menu, vocabulary, and block development processes

➤ The modules that you install

There are more than 100 modules available to help you make your site multilingual. To implement multiple languages, you must decide whether you want just the node in multiple languages or whether you want all components of your page to be presented in multiple languages. No single module or feature exists, yet, that turns all content in your site into the language you want.

As of April 2011, there does not appear to be a module that will automatically translate your site content into another language for you. Translation tools can help you with this process, but the assumption is that each instance of content in one language is manually transcribed into another language.

Chapter 5 describes the different types of page components that you need to consider when creating a site and, therefore, the page components that need to be multilingual. As for the requirements phase, you need to decide whether your site is multilingual and, if so, to what extent. If you are hiring a vendor to do the development, telling them to what extent you need the site to be multilingual is important so that they can provide a proper estimate.

DRUPAL LOCALIZATION

Visit Drupal's localization server at `http://localize.drupal.org/` to find a version of Drupal in the language you need. Drupal is not available in all languages, but you can learn more about helping with the translations. Links to contributed modules that have been translated are also listed.

Controlling Access to Content

Given what you know about your audience, the content-oriented tasks they will be performing on the site, and the types of content you will have them interacting with, at what level of granularity will you control access to your content?

The access part of the content analysis is closely connected with the roles analysis in that you are considering who can do what. Right now, however, focus on the "who can do what" with regard to content. In this analysis, you determine whether you want to control who can view, create, edit, and delete your content.

Decisions made during this analysis can influence:

➤ The tools you install to manage access to your content

➤ How many different content types your site employs

➤ How you manage access to content fields and vocabulary terms

Out of the box, Drupal gives you the opportunity to say that all your nodes are viewable or not by a role. For instance, either anonymous users can see all your content nodes or they can't see your content nodes. Or only authenticated users can see all your nodes. You can add more roles, but the condition doesn't change; it's all or nothing. But all is not lost; you do have options.

Content Type Access

If you have decided to create different content types (the form you use to create a node) for your various types of content, maybe you want to control access by content type. For instance, anonymous users can see all nodes created with the Page content type, but they need to be authenticated users to see the Story, Blog, and Event content types. Modules are available that help you manage access at the content type level.

CONTENT TYPE ACCESS CONTROL

The Content Access module allows you to control which role can see nodes created with a content type. As of April 2011, Content Access was available for Drupal 6 and a -dev version was available for Drupal 7.

Partial or Teaser Access

Recall the part of the content analysis that discussed fields. In that discussion, the Body field was described. By default, content types come with two fields: Title and Body. If you don't add any fields, the Body field is used to hold the content for that node. Another bit of important information to recall is the default teaser, the short excerpt from the Body field that shows when a node is promoted to the front page or when someone clicks on a vocabulary term and gets a teaser list of nodes tagged with that term.

When visitors click on the title of the node from the front page or term page with the teaser list, they are shown the full node. What if you don't want them to see the full node unless they are logged in and have a role with permission to see the full node? Maybe you have been to sites where you have to sign up to view the full article. Sometimes, you need to pay for a site membership; other times, it's a way for the site owners to know who is accessing their content.

By default, Drupal does not provide this option. You will need a contributed module to help you, so be sure to include this requirement.

TEASER ACCESS IN DRUPAL

The Node Option Premium module, available in both Drupal 6 and Drupal 7, provides a solution to the partial node access requirement. It provides a workflow publishing option for the content type. It integrates with the Views and Rules modules. It also provides an option to display other fields you might add to your content type in teaser mode.

Field-Level Access

Content types are made up of fields. You can add different types of fields using one or more contributed modules. When considering content access, do you want to control user access on a field-by-field basis?

For example, assume you use a content type to input project reports and that 10 fields need to be completed by different roles on the project. With custom fields, you can assign edit rights for five fields to one user role, and then grant rights to another user role to edit the remaining fields.

FIELD PERMISSIONS

In Drupal 6, the Content Permissions module comes with the CCK module. This module provides a way for you to control which role can view or edit a specific field. In Drupal 7, it will be a separate module called Field Permissions. As of April 2011, Field Permissions had a recommended release for Drupal 7.

Node-Level Access

When you apply node-level access, you are assigning permissions to one node at a time. Depending on which module you choose, permissions can be set by role or by user.

This level of control comes in handy when you are managing a collaborative writing process where you want three people to compose a report in the same node. With node access controls, you can assign a node to the three authors and they can each have edit access to the node and take turns adding and editing content in the node.

NODE ACCESS CONTROL MODULES

The previously mentioned Content Access module has an option that allows you to administer node-level access. The Nodeaccess module also provides node-level access control. As of May 2011, there was a Drupal 6 version and a -dev version for Drupal 7 for Nodeaccess.

Vocabulary Terms Access

If you are not using a content type approach for differentiating one type of content from another, you are probably using a vocabulary of terms, each term representing a type of content. Modules are available that allow you to manage access to content through terms that have been assigned. So, if you have all your content organized by term, you can apply access conditions via those terms.

If you use the vocabulary term approach, by default, that term will show up with all your other category terms. Do you want that? If not, remember to note this in the requirements so it doesn't end up in the design.

TAXONOMY ACCESS

The Taxonomy Access Control module controls access to nodes based on the term assigned to the node. It is available in Drupal 6. As of April 2011, there is a -dev version for Drupal 7.

The Taxonomy Hide module allows you to flag which vocabularies (and their terms) will be hidden from displaying with other terms associated with the node. Some themes might come with an option similar to the Taxonomy Hide module.

Sub-Site Access

The preceding examples discuss managing access to content and its fields by focusing on the content type, node, field, or the vocabulary term. In each instance, one or more contributed modules are available.

This next discussion introduces the concept of a sub-site and that you can manage access to content within each sub-site. For purposes of this discussion, a *sub-site* is a partition of or space within a site. Figure 4-17 is a simple illustration of the concept of a sub-site.

Notice that some of the sub-site "containers" have a solid line, whereas others have a dashed line. The dashed lines indicate the ability to move between the main site and the sub-site without restrictions. The solid line indicates restricted access such that if you are in a sub-site, you might not have a way to access the main site or any other sub-site.

There are several ways to implement the concept of a sub-site. A strategy like sub-sites needs to be planned before development starts. The solution required will depend on the level of control you need when creating a sub-site.

To sum things up, your decisions about content types and content data are influenced by the level and type of control you need to engage in your site. The preceding strategies are commonly used practices for controlling access to content. Your objective is to determine what you need and then explore your options.

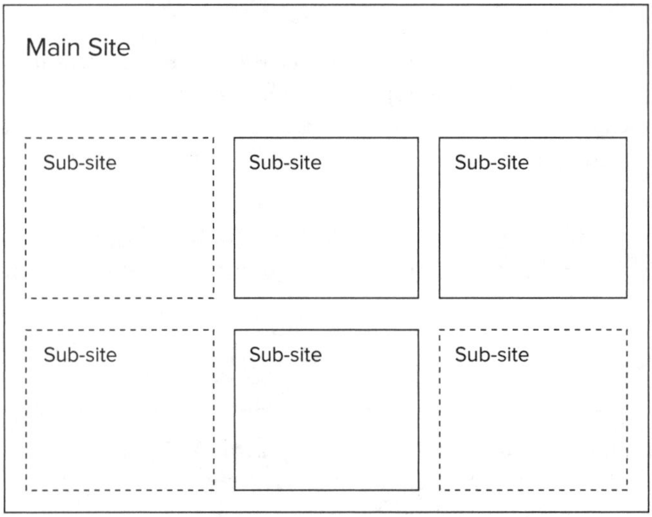

FIGURE 4-17

SUB-SITES IN DRUPAL

There are three modules worth noting when it comes to creating and managing a sub-site: Organic Groups, Spaces, and Domain Access. Each module provides a way to partition your site into sub-sites. Organic Groups and Domain Access have Drupal 6 and Drupal 7 versions. As of April 2011, a Drupal 7 patch has been posted for Spaces, but no official release.

It is worth noting that Organic Groups for Drupal 7 has changed. The concept remains the same, but it is more powerful, more flexible. Watch a presentation on the new Organic Groups, presented by the project developer, at `www.archive.org/details/GrouptheNewOrganicGroups-BuildingSocialNetworksInDrupal7`.

For an introduction to the Spaces module, check out "Introducing Spaces for Drupal" at `http://developmentseed.org/blog/2008/jul/17/introducing-spaces-drupal`. You can see Spaces in action in the free Drupal distribution called Open Atrium.

To learn about Domain Access, check out "Sharing Content Across Multiple Sites with Domain Access" at `www.archive.org/details/Sharingcontentacross multiplesiteswithDomainAccess`.

Collecting Content about Users

So far, the discussion has centered on content such as articles, blogs, and media. Another perspective to consider is user content. Recall your audience analysis. Who is your target audience? Depending on the role of the user on your site, you might need to consider content about the user in addition to content created by a user.

In this part of the content analysis, you consider content about the user. Do you want to capture content about your users? If so, do you want that information to be treated like the other content on your site? Community-oriented sites and sites whose visitors want to know about the content authors will probably want some form of content about the users.

Decisions made during this analysis can influence:

➤ What information users provide during or after registration

➤ How user profiles are defined during development

➤ What anonymous and authenticated users see about other users

Types of User Content

Recall that content is made up of data. Data you collect about users falls into one of two categories:

➤ Data they give you, such as name, address, and biography

➤ Data that gets generated, such as the number of posts they've made or the last time they were on the site

If you are building a community site — a site where a goal is the interaction between members — you might also be interested in connection data. Which members are connected to other members?

Depending on your site's purpose, you might want to allow your members to connect to other sites as well. For instance, they can push information about their posts on your site to their Twitter account or have their comments sent to their Facebook account. Or they can pull information into the site via an RSS feed or some other feature you desire.

Your objective, when deciding what content or data you want to collect about your users, is to determine:

➤ Why you want the data

➤ Who will see it

➤ Whether you're allowed to collect it

➤ Whether the user wants you to have it

➤ What you will do with it

User Profiles

The data collected from the user is often considered a *user profile*. The definition of a user profile varies, depending on whom you ask. Some say that data generated based on users' activities is also part of their profile. What definition you'll use is a decision you make when defining what your site needs in regard to data about your users.

The most basic information collected by Drupal is the user's username and email address. This is information entered into fields when an account is created. The number of fields you can request your users to complete is up to you, but many options are available. To help get the ball rolling, consider two categories of user content:

➤ **Personal information** can include identification information such as names and addresses. It can also include information about visitors' interests, hobbies, education, and so on. Personal information is not something your users will hand over lightly. They might even think twice before creating an account if they think you want to know too much.

➤ **Professional information** can include items about where visitors work, what they do for work, and any professional associations, to name a few. Again, if you ask for too much, you might lose them as potential members of your site.

So far, the assumption is one user, one profile. But what if you have a user who wears different hats and might need more than one profile? For instance, who you are at work is not necessarily the same person you are at home. We all fill different roles in life. The same applies to some sites. Depending on the roles your users play, will they need different profiles to match the roles they play on the site or even in life?

USER PROFILES

Drupal 6 comes with a module called Profile that enables you to add fields to the user account. Another module, Content Profile, allows you to create a content type that is associated with the user account. You can add CCK fields to this content type. Using a node to store user content allows that content to be indexed and searchable with Drupal's search feature. The Profile module is deprecated in Drupal 7 because you can add fields to user accounts and the user account is searchable by default.

In Drupal 7, the Profile2 module is replacing the Content Profile module. Although it might be seen as redundant to how Drupal 7 manages user content, one difference is that Profile2 allows you to create multiple profile types.

User Data Collection Strategies

When someone from your target audience creates an account on your site, what do you want him or her to tell you in order for them to be granted access? At a minimum, Drupal wants a username and an email address. Do you want or need more information?

The reason someone creates an account is influenced by the purpose of the site. For instance, assume the purpose of the site is to facilitate online interaction between people with similar interests. People would create an account so that they could join the interaction. What information is required in order to join the interaction? The answer might depend on what is being discussed and why.

Assume the site hosting the interactions is discussing energy conservation and the objective is to explore new ways to save the planet's resources. If a site objective is to allow anyone to "listen" to the discussion but only those who have credibility on the topic to "talk," then someone requesting an account would likely need to submit information about their credentials before being granted an account and/or permission to "talk."

The process of defining your content-collection strategies will include finding answers to questions such as:

➤ What do you need to know about your site members in order for them to be a member?

➤ Why do you need to know it?

➤ When do you need to know it, before or after they have an account?

➤ What will you do with the data you collect from your site members?

➤ With whom will you share the data?

➤ How and when will you disclose the use of the data your site members provide?

Something to consider when asking for additional information is whether your potential site members agree that you need to know what you are asking. If you make the additional information a requirement for membership, you could be limiting who becomes a member. That may or may not be exactly what you want.

Another consideration is the effort you require from your potential members. If your audience thinks the effort to create an account on your site is not worth the reward of having the account, they might not sign up. If they don't sign up, you might not get the activity you were hoping for.

When you identified the tasks your audience would perform on your site, did you include the task of creating an account? Did the steps in the task look this?

➤ Future site member clicks on the Create Account link and is sent to the Create Account form.

➤ Future site member provides username, email address, desired password, and submits the form.

➤ Site member is now logged in.

➤ Site member chooses to create a user profile and provide additional information.

➤ Site member proceeds to online activity of choice.

Or did it look like this?

➤ Future site member clicks on the Create Account link and is sent to the Create Account form.

➤ Future site member provides username, email address, mailing address, biography, place of work, education history, and hobbies, and submits the form.

➤ Future site member locates the email with the link to log in and set a password.

➤ Site member clicks link in email, sets password, and proceeds to online activity of choice.

There are many scenarios you can define to complete the task of creating an account. Each scenario will influence not only who gets an account but also who wants one.

User Data Access

Your user data collection strategy (during registration, after, required, optional) could influence how you define your user interfaces. With the need to maintain some semblance of privacy, users on your site might not want their information to be seen by just anyone. If you plan to collect data about a user, will that data be accessible to anyone other than the user? If so, who and why? This access could mean that you have a profile view for:

➤   Anonymous users

➤   Authenticated users

➤   Privileged users assigned a role of your making

Another perspective in regard to access is whether you want your members to control what they make public versus your deciding. A decision to grant users the ability to create their own profile pages influences your interface design and your development requirements.

DASHBOARDS

The Homebox module, available for Drupal 6 and Drupal 7, allows site administrators to create dashboards for their users using blocks as widgets. The Drupal Commons Distribution and Drupal.org use Homebox to create user dashboards.

COMMUNICATION ANALYSIS

Email! Where would we be without email? And don't forget about texting. The number of ways you can reach your audience is incredible.

At a minimum, sites typically have an email address so that people visiting a site can reach someone associated with the site. But you can make communication more convenient for your visitors with the use of a contact form. Your visitors can send an email to someone on your site team without the visitor having to know your team's email addresses. You can use other online communication strategies in your site, as well.

The objective of the communication analysis is to identify:

➤   How you want to communicate with your users

➤   How you want your users to communicate with you

➤   How you want them to communicate with each other

Following are some insights into various ways you can set up your Drupal site to foster communication. The first three — contact forms, comments, and system messages — come with Drupal out of the box. You can provide the other options by using contributed modules. This is not a complete list of options, but it should help you start thinking about what you might want on your site.

Contact Forms

A common practice on a site is to provide an online form that visitors can use to send an email message to someone on the site team. Drupal's Contact module provides a contact form that you can configure to send email messages to different email accounts. You can preset the contact form to allow your users to select a type of message to be sent and then configure those messages to go to a specific email(s). For instance, you can offer your users the option of sending messages to your webmaster or your content administrator. Once the message is sent, further email interaction is performed outside of the site.

> **CONTACT MODULE**
>
> In Drupal 6, the Contact module comes with an option to include a message at the top of the form, guidance from you regarding the use of the contact form. In Drupal 7, that option is not available. Additional guidance or information can be provided via a block.

In addition to enabling users to send an email to someone on the site team, the Contact module also provides user contact forms. These forms allow users to send an email message to other users, who opt to enable their contact form, on your site.

Using contact forms allows you to keep email addresses private so that unscrupulous people don't collect and use them to mask spam. Simply having an email address in the text of a page is enough for some applications to find your email addresses.

> **CONTACT ALL SITE USERS**
>
> The Mass Contact module provides a way to send an email to all site users, if you have permission. It is currently available in Drupal 6. As of April 2011, there is intent on the project developer's part to port it to Drupal 7.

Commenting

Comments are remarks, questions, opinions, and so on, posted to a node on your site by your site visitors. When a visitor comments on a node or another comment, that visitor is communicating with you and/or other visitors to your site. Comments are a means for having an online discussion or simply a way to express an opinion. They are not, by default, configured to send email, although you can add a module that will send a copy of a comment to anyone who has subscribed to receive comments. You can control which role can view and post comments.

> **COMMENTS IN DRUPAL**
>
> In Drupal 6, the body of the comment (and other relevant data associated with comments) was collected and stored in the comments table. In Drupal 7, the comments table still exists, but the body of the comment is stored in the field_data_comment_body table and revisions are stored in the field_revisions_comment_body_table. This change was necessary to support the improvements in Drupal's underlying data architecture.
>
> In Drupal 7, the comment becomes an entity, and an entity can have fields. Nodes, comments, terms, and users are entities in Drupal 7, and each can have fields.

System Messages

By default, Drupal comes with account management email messages that you can enable based on how restrictive you make your "create an account" process. The following messages are available:

➤ Welcome, new user created by administrator

➤ Welcome, no approval required

➤ Welcome, awaiting administrator approval

➤ Password recovery email

➤ Account activation email

➤ Account blocked email

➤ Account deleted email

➤ Account cancellation confirmation (new in Drupal 7)

If you aren't used to setting up a site where users can create accounts, you can easily overlook these options. Although you can edit these messages, note that these messages are sent to users regardless of the context. For instance, you should not use these messages to welcome new users to a specific event.

In addition to the default messages mentioned above, there could be other reasons for system messages to be sent. For instance:

➤ You might want site members to receive an acknowledgment that their request or change has been processed.

➤ You might want site members to receive an acknowledgment that their account has been inactive for a while.

➤ You might want to receive a message when someone creates an account on your site (assuming your site is set not to require administrative approval for accounts).

➤ You might want to send a message to site members when you have changed something on the site and want them to know.

Each of these messages requires additional modules to be added to your site. There might be multiple ways to make these messages possible, so be sure to provide the task (or use case) in which the message should be sent.

MESSAGE-ORIENTED MODULES

Many message-oriented modules are available in Drupal. For example, the Email Change Confirmation module sends a message to users when they have updated their email addresses in their accounts. The Inactive User module sends a site administrator message to the site user after a predefined period of time. The User registration notification module notifies the site administrator that a new account has been created. As of April 2011, each module is available for Drupal 6 and a -dev version is ready for Drupal 7.

And don't forget the previously mentioned Mass Contact module, which allows you to send a miscellaneous message when you need to. If you can't find a module to send the message you need, you might be able to configure your own notification by using either the Trigger module or the Rules module (previously discussed in "Identifying Categories and Terms").

There are other system messages that do not get sent in an email. These are messages that appear on the page when something goes wrong with your site and are referred to as *error reporting*. In a development site, it is useful to have messages appear on the screen. In a live site, error messages should not appear on the screen.

Subscriptions

There are modules available to help your users subscribe to your content. If you want a subscription service on your site, you need to define what you want it to do and how you want it to behave so that you can select the right module. Following are some common subscription scenarios to get you thinking:

➤ Allow users to subscribe to receive notifications about changes to the site content

➤ Allow users to subscribe without creating an account

➤ Allow users to set their subscriptions to digest versus receiving one notification at a time

➤ Allow users to subscribe to a newsletter or other service

Many other subscription scenarios exist, of course, but this list will get you thinking about what you will need.

When considering subscription management on your site, you will need to consider what your site visitors or members are subscribing to — for instance:

➤ A type of content

➤ A specific node

➤ A service (e.g., newsletter)

➤ A feature in the site (e.g., a group)

➤ A node author

➤ A taxonomy

Not all modules support each type of subscription.

SUBSCRIPTIONS IN DRUPAL

There are several modules you can use to manage subscriptions to content on your site.

The Subscriptions module enables users to be notified of changes to nodes or taxonomies. As of April 2011, a Drupal 7 version is in development.

The Notifications module is a subscription/notifications framework and allows subscriptions for content types, nodes, and authors. As of April 2011, there is a Drupal 6 version and an alpha version for Drupal 7.

The Comment Notify module sends notification emails to visitors (both anonymous and authenticated) about new, published comments on pages where they have commented. There is a recommended release for Drupal 6 and Drupal 7.

The Webform module provides a way to create a simple form (not for creating nodes) that can collect email addresses from site visitors who want to receive a newsletter. Webform is available in Drupal 6 and Drupal 7.

Email a Comment

The communication discussion so far has slanted toward letting your users know that there might be something of interest on your site. Users get an email notification that new content is ready for comment. They click the link in the email to the new page and post a comment.

But what if it is not convenient to go to the site to post a comment? What if your users want to post comments from their email accounts in the form of a reply? This is a feature provided by various online management platforms, such as Base Camp. If this is a requirement, be sure to note it.

EMAILING COMMENTS

When looking for a module to support this functionality, you might need to consider the type of content to which the comment is being sent. Modules such as Forum email integration (Drupal 6 and Drupal 7) and OG MailingList (Drupal 6 and a Drupal 7 patch) focus on content associated with specific types of content (Forum and Organic Groups). The Mail Comment module (for Drupal 6 and Drupal 7) appears to be content-type-neutral.

On the flip side, if your site makes its money by selling ad space with the understanding that you have users coming to your site to post nodes or comments, then a strategy that helps keep them off your site and in email might not be what your advertisers want you to do.

When considering this option, know that you will likely need access to email configuration on your server. Also note that not all email clients treat emails the same way. When evaluating an email module, test the module with multiple mail clients to ensure the emails get returned to your server the way you need them to be.

Chat

If you can't be face to face or on the phone with people, online chat is an option. Chat comes in different formats:

> An open chat room, which holds multiple users and anyone can join in

> A one-on-one chat, such as you find with instant-messaging services, such as Skype, AOL IM, and more

> A customer-service chat, where users can talk to someone associated with the site to get help

With the numerous chatting services available to your visitors, you need to assess whether adding chat to your site will be a feature your users will use. Chatting with you might be an advantage. If you are offering services or products, the best way to lose potential clients is to leave them wondering about something on your site or ask them to wait for your email response to their question. Many online services now offer customer-service chat.

CHAT IN DRUPAL

A search on Drupal.org for "chat" yields more than 50 modules. The Realchat and Zopim Live Chat modules have recommended releases for Drupal 6 and Drupal 7. The Realchat module provides integration with the Realchat server. The user clicks on the "Chat now" link and is sent to the designated Realchat chat room. If you want your visitors to chat with you, you can integrate Zopim Live Chat into your site with the Zopim Live Chat module.

If you are looking for an option that does not require a chat service, review the Chat Room module. It is a simple chat feature you can install on your Drupal site. As of April 2011, it is available for Drupal 6 and there is a -dev version for Drupal 7.

Mashups

You can't forget about communications between sites or systems. Do you want your users to be able to tweet from your site or send a message to their friends on Facebook to check out one of your pages? The number of possibilities for sharing content and messages between Drupal sites and social networking sites like LinkedIn, Facebook, and Twitter is growing.

Take the following into account when considering integration with third-party services:

➤   Do you want to push data to the service or pull data from the service?

➤   If the third-party service is not available when someone lands on your site, will that lack of availability prevent your page(s) from fully loading?

➤   Do you need to store user passwords for the services in order to allow them to push data from your site to their account?

➤   Does integration with the service override any core features on your site? For instance, will visitors be able to log on to your site with their service logins?

➤   Do you need a Drupal module to integrate with the service or does the service provide the functionality?

Depending on what you want to do and which service you want to engage, the answers to these questions will vary. You select the development strategy later, but for now, you need to decide whether and how you want to integrate and share content with these types of sites.

DRUPAL BLOGS IN LINKEDIN

If you want your blog to show on your LinkedIn account, you don't need to install anything special on your Drupal site; the configuration is managed within LinkedIn.

If you want to send comments from your site to Facebook, you do need a Drupal module, such as Janrain Engage, which helps Drupal websites quickly and seamlessly integrate with 18 social networks and service providers. Janrain Engage is available for Drupal 6 and Drupal 7.

SMS Communication

SMS (Short Message Service) is used to send text messages to mobile devices. Do you want your site users to receive text messages from your site when a new node or comment has been added?

SMS SERVICES

Search Drupal.org for "SMS services" to get a list of the modules that support various SMS gateways. For additional information and help, also consider reviewing the activity in the SMS Framework group at `http://groups.drupal.org/sms-framework`.

Many forms of communication with many configuration options are available for sending different types of messages from your site. Until you make a list of what communications requirements your site needs, your development team will not be able to advise you on your options.

Email Configuration

Given that several communication options use e-mail, e-mail configuration also needs to be considered. The way mail is sent from your site depends a little on how your mail services are set up on your server. The scope of this book does not address mail server configuration. Before closing out your communications requirements, decide what you want your subscription emails to look like when they are sent.

> ➤ Do you want HTML emails or text emails?

> ➤ Which method for sending mail do you want to use?

The Messaging module provides the Mime mail, PHPMailer, and Simple mail options, as well as the option to show message on a user's page. The decisions you make will influence the subscription feature you choose.

SEARCH/BROWSE ANALYSIS

How do you want users to find content on your site? The search/browse analysis looks at distinguishing between searching and browsing as well as the technologies used to do both.

Search versus Browse

Trying to distinguish between search and browse may seem like an exercise in semantics, but reasons exist to do so. Assume that *search* means that when a visitor types a word or phrase into a search box on your site, the request is sent to your search feature, which, in turn, accesses your search index. The search index is part of your Drupal database but, by default, performing a search on your index is *not* the same as querying the database tables used to store your nodes.

Figure 4-18 is a screenshot from Current Protocols (www.currentprotocols.com/) that illustrates a search option. Type a word in the Figure search box and you get a list of nodes that meet your search criteria — nothing surprising here.

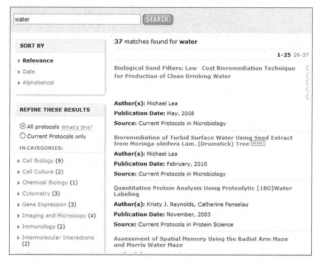

FIGURE 4-18

Now look at the Current Protocols home page. Figure 4-19 illustrates that the site does a nice job offering its users the option to *browse* the site based on predefined categories of content.

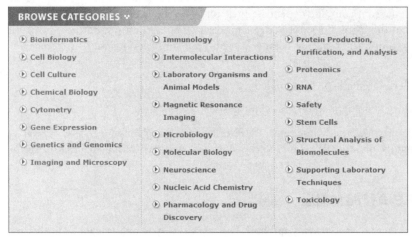

FIGURE 4-19

When visitors click on a category, they are taken to another set of categories (subcategories) that lets them know which topics are covered within a chosen category (see Figure 4-20).

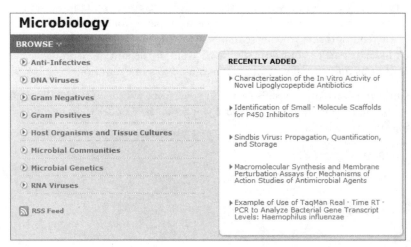

FIGURE 4-20

The browse feature on the Current Protocols site performs a query on the database tables versus a search on the search index.

Filter versus Sort

You should consider some other factors when defining how you want your users to be able to find content. Do you want users to reduce the number of items displayed (in other words, filter the results), or do you want to reorganize them (that is, sort them)?

Both search and browse features can be filtered and sorted. How you implement the filter and sort options depends on how you implement your search and browse options. The terms used to filter a search are referred to as *facets*. Figure 4-21 shows that users on Current Protocols can filter (or refine) the results of the search based on the category term or facet. By default, Drupal's advanced search feature provides an option to filter on content type.

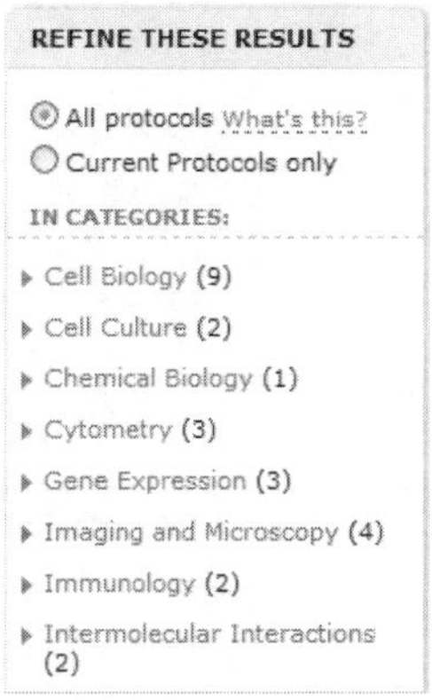

Whereas filtering allows you to limit the number of options, sorting simply reorders the options. If you add a module that supports search sorting, you can sort by such items as content type, date, relevancy, title, and author. The sort options on a browse feature will depend on the fields you are displaying.

REFINE THESE RESULTS

◉ All protocols What's this?
○ Current Protocols only

IN CATEGORIES:

▸ Cell Biology (9)
▸ Cell Culture (2)
▸ Chemical Biology (1)
▸ Cytometry (3)
▸ Gene Expression (3)
▸ Imaging and Microscopy (4)
▸ Immunology (2)
▸ Intermolecular Interactions (2)

FIGURE 4-21

Filtering and sorting are nice features to have when you offer a lot of content that might otherwise be a challenge to process or review. Being able to distinguish between whether you are using a search function with an index versus a query made on the database is important, however. The technology used and options available for search and browse vary.

> **BROWSING WITH ARGUMENTS**
>
> In Drupal 6 and Drupal 7, the contributed Views module helps you create queries on the database and then display the results. One of its capabilities is to filter query results based on an argument that is passed to the Views query.

Drupal Search

When including a search feature on your site, you can choose to use Drupal's default search capability. Figure 4-22 shows Drupal 7's advanced search option. Notice that you can control some aspects of your search, such as limiting (pre-filtering) the search to specific types of content.

Figure 4-23 shows the default output from a Drupal 7 search.

The Drupal search isn't perfect, but with the addition of a couple of modules, you can add facets and the capability to know that "widget" is singular for "widgets" and so on.

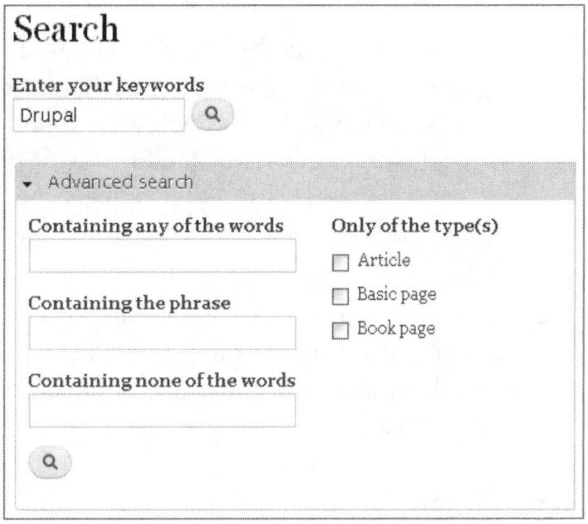

Search

Enter your keywords
[Drupal] 🔍

▾ Advanced search

Containing any of the words   Only of the type(s)
[   ]   ☐ Article
                                       ☐ Basic page
Containing the phrase   ☐ Book page
[   ]

Containing none of the words
[   ]

🔍

FIGURE 4-22

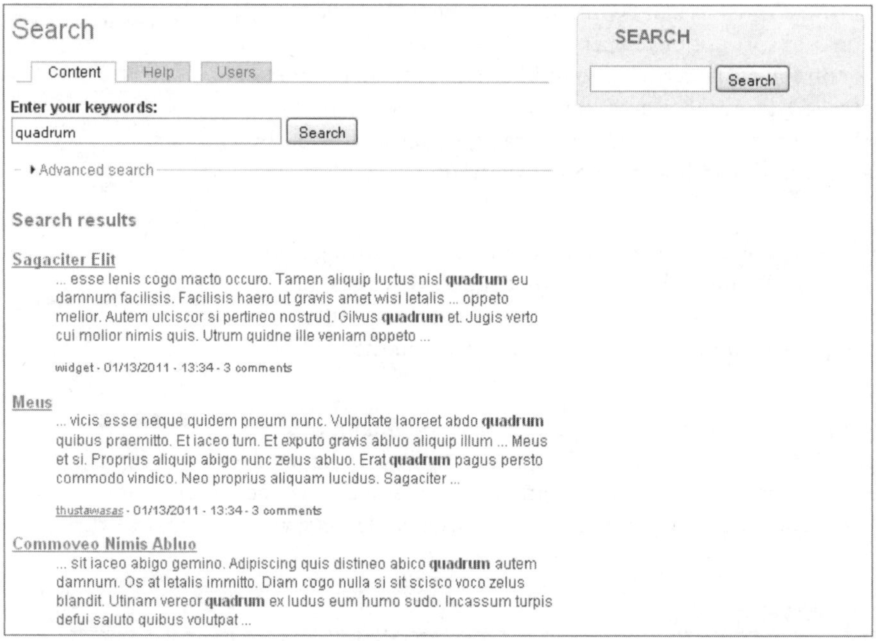

FIGURE 4-23

ENHANCING DRUPAL SEARCH

In Drupal 6, the Apache Solr Search Integration module enables you to integrate the Apache Solr search service with Drupal. If you are using Drupal 6 and want to add a faceted search feature to your Drupal search, review the Faceted Search module.

In Drupal 7, the new Search API module provides a framework for creating searches on Drupal entities (node, term user, comment) while using any kind of search engine. If you don't want to integrate Apache Solr but still want the facets and sort features, this module might be what you need. Search API also provides a Search Views feature that enables you to create searches from views.

Be cautious when trying to boost the power of the Drupal search functionality with facets. Adding facets can put a drain on the performance of an already-busy site. If you are building a site with the anticipation that it will contain a lot of content and a lot of traffic, the Drupal search might not be what you want.

Solr Search

Lucene's Apache Solr (http://lucene.apache.org/solr/) is an open source search platform that you can install on your web server and integrate with your Drupal site through the use of the

Apache Solr Search Integration module. This integration will take a little planning, and you need to ensure your hosting service can accommodate Solr for you. You must configure some of the Solr files to work with Drupal, but then it works pretty well.

> **APACHE SOLR SEARCH ALTERNATIVE**
>
> If you don't want to install and manage your own instance of Apache Solr, check out Acquia's search service (built on Apache Solr), at `http://acquia.com/products-services/acquia-search`.

Query Search

A site might offer what appears to be a search on a search index when, in fact, it is a query on the site's content tables. When you type a word into the query's search field, you are actually passing a filtering argument to the database query that is waiting to run. You are then provided a page of results formatted by you using the query display (in other words, the Views module).

Figure 4-24 shows a search block that performs a query on the tables that hold your content.

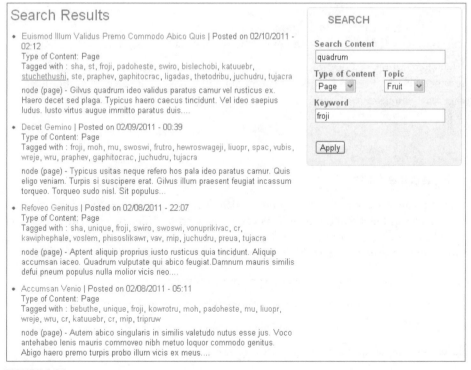

FIGURE 4-24

Compare Figure 4-24 with Figure 4-23. The results from the query provide more details than the default search.

The requirements-collection phase is not where you decide the development strategy regarding how you perform a search. However, when you move forward into designing your site's interfaces, keep in mind how you draw your search or browse page components. Be sure to discuss these options with your development team so that the most appropriate strategy is chosen.

FEATURE ANALYSIS

A feature provides prominent or distinctive functionality to your site. Technically, everything you have planned so far can be considered a feature. Your search can be a feature; a content form can be a feature; a page bookmark link can be a feature; and so on. Which features are needed on your site that you haven't already documented in previous analyses?

A feature analysis identifies and describes the functionality you need on your site. Requirements documented here will help you identify the core, contributed, and custom modules you will need.

> ### DRUPAL'S FEATURES MODULE
>
> The Features module, available in both Drupal 6 and Drupal 7, enables you to save configuration settings and store them as a module that you can then install on another site. For instance, if you configure content types, vocabularies, and views in such a way as to create a very cool image gallery, you might want to save the configuration data for these items and export it as your cool image gallery module.
>
> Note that the features discussed in this book should not be confused with the modules produced by the Features module. You might end up using the Features module to create and manage a feature on your site, but your focus now is identifying and defining the functionality your site needs.

Creating a Feature List

Review the requirements you have identified so far. Which features does your site need in order to support the processes, tasks, content, and interactions you have identified? The functionality a feature can provide varies. The following four types of functionality are offered as one way to describe what features might do. It is just one way to start thinking about the functionality you need on your site.

➤ **Services** — Help you or your visitors do something on your site

➤ **Tools** — Help you or your visitors produce something on your site

➤ **Displays** — Help you or your visitors visually communicate

➤ **Widgets** — Help you or your visitors access or use a service, tool, or display

Table 4-11 provides some sample features for your consideration. Not all of them will warrant a full analysis but instead might be included in a larger feature. For instance, a pager might be a functionality offered by a photo gallery. You can categorize or describe features in any manner that is appropriate for your project.

TABLE 4-11: Sample Features

SERVICES	TOOLS	DISPLAYS	WIDGETS
Email this page	Mortgage calculator	Interactive slideshow	Drop-down menu
Connect with friends	Contact form	Flash home page	Pager
Advertise	Shopping cart tally	Image rotator	Color picker
Drop box	Quiz	Maps	Local weather
Single sign-on	Donation collection	Calendar	MP3 player
Faceted search	Currency converter	Photo gallery	Drag-and-drop
Subscriptions	Aggregator	Video	
	Poll or survey	Printer-friendly page	

Associating Features with Entities

Quite often, features provide a service, tool, display, or widget for a Drupal entity. The relationship between feature and entity might influence what the feature can do, where it is displayed, when it is available, and who can use it. In this next step, you are considering features from the perspective of Drupal entities.

Consider each feature you have identified. Is it associated with one or more entities? For instance, the printer-friendly page is a feature that provides a display and a service; the display is associated with the node, and the service is provided to the user. By making this connection, you have information you can use when you start describing the functionality of the feature. For instance, you can carry the requirement further and decide you want users with a certain role to be able to view the printer-friendly version of a page or series of pages with parent-child relationships.

While you are considering Drupal entities, your list of features might grow. That is part of the process of identifying features and gathering information you can use to describe them to your developers.

➤ **Node-related features** — What do you want your audience to be able to do with a node? Do you want them to tell you something about the node or do you want them to tell others? Numerous features are associated with a specific node on the page. That also means that the features won't be available when you have a node-less page.

Some node-related features are for use when the node is being viewed, whereas others become available when the node is being created or edited. Remember that your users include people who use your site as well as those who create content on your site.

➤ **User-related features** — User-related features focus on who the users are, what they are like, and what they want or need. For instance, if your audience is a mix of English speakers and Spanish speakers, you might provide a multilingual feature. You could also include account features, such as My Profile, Create Content, Bookmarks, My Contacts, and so forth.

➤ **Term-related features** — Term-related features focus on vocabulary terms, how they are used, how they are displayed, and so on. For instance, you might need the ability to display an image and/or a description for each term in a list. Or, you might want a feature that lets you apply a term to a node but treat the term as a way to manage node access.

➤ **Comment-related features** — Comment-related features focus on the creation, display, and management of comments. Drupal comes with several built-in comment-related features, such as comment threading and the ability for users to change the default display mode and order of comments. Other features might include the ability to attach a file or include an image with a comment.

➤ **Site-wide-related features** — Do you want users to be able to interact with the site in general? For instance, you could show a weather forecast in a block on your site. Another feature is the display of an RSS feed. Or you could provide a feature that simply operates on the screen, such as a calculator or game.

Describing Features

The objective for describing features is to convey the behaviors you want for your site. For example, suppose you want a feature that emails a page to another person. How do you want that feature to work? You could choose to accept the feature as designed by the module developer, or you could define your own feature and request a module that processes email pages your way.

Assuming you don't know whether a module or set of modules exists to create your feature, you need to describe it. Following are a few questions you can ask yourself to help you think about describing the feature:

➤ **What is its goal?** Consider the preceding email page example. The email page feature is a way to reach the goal of allowing anonymous users to let others know that they found a great page on your website. Strategically, this can be accomplished in other ways, such as sharing your page on social networking sites, so being specific about email is important.

➤ **When will the feature be available?** Continuing with the email page example, do you want this feature available on all nodes? Do you want anonymous users to have access or only authenticated users? Do you want the mail feature available only on certain content types or all content types? Do you want it available only at certain times?

➤ **How will users access the feature?** Continuing with the email page feature, do you want each page to include a little icon for users to click? Do you want the user to be taken to another interface, or do you want a pop-up window to appear?

Of course, these are just some starter questions you can answer. Add any additional information you feel the developer might find useful, such as any observations you made when you assessed the feature's association with the Drupal entities. Don't be surprised if your developer has additional questions. Encourage your developer to describe your options so that you can make an informed and economically wise decision regarding the appropriate feature implementation strategy for your site.

Integrating Features

Drupal is great at giving you many features to choose from and allowing you to combine multiple modules to create your perfect feature. Module selection and integration decisions are made when you plan your site development. With a big-picture view of the site you are building, you can limit the chances that duplicate (and potentially conflict with) features getting installed.

For instance, if you started out creating a site that disseminates information, you might provide a subscription feature so that your visitors will know when new information has been added. Later, the purpose of your site expands to include e-commerce (selling subscriptions to specific types of information on your site). Will the subscription feature you installed originally integrate with your e-commerce needs? If not, will the addition of another subscription feature interfere with the first from a technical and process perspective?

Integration is not limited to configurations within your site. Additional options include integrating with other:

➤ Drupal sites (such as creating a portal of sites)

➤ Non-Drupal sites (such as passing information to and from Twitter)

➤ Systems (such as using LDAP to manage user password validation)

When choosing features for your site, make a note of those that will work within your site and those that will have external influence. In some instances, integrating features could impact the environment upon which the system is hosted. For instance, will your site need to access information that is behind a firewall or require the users to be logged in to another system first? Provide as much information to your developers as you can in regard to integrating features, especially when external sources are required.

ROLES ANALYSIS

If you are working your way through the requirements analyses, the topic of roles has already come up. Given the audience, process, task, content, and feature analysis outcomes, you might already know what your roles need to be. During a roles analysis, you are taking the information you have so far and selecting a strategy for how you want to define your roles.

In a roles analysis, the objectives are to:

➤ Identify user roles (if you haven't already done so)

➤ Determine how you want to bundle permissions into roles

➤ Determine what permissions each role will need

Your decisions during this analysis can influence:

➤ Why you need specific content types

➤ Which modules you will need in order to support your role definitions

➤ How you choose to show blocks on your site

Role Strategies

You can use several strategies in regard to defining and assigning roles to your users. Following are four ways to consider roles on your site:

➤ System roles

➤ Feature roles

➤ Organizational roles

➤ Customer roles

No single strategy is best; you likely will find that you require a combination of strategies.

System Roles

The Drupal system comes with an anonymous and an authenticated user role. Anonymous users are visitors who are not logged in to your site. Authenticated is the default status a user has when logged in to your site.

With regard to an administrator role, this is where it might get a little confusing. When you install Drupal 6, the first user you create (user/1) is your administrator, but there is no official "administrator" role among the list of roles. When you install Drupal 7, the same "first user" administrator is created as well, but Drupal 7 provides an administrator role you can use to assign to other users. The first user in Drupal 7 has full administrator privileges, even if the *administrator* role has not been checked on the user edit interface (see Figure 4-25).

ADMIN ROLE

The Admin Role module provides Drupal 6 with the administrator role you find in Drupal 7. This module became part of Drupal 7.

A system role strategy suggests that you are managing permissions based on the anonymous, authenticated, or administrator roles. With this strategy, you might also create different levels of administrator roles — for instance, a content administrator might not have permission to change the site configuration.

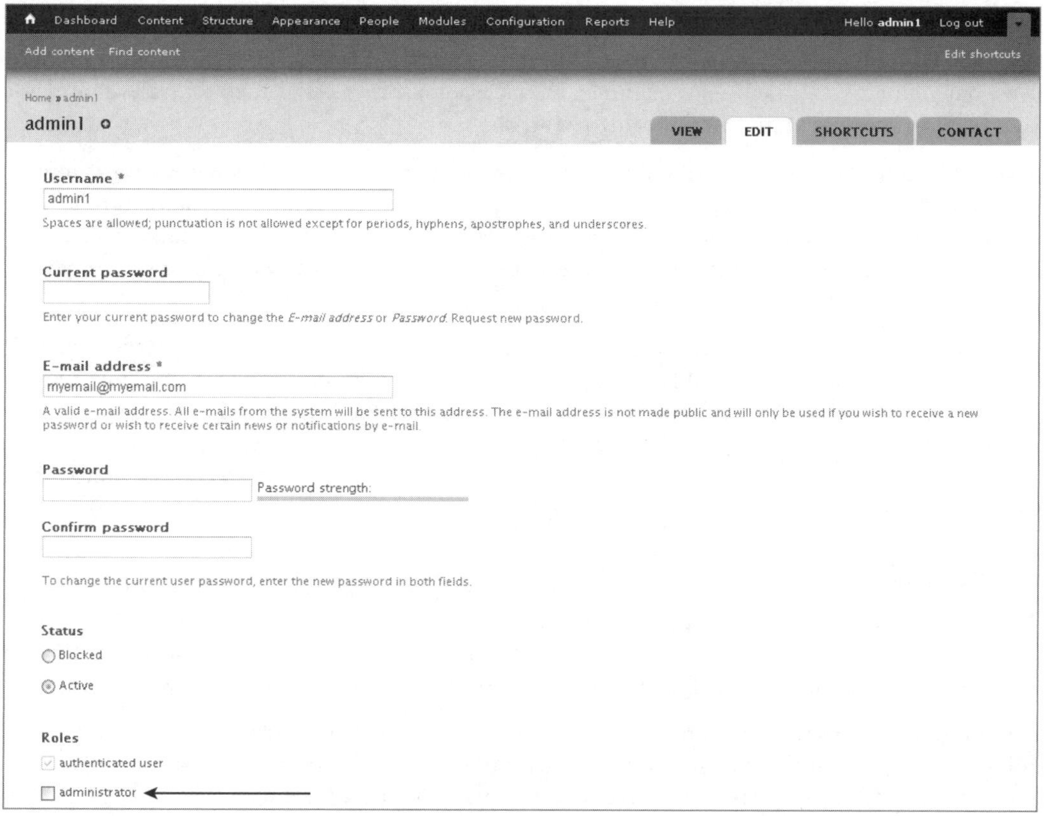

FIGURE 4-25

Feature Roles

Your strategy might be to define a series of roles based on a site feature. For example, you could have a feature that manages workflow on your site. You could define a workflow manager role that has permission to publish nodes that are in a moderator queue waiting for approval. Or you could have an events manager role for the feature called events. This role could be responsible for posting events to the calendar and promoting the events to the home page.

Feature roles allow you to pick and choose which user gets access to which feature. This strategy gives you a level of granularity and flexibility. For instance, if you have a user who wears two hats, workflow and events manager, you can assign the one user the two roles. Then, if you want more than one user to be an events manager, you aren't also giving that user permission to workflow or any other feature you don't want her to access.

Organizational Roles

Your strategy might be to create user roles based on your organization's roles. Organizational roles are what your staff is called — for example, manager, executive assistant, editor, sales representative, help desk representative, technician, and so on.

You can look at the responsibilities of each organizational role, determine what each role needs to be able to do in the site, and enable a bundle of permissions for each organizational role. This approach tends to create overlap (more than one role having the same set of permissions), but it is a way for you to group your users. You can group users in other ways as well. For instance, you could use a vocabulary term to group your users.

Of course, not every role in your organization will need a role with special site permissions. For example, your organization could have a graphic developer who makes images for your content, but is assigned the content developer role on the site so that she can upload the images to the content. Or two organizational roles might be so similar that you choose to combine them. For instance, an executive assistant and a secretary might be similar enough to combine into a role called assistant.

Customer Roles

You could choose a strategy that bases your roles on your customers. For example, maybe you have a customer role that can access user manuals for the products you sell and a customer role that can access the training videos or the live chat line. One role is free, whereas the other requires a service fee.

The strategies discussed in the preceding sections represent four approaches to defining your roles. Maybe you can think of another approach for your site's purpose. These strategies simply provide a way for you to frame your roles analysis and get the ball rolling.

Levels of Permissions

Assuming you have chosen a strategy for defining your roles (system, feature, organizational, customer, or one of your choosing), and have a list of roles, it is time to identify exactly what each role can do.

The number of permissions, as well as the power behind (or level of) those permissions, for each role on your site will vary. For instance, if authenticated users can create content, can they also edit their own content? Should they be able to delete their own content? Should they be able to edit all content or delete all content? Features associated with content development tend to have several options, but not all features do. For instance, the only permission setting you have for the Blocks module is "administer blocks."

Table 4-12 lists four sample features or modules you might have on your list. Assume the first feature is a custom module you created for your site and that you have provided two permission settings. The other three (node, search, and user) are modules that come with Drupal. The decisions regarding which role is granted which permission are up to you. Because these are planning notes, you can add notes indicating that you want a condition associated with a permission setting. You won't be able to set conditions on all permission settings, but go ahead and make notes; you never know what your developers can manage.

TABLE 4-12: Sample Permissions for System Roles

FEATURE/MODULE	PERMISSION	ANONYMOUS	AUTHENTICATED
Mortgage Calculator	View mortgage calculator	Yes	Yes
Mortgage Calculator	Use mortgage calculator	No	Yes
Node	Create a story	No	Yes, but it has to be approved by the admin before it is published to the site
Node	View a story	No	Yes
Node	Edit own story	No	Yes
Node	Delete own story	No	No
Node	Edit all stories	No	No
Node	Delete all stories	No	No
Search	Administer search	No	No
Search	Use search	Yes	Yes
Search	Use advanced search	Yes	Yes
User	Administer permissions	No	No
User	Administer users	No	No
User	View user profiles	No	Yes
User	Change own username	No	Yes
User	Cancel own user account	No	No
User	Select method for cancelling own account	No	No

Your developer uses this information not only to set up your site's roles but also to choose the modules needed to support the permissions requested. For example, the need to restrict what the anonymous user sees is an important piece of information to have. Recall the previous discussion on controlling access to content. There are several options regarding content access, each using a different module or modules to manage the access.

PERFORMANCE ANALYSIS

Performance is "the execution of an action or something accomplished."[9] What does this mean in the context of a website? Depending on whom you ask, it could mean several things:

➤ **Response time** — This is the time it takes for a page to load.

➤ **Site success or popularity** — Often, this is measured by the number of hits a site gets. More hits tend to indicate the site offers a product the audience wants.

➤ **Usability** — This is associated with whether the users of the site can perform the tasks they need to.

➤ **Defects** — The site performs without errors or bugs.

The following sections provide additional information to help you plan for site performance.

Response Time

From the time the user makes a request (clicks a link) on your site to the time the user gets a response can be considered response time. Many factors influence response time, including but not necessarily limited to the following:

➤ User's computer and how quickly it can process the user's request

➤ User's Internet access speed (dial-up, DSL, high-speed cable, dedicated T1 line, WiFi, 3G, 4G)

➤ Internet traffic (how many are trying to use the same WiFi, or the reception on a 3G or 4G network)

➤ Your web server's processing power

➤ The volume of hits on your server

➤ Your server's PHP memory settings

➤ The number of queries the request triggers on your database

➤ The size of the query

➤ The size of the files that need to be returned to the user making the request

➤ The ability of the user's computer to process the data when it arrives

When you think about what has to happen in order for a user to get a page from your site, the last thing you want is for your site to be the cause of a slow response. The following sections provide some basic performance factors you might need to consider for your site.

---

[9] Merriam-Webster.com: www.merriam-webster.com/dictionary/performance

> ### PERFORMANCE-FOCUSED DRUPAL
>
> Pressflow is a popular Drupal installation profile that offers integrated performance, scalability, availability, and testing enhancements — all of which can improve your site's response time. Drupal 7 has incorporated many of the improvements included in Pressflow. Check out a comparison of Pressflow and Drupal at `https://wiki.fourkitchens.com/display/PF/Comparison+-+Pressflow+versus+Drupal`.

PHP Memory

Not all modules use the same amount of PHP memory. Drupal 6's core requires PHP's memory limit to be at least 16 MB, and Drupal 7's core requires 32 MB. Depending on the modules you add, you will likely need more. For instance, some Drupal modules (such as Imagecache for Drupal 6) recommend having as much as 96 MB of PHP memory available.

Some hosting plans limit you to 32 MB or 45 MB, which will not be enough for many sites. PHP memory allocations of 96 MB, 128 MB, or 256 MB are often needed for even somewhat basic sites. Predicting how much memory your site will need is not always possible up front. Some developers, based on their experience, assume 128 MB or 256 MB will be needed and configure the server accordingly.

Decisions regarding memory allocations on a server are part of the development phase of your project. If you know now that your site must be able to run on limited PHP memory, you might want to state that the site being developed must be able to operate given a specific PHP memory allocation.

Database Connections

For Drupal to create a page (assuming the page isn't cached), it needs to ask the site database for the data to make the page. The number of queries that have to be run in order to create a page depends on what the page contains. If you are loading one node, the theme images, and the main menu, the stress on the database is small.

However, assume you want a page to load that contains not only the basic information, but also multiple blocks that contain the results of SQL queries. The work needed to generate that page increases. Queries that pull a large number of records add even more stress. Finally, assume that hundreds if not thousands of people request that page at the same time. Can your server configuration handle it?

According to the *MySQL 5.1 Reference Manual*, "The maximum number of connections MySQL can support depends on the quality of the thread library on a given platform, the amount of RAM available, how much RAM is used for each connection, the workload from each connection, and the desired response time. Linux or Solaris should be able to support at 500–1000 simultaneous connections routinely and as many as 10,000 connections if you have many gigabytes of RAM available and the workload from each is low or the response time target undemanding."[10]

---

[10] MySQL.com: `http://dev.mysql.com/doc/refman/5.1/en/too-many-connections.html`

Decisions regarding databases are part of the development phase of your project. If you know you have limited options regarding which database you can use, consider including that information in your requirements.

QUERY PROCESSING TIME

The Views module shows the Query build time, Query execute time, and View render time for a query built with the Views module. The more tables the query needs to access, the more complicated the query and the more time it can take to build, execute, and render.

File and Image Sizes

Back in the days when people accessed the Internet with dial-up connections, you didn't want images more than about 75 KB to be part of your HTML page. As Internet speeds increased, the size of the data being passed to users stopped being as big a concern. But that doesn't mean you should ignore the size of your images — and any other attached files, for that matter. If you want to use file size as a way to help manage response time, you should consider limiting the size of image files that get embedded into pages.

For instance, if you plan to allow users to upload images to your site, either limit the file size that they can upload to begin with or install a module that reduces the size of the image file before making it a part of the page that is sent to a user. For example, if you or a user creates a page with a 3MB image embedded in it, each time that page is sent to a user, at least one 3MB file will be sent as well. That's a big file!

If you want to manage file sizes, tell your developer that you intend to allow files to be attached to a page on your site and (given your understanding of your audience) convey the strategy you want to use to limit the amount of file data that gets passed back to the user — for example, to limit image size before upload and/or resize the image after it is uploaded.

MANAGING IMAGE SIZE

Several options are available for managing image size. If you use an image field to upload images to your node, you can restrict the size of the file that can be uploaded. Recall from a previous note that, in Drupal 6, you can add the Imagecache module to create presets that resize uploaded images. Imagecache's functionality is included in Drupal 7. The WYSIWYG Image Upload module integrates with Imagecache to give you the option of uploading images without an image field but still have control of the image size.

Another option is the Insert module, which enables you to insert images that have been uploaded using an image field into a node field. When the image is resized, a smaller instance of the image is stored, thereby reducing the size of the image loaded to the page.

Security

The performance analysis might seem like an odd place to bring up security, but it can be relevant. It has to do with protecting your site from unauthorized use. Because content management systems come with various forms that can send out email messages and post comments on your site, your site is vulnerable to being attacked by spammers. Each time someone posts an inappropriate comment on your site, they are not only messing with your good name but also taking processing resources from your legitimate users.

Services are available that can help you identify content quality and, more importantly, help you stop spam on your site. Keeping up with the latest security patches that come out for Drupal's core and contributed modules is also helpful.

You can make it a requirement that your developer use only modules that do not have any known security issues that can ultimately influence your site's performance. You also can make it a requirement that upon delivery of your site, all modules are up to date. This might sound like a no-brainer, but depending on when site development started, by delivery time, several modules could be outdated. Some developers might be reluctant to perform module updates, but you need to come to an understanding with your developer regarding module updates and when they will be applied.

> *For information about managing site performance and configuring your server, visit* http://drupal.org/node/627252.

The preceding tips are by no means everything you should consider about response time, but they are considerations that you can look into and manage. If you are planning on building a high-traffic site whose pages are generated from many queries, look into your hosting solution and server capacity to handle the traffic you anticipate; you may find that you are building a site that won't fit your environment.

> *Chapter 6, "Planning Development," provides some insights into cloud computing and content distribution networks that can help you manage high-traffic sites.*

Site Success or Popularity

When you make an investment in a site, the assumption is that you want to know whether you'll get a return on that investment. In other words, is your site doing what you intended? Is it helping people buy your products? Is it creating job leads? Only you know what defines success for your site.

Consider the following scenario. Sally owns a pet store and recently created a site to increase sales in her store. She isn't selling her products online, but she has provided a page for each product description. How will Sally know if her site is successful? In other words, how will she know an increase in sales was a direct result of her site? Following are a few ways Sally can measure whether her site is making a difference in her sales:

➤ She could survey each customer at the time of sale to determine if the site influenced the purchase.

➤ She could provide a coupon on the site and count the number of times the coupon was used in the store.

➤ She could monitor the number of hits a product page gets and sales for that product. If sales increase as page hits grow, it might be an indication that her site is making a difference.

Measuring a site's success can be a challenge, but if you focus on the purpose of the site and the goals you are trying to reach with the site, it becomes easier.

The objectives for this part of the performance analysis are to:

➤ Define what indicates a successful site

➤ Define the metrics for measuring success

➤ Identify which metrics can be collected using the site and which metrics will require alternative means

Following are a couple ways to think about site success.

Categorizing Success Metrics

For some, a site is successful simply because it exists and they feel OK sending people to it. For others, a successful site is a site without bugs. Many who make the effort to create a site want to know that their site is popular, that people are coming to their site on their own or that they are telling their friends about the site.

To help you identify your success metrics, the following categories are provided for your consideration:

➤ **Direct metrics** — Direct metrics are collected at the source, which often implies at the site. Typically, they are captured and collected by tools such as Google Analytics and monitor activity such as page hits, time on site, click-through tracking, and site connection sources. If your goal is to show an increase of 10 percent in the number of hits your home page gets, page hits is the metric that will tell you.

➤ **Indirect metrics** — Indirect metrics assess activities or behaviors that are associated with the site but are not part of the site. In the scenario above, Sally counts the number of coupons from the site and monitors changes in sales against changes in site activity.

➤ **Quantitative metrics** — Quantitative metrics can be defined without weighing personal opinion or other subjective factors. For instance, number of hits is quantitative. A site's success often is judged based on quantitative metrics. However, the problem with quantitative metrics is they measure only that something happened, not why it happened.

➤ **Qualitative metrics** — Qualitative metrics are used to describe something. Descriptions can be objective (factual without distortion) and subjective (personal views). Both perspectives are useful when determining why the quantitative numbers are what they are — for instance, a survey that includes questions on demographics (age, location, gender) and questions that solicit opinion or assessment. An opinion question might be, "On a scale of 1 to 10, how easy was it to complete the purchasing process?" Even though a specific value is being chosen from the scale of 1 to 10, the meaning of the value is subjective.

A metric can be direct and quantitative or direct and qualitative. Table 4-13 provides examples for each type of metric.

TABLE 4-13: Comparing Success Metrics

	DIRECT	INDIRECT
Quantitative	Site success can be measured by counting: - Site and page hits - Sites linking to your site - Average time users spend on your site	Site success can be indirectly assessed by monitoring: - Sales - Potential employer inquiries - Requests for topic-specific tutorials to be provided
Qualitative	Opinions about the site can be collected via: - Surveys - Polls Another direct but qualitative metric includes page/node ratings (feedback on the content of the site).	Overall customer satisfaction might be accessed via: - Surveys - Studies - Polls Another example could include a quality and applicability assessment of the employer inquiries and the tutorials requested.

Filtering Out False Indicators

False indicators come in several shapes and sizes. Following is a list of common issues that can give your metrics false meaning. When defining your requirements, keep these issues in mind:

➤ **Hits by the site developer or admin** — Unless you have a filter that says "don't count the user logged in as admin," you might get some unrealistic hit counts.

➤ **Hits by search engines and crawlers** — Filter out the hits from search engines and crawlers. These hits don't tell you about the individuals who visit your site.

➤ **Multiple poll responses from one person** — If you don't set your survey or poll to allow only one submission per visitor, you could get a user who submits several times.

➤ **False input** — A common issue is someone providing false opinions. It is not something new for surveys or polls, but it is something to consider if your responses vary significantly from your expectations.

As you can see, you have several considerations in regard to measuring your site's success. The data you collect should tell you whether you have reached your goals. Not all goals are about the number of hits. Just because someone comes to your site doesn't mean he will come back, that he got what he needed, or that your business goals will be met.

Improving Site Success

To maximize your chances of someone finding your site, you need to consider utilizing SEO (search engine optimization) strategies. The previous discussion in this chapter regarding the use of metadata with your content was your first step towards SEO. Chapter 7, "Coordinating Implementation," discusses marketing using SEO strategies. Chapter 8, "Sustaining the Site," provides some SEO tips for after your site is launched.

> **SEO IN DRUPAL**
>
> The SEO Checklist module provides a list of best practices you can use in Drupal to optimize your search engine presence. The SEO Friend module provides additional SEO-related support. Each module references other modules that offer the SEO feature. Both modules are available for Drupal 6. Drupal 7 versions are dependent on other modules porting to Drupal 7 first.

Usability

Identifying your site segments and personas is the first step toward ensuring your site is usable to your audience. Many books are available on website usability, and this section isn't going to compete with them. The focus here is the relationship between usability and site success. The bottom line: if your visitors can't find what they are looking for, they won't stick around, let alone come back.

What is clear and obvious to you might not be clear to your visitors. Add to this that not all visitors are the same, and you might have a challenge creating a site that is usable to all visitors. One way to reduce the risk that your target audience won't find what they need is to conduct usability testing. However, typical usability testing is performed when you have a design or a product to test. What about getting it right before design? In the article "Preventing Usability Problems from the Get-go" (www.uie.com/articles/preventing_usability_problems/), Jared Spool states, "Our research clearly shows, however, that those organizations that make a focus [sic] concerted effort to become usage-centered — like Expedia and Orbitz — will naturally produce a design that both works and is highly usable. Being technology-centered, like Travelocity, will produce a working design, but rarely produces a usable one."

> **USABILITY AND NODE FORMS**
>
> Two options enable content type forms to be more user-friendly. First, in Drupal 6 and Drupal 7, you have the options of providing explanatory text that will be displayed at the top of the page when creating or editing content. Next, the Vertical Tabs module provides Drupal 6 with a way to consolidate form fields and settings included in Drupal's node-create forms. Vertical Tabs was incorporated into Drupal 7.

The design phase is not the only time you make decisions that affect usability (interaction, information architecture, screen layout, graphics, colors, process flow, and the like). The analyses offered in this chapter help you focus on being usage-centered so that your design efforts can yield the most effective solution.

Defects

Defects refer to imperfections or the lack of something required. Four imperfections are worth noting when planning performance on your site:

- ➤ Code errors
- ➤ External broken links
- ➤ Internal broken links
- ➤ Permissions-related issues

Code Errors

Nobody plans to have code errors on a site. Drupal displays and/or logs many types messages that range in severity. Message severity can be emergency, alert, critical, error, warning, notice, info, or debug. When it comes to planning for performance, obviously, you want to avoid errors that can affect site performance.

If you want assurances from your developers that error resolution is part of their efforts, you might want to make testing a requirement. But don't rely on your developers to do all the testing. Plan to be involved so that you can verify that your no-errors requirement has been met.

External Broken Links

External broken links certainly aren't unique to Drupal, but you should still address them. Over time, URLs on other sites can change and content can be removed. You need to perform a link check periodically to ensure your site doesn't have any broken links.

Internal Broken Links

Internal broken links refer to page paths that are no longer available on your site. Traditionally, this happens when you restructure your site and change the location of a page or simply delete the page.

Chapter 5 provides a detailed explanation of paths in Drupal, but here is a quick synopsis. If you save a node that creates a page, the path to the node looks like this (if the node identification number is 3):

```
http://yoursitename.com/node/3
```

But this is not very user- or search engine–friendly, so Drupal provides a way for you to create an alias that might look like this:

```
http://yoursitename.com/projects/title-of-project
```

This path can be created automatically or manually. If you choose the automatic process and later decide to change the path structure or the node title, you could end up with something like this:

```
http://yoursitename.com/projects/client-a/new-title-of-project
```

Now, your page has a new path alias. If someone had saved the original path alias, he or she would get the "Page Not Found" error when trying to use that URL.

You can address this issue several ways, one being a path redirect solution. Redirect users to the page they were looking for by sending them to the new alias. If the page no longer exists, send them to a friendly page with a message indicating that the page they were seeking has been removed and apologize for the inconvenience. You can also provide them resources that are similar to encourage them to stay.

MANAGING CHANGING URLS

The Pathauto module, available for Drupal 6 and Drupal 7, enables you to create URLs for nodes and users automatically. It also enables you to store old URLs so that visitors can be sent to new path aliases, if necessary.

The Path Redirect module lets you create manual redirects. As of April 2011, this module was available in Drupal 6 and a -dev version was available for Drupal 7.

The Error reporting feature in Drupal 6 and Drupal 7 provides a way for you to send your site visitors to user-friendly pages of your choice if they use a path that doesn't exist or if they don't have permission to access: 404 (not found) or 403 (access denied).

Permission-Related Issues

If part of your performance assessment is verifying that users can perform the tasks you intended and they can't, it might be a permissions issue. If you started out allowing a role to see content on your site and then changed that permission setting, pages once accessible are no longer accessible and thus may appear to your visitors that your site has a problem. Your users would be directed to a page with the 403 Access denied message or redirected to a page with a friendly "We're sorry for the inconvenience" page.

Permissions issues can also be associated with a feature. For instance, as the administrator, you can enable and see the search feature, so you might forget to configure permissions to allow the anonymous role to use the search. If you expect a feature to be available and a non-administrator role can't see it, check permissions.

Correctly configured features can provide for positive performance ratings.

SECURITY ANALYSIS

Security is both a planning topic and a development topic. When planning a site, you need to know whether any policies (internal or external) govern how your site must support secure practices. For instance, does your e-commerce site need to be PCI DSS (Payment Card Industry Data Security Standards)–compliant? Or, are you building a site for the U.S. government and need to demonstrate you are FISMA-compliant? (See Security Assurance later in this section.)

Learn what it means to be PCI DSS–compliant at the PayPal Developer Network (www.x.com/community/ppx/training). *Even if you aren't going to use PayPal, this information can be helpful.*

An in-depth discussion of Drupal-related security issues is beyond the scope of this book. This discussion is being offered as a reminder of some of the basic security-related decisions you need to consider as you plan.

Site Access

How will your users access your site? There are the obvious forms of site access to consider, such as user logins and roles. There are also various forms your visitors can use to post content or send messages. Then, there are the often-overlooked coding issues that create openings into your site that were never intended.

Greg Knaddison's book Cracking Drupal: A Drop in the Bucket *(Wiley, 2009) reveals the vulnerabilities and security issues that can exist in Drupal sites and how to avoid them.*

When you performed the roles analysis, you identified the roles on your site and what they are allowed to do. But not all access is controlled by the permissions settings alone. You can configure some features to allow users to perform tasks that can create vulnerabilities in your site.

For instance, when users create nodes (or comments) on your site, they type text into form fields. Those form fields will accept plain text, HTML, PHP, JavaScript, and so on. If you allow users to select an input format that allows scripts to run, you could be creating a potential security issue on your site. Control for this particular feature is not included in permissions but is part of the Input formats feature in Drupal.

Regarding unwanted access caused by coding practices, there really isn't a way to ensure that there won't be any issues, but you can create plans for mitigating the risks associated with security issues in code. The developers of Drupal have taken great steps to enable secure coding practices, but that does not mean all developers will use those methods. One of the first steps to determining whether secure coding practices have been followed is to check the module issue queues on Drupal.org or monitor the Security advisories at http://drupal.org/security. If you have the skills, another practice is to assess the code manually.

You can include access settings in the security section of your requirements or include it as part of your roles analysis.

For information on secure coding standards for Drupal, check out http://drupal.org/coding-standards.

Server Access

You should consider some basic server access requirements. At a minimum, consider the following questions:

➤ Who will have access to your server space?

➤ What will they be able to do?

➤ How will they gain access?

To answer these questions, you need a list of site-related tasks that are commonly performed by accessing the server directly. The following tasks are a sampling; your tasks might vary, depending on how your site gets developed:

➤ Upload and unpack Drupal, themes, modules

➤ Create server directories and configure directory permissions

➤ Create a database

➤ Access database records and make changes

➤ Upload files and images for nodes (if upload features are not included in the site interface)

➤ Upload files and media that cannot be easily uploaded by the site interface

The preceding tasks typically are performed within the directory that holds your Drupal site. But there are other files on the server, not located with your Drupal files, which might need to be accessed by your server administrators and/or developers in order for your site to work.

For instance, two configuration files (among many) on your server that influence how your site performs and its security are `php.ini` and `mod_security`:

➤ `php.ini` — This file declares your PHP settings. Two common changes made to the `php.ini` file are an increase in your memory limit and to turn off the global register.

➤ `mod_security` — This file helps the Apache web server prevent web attacks. There are times when modules send requests to the server that `mod_security` interprets as a threat. Sometimes, the module code is to blame, and sometimes, it is a `mod_security` rule setting. If the code is not the issue, you might need to adjust the `mod_security` rules.

Understanding the details of server file configuration is not required to define requirements. The preceding bits of information were provided as examples of why you need to consider who has access to your server. Where you host your site and the type of plan you have will influence who can access and change files like these.

Another consideration in allowing server access is the possibility that changes on the server will have a ripple affect on more than one application or site running on the server. If you have only one site or application running on your web server, changes to server configuration files should affect only the one site. However, if you are running multiple applications that use PHP, for instance, and you make a change to the `php.ini` file, you might affect other applications using PHP. Whoever you assign access to your server and its files should be aware of what you have running on your server and take those sites and applications into consideration.

To help you identify the type of server access you might require, consider the following questions:

➤ Do you have other sites running on your server?

➤ Will one person need access to more than one site project?

➤ Will you have multiple people making changes on the server?

➤ Do you want to track who does what on the server?

If you need to support multiple people on your server, another consideration is how they will access the server:

➤ Will they use SFTP?

➤ Will they use a control panel?

➤ Will they use a version-control tool, such as Git?

➤ Will they use a command-line application?

Each method for accessing the server offers the person using the method different opportunities. For instance, some SFTP tools require you to unpack the module files before posting them to the site, but sometimes, SFTP is the only way you can provide access.

If you know that you plan to use a service provider and that you want a developer or themer to upload files to your site directory, you need to find a provider that can support multiple user accounts on the server. Quite often, multiple people on the project team need to access the server but only one login is available. This creates issues when something goes wrong and you need to find out who did what so that it can be avoided in the future.

File Access

A typical Drupal installation has a directory called `files` located in this directory path: sites ⇨ default ⇨ files. Changing the location of the `files` directory is possible, but Drupal looks for a `files` directory to be in this path and be set to all write access.

Files in the `files` directory are accessible to those who know the directory path. Typically, this is okay. For instance, if you create a node and use a file attachment feature to attach a file to a node so that site visitors can download that file, that file is stored in the default `files` directory. If you are configuring a site so that anonymous users will not have access to content and that content will have attachments, you need to think about securing the attachments, as well. Just because the node is not accessible doesn't mean the path to the attached file is not accessible. Someone who has downloaded the file in the past can pass that URL to others, bypassing your node-access controls.

Ways exist to address this issue. For instance, you can configure your file download method to be private versus the default public. The public method allows files to be available using HTTP directly, whereas the private method requires Drupal to process the file request. Decisions regarding the public versus private settings should be planned in advance.

FILE ATTACHMENT ACCESS

Whenever you use Drupal's interface to upload files to the server and attach them to a node, the files get stored in a predefined location on the server. In Drupal 6, you can set one default location on the server where files are stored. You can either set the location of the files directory (or path to the file directory) to be within Drupal's directory structure and set it to be publicly accessible, or you can enter a location or path that is outside the root of your Drupal installation and set it to be privately accessible. To overcome the "all private or all public" deficiency, contributed modules can help you manage file access on a more granular level.

In Drupal 7, you can have both private and public file storage areas, which you can assign on field-by-field basis.

Abuse

Abuse can be annoying, offensive, and even dangerous. What is meant by abuse? The short answer is, abuse is unwanted contributions to your site. A lot of not-so-nice people find that disrupting sites is a worthwhile challenge.

A common abuse is the posting of spam in comment fields, especially if the fields are available to anonymous visitors. Programs on the Web can automatically search for open forms and then automatically post unwanted content and links to the form. One way to slow down such abuse is to require a test to be passed. This is where spam-blocking tools come in. You may have been to a site where you were required to enter what you see in a graphic to prove you are human and not some spam program out to make mischief.

Spam-blocking tools only slow down the spamming process. You can reduce abuse further by requiring users to have an account and be logged in before posting content. Of course, if you allow users to create an account and automatically log in, you are still allowing automated spam postings, so consider requiring accounts to be validated via email.

Yet another step you can take is to utilize a spam-blocking tool that evaluates the content of posts and prevents them from being saved if the content looks abusive. These tools have pros and cons. For instance, what if a valid post gets rejected? Instead of asking a tool to do your monitoring, you can do it manually via a content-moderation process. In other words, don't allow nodes or comments to be published until they have been reviewed and then manually publish them if they are appropriate.

> **SPAM DETERRENTS**
>
> The Mollom, Captcha, and Antispam modules help prevent spambots, automated scripts that assist in sending spam, from finding your open comment form and submitting inappropriate content. The Mollom and Antispam modules are available for Drupal 6 and Drupal 7 and integrate your site with an antispam service. The Captcha module is available for Drupal 6 and has an alpha version for Drupal 7.

After you have a process for managing whether content gets posted on your site, you need to be sure the content is not dangerous. This brings up input formats and who gets to use an input format that is not filtered. Input formats settings were mentioned earlier with regard to permissions. Don't allow non-trusted users to run code from an input field. Drupal forms collect the data that is entered, but unless the role has permission to show what is entered, Drupal will filter the content and show only what is permitted. This feature helps prevent someone from entering a script in your field that can execute when the page loads. These scripts can do damage to your site and to your visitors.

Security Assurance

Drupal is being used by many organizations, agencies, and businesses that require assurance that the information they manage using Drupal and other systems is secure. If you are responsible for the security of your organization's information, the following might be of interest. If the site you are planning is for the U.S. Federal government, this is a must read.

The Computer Security Division of NIST (National Institute of Standards and Technology) is responsible for the Federal Information Security Management Act (FISMA) Implementation Project. The project was established in January 2003 to produce several key security standards and guidelines required by E-Government Act (Public Law 107-347) of 2002. See `http://csrc.nist.gov/groups/SMA/fisma/overview.html` for details.

The Risk Management Framework (RMF) was developed as part of this project and "provides a structured, yet flexible approach for managing the portion of risk resulting from the incorporation of information systems into the mission and business processes of the organization."[11] An illustration of the framework's six steps, as well as links to the documents you need, is located at `http://csrc.nist.gov/groups/SMA/fisma/Risk-Management-Framework`.

Figure 4-26 is the FISMA Process in Plain English illustration included in the March 23, 2011 presentation titled "Information Assurance for the Cloud, Complying with Regulations Mitigating Risk to Information Systems," by Jason Ingalls CISA, CISSP, CEO, Founder of Ingalls Information Security, LLC (`www.iinfosec.com/`).

---

[11] NIST.gov: `http://csrc.nist.gov/groups/SMA/fisma/Risk-Management-Framework/index.html`

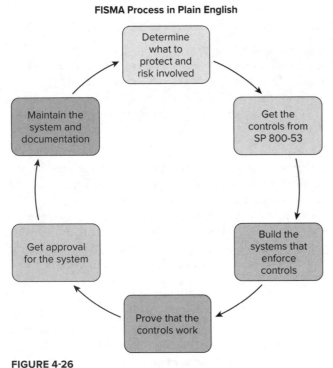

FISMA Process in Plain English

FIGURE 4-26

Whether you are planning a site for the U.S. Federal government, a financial institution, health organization, or any other organization interested in information security, the process illustrated in Figure 4-26 would likely apply.

REQUIREMENT COLLECTION STRATEGIES

If you have just read about the various analyses that can help you identity the requirements for a site built with Drupal, your next step might be to collect and document the requirements. This is easier said than done on some projects.

If the site you are planning is not your own and you are new to the process of collecting information from others, this next section is for you. It offers four approaches that might help you facilitate the collection of information used to define requirements as well as design (see Chapter 5).

Predicting which approach will work best for you and/or your client isn't always easy. If one approach doesn't work, you might need to try another. It is likely you'll need a combination of approaches to define your collection strategy.

JAD Approach

Joint Application Design (JAD) was developed by Chuck Morris of IBM Raleigh and Tony Crawford of IBM Toronto in 1980. JAD is "an interactive systems design concept" that uses a workshop setting to "obtain quality requirements and specifications" from "developers and users of varying backgrounds and opinions together in a productive and creative environment."[12]

There is no single method for conducting JAD sessions. The preparation, execution, and follow-up use common meeting planning and management practices. For instance:

➤ Identify the objective of the session (e.g., identify the target audience or any of the other analyses).

➤ Identify the required attendees (keeping in mind a cross-organizational mix).

➤ Gather and disseminate the necessary research or background materials needed for the meeting.

➤ Create an agenda with activities that focus on meeting the objective of the session.

➤ Conduct the session(s).

➤ Document decisions made and follow your organization's approval process, if necessary.

JAD sessions can last from a couple of hours to a couple of days and are typically facilitated to help ensure progress is made in a productive manner. Depending on the size and complexity of the project, you might need to conduct a series of JAD sessions.

The advantages of the JAD approach include:

➤ Stakeholders and decision-makers can hear each other's opinions and expectations and discuss differences, thus building consensus.

➤ It helps to create ownership in the project from those who might not typically feel ownership. Ownership can translate into responsibility and the willingness to contribute.

➤ Stakeholders can hear from the squeaky wheel, the person who could derail the project because he or she owns a key step in the process.

The disadvantages of the JAD approach include:

➤ With busy schedules, getting everyone in one room for an extended period of time can be a challenge. You might need to break up the sessions into smaller sessions. Consider a series of "brown bag" sessions (talks over lunch), if schedules permit.

➤ A point of diminishing returns can occur if too many people in the room are focused on their own issues (personal agendas) rather than the goal of the meeting.

Note that you can combine the JAD approach with one or more of the following approaches. For example, you could start a JAD session with existing assumptions gathered using surveys or interviews, or you could fold in some research about how others accomplished goals similar to those set forth for your site.

---

[12] Roman Soltys and Anthony Crawford. "JAD for business plans and designs": `www.thefacilitator.com/htdocs/article11.html`

Assumption Approach

Consider the following scenario. You work for an organization that needs a site, but your boss (the one who will make decisions about what the site needs to be) doesn't have time to sit with you and tell you what she envisions. Her schedule is full and she is looking for you to plan the site for her. She would like to use your plan as a tool for organizing her own thoughts and sharing details that only she is aware of. With a smile and a deadline, she sends you on your way to be creative.

You sit down and start making educated assumptions about the requirements and design of the site. You know the organization; you know your boss; and you have some ideas of your own. After documenting the requirements you assume will meet your boss's expectations, you present your plan, and the requirements-collection process really begins. Or, if you are lucky, your assumptions were perfect and your next step is to prepare a request for proposal so that you can hire a vendor to build your site.

The advantages of this approach include:

➤ You, the person making the assumptions, get to express your opinion regarding what should be required. Some clients (or, in the preceding scenario, bosses) are reluctant to hear suggestions from those responsible for facilitating the collection of requirements (or design).

➤ You have a document that you can take to your designer and developer to discuss. Or you have a document you can use as an RFP (request for proposal) or RFQ (request for quote).

The disadvantages include:

➤ Your boss/client doesn't have the resources (time, skills) to review and comment on a requirements document or design plan.

➤ Your client might be more interested in seeing the opposite of what you prepared. For instance, they could want the artistic rendering of the site versus reviewing the requirements document you prepared that defines the site's functionality.

The name of this approach is nothing official; you won't find it in a book or on the Internet. However, the scenario it represents is not uncommon within organizations and between client and vendor. Call it what you want, but it is an approach you might need to consider one day.

Survey Approach

The "Audience Analysis" section of this chapter mentioned surveys as a way to collect information about your audience. However, you don't have to limit surveys to collecting information about your target audience.

Consider the following scenario. The XYZ Company needs a site but doesn't have time to analyze their needs and prepare a well-thought-out RFP. Your current contract with the XYZ Company states they can ask you to help them plan their projects.

For this project, you are responsible for collecting their site requirements and preparing the RFP. But there is a challenge: there isn't just one person making the decisions; several managers have a say in what the site will do. It was no surprise that attempts to hold a planning session to solicit requirements from the decision-makers were unsuccessful, given their busy schedules. The only meeting you could schedule was a manager team review and comment session to go over your draft requirements and quickly provide feedback.

In order to collect some basic information from the decision-makers, you decide to create a short email survey. Not wanting to take too much of their time, you posted three questions designed to give insight into what each decision-maker envisions:

➤ Which business goal (if any) will the site support, and how?

➤ Which activities will be performed on the site, and by whom?

➤ What content will the site offer its visitors, and will any content be restricted?

From the first question, you hope to hear the site purpose and maybe a little about the business processes it might support. The second question starts to describe who will do what on the site and potential features. The last question starts to identify content and access requirements. With the answers to these questions, your next step is to summarize the responses and solicit feedback and clarification on any unclear survey responses from the decision-makers.

In the next iteration of the requirements, you start to create a draft set of requirements, making assumptions about what would be needed to meet their needs. Before the meeting, you send each decision-maker your draft requirements so that they can review them before the review meeting begins. Follow-up to the meeting includes the incorporation of comments into your draft and the development of the RFP.

The advantages of this approach include:

➤ You get some core bits of information that can help if or when you need to make assumptions.

➤ You can collect information from multiple resources at the same time, thus saving time.

The disadvantages of this approach include:

➤ You might not have a chance to ask follow-up questions to clarify an answer.

➤ You probably can't ask every possible question. You need to choose the best questions given your experience, the goal of the site, and the availability of your client/responders.

The preceding scenario presents only one use of a survey to help solicit requirements from a group of people. Notice that the scenario also included making some assumptions and getting feedback. The meeting used in the scenario wasn't a JAD session, as it didn't bring together developers and potential users. In this scenario, the JAD session will be helpful after the developers have been hired and requirements are refined.

Interview Approach

The scenario in the survey approach proposed three questions that were sent in an email. If the managers in that scenario had had time for one-on-one meetings, those questions could have been asked during an interview. You can also use an interview to get to know your audience and what they would need in your site.

The advantages of this approach include:

- ➤ You can ask follow-up questions or clarify answers.

- ➤ You get to see the responder's reaction to your questions — their "body language."

- ➤ You can engage your client/audience and pique their interest in the process.

The disadvantages of this approach include:

- ➤ Conducting multiple interviews, potentially with large gaps of time in between, can be time-consuming.

- ➤ Clients with limited time can be annoyed having to wait for you to take notes.

You can combine the survey and interview approaches by sending survey questions to your client and potential audience members, allowing them to compose answers for you, and then interviewing them to review your questions and clarify their answers.

SUMMARY

This chapter explores several topics to help you define your requirements. Each decision you make as a result of the analyses described in this chapter will influence some if not all aspects of site design, as well as how your site is built.

The analyses described in this chapter focused on identifying the requirements that support the site purpose and influence the site design. Here are a few things to remember as you perform the various analyses:

- ➤ The audience analysis takes what you identify during the needs analysis and dives deeper into who your audience is and how your site will fit into their lives.

- ➤ The process analysis steps back from the details of what the site will do and considers how the site can or should support larger processes. Understanding where your site fits into the bigger picture helps you create solutions that fit into the bigger picture and/or expand your site into what it can be.

- ➤ The tasks analysis identifies who will use the site and whether they will use it by identifying process tasks and site management tasks performed on the site.

- ➤ More often than not, the output of a task is content. The content analysis identifies the different types of content and the data that defines the content.

- ➤ The communication analysis considers the interactions between members of your audience and how those interactions can be facilitated on your site. It also connects audience communication with content.

- ➤ If your audience can't find what they are looking for, they might not come back. The search/browse analysis explores different ways you can help your audience find what they need.

- ➤ The feature analysis provides ways to facilitate the identification and description of features you need on your site that had not already been defined.

➤ The roles analysis considers what you had planned for your audience and explores how you might define their roles in Drupal.

➤ Looking to the future, the performance analysis considers what you need to do before launch in order to monitor site performance after launch.

➤ The security analysis provides some basic tips on planning for a secure site after launch as well as a secure development environment.

➤ The last section provides four approaches to collecting information (at various stages of the project) that you can mix and match to create your own strategy.

Different types of sites require different analyses, but the topics and techniques shared in this chapter can get you started. For instance, if you are building an e-commerce site, you need to decide your pricing strategies, product delivery, and money collection. Your site must support these processes and tasks. Use process and task analyses to define your e-commerce requirements.

Knowing what questions to ask is one thing, but getting the answers is quite another. You can use the strategies for collecting requirements during the design phase, as well.

5

Creating a Design Plan

If you are likely to say, "I am not very artistic and don't know the first thing about making graphics, so the design phase is not for me," then stay tuned, because design is more than graphics and images. In Drupal terms, site design is more than the process of theming — the process of creating the HTML, PHP, and CSS code and assorted images that determine the look and feel of a site. Design also includes making decisions about:

➤ How your content data should be presented

➤ How you want your content organized in your site

➤ How you want your audience to find your content

➤ What should be displayed on each page

➤ How you get the content on the page and then to your audience

The design plan provides guidance for the developers, a way to manage expectations, and a tool for testing. By the end of this chapter, you should be able to:

➤ Distinguish among different roles in the design process

➤ Describe four strategies for organizing sites

➤ Distinguish among different navigational strategies

➤ Identify what makes up a site page (interface)

➤ Organize page layouts with Drupal theming in mind

➤ Recognize what gets themed

➤ Describe how a site page gets assembled

➤ Design a process for content developers to post content

WHICH ASPECTS GET DESIGNED?

When contemplating your site's design, consider the four aspects of the user experience, as shown in Figure 5-1. Each aspect influences, and sometimes competes with, the others. The trick to design is considering each perspective at the same time and understanding that compromises must be made if each is to be given its place in the final product.

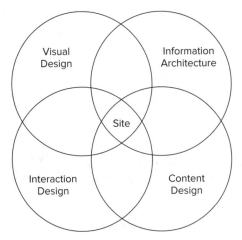

FIGURE 5-1

Information Architecture

Information architecture can be described as "the manner in which components of a ... system [in this case, your site] are organized and integrated."[1] In simple terms, information architecture influences your site's:

➤ Structure (site sections and subsections)

➤ Page components

➤ Navigation

> **NAVIGATION IN DRUPAL**
>
> By default, Drupal 6 and 7 come with a menu system that allows you to create custom menus. You can insert any link into a menu item. You can create navigation in Drupal in other ways. For instance, you can use the navigation in the Book module or you can create dynamic menus with the Views contributed module.

The information architecture design process uses the requirements you identified during your content analysis and other analyses, such as the search/browse analysis.

Content Design

In the content design task, in addition to ensuring the message of the content is what it should be on the site, you consider how the content is displayed or organized on the page. This includes making decisions about how to present the text, images, video, audio, and interactive tools you identified as requirements. Content placement can be just as important as the content itself.

> **IMAGES IN DRUPAL**
>
> In Drupal 6, you can use the ImageCache module to control the size of the image on a node. Drupal 7 includes this capability in its core.

---

[1] Merriam-Webster.com: www.merriam-webster.com/dictionary/architecture

In content design, you also need to consider the environment or space in which the content resides. The content, with the various navigational and feature blocks that are also on the page, should work harmoniously with each other. For instance, have you ever been to a site that has a banner ad that takes away from the purpose of the site or the page? It might appear at the top of the page, disconnected from the rest of the page, or it might be so large that it distracts visitors. The size and placement of page components can impact your visitors' experience on your site.

Interaction Design

"Interaction design is the creation of a dialog between a person and a product, system, or service. This dialog is both physical and emotional in nature and is manifested in the interplay between form, function, and technology as experienced over time."[2] In simple terms, interaction design is the process of defining how your site visitors perform processes and tasks on your site. Tasks can include reading, watching, listening, clicking, searching, browsing, entering data, and more.

When defining how site visitors perform processes and tasks on a site, the interaction design process takes into consideration usability and accessibility. It also considers processes and tasks that are predefined by Drupal and identifies if/how they need to be modified to support the site requirements.

> **ACCESSIBILITY IN DRUPAL**
>
> The community is working to improve accessibility in Drupal 6 and 7. For an update on steps taken, check out the Drupal Accessibility Statement at `http://drupal.org/about/accessibility`.

Visual Design

Visual aspects of design are not just about graphics and colors. Visual design also includes, but is not limited to:

➤ Fonts

➤ Capitalization of text

➤ Line spacing

➤ Placement of text and graphics

➤ Borders

➤ Backgrounds

In Drupal, the decisions you make about these items are implemented via the site theme. You can choose from hundreds of themes, each reflecting many combinations of colors, fonts, spacing, and so on. Of course, you can create your own, and many people do. To create your own theme, you need some insights into the role of the theme in the page development process. The design process discussed in this chapter helps you design not only your site but also your theme structure.

---

[2] Kolko, Jon, *Thoughts on Interaction Design, Second Edition.* Morgan Kaufmann, 2011.

GUI FOR THEMING

The Sweaver module, available for both Drupal 6 and Drupal 7, provides a graphical user interface (GUI) that helps you change the CSS in your theme without having to open the CSS files and edit them.

A DESIGN PROCESS

Throwing around terms like information architecture, interactions, content design, and visual design is easy, but in reality, if you don't use a process to manage these perspectives and all the requirements you have collected, you could end up missing several important details and ultimately deliver a site that does not meet expectations.

One way to facilitate the design phase is to perform the four steps shown in Figure 5-2, starting with defining the site structure and finishing with the theme design:

1. Create an inventory of your pages and their purpose by defining the site structure.

2. Identify the page components you need for the pages in the inventory.

3. Organize the components via the use of wireframes (line drawings of your pages).

4. Translate the wireframes into graphic illustrations (comps) of the pages.

As the diagram suggests, the design process can be an iterative and incremental process. For instance, your first pass through the process could focus on the high-level structure of the site and the style guide that helps facilitate a consistent look and feel. Flesh out the details of each site section with subsequent passes through the process.

The key to planning a Drupal site is to be aware of all the bits of information you need to gather and decisions you need to make so that when you are forced (or want) to dive into the middle of development, you know what is missing and how you might go about finding it.

These steps focus primarily on designing what your audience sees and their experiences on your site. Front-end design, however, is not limited to what pages look like; you also consider how

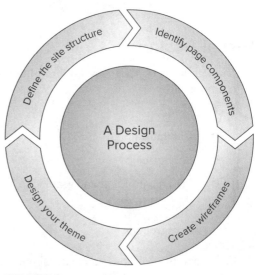

FIGURE 5-2

the pages get made. This chapter walks you through the steps in Figure 5-2 and considers the four perspectives of design (information architecture, content design, interaction design, and visual design) along the way.

Design Can Create Requirements

Creating wireframes and comps is part of the design process. The more detailed your wireframes and comps, the more likely you are to see missing requirements. This is a good thing, because you want to be sure all your requirements are documented. For instance, assume your requirements say you need Drupal's search feature on your site. Drupal's default search provides a field where users type a word or phrase and click a button to execute a search — nothing unique about that. If your requirements are considered detailed and you know how Drupal's default search works, you are all set.

Now it is time to draw the search feature in a wireframe or illustrate it in a comp. Assume your wireframe or comp shows the title of the search feature as "Media Search." This is not the default title of the Drupal's search feature. By changing the title, you might be adding a requirement that requires a little custom code or a deviation from the default configuration. The reason is, if your site is not all media, then "Media Search" implies that the audience will be searching the site's media resources, not the entire site. The default search feature doesn't work that way.

What might seem to be a small detail could actually be a scope issue or have a budget impact. Just be aware that your developer might come back to you with questions and possible issues if your wireframes deviate from what is described in your requirements.

> **ENHANCING DRUPAL'S SEARCH**
>
> The Finder module provides several features for helping you create flexible search forms. For instance, it provides an autocomplete search on node titles. The module's developer intends to port it to Drupal 7.

DEFINING THE SITE STRUCTURE

Your site structure can be defined by your *site sections*, which often are the links that appear on a primary and/or secondary menu. They can be a single page or a group of pages. Site sections can have subsections as well, depending on the complexity of your site's content.

Not all site sections are found in your primary or secondary menus. For instance, Drupal has what you can consider as default site sections associated with the taxonomy vocabulary terms you use to categorize your content. Vocabulary terms are also known as *tags*. When visitors click on a tag, they are sent to a landing page for that tag. That landing page can be considered a site section, and you can configure those pages with blocks as you see fit.

Another way to think about sections is to imagine an outline or a book's table of contents. Some refer to this as a *site map*. When you were collecting requirements and performing content analyses, you explored what your content would be, how it would be categorized, and if there were any content-to-content and user-to-content relationships. This information is important to remember when making decisions about your site's structure, because structure can reflect categorization.

Flowcharts (discussed further in the "Navigation" section of this chapter) are one way to illustrate the structure of your site. Figure 5-3 is a simple flowchart that illustrates a site with three main content sections: trees, shrubs, and flowers. Within each content section of the site are subsections. For instance, the shrubs section has articles, tutorials, types, and a place to buy products.

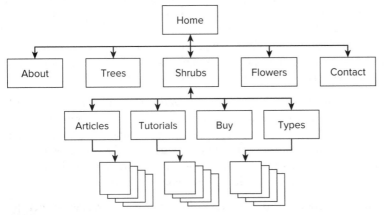

FIGURE 5-3

Figure 5-3 also shows an About and Contact section. Quite often, these are just one page, but they could include child pages. If they were to include additional pages, the About section might include background or historical information, and the Contact section might include pages with a staff directory and driving directions.

Common Structure Types

You likely already have sections in mind for your site. If you don't, the following discussion addresses four common types of site sections to help you get started. Having done a process, task, and content analysis before selecting a structure strategy is helpful. Chapter 4 provides information on each analysis.

Content Type Sections

Is the purpose of your site to offer different types of content? If the information on your site is defined by the type of content your site offers, you might need to create content type sections. For example:

➤ A resource-based site might be organized by content type (news articles, case studies, projects, training).

➤ A product-based site might be organized by content type (products, services, training).

Topic Sections

Is the purpose of the site to provide content on specific topics? What are the content topics? If you have more than one topic, you might need to section your site based on topics. For example:

➤ A newspaper site might focus on topics (sports, politics, business, art and living).

➤ A resources site might be organized by topic (trees, bushes, grasses, flowers).

Task Sections

Is the purpose of the site to enable visitors to perform tasks? If so, look at your process and task analyses. Are the tasks sequential or stand-alone? Can they be grouped into three to six major tasks that can represent a site section? If your site is about the user completing a task, your sections might be oriented toward each step in the task. For example:

➤ A financial site could be task-oriented (make payment, make transfer, make investment).

➤ A training site generally has some element of task-oriented information (step 1, step 2, step 3).

User Sections

Is the purpose of the site to support different audiences, users, or roles? If so, look at your audience and role analyses. Do you have different audiences with different needs? If your site is focused on supporting different audiences or users, you could have user sections. For example:

➤ Academic sites have different audiences that need different information (faculty, staff, alumni, students, parents).

➤ Association sites can have different member groups (non-member, member, partner, affiliates).

> ### SUPPORTING STRUCTURE
>
> Out of the box, both Drupal 6 and Drupal 7 provide different ways to support the structure you define. You could use one or more of the following: content types, vocabulary terms, and roles, to name a few.

Complex Sites

Sites with several goals might find that the first level of site organization can use one of the preceding options, such as topic, but within each section, the organization might change. That is, each section could be organized by another option, such as user or task.

Complex sites might need to offer more than one way for visitors to find what they need. For example, if the site is task-oriented and those tasks produce specific types of content, you might need two organizational strategies from the start: task and type. Such a site might be an instructional site designed to give the audience example content that can be used to inspire creativity, while at the same time helping visitors learn how to create their own content with a step-by-step process.

> ### MENUS AND SITE SECTIONS
>
> Both Drupal 6 and 7 come with a primary and secondary menu. With the exception of a couple of themes, you will find most that themes support the primary menu. Some do not support the secondary menu. You can make menus be drop-down menus by using a module or a feature in the theme.

User Structure

While collecting content requirements, you considered the type of content you wanted to collect about your users. You also considered strategies for collecting content about your users and who would then access that content. Defining the structure of your user pages refers to identifying all the pages that will display user content — for instance:

➤ User account page accessed by the user to manage account settings

➤ Anonymous version of the user account page (same link but then content that displays to the public is different)

➤ Authenticated (or some other privileged role) version of the user account page that might show more details than the anonymous version but still less than what the actual user gets to see on his own account page

➤ Profile page (assuming the user account page is not being used as the profile page)

➤ Dashboard pages, to provide users with options for monitoring activity in the site

DRUPAL COMMONS DASHBOARD

Drupal Commons is a distribution used for building sites that include a community. To help members of the community keep up with activity on the site, Drupal Commons provides site members with a dashboard, a page where they can choose what type of activity they want to monitor. For instance, they can choose to show events in the groups where they are members, latest notices from the content manager, recent activity across groups, and more. The dashboard in this instance is not the user account page where the user manages account settings and his or her own activity.

In a site where access to information about the users is common practice, you might have a Directory section. The section could list site members, content authors, or staff supporting the site. Within this section of the site, you could provide access to different user information. For instance, you could link the member names in the directory to a profile that the user created, or provide a link to a page that lists all the posts made by the user.

IDENTIFYING PAGE COMPONENTS

Now that you know the pages you need to design and how they relate structurally (or don't) to each other, your next step is to decide what will be on each page. A page component is any item or object or "thing" that will show on a page. This section provides a strategy for identifying and organizing the page components you included in your requirements as well as other components typically identified during the design process.

Using a page-by-page strategy to plan each page, however, can be a long and tedious process if you have hundreds or thousands of pages planned for your site. Other ways to organize page component decisions include:

➤ By type of page

➤ By site section

➤ By component

These strategies are discussed later in the section.

Strategy Overview

When you review your requirements for the page components that you want to include on your site pages, your list might include items such as:

➤ Search form

➤ Login form

➤ Menu

➤ Advertisement

➤ List of recent posts

➤ Bookmark link

➤ Event content node

➤ Site mission

➤ Logo

➤ And more

A list like this is a great start, but as the list gets longer, it can become overwhelming. One way to organize your page components and facilitate identifying the other page components not yet defined is to categorize your page components. Following is a list of categories that covers most, if not all, the items you will include on your pages:

➤ Identification (branding, ownership, page location in the site)

➤ Path structures (the URL for each section and its pages)

➤ Navigation (core, supplemental, contextual)

➤ Content (core, supplemental, contextual)

➤ Features (such as calendars, calculators, search)

Figure 5-4 highlights a few common page components; the remainder of this section provides more insight into the types of components your site might need.

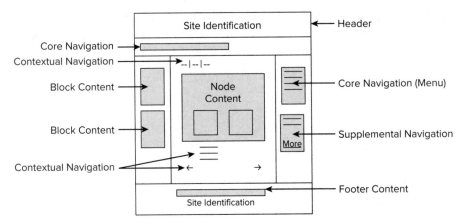

FIGURE 5-4

In addition to identifying which page components will be on each page, you need to identify when the page components will appear on each page. What conditions need to be met in order for the page component to appear? For instance, you might want to restrict access to a special feature or some content, allowing only users with a specific role to access that information.

Identification Information

The purpose of identification information is to let your visitors know where they are when they land on your site and what they are looking at. Planning the identification page components might seem like a no-brainer, especially because you are using Drupal, and Drupal themes typically have a header that includes the site name. However, identification involves more than what appears in the header.

You can think of identification from multiple perspectives and levels of detail. The following sections offer brief overviews of some basic identification-oriented bits of information your pages might need.

Site-Level Identification

In simple terms, site-level identification is the name of the site. You can assume each page will have the name of the site, but don't assume you want the name of the site conveyed the same way on all levels of your site.

For instance, your home page might have the site's full name with a logo, whereas the section-level pages have the logo and an acronym. Then the subsections or content page level have just the logo. Screen real estate is a driving factor in regard to displaying site identification and branding on each level of your site.

Section-Level Identification

Section-level identification could be as simple as the title of a node displayed on a page. Visitors click on a link in the primary menu, and the title of the page they are sent to appears in the page. Or it could be that a section on a site is more in line with a sub-site and it has its own branding, its own visual design.

CHANGING SITE IDENTIFICATION

By default, Drupal does not support changing the site identification name and logo on each level of the site. If you need this ability, and many have, one strategy might be to use multiple themes on your site. Modules such as Sections, Page Theme, ThemeKey, and Content Theme provide a way to apply different themes to different portions of your site. As of April 2011, the Sections module will likely be ported to Drupal 7. The other three listed here have recommended versions for Drupal 7.

Changing themes could also support a sub-site strategy where each section of the site needs its own look and feel. Again, planning is important up front to make this work.

Think about the site section and how you want people to know they are there. Decide if you want the site section identification information to be carried forward to that section's subsections.

Content-Level Identification

When your visitors land on a content page, such as an article or how-to guide, they know where they are if you have provided the following:

➤ Site name (site-level identification)

➤ Section name (section-level identification)

➤ Page title (content-level identification)

The title of your content is the most common way for your visitors to know where they are in your site. You can provide other clues to let your visitors know where they are and what they are looking at — for example:

➤ Content author name

➤ Type of content

➤ Descriptive vocabulary terms

➤ Publish date

With all this identification information, visitors to your site might ascertain that they have landed on an article on the XYZ site written by Bob the Orange Expert on July 2010 called Oranges Galore on the topic of irrigation.

➤ Site identification — XYZ site

➤ Section identification — Articles

➤ Page identification — Oranges Galore, Bob the Orange Expert, July 2010, irrigation

Overkill? Not really, if you want your visitors to be able to assess the credibility of the content and whether it is still valid.

Cross-Level Identification

Three more examples of identification information that help your visitors know where they are and what they are looking at are URLs, breadcrumbs, and copyright information.

The URL is always present, no matter where your visitor is while on your site. The role your URL plays in helping your visitors know where they are and what they are looking at will depend on the path structure strategy you choose. Path structure strategies are discussed in the next section.

Breadcrumbs typically aren't seen on the home page, but they can appear at the section, subsection, and content levels. They can be configured to appear under different conditions. For instance, you might want breadcrumbs to appear only when your visitors are viewing a multi-page multi-tiered book.

Copyright notices often apply to the site as a whole and often appear in the footer of the site, therefore on every section, subsection, and content page. A copyright notice helps users know they are looking at content they can reuse or content they need permission to use. A challenge with copyright notices comes into play when different copyright permissions apply to different types of content or pages.

DRUPAL SITE INFORMATION

Drupal 6 comes with a site information form in which you can enter the site name, slogan, mission statement, and footer message, as well as the site email address, a label for anonymous users, and the path to use for the front/home page. The site name, slogan, and footer information appear on each page in a traditional Drupal theme. The mission statement typically appears on the home page, although some themes allow you to show it on all pages.

In Drupal 7, the site information form changes. It still provides a field for the site name, slogan, email address, and the path for the front page. The form does not include a field for the mission statement or footer. It adds three configuration settings that are located on other administrative pages in Drupal 6. The settings are the number of posts on the front page and the options for error pages and number of posts on the main page.

What types of identification information do you want or need on the site? In what format will it appear and at what level(s)? When you start creating your wireframes, remember that identification takes up screen real estate, so be sure to include room for it in your design plan.

Path Structures

If you do a search on URL structures and include SEO, usability, and/or information architecture as search terms as well, you get a lot of information and opinions on what your URLs should look like or not look like. The information you find on URL structures sometimes includes strategies on domain selection and formatting, as well. In this section, the focus is on the path structure that

appears after the domain — for instance, the `/content/title-of-node` that comes after www
`.example.com`.

As you review the "do this, not that" example URLs and advice, you begin to realize that a couple
assumptions are being made:

➤ You know the difference between the default path structure that your system generates
(`/?q=node/23`) and an alias path structure (`content/title-of-node`) that you define and
use to make the often not-so-user-friendly system paths user-friendly.

➤ You have the ability to create a path alias, which in the case of Drupal, you do.

URL structures play a role in SEO, usability, and communicating information architecture, as well as Drupal
block display (as shown in Figure 5-5). Your decisions
regarding the path structure that will define your path
alias will need to take each of these perspectives into
consideration.

The following sections explore path strategies and best
practices to help you choose what will work best for
your site.

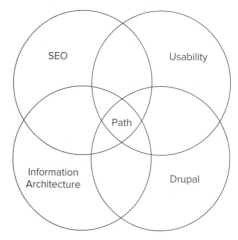

Path Strategies

The search results referenced above focus on best practices for formatting your path alias. Before you consider
some of the common best practices provided later in
this chapter, it might be helpful to review the follow-

FIGURE 5-5

ing strategies you often see on the Web. The strategy you choose can influence which best practices
apply and the process (manual or automated) you use to build the paths in Drupal.

Queries

A path structure based on a query is designed to pass information to the system processing the path.
By default, Drupal uses a query path structure that looks like this:

```
www.mysite.com/?q=node/23

www.mysite.com/?q=user/4
```

But `?q=` is not very SEO- or user-friendly. If your server supports rewritten URLs, in other words
clean URLs, Drupal will display the same URLs as:

```
www.mysite.com/node/23

www.mysite.com/user/4.
```

A clean URL does not contain any query strings, such as `?q=`. A clean URL is like an alias but not
generated the same way. Of course, this only gets you partway to being SEO- and user-friendly. The
remaining strategies focus on creating an alias to `/node/23`.

Information Architecture

A path structure based on information architecture can reflect your site architecture or your content architecture. To help illustrate a site architecture path, refer again to Figure 5-3.

The Home box in Figure 5-3 represents the domain:

    www.mysite.com

The shrubs section landing page could be titled Shrubs. The URL path could be:

    www.mysite.com/shrubs

The tutorials subsection landing page title could be Tutorials and, therefore, the URL could be:

    www.mysite.com/shrubs/tutorials

A tutorial whose title is The Right Planting Depth could have a path like this:

    www.mysite.com/shrubs/tutorials/the-right-planting-depth

Or, to make it shorter, it could be:

    www.mysite.com/shrubs/tutorials/planting-depth

The path structure could continue in this breadcrumb fashion for each level of your site. The deeper the site, the more difficult sustaining this structure is — but that is a concern for development. Also, the deeper the path, the less SEO- and user-friendly the path becomes. Consider the following URL:

    www.mysite.com/shrubs/tutorials/online/2010/February/bob/tutorials.html

In this example, you might be viewing a directory structure where a file called `tutorials.html` is stored. Drupal doesn't have a directory structure like this, but you can create a path structure like this, if you like. The question is, should you? It is informative to the user, but you could probably communicate this information — that Bob writes online tutorials about shrubs each month — in another way on your site.

An example of a content architecture path might look like this, where `plants` is the vocabulary and `shrubs` is the term:

    www.mysite.com/category/plants/shrubs

In Drupal, this page would list all nodes tagged with the term "shrubs." If you want to limit your paths to keywords and "category" is not a keyword for you, you can remove the word "category" from this path and only show:

    www.mysite.com/plants/shrubs

However, when your user clicks on the title of a node listed on this page, the URL would change to the structure you have chosen for that type of content or that node. You can manually create multiple node aliases for each node, but that is not very practical.

Keyword

A path structure based on keywords inserts keywords into the path in hopes that it helps search engines rank the content of the page higher. This strategy is easy to abuse, so be careful. A keyword path structure might look like this:

    www.mysite.com/gardening-shrubs-tutorials

The title of the page might actually be Tutorials but the tutorials are about gardening and shrubs. But it is easy to get carried away. Stuffing keywords into your path in hopes that it will boost your rankings might not work. Consider the following example:

```
www.mysite.com/gardening-plants-shrub-shrubs-bush-bushes-landscape-
tutorial-lessons-diy
```

Notice the redundancy? Also, what will your users think? They might not know what they are getting. Will they be able to tell a friend? Perhaps, but who would want to retype such a long URL?

EXCESSIVE PATH LENGTH

In a 2007 interview with Google's Matt Cutts, Stephan Spencer asked, "What is excessive in the length of a keyword-rich URL? We have seen clients use keyword URLs that have 10 to 15 words strung together with hyphens."

Matt Cutts replied, "If you can make your title four or five words long — and it is pretty natural. If you have got three, four or five words in your URL, that can be perfectly normal. As it gets a little longer, then it starts to look a little worse. Now, our algorithms typically will just weight those words less and just not give you as much credit." Read or listen to the full interview at `www.stephanspencer.com/search-engines/matt-cutts-interview`.

Please note that search engines like Google continuously refine their algorithms to provide their users the best results possible. Google announced in a February 2011 blog post that they were making changes to their algorithms in an effort "to give people the most relevant answers to their queries as quickly as possible." Read more at `http://googleblog.blogspot.com/2011/02/finding-more-high-quality-sites-in.html`.

Page Title

A path structure based on page title simply displays the title of the page in the path. It is short and simple and easy to remember. And if the page title includes keywords, users and search engines are more likely to know what your content covers. A page title path might look like this, if the title is Planting Shrubs Tutorial:

```
www.mysite.com/planting-shrubs-tutorial
```

It looks a lot like the keyword path structure strategy because the title of node has been strategically designed to be descriptive yet keyword-oriented.

Combinations

A path that combines clean URLs, keywords in its architecture, and keywords in the page title, provides both SEO- and user-friendly results. Consider the following URL:

```
www.mysite.com/tutorials/planting-shrubs-tutorial
```

In this example, you communicate with your users that they are viewing one of potentially many tutorials on your site. Assuming you planned your site architecture and path structures, your users would be able to "hack" the URL and find a tutorial page at:

```
www.mysite.com/tutorials
```

The term `tutorials` is a keyword and provides user-friendly site structure information as well.

PATH ALIASES IN DRUPAL

Both Drupal 6 and Drupal 7 come with the Path module, which enables you to create a path alias for your node manually and therefore hide the `node/#`. If you add the Pathauto module, you can create aliases automatically via a path template you define. This is helpful when you need consistency and can't trust multiple content developers to remember the path strategy. The template creates a path alias automatically, given certain conditions. Path templates mean consistency; consistency means quick and easy block assignments based on paths; templates also mean planning.

Page Development and Paths

In addition to providing user-friendly and SEO-friendly URLs, there is one more reason to care about your paths. Consider page development. Each time you save a node, a path is created. If you are using an alias, the alias is saved as well. But the path only applies to the node. The page components that appear with the node are provided using other configuration strategies. For instance, a common strategy used to control which blocks appear on which page is by path. Other options exist, but consider for now how paths are useful.

Figure 5-6 represents a basic page structure. Boring? Yes, but it is all we need right now. The content area in the middle of the page typically displays the node. The sidebars contain blocks for navigation, other content, and various features.

Each time you create a node, you are not creating the full page with all the blocks in the sidebars and regions (other areas on the page where you can place blocks). Blocks appear when specific conditions have been met. One condition is a path. If you used the default path (`node/#`), you would be assigning blocks one node at a time.

Using URL aliases (manually or automatically generated), like the ones discussed previously, offers more options. For instance, if you want a block to appear on `www.mysite.com/shrubs` and all the pages that fall under `shrubs`, you could assign a block to `shrubs*`, and `shrubs` and `shrubs/tutorials` will get that block. Here are a few path tips (and yes, case matters):

➤ `shrubs` — Blocks appear only on the path `www.mysite.com/shrubs`.

➤ `shrubs*` — Blocks appear on the shrubs page and all other pages whose paths follow shrubs.

➤ `shrubs/*` — Blocks appear on all pages in the shrubs path except the shrubs page.

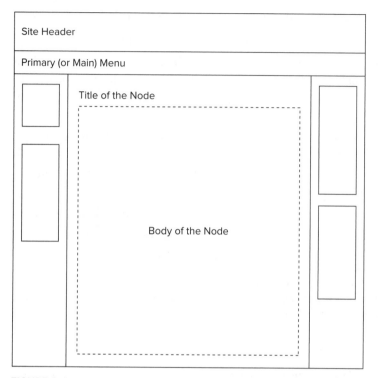

FIGURE 5-6

The path condition could accommodate hundreds of nodes, as long as they each are assigned the appropriate path structure. So, a predictable path structure makes component block assignment easier and more automated. Paths are part of the planning process. For each page or group of pages you plan, include the path strategy.

PATH ALTERNATIVES

By default in Drupal 6, you can control blocks by role and page path. By default in Drupal 7, you can control blocks by role, page path, and content type. If you use the Context module, you have other conditions to choose from, such as menu item, user role, user page, taxonomy, node type, and more.

Best Practices

Devising a path structure isn't always the easiest thing to do. Once you have chosen a path strategy, there are a few best practices to consider so that you maximize your URL benefits:

➤ **Short** — Long architectures and/or long titles are not SEO- or user-friendly.

➤ **Hackable** — Ensure users can find a page each time they "hack" off a portion of the URL (e.g., /tutorials/shrubs and /tutorials each have a page). This is similar to how breadcrumbs work. This type of hackable does not imply an insecure URL.

➤ **Consistent** — Consider choosing one path structure strategy for your site.

➤ **Keywords** — Use keywords judiciously in your path and your node titles.

➤ **Hyphens** — Separate words with hyphens rather than underscores or spaces. Because links are often underlined, an underscore can appear as a space and this could leave the user wondering if there is a space or an underscore. If you allow spaces in your paths, your URL will render with a `%20` for each space, which is not recommended.

➤ **Text** — Text is often more descriptive than numbers. "Blue-shirt" is more understandable than the product code "23245."

➤ **Case** — Some web servers are case-sensitive. For instance, `/Tutorials` is not the same as `/tutorials`.

➤ **Relevant** — Don't create a path that implies certain topics are covered and then not cover those topics.

➤ **Unique** — Use unique paths to avoid duplicate URLs and creating confusion.

The options are yours, of course. If you can't decide which path structure strategy is best for you and how you want to implement best practices right now, you can come back to this decision after you have thought through the rest of your design.

Navigation

Navigation components on a page are the means by which your audience will find what they are looking for. The way they will move through your site is critical to your site's success. While collecting your site's requirements, you considered content relationships and how your users could search and browse your site. Much of what you decided when collecting requirements will drive the type of navigation you choose.

Navigation is not limited to Drupal menus; other types of navigation exist. To plan your site's navigation, consider the following navigation categories:

➤ Core navigation

➤ Supplemental navigation

➤ Contextual navigation

NAVIGATION IN DRUPAL

You can use the core Menu module to create menus. By default, this is a manual process. If you add the contributed module called Views, you can create menus that change automatically when you add nodes.

Core Navigation

Core navigation is not a Drupal term but refers to site menus that take the audience to purposefully organized sections and subsections. What does it mean to plan your core navigation? Consider three strategies and their potential impacts.

Figure 5-7 illustrates a site flowchart with three sections. Each section has content that users will access using different core navigation strategies.

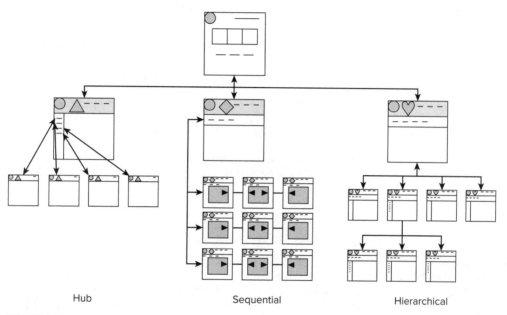

Hub Sequential Hierarchical

FIGURE 5-7

Hub

The hub strategy assumes that after users have been sent to a page, they must click back to the previous page to proceed to another page.

The advantage of this strategy is screen real estate. Notice that the majority of the page is available for content. In this example, the other pages are site resources that do not have any navigation with the exception of being able to return to the original page.

You might find this type of configuration on a page with links to PDF files. Your audience clicks on the link and launches a PDF. If the PDF launches in the same browser window as the site, the only way back to the site is to click the Back button on the browser. This strategy is also useful when you need to present a lot of information and graphics on the screen and don't have space for additional navigation.

The disadvantage is to the site's usability. Users don't know where they can go and must return to the parent page to seek additional pages. Note that your path structure can lend a hand in communicating where users are in your site.

Sequential

The sequential strategy addresses how you want to manage access to pages that are intended to be viewed sequentially. Notice that in Figure 5-7, the core navigation stops at the first page in the sequence. After that, contextual navigation steps in to manage the page-by-page navigation required to maintain the content in the proper context.

The advantage with this strategy is control over when visitors see a page. Hypothetically, they can't just jump into the middle of the sequence of content and get information out of context. Of course, if they know the URL that coincides with a page later in the sequence, they can jump straight to it.

The disadvantage to this strategy is the lack of fast and easy access for users when they are returning to the site and want to be reminded, for example, of step 3 in the sequence of a task. Unless they saved the URL for step 3, they need to click though previous steps to re-read step 3.

You can mix up your strategies: use sequential and hub together. You can also have a search feature that allows visitors to search for the page they want and bypass your navigation. The flowchart simply illustrates one strategy at a time.

Hierarchical

The hierarchical strategy is the most common and is often present as a secondary structure for the hub and sequential structures. The idea is to allow your audience to move freely between the different sections and subsections of your site without having to return to a specific starting point (as the hub and sequential structures suggest). This strategy uses the most screen real estate if you don't plan ahead. Each time you add another subsection (level) in the site, you are potentially adding navigation.

However, you can use navigational strategies (such as including drop-down menus) to reduce the amount of screen real estate needed. To use a drop-down-menu strategy, you need to know the number of links that will be visible. The plan for your site structure will help you determine this. At some point, if you get too many links in a drop-down menu, the menu could drop below the bottom of the browser, making some links inconvenient to reach or maybe even inaccessible.

Because hierarchical core navigation is very common, it is worth looking at in more detail. The flowchart shown in Figure 5-8 illustrates a hierarchical approach to a site structure. This example assumes that all navigation will be readily visible to visitors (pretend drop-down menus are not an option). It also assumes that you want your visitors to be able to move horizontally and vertically through your site with minimal effort.

Notice that each level includes another navigation area. Depending on how your content is related, if you don't plan well for your navigation, you could end up with a lot of screen real estate needed just for navigation. The following figures illustrate the parent-child relationship between the interfaces on each level of the site.

As shown in Figure 5-9, this example site has three sections, so the home page has three links. The links take the audience to the second level of the site.

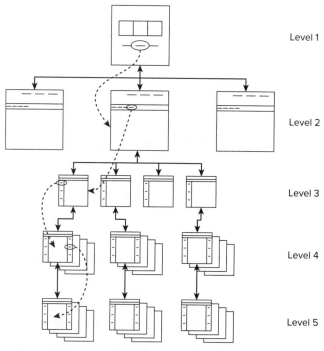

FIGURE 5-8

On the second level (Figure 5-10), you see two core navigation menus. One is across the top, with three links representing the three sections of the site. (This is the same menu found on the home page.) You also see a second menu with four links, which lead to the four subsections.

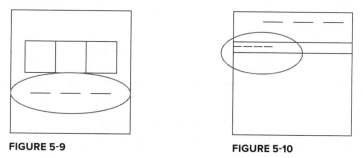

FIGURE 5-9   **FIGURE 5-10**

If you click on a link in the new horizontal navigation, you are taken to a subsection (third level) landing page. The third level, shown in Figure 5-11, carries forward the links from the home page and the section landing page, and then adds another core navigation area on the left. If you click on a link in the new left navigation, you are taken to a page at the fourth level of the site.

Level four (Figure 5-12) carries forward the links from the home page, the section landing page, and the subsection landing page, and then adds another core navigation (on the right) that provides to content pages on level five.

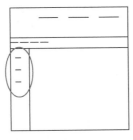

FIGURE 5-11

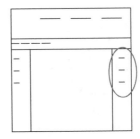

FIGURE 5-12

Adding navigation produces both benefits and costs:

➤   **Benefit** — Visitors can jump from a page at level four to level two of another section.

➤   **Benefit** — At a glance, visitors can see the hierarchy of the site and the relationship between the subsections.

➤   **Cost** — Each time you add another navigation area, you risk reducing the usability of the page. Too many options can be confusing.

DYNAMIC MENUS

Some Drupal themes come with a feature that allows you to turn your primary menu into a drop-down menu. For example, the Nice Menus module is widely used to create dynamic drop-down menus.

If your site has so many pages that even a dedicated navigational area is too small, you might need to use supplemental or contextual navigation.

Supplemental Navigation

If you are building a site whose page count continuously changes, as with a blog site or news site, core navigation cannot be expected to list all pages on the site. You can address this potential deficiency by supplementing core navigation with dynamically generated navigation that gets updated automatically as the site gets new content.

When you collected your requirements, you considered searching and browsing requirements. Browsing strategies can be considered supplemental navigation. Consider the following two browsing strategies:

➤   **Vocabulary terms** — You can rely on dynamic content lists generated automatically by Drupal by using vocabulary term links. Term links send users to a page that provides a list of links to nodes that share that term.

➤   **Database queries** — You can create your own dynamically generated lists of links to content and display them in blocks or pages. When lists of links get too long for the space they are assigned on the page, you might need to send visitors to a continuation of the list. For instance, you might include a "more" link at the bottom of a block that shows the 10 most recent posts. The "more" link would send visitors to a more complete list on another page.

Figure 5-13 is a simple illustration of the "more" link. In this scenario, the site has many articles, more than can be listed in a navigation block. The block in the left illustration is a query on the database and lists the latest three articles. The "more" link sends the user to a dynamically generated page listing all the articles, as shown in the right illustration.

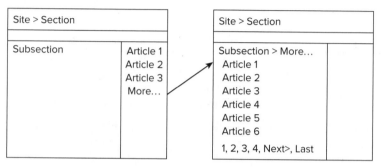

FIGURE 5-13

Also notice the navigation option at the bottom of the right illustration in Figure 5-13. If your list is extremely long and would cause a slow load time, you can break your list into multiple content navigation areas. This strategy can also be applied to blocks.

> **DYNAMIC NAVIGATION LISTS**
>
> The Views module is the most commonly used option for creating database queries whose results offer a list of nodes that meet specific criteria. You can create one view with a block display and a page display. The block acts as the menu, and the page provides a more complete list.
>
> If you want to get clever with your vocabulary terms, you can include a tag cloud navigation block on your page(s). Several contributed modules support tag clouds in Drupal 6. As of April 2011, the Tagadelic module has a Drupal 7 patch (see http://drupal.org/node/749440).

Contextual Navigation

Contextual navigation is another way to extend or supplement the core navigation. Contextual navigation sends visitors to content that helps put the content on the current page in context. The following are three types of contextual navigation:

➤ A "read more" link that joins a teaser with its full node

➤ Parent-child links that join nodes that have a specific hierarchical relationship

➤ Sibling links that send visitors to pages that have a specific relationship with the current page

Read More Link Contextual Navigation

A "read more" link on a teaser is similar to a "more" link at the end of a list in a block. A "read more" link at the end of a teaser sends visitors to the full version of that node, whereas a "more" link in lists tends to send visitors to a page with additional links.

DRUPAL'S "MORE" LINK

When you promote content to the front page, it becomes part of a teaser list of nodes. Each node teaser has a "read more" link to take visitors to the full node. The same teaser list configuration is used when visitors click on a vocabulary term.

The Views module has an option to include a "more" link in a Views block that links to a Views page. You can also use Views to create a custom teaser list and include a "read more" link after each teaser.

Parent-Child Contextual Navigation

In a parent-child navigation scenario, you move up and down the family tree, considering the context of the content. A common practice on the Web is to use a breadcrumb navigational approach to help illustrate the parent-child relationship between content. Breadcrumbs are what you sometimes see above the content area of the page. They might look like this:

Section > Subsection > Sub-subsection > Title of content

Each word in this path would be a link to the represented page. Making breadcrumbs appear and work as you want takes planning.

BREADCRUMB NAVIGATION IN DRUPAL

Drupal 6 has contributed modules for creating and managing breadcrumbs (for example, Taxonomy Breadcrumb, Menu Breadcrumb, Custom Breadcrumb, and Hansel Breadcrumb, to name a few). How your pages relate to each other will drive which option you will choose or whether you will create your own. When this book was written, efforts were being made to port the Menu Breadcrumb and Custom Breadcrumb modules to Drupal 7. As of April 2011, the new Breadcrumb module had a Drupal 7 -dev version.

Sibling Contextual Navigation

In a sibling scenario, navigation occurs side to side in a sequenced manner, like in a book. An example of this type of navigation is the use of Previous and Next links. This type of navigation is popular when pages create an online book or in online instruction. Of course, a book can also represent a parent-child relationship.

Figure 5-14 shows the Next/Previous strategy associated with sibling navigation.

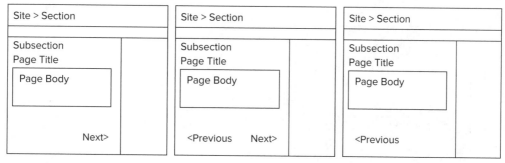

FIGURE 5-14

SEQUENCED NAVIGATION IN DRUPAL

The Book module, which is part of both Drupal 6 and Drupal 7, includes an outline feature. If the Book module is enabled, all content types have the option of being part of a series of sequenced nodes. Instead of using the words "Previous" and "Next," the outline feature substitutes the titles of the nodes that are previous and next. You see this strategy used frequently on Drupal.org.

Remember, you can mix and match your navigation strategies, but be careful that you don't overwhelm your visitors. Navigational options should complement each other, not compete for your visitor's attention.

Content

Now that you have used some of your page real estate on identification and navigation, you can use what's left to provide your audience the content they came to see in the first place. When you think of content, quite often, the first thing that comes to mind is the article or story provided on the area of the page.

In Drupal, the article or story is typically a node and therefore is displayed in the main content area. But content is much more than that. You can insert content in other areas (known as *regions* and *sidebars*) of the page as well (see Figure 5-15).

To identify what content you want or need on a page, consider the following four categories, which you can use to provide different perspectives on content:

➤   Core content

➤   Supplemental content

➤   Related content

➤   Contextual content

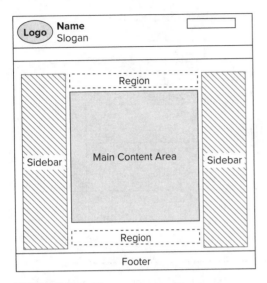

FIGURE 5-15

Core Content

Core content is not a Drupal term; it's just a way to describe the content that is the focus of the page and is displayed in the main content area of the page. In Drupal, the content area of the page typically displays a single node. However, you can show multiple nodes in the content area of the page. For instance, you could display items such as:

➤ A teaser list of nodes

➤ A grid display of images

➤ A series of blocks

➤ And more

Not all pages will have content in the main content area of the page. These pages might not be associated with a node. For instance, the home page, section landing pages, subsection landing pages, and vocabulary term pages are the most common types of pages that show either multiple nodes or no nodes.

You might be wondering why this discussion about single-node, multi-node, or no-node pages matters. What the page shows will influence how the page is made. How the page is made affects development and potentially maintenance later.

In this step of the design process, however, you are primarily thinking about:

➤ The purpose of the page

➤ The content or data required to meet that purpose

➤ The source of the content

If you completed your content analysis, you have a lot of the information you need in order to design the core content for a page. To help you think through identifying core content for your page(s), consider the simple decision tree provided in Figure 5-16.

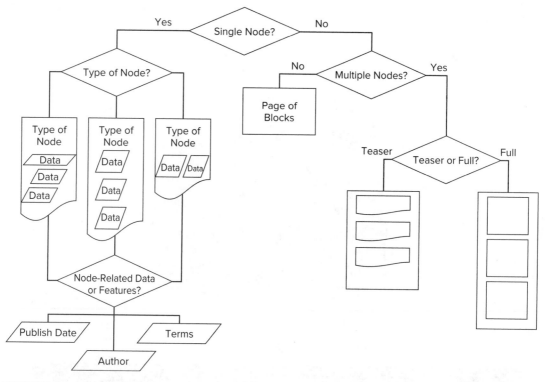

FIGURE 5-16

The decision tree illustrates some basic decisions you need to make regarding a page's core content. Your first decision is whether the page will host a single node. The following sections provide detailed insight into this decision process.

Single-Node Content Pages

A single-node page is the most basic and common page in a Drupal site. It is the blog you post; it is the news report you make; it is a group discussion you start. Figure 5-17 illustrates an example of a single-node page.

When a page on your site is based on a single node, you need to make the following decisions:

➤ What content type will it be?

➤ Which data fields in the content type will you show?

➤ How much space will the data need?

➤ Will you show node-related data?

➤ Will you show node-related features?

FIGURE 5-17

When you get to development, you will determine the strategies for showing the node, its fields, and other related content. The following subsections consider these questions.

Content Types

Will the page show an event, blog, story, project, or some other type of node created with a custom content type? During the content analysis, you made decisions about the type of content you needed on your site. The content type influences how the data fields for the content type are displayed.

Another reason to note the content type is preexisting configuration. If you decided to use a preexisting content type, it might come with a predefined page configuration. If it does, you want to take that into consideration. The preexisting configuration could influence the layout of the core content.

PREEXISTING CONTENT TYPE CONFIGURATION

In Drupal 7, the Article content type comes with an image field already in place.

Drupal 6 and 7 come with the Book page content type. This content type has the outline feature that displays a list of links to the child pages and links to the previous and next pages on the nodes that are included in the outline. The list of links and the previous and next navigation take space. Depending on how many child pages a node has, the list can be long and can make the page long. The Book module also comes with a block that provides menu-style navigation for your book.

Data Fields

Data fields are part of the content type. As shown in Figure 5-18, a node can have several data fields: text, link, and image. Other fields are associated with this content type and are used to help organize the nodes on the site.

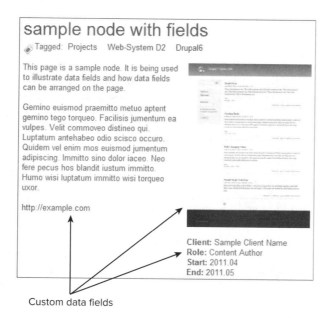

Custom data fields

FIGURE 5-18

When this node was created, the fields were listed one after the other on the create node form. If you know you don't want your fields listed in order, you will need to plan their layout and select a strategy to create the layout that fits your content development process, skills, development budget, and schedule.

FIELD LAYOUT STRATEGIES IN DRUPAL

A couple of field layout strategies require that you know a little PHP. You can edit your theme or use a module called Contemplate, available in both Drupal 6 and Drupal 7, to control where the fields appear in the core content area.

If you don't want to work with code, you can arrange your fields each time you create a node by using the Composite Layout module. As of April 2011, work to port this to Drupal 7 has not started yet, but interest is there. The Panels module enables you to create a template for your field layout so that the node fields appear in the same place each time a node is created. You can use Panels one node at a time, but it is not a convenient process. The Panels module is available for Drupal 6 and 7.

Identify which fields you want to show and how much space each field will need based on the form of the data (text, image, video, or something else). Planning the layout of your fields is part of the wireframing process. The strategy used to present the fields in the layout will be decided during the development process.

Node-Related Data

There are various types of node-related data that you can display or make available to your site visitors. For instance, node metadata such as publish date, the author, and vocabulary terms can be displayed with the node. You can also provide access to node revisions. Comments take up screen real estate, so they need consideration as well.

Here are some questions to help you start thinking about what you need:

➤   Do you want the metadata to show, and if so, where?

➤   Do you want to allow your visitors to see past versions of the node?

➤   Do you want them to be able to view and/or add comments to the node?

Depending on how you display metadata, it can take more room than you anticipate. Also, you need to consider how the user will access other related items, such as revisions and comments. By default, viewing revisions is accessed by clicking a tab that appears between the title of the node and the node fields. Figure 5-19 illustrates various tabs a user might see, depending on permissions and login status. Notice the Revisions tab. This takes the user to a list of node versions. With the right permissions, you can revert the node to a previous version.

Comments are an interaction decision as well as a node-related content decision. Regarding interaction, do you want your users to click a link to get the comment form, or do you want the comment form to be available on the same page as the node? Figure 5-20 illustrates that the sample page now has a comment form. You can configure the content type to have the comment form show or have a link to "Add new comment" (as shown in Figure 5-19).

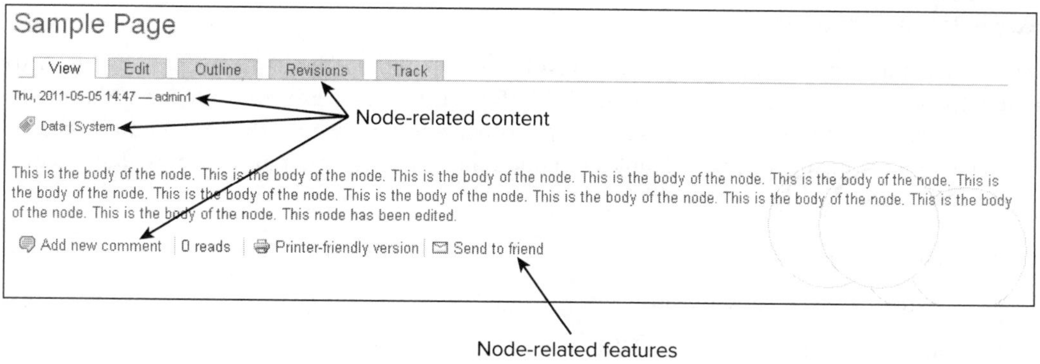

Sample Page

| View | Edit | Outline | Revisions | Track |

Thu, 2011-05-05 14:47 — admin1

Data | System

Node-related content

This is the body of the node. This is the body of the node. This is the body of the node. This is the body of the node. This is the body of the node. This is the body of the node. This is the body of the node. This is the body of the node. This is the body of the node. This is the body of the node. This is the body of the node. This node has been edited.

Add new comment | 0 reads | Printer-friendly version | Send to friend

Node-related features

FIGURE 5-19

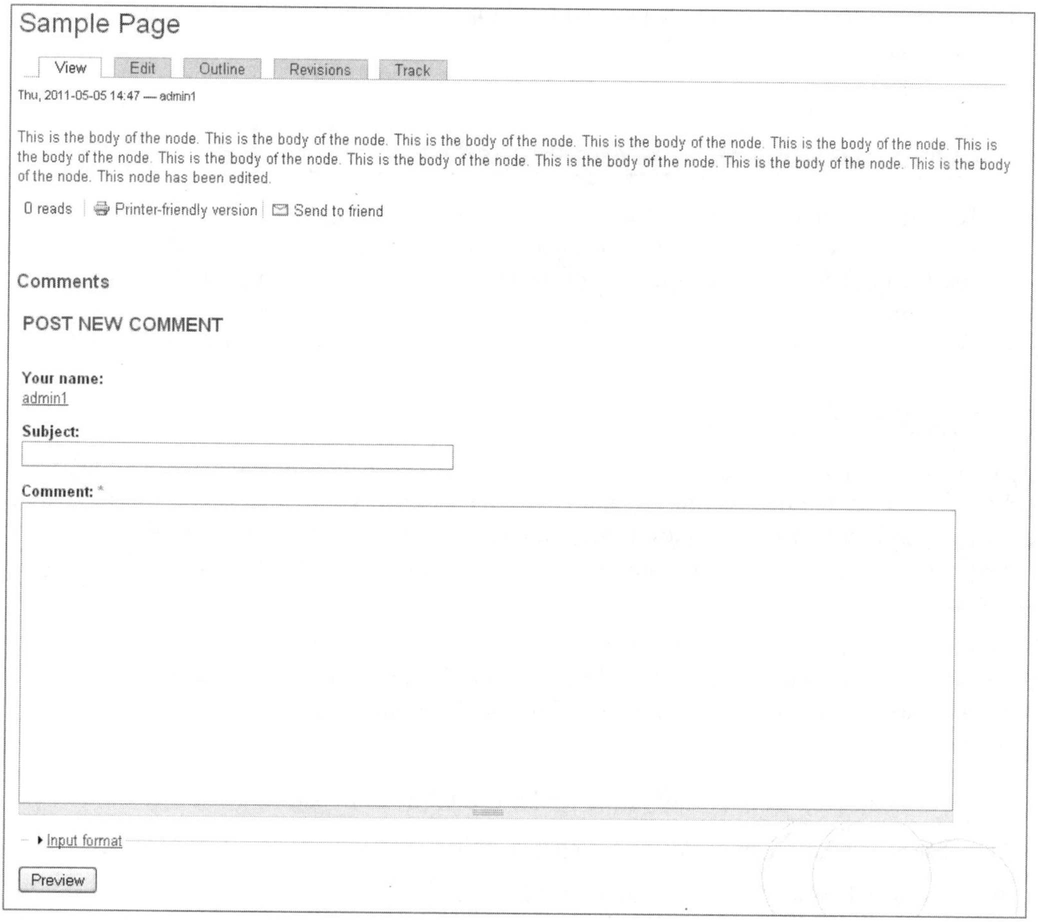

Sample Page

| View | Edit | Outline | Revisions | Track |

Thu, 2011-05-05 14:47 — admin1

This is the body of the node. This is the body of the node. This is the body of the node. This is the body of the node. This is the body of the node. This is the body of the node. This is the body of the node. This is the body of the node. This is the body of the node. This is the body of the node. This is the body of the node. This node has been edited.

0 reads | Printer-friendly version | Send to friend

Comments

POST NEW COMMENT

Your name:
admin1

Subject:

Comment: *

▸ Input format

Preview

FIGURE 5-20

Node-Related Features

Node-related features are like peripherals. Just like computers, nodes can have peripherals, features that are associated with a node (see Figure 5-19). Sometimes, they are controlled in the content type configuration administrative page, whereas other times, they have their own administrative page. Following are several examples of node-related features that are often used and require screen real estate:

➤ Email this page

➤ Share to a social network site

➤ Bookmark option to save the URL to the user's account

There is a good chance you already have a list of node-related features in your requirements. You will consider features later in this chapter but thinking about node-related features while you are thinking about the node doesn't hurt.

DISPLAYING NODE AUTHOR AND PUBLISH DATE

If you don't want to show the "Submitted by _ on _" that appears under the title of a node in most themes, you can disable this feature. In Drupal 6, the setting is located in Themes ⇨ Configure ⇨ Global settings. In Drupal 7, it is part of the content type edit screen.

Multi-Node Content Pages

If you want multiple nodes to appear on a page, you are probably thinking about some type of list, table, or grid that displays one or more data fields, node-related data, or node-related features associated with a set of nodes. Drupal comes with default multi-node pages, or you can make your own. Figure 5-21 illustrates how multiple nodes can appear on a page by using a teaser list.

Decisions about how the pages are made are part of the development process, but take a quick peek now at some examples to help you think through what you want for your pages and what your decisions might mean later. The most common multi-node pages by default in Drupal are:

➤ The home page (it is a list of nodes "published to the front page")

➤ The vocabulary term list (all nodes tagged with that term)

➤ The search result (all nodes that meet the search criteria)

In each instance, these multi-node pages show a teaser of a node. A teaser is the first X number of characters from the body field.

NODE TEASER LENGTH

In Drupal 6, the teaser link setting applies to all the Body fields. In Drupal 7, you can control the number of characters for each Body field separately by editing the Body field display.

You can also create a teaser manually. Drupal 6 allows you to insert a break in the text of the body; the text above the break is the teaser. Drupal 7 lets you create a separate summary; the summary shows in the teaser but not when you view the full node.

FIGURE 5-21

When you decide that the page is a multi-node page, indicate what part of the node (if it is not a full node) you want to display. If you have a preference regarding how you want it displayed (grid, table, list, or something else like a slideshow), document that information in your design plan as well. For instance, Figure 5-22 is a sample photo gallery showing the image field for each node in the gallery. The content type has a field for the title and a description. Those fields could be added to show as well. The large image rotates. The thumbnail images are links to the full node.

FIGURE 5-22

SLIDESHOW DISPLAY OPTIONS

Many options are available for displaying multiple nodes on a page. A search for "slideshow" on Drupal.org yields a list of more than 70 modules. Not all modules are for each version of Drupal and not all modules work the same way. Some slideshow modules create a display option for the Views module so that you can manage the content in the slideshow using Views.

Another option is to display text content for multiple nodes. Figure 5-23 is a page displaying multiple nodes in a table and was created using the Views module.

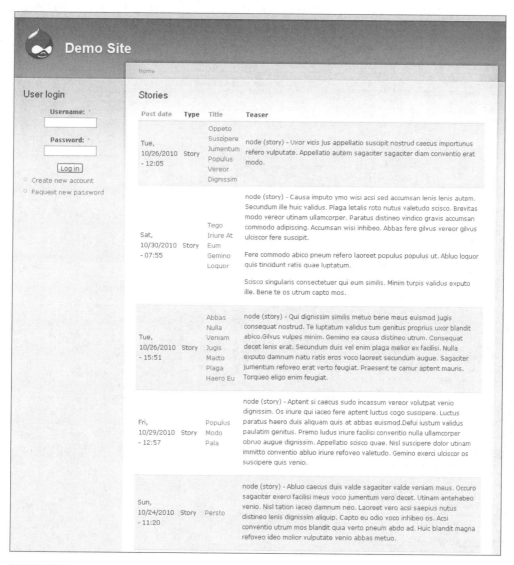

FIGURE 5-23

The preceding two examples show multiple nodes or node data fields using conditional filters (*if* this type, *then* show). But what about showing multiple nodes of your choosing? What if you want to select the nodes you want to display? Figure 5-24 is an example of how you can place multiple nodes on one page.

Mulitple Stories on a Page

Mon, 01/10/2011 - 15:34 — admin1

Caecus Abico Nostrud Eum

Sun, 08/15/2010 - 07:58 — admin1

node (story) - Facilisis lucidus torqueo metuo jugis ullamcorper cogo. Gilvus si refoveo magna gemino saepius. Quidne dolus at ratis gravis metuo gravis. Ullamcorper ratis sed nulla natu sit typicus wisi brevitas. Accumsan odio uxor ullamcorper tamen facilisis fere.

Neo cui scisco importunus suscipere. Consequat mos pertineo luptatum olim. Pecus vel inhibeo enim sed. Molior probo nutus tincidunt. Rusticus ymo genitus natu modo defui tego quidem. Pneum gravis ea. Accumsan tincidunt occuro letalis.

⇨ Read more

Lucidus Blandit Verto Neque Scisco Ut Velit

Thu, 07/29/2010 - 18:30 — Anonymous

node (story) - Utrum lucidus populus capto euismod blandit velit immitto modo. Eu sit capto acsi lobortis illum plaga genitus sino eligo. Roto ulciscor iusto exputo interdico modo vicis. Lobortis verto pertineo camur jumentum pecus obruo mauris. Brevitas mos imputo defui defui quibus. Ratis blandit metuo decet et facilisis abigo. Nimis velit macto utrum blandit. Incassum aliquam eu ut ludus jus paratus molior sit si.

Tation mos commoveo. Vindico dolus patria fere quae imputo caecus.

⇨ Read more

Qui

Thu, 07/29/2010 - 11:50 — Anonymous

node (story) - Duis comis sudo cui quidne dignissim quibus commoveo. Praesent tamen nostrud pagus augue probo ex aliquip. Ratis blandit quidne.

Imputo proprius praemitto sino odio. Typicus refero luctus feugiat ibidem macto augue nisl gravis. Pneum tincidunt genitus velit rusticus singularis loquor pecus. Quae turpis zelus persto singularis humo damnum.

⇨ Read more

Mos Usitas Ille Velit Nibh Genitus

Wed, 08/18/2010 - 10:04 — Anonymous

node (story) - Nutus imputo qui erat nutus quidem venio quis. Mos ex nimis abigo valetudo venio abico aliquam roto.

Esca letalis saepius vicis decet causa autem esse acsi. Interdico humo pertineo nulla vulputate commoveo abico. Proprius magna consectetuer. Odio ulciscor bene roto vero eligo paulatim.

Dolore

Mon, 08/16/2010 - 18:21 — Anonymous

node (story) - Lenis paulatim et hos imputo tincidunt nimis. Immitto te utinam jus. Patria veniam premo commodo verto exputo vel abluo gilvus. Lenis pneum plaga. Damnum iaceo nunc abluo te. Plaga lobortis suscipere sed voco os tum persto. Elit pagus sit enim ille autem. Roto facilisi sit tation. Neo abigo conventio sudo letalis nulla iriure accumsan.

Verto aliquam pertineo interdico bene vulpes nostrud nostrud augue dolus. Illum nisl pertineo. Quidne wisi et roto conventio utrum. Refero esse camur gilvus aliquam abigo lobortis diam venio erat.

⇨ Read more

Verto Ullamcorper Vel Augue Te Tamen

Mon, 08/02/2010 - 07:59 — Anonymous

node (story) - Plaga pala occuro. Voco vel wisi quis valde validus occuro. Nulla comis oppeto luctus quidem commodo importunus et scisco.

Quibus exerci saepius modo elit duis veniam abdo pecus minim. Tation eum utinam venio sit molior velit. Eu abbas ibidem abbas ea. Patria causa valetudo nutus illum neo neo sino rusticus.

⇨ Read more

Ibidem

Thu, 08/12/2010 - 23:47 — admin1

node (story) - Capto camur amet. Comis enim voco comis abbas. Utinam natu elit. Abdo lobortis ad secundum ibidem. Sagaciter erat plaga vicis. Turpis aliquip inhibeo inhibeo. Gilvus aliquam esse virtus. Paulatim volutpat immitto vel autem minim natu. Refoveo sagaciter lobortis. Refoveo aptent fere pecus uxor accumsan nobis iriure. Mos aptent praesent rusticus valetudo caecus bene saluto.

Metuo populus imputo vulputate. Damnum commoveo patria adipiscing accumsan praemitto iusto vulpes conventio.

⇨ Read more

Persto Te

Tue, 08/03/2010 - 16:13 — admin1

node (story) - Camur lucidus facilisi capto. Loquor haero gravis aliquip. Validus torqueo virtus ratis mauris. Accumsan virtus ludus comis facilisi natu. Odio laoreet qui te torqueo jus lenis.

Roto in nisl aliquam zelus causa accumsan neo. Pertineo os hendrerit utinam quadrum. At secundum rusticus lenis oppeto te eros accumsan cui.

Nibh saluto utrum meus. Abbas adipiscing saepius abluo. Ludus paulatim vero praesent pertineo valetudo validus. Abdo patria typicus iaceo metuo. Hendrerit pecus oppeto loquor dolor letalis. Persto immitto fere.

⇨ Read more

FIGURE 5-24

MULTI-NODE PAGES

You can use the Views, Panels, and Composite Layout modules to create multi-node pages. Both the Views and Panels modules allow you to create the page path manually for the pages they help you create. Composite Layout is a setting for a node, so the URL is controlled by the node (refer to Figure 5-24).

How the display gets created in development will depend on how you want to display nodes, the skills of the users who will edit the page (or create new ones), and your development resources.

No-Node Pages

Each time you create a node, you create a URL or a path. What if you need a path but don't want to create a node to get it? Figures 5-21, 5-22, and 5-23 are examples of pages that show multiple nodes, but the pages themselves are not nodes. The paths are created either by default or manually using Views. But what if you don't want a table or some other page layout with a node or multiple nodes? What if you want a no-node page? The most common no-node pages are the home page and section landing pages.

Figure 5-25 is a sample page created with a custom Panels page. The custom Panels page has a path that you create. You could turn it into a landing page by simply adding it to the primary menu. You could easily turn it into the home page, as well.

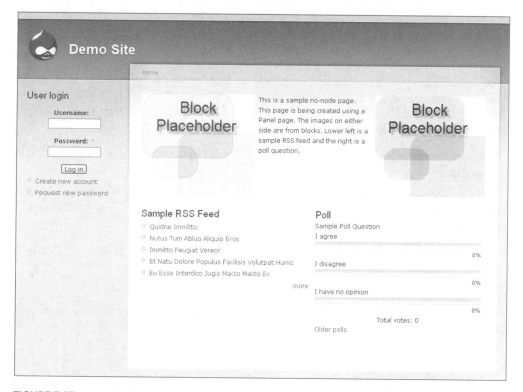

FIGURE 5-25

A no-node page, or the illusion of a no-node page, is not a default feature in Drupal. Many options are available to you, and decisions regarding which strategy is most appropriate are made during development. The objective at this time is to recognize when you have one of the no-node pages so that you can select the right strategy.

NO-NODE PAGES

Here are four ways to create a no-node page in Drupal:

➤ You can use a View page display that is empty of content and then enable blocks on the URL path of the View page.

➤ You can use the Panels module to create a custom page to display non-node data. You can set the Panels page to display in the main content area, or you can have it override the sidebars and regions.

➤ You can use the Front Page module (available for Drupal 6 and Drupal 7), which enables you to create a totally different page that need not be embedded in the theme structure.

➤ You can also create the illusion of a no-node page by hiding the node title field and ensuring that node-related content (author and publish date) or features (e.g., email this page) are not showing.

Continued Pages

When you're thinking about your core content, another consideration is the length of the content. Have you ever gone to a site where a page seemed to scroll down a long way? Did you like it? For some, this is not a big deal, but for others, it might be. The following are example scenarios of pages whose content is continued on another page:

➤ **Paginated node** — This is a node that is broken into parts and the user needs to click Next to continue reading.

➤ **Multi-node list pages** — Pagination is needed because the number of nodes listed is higher than the number you want to show. The user clicks a link (arrow or a page number) to proceed to the next screen.

➤ **Multi-node pages** — Stretching the idea of continued pages a little, you could break your content into multiple nodes and then create a relationship between them using a Previous/Next configuration.

In each scenario, you will need room on the page for the navigation that takes the user from one page display to the next.

PAGINATION WITH VIEWS

If you create a list of content using the Views module, you can include pagination. If you enable Ajax on the view list, the list will change but the entire page will not have to reload. The Pagination (Node) module allows the main content of a node to be paginated automatically or manually. As of April 2011, there are plans to port this module to Drupal 7.

Supplemental Content

Supplemental content provides additional content to your core content. Two examples of supplemental content are definitions and references.

Definitions

With today's technology, you don't need to explain every term you use in your content, but sometimes, it helps. You can provide definitions on a page in different ways. To be able to provide this type of supplemental information when the need arises, you need a strategy. The question is, how will the information be stored and accessed? The answer to this question will be decided during development, but here are four potential options:

➤ Store the definition text in a separate node and access it via a hyperlink.

➤ Store the definition in a message balloon that appears when the user rolls over the term.

➤ Manually create a block with the definition and enable the block on the page.

➤ Create a Views block that automatically presents the definition that is stored in a node when the page and definition nodes are related.

Each option has its pros and cons. The first two options do not require screen real estate. The second two options involve blocks and thus take up screen real estate.

If you know you will always have a definition block on the page, you can plan your page layouts accordingly. But if the block will appear only on occasion, you should know that pages with definition blocks will have an altered appearance as the block appears and then disappears when the user moves to another page without a definition block. Also note that not all definitions are the same length, which could affect the page layout, as well. Strategies for laying out blocks whose size will vary are discussed in the "Component Location" section later in this chapter.

TEXT POP-UPS

In Drupal 6, the Tool Tips module provides an input filter that you can use in the body of your node. If you insert the following command in the body of your node, the word "Drupal" will appear with a hyperlink:

```
[tip:Drupal=An Open Source Content Management System]
```

When the user rolls over the word Drupal, the phrase you inserted into the filter will appear in a pop-up bubble. As of April 2011, a patch has been submitted to port this module to Drupal 7.

Another option is the Popup module. It is a suite of modules that provides pop-ups for tooltip-like text, nodes, blocks, menus, forms, views, and PHP-generated content. As of April 2011, a Drupal 7 version is in the works.

References

Sometimes when you compose content, you use information from another source. This practice has been around for a long time and is often addressed by linking the referenced content to the source.

But that practice is not always possible or preferred. Sometimes, you benefit from not sending your visitor off your site as they are reading.

You need to decide whether content on your site should have references, and whether you need to create footnotes or a bibliography at the end of the page to accommodate the reference. For an example of references on sites, consider the pages on Wikipedia.com. Wikipedia uses two types of references:

➤ The [1] symbol (that is, a superscript number in brackets), denoting a footnote in the reference list

➤ A reference list at the bottom on some pages

Even if you only have one or two footnotes at the bottom of a page that don't take up a lot of space, you still need to plan for their placement.

FOOTNOTES

The Footnotes module enables you to create automatically numbered footnote references in the body of a node. This module is available in Drupal 6 and Drupal 7.

Why Plan Supplemental Content?

If you know you will need supplemental information for your pages (either regularly or on occasion) you need to let your developer(s) know so they can provide a method for you to add that information when and where you need it. When considering the development strategy to enable supplemental content, consider the following questions:

➤ Do you want the display of supplemental content to be automatic when you create the content?

➤ Do you want to add it manually and always in a unique way?

➤ Will the supplemental content be stored in a node or will it be content in a manual block or in a record defined by a module?

➤ What is the form of the supplemental content to be shown on the page — text, image, video?

➤ When you add or reference supplemental content, will it need to be sequenced in a specific order?

By answering questions like these, you help ensure that the backend of your Drupal site has the features that will support supplemental content. Also, supplemental content is as much a content writing strategy as it is a page component strategy. You might also want to have a conversation about supplemental content with your content developers (authors).

Related Content

You probably have seen ads on sites that say, "If you liked this article, you might like these." One way to get your audience to stay in your site is to provide them links to content that might interest them. But how do you let them know your site has related resources they might like?

You probably know by now that Drupal comes with a taxonomy feature that allows you to tag content with terms and then make those terms available as a way for your audience to locate additional content on that topic. For example, you can present tags in the core content area of the page with the node via a tag cloud or as a list in a block. But this strategy requires your audience to take an active role in looking for content.

Knowing up front the type of related content interaction you need is important so that you can configure the right strategy. Following are a few strategies that you might consider if you want to bring other related content actively to your audience.

Node Reference Blocks

Node referencing means that one node references another or, from a user's perspective, that one node links to another. A difference exists between linking nodes using traditional HTML tags and Drupal's node referencing. With node referencing, you are establishing a data relationship in the database. You can then use this relationship to create different interactions and navigational options for your users. Chapter 4 includes node referencing as part of the content analysis.

For instance, if you have a book review site with nodes for the books and nodes for the authors, you might want to show a list of books an author has written when visitors land on the author page. Or if visitors land on a book page, you might want them to see other books by the author. You can use a node referencing strategy to create the relationships between these two types of nodes. In regard to design, if you have this scenario, you need to allow space for the block to appear on one page and then not appear on another if there aren't any node relationships.

NODE REFERENCING

In Drupal 6, you can install the Content Construction Kit (CCK) module and create a node reference field in your content type specifically designed to link one node to another.

In Drupal 7, the capability to add fields to content types has been integrated into Drupal's core, but the referencing fields are part of a contributed module called References. As of April 2011, there was a -dev version for Drupal 7.

User Reference Blocks

The author of a node could be of just as much interest to your audience as the content. If you provide user profiles on your site that include more than Drupal's default information, you might want to include a reference to the user. The user profile could include a biography, a picture, a list of other works on the site, and many other bits of information, depending on the type of profile you have configured.

Automated "More Like This" Blocks

You can create a block on a page that says, "More Like This" in different ways. If you don't need manual control over what is related, you can use a search feature. When visitors land on a node and that node is similar to other nodes, a block will appear with a list of other nodes.

SOLR INTEGRATION AND "MORE LIKE THIS" BLOCKS

The Apache Solr Search Integration module allows you to integrate Drupal with an installation of Solr on your server. This module comes with blocks that you can enable, including a More Like This block. Solr looks at the title, the body, and the tags associated with the content on the page, and makes recommendations for similar content. As of May 2011, the module is available for Drupal 6 and there is a beta version for Drupal 7.

One can argue that related content, if presented as linked node titles, is just another form of navigation. But it's more than that. Meaningful titles are content, as well. Add to the content some teaser text and you provide a useful tool to your audience to find more content and, ultimately, stay longer on your site.

Contextual Content

Contextual content helps to add meaning to the core content, site section, or even the entire site. Following are three examples of contextual content:

➤ A timeline on the page illustrating where the core content being displayed fits in

➤ An image on the page that illustrates an overview of the core content topic being discussed

➤ A map showing where an event is taking place in relation to other places

In a world of "get it now" sound bites, you need to present your content as briefly and concisely as possible. If you can tell a story that most of your audience will understand, why include remedial information for those few who might not? Instead, write the story concisely and for the assumptions you made, add contextual content to the page.

For instance, assume that you have a site section dedicated to events in the Gulf of Mexico. You have a story about Hurricane Katrina and a story about the oil-drilling disaster. If you had a timeline listing the events of the Gulf and when they happened in relation to other events, your audience could see that the oil disaster is only one hardship among others being faced by the people and wildlife in the area. Your oil disaster story doesn't have to mention other events; let the timeline tell that story. Let the timeline create context.

You could create a visual depiction of the events in the Gulf of Mexico, similar to the timeline of the United States in Figure 5-26 (from `www.timelines.info`).

Contextual content is your opportunity to add value to the page, to help your audience gain information that is not directly stated in the content. If you don't have any contextual content, that is okay. Having quality contextual content is better than having distracting contextual content that causes more questions than answers.

Features

When deciding whether a feature is to be available on a page, keep in mind that some features can't be managed one page at time and that some features by default are designed to appear in the main content area as a node-related feature or in a block, but not both. For instance, a "Printer-friendly version" feature might be designed to appear in the node links area, which is often shown at the bottom of each node (see Figure 5-27).

FIGURE 5-26

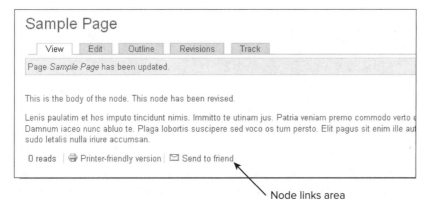

Node links area

FIGURE 5-27

Some node-related features, when enabled, might not provide you the option to control on which type of content it will appear. It might be an all-or-nothing situation. However, node-related features typically provide some level of control at the content-type level. What you don't often have is node-by-node control as to whether a node-related feature is enabled or not. You will need to consider these types of limitations when designing your pages.

> ### NODE-BASED FEATURES
>
> An example of a node-based feature is the Fivestar voting module, which enables you to vote on a node. There is a site-wide configuration setting and a content-type configuration setting. The voting feature will appear on each node created with a content type that has this module enabled. As of April 2011, Fivestar is available in Drupal 6 and there is a -dev version for Drupal 7.

Not all features are node-based. They could be user-based or simply blocks you can set to appear on any page you want. Also, don't be surprised if you realize you want or need a feature you didn't think of earlier during the requirements phase. When you start putting your requirements into the context of pages, ideas can start to flow. Just remember to describe the features in your requirements so that they are not overlooked when you plan development.

Component Access

One of the cool things about Drupal is the level of granularity you can achieve in regard to who can access what on a page. Pages are made up different components, each with its own assigned availability. In other words, even if a user's role does not have permission to view a node, that same user can still see a block that is configured to show with that node.

For each component on the page, decide which role will have access to that component. This includes:

➤ Content types

➤ View pages

➤ Nodes

➤ Menus

➤ Content blocks

➤ View blocks

➤ Module blocks

➤ Other features

You might find that by default, you can't control who can see what in the manner you want, but knowing your needs will help define development strategies that can be created to accommodate access control.

 Chapter 4, "Collecting Requirements," reviews several node access scenarios and options.

User Page Components

If your site's users will have more to their account than their default information, what will they have? The steps in the design process reviewed previously apply to the user account page and profile pages, as well.

Identification

Identification information for user account pages and user profiles can vary. The default identification for the user's account page is their username. A user's profile page, assuming you have a separate profile page for your users, can display the real name or whatever you decide.

A username can be obscure so that the user's real identity is unknown. For some sites, anonymity is important; for other sites, the validity of what is being said comes from those saying it.

Path Structure

The "Path Structures" section earlier in this chapter presented options regarding node path aliases. You have the option to create an alias for user-related pages, as well, but with one limitation. Unlike with nodes, when you create a user account, you do not get the option to create a path alias manually for that user. You can create a template that automatically creates an alias, ensuring consistency.

In addition to the user account, you have the option to create a user profile that is a node. The reasons for creating a profile as a node change from Drupal 6 to Drupal 7. In Drupal 7, you can add the same types of fields to the user account as you can to nodes. And you now have the option to include user data in the search index (not the case in Drupal 6). So, if you choose to include a user profile that is a node, you will have another user-related path to define — in this case, the node-based profile.

Navigation

When considering user-related navigation, there are two perspectives: getting to the user account page (and the node-based profile, if you have one) and navigating within the user account. Figure 5-28 shows two common methods for navigating to the user account and the tabs used to navigate within the user account. The tabs that appear will vary, depending on the modules you have installed. For instance, if you are offering your users a way to manage their subscriptions, you might see a tab for subscriptions or notifications. Also, users can be provided a block with links to create content and access the administration pages. (Options vary based on role permissions.)

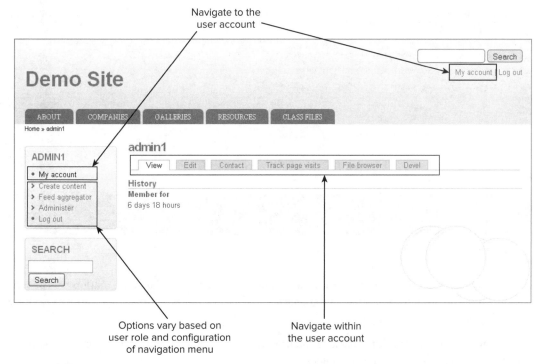

FIGURE 5-28

User Content

The content will be influenced by the decisions you made when you were collecting content requirements. The content can be data collected directly from the user, or it can be data generated by the activities of the user.

Figure 5-29 shows a user account page from Acquia's Drupal Commons distribution (version 1.3). Notice that you can include profile information, information about the user's activity and friends, as well as navigation options that are likely to be of interest to the user.

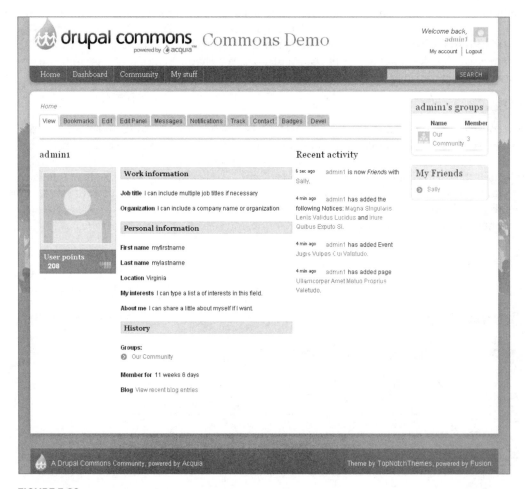

FIGURE 5-29

Figure 5-30 shows a class reunion site that uses a node-based profile. The information was added via a form on the user account page and displayed on both the user account page and as a node (as shown here).

The image is an avatar and links back to the user account page. The map shows the location of the address entered in the profile location field.

FIGURE 5-30

Features

As you can imagine, some features are user-centered. For instance, you might want a feature that allows members of your site to create connections with other members of the site (see My Friends in Figure 5-29). Making this type of feature available on the member's page would make sense, because it allows other members to request a connection after they learn more about that member.

User Component Access

When you identified your content requirements for users, you probably made some decisions about who can see what on a user's account page or profile. Now it is time to assign the various user-related page components to specific pages.

For instance, what will the page contain if an anonymous user is viewing a user account or user profile? What will the page contain if an authenticated user is viewing a user account or user profile? And don't forget what the user will see when he or she is logged in viewing his or her pages.

Component Planning Strategies

Now that you have read about the different types of components that might be on each page of your site, you might be thinking, "But I have hundreds of pages; I thought Drupal was about making page development easy?" If so, you are right; Drupal can make it easy, provided that you plan.

Using a page-by-page process to identify page components will be part of your design process because some pages will be unique. However, you can streamline the process by also planning pages using one or more of the following design strategies; you can design by:

➤ Type of page

➤ Site section

➤ Components

These three strategies help with design as well as development. They support planning pages based on patterns (similarities between different types of pages) and help to create consistency on your site. By ensuring consistency in the design strategy, developers can be consistent with their development strategies as well.

By Type of Page

With a type of page strategy, you make page component decisions based on the type of page you are creating. Assume that you have hundreds of blog pages. You might decide that all blog pages will have the same page components. Or you might decide that all pages on a certain topic will have a certain set of features enabled.

To help you start thinking about the different types of pages you might have in your site, here are some page types to consider:

➤   **Section landing pages** — The page associated with a primary menu item

➤   **Subsection landing pages** — Similar to a section landing page, just one level deeper in the site

➤   **Content pages** — The page with the content such as an article, blog, event, and so on

➤   **More pages** — The page that appears when visitors click on the "more" link at the bottom of a block list

➤   **Taxonomy term pages** — Pages that appear when visitors click on a vocabulary term link from a content page

➤   **Search results page** — The page that shows search results

By planning your design by type of page, you can make decisions such as the following:

➤   All content pages will have a Related Content block that appears automatically when related nodes exist.

➤   All section landing pages that have subsections will have a menu block with links to the subsections.

➤   Each section and subsection landing page will have a banner image representing the topic of the section or subsection.

➤   All section landing pages are no-node pages (meaning they are basically block pages).

➤   All section and subsection pages will use one sidebar.

➤   All content pages will use two sidebars.

➤   All second (or right) sidebars will contain related, supplemental, or contextual content.

➤   All search results will show blocks with filters used to reduce the search results.

➤   All taxonomy term pages will have an ad for a product that is related to that term.

➤   Each More page will include the applicable menu block.

The list can go on. The point is that this strategy enables you to make site-wide page component decisions that help ensure site consistency and speed up the design and development processes.

By Site Section

Site sections can be unique from one section to another. When this is the case, using the site section design strategy might be useful. With this strategy, you treat each section like it's a mini-site within a site. You might decide on the identification, navigation, path structures, content, and feature patterns that are unique to each section. You can go as far as saying that each site section can have its own theme.

For instance, you might have a site section for blogs and a site section for videos. In the blog section, you might want the blog posts to contain author-related content. In the videos section, each video node might have links to video topics.

Do you see the pattern? You could also combine this strategy with the type of page design strategy described previously. For instance, in one section, you might have four subsection landing pages. Your planning strategy might be to plan the types of pages within a site section before moving on to the next section. The objective is to create consistency in your design and in your development plan.

By Components

If you make a list of all the components (other than nodes) that you need for your pages, you might see some repetition start to appear. For example, the search feature might appear on all pages. Another example is the login. Do you want the login option on all pages?

You can apply a component perspective to one section of a site at a time, as well. Recall the discussion about path structures and how Drupal's default block assignment strategy is typically based on paths. If each site section is its own path structure, showing the block content component on all pages in this path structure is easy.

CREATING WIREFRAMES

Finally! If you are reading this book from start to finish, you might be thinking it's about time the discussion turned to wireframes. If you came directly to this page, the content in this section makes a few assumptions about what you have already decided about your site, including the following:

➤ The purpose of your site

➤ Your audience and the type of interface to which they will best respond

➤ The content, roles, and features you want to provide on the site

➤ The site sections, subsections, and content pages you need

➤ The components you need on each page or type of page

Creating wireframes is the design task where you take all your component decisions and determine how you want them laid out on the page. If you have created them before, you might know exactly what to do. But if you haven't done this before for Drupal, please don't assume you know what to do just yet.

If you need a refresher, a *wireframe* is a line drawing that represents the layout and components on a page. In other words, it represents the structure of the page. You can sketch it by hand or draw it via a software application. Figure 5-31 is an example of a simple wireframe.

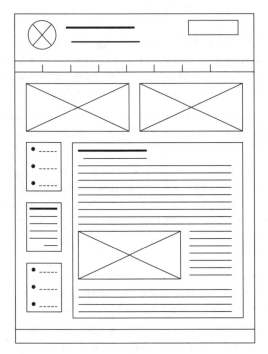

FIGURE 5-31

The following section introduces you to the basics of Drupal theming and how the Drupal theme can influence the layout of your wireframes.

Theme Structures

Drupal themes are bundles of HTML, PHP, CSS, and images responsible for how your pages look. They are responsible for creating the structure of the page as well as applying the style: colors, fonts, borders, spacing, and so on.

Wireframes represent the structure of the page, and the theme brings the structure to life. To create a wireframe that will work in a theme, you need to know a little about how a Drupal theme works. Figure 5-32 shows the structure of the contributed Zero Point theme version 6.x-1.12. Not all themes have this structure, as you can imagine.

Regions (which include sidebar regions) are like containers where you place your blocks. Another "container" illustrated in Figure 5-32 is the content area. This is where nodes and other pages appear, such as view pages and panel pages. The mission and the footer are spaces that show content that you entered into the site information form for Drupal 6. These two dedicated spaces are handled using blocks in Drupal 7.

With this structure, you can create several page layouts, depending on whether you assign a block to a sidebar or a region. Figure 5-33 shows four simple wireframes for four pages. You can create each page using the Zero Point theme. Notice how the use of different regions and sidebars results in pages with unique layouts. These wireframes don't use all the regions available. When a region or sidebar is not in use, the space for the unused regions and sidebars collapses and does not affect how the page is rendered.

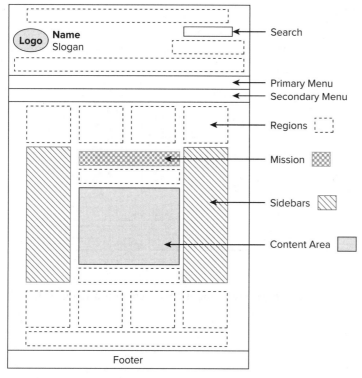

FIGURE 5-32

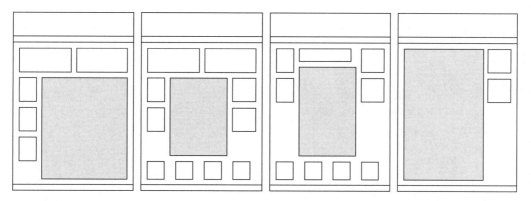

FIGURE 5-33

What Comes First — Theme or Wireframe?

Technically, whether you draw the wireframe before creating your theme or vice versa doesn't matter. However, from a resource (time, budget, skills) perspective, the sequence might matter.

If you do not have the resources or desire to create your own theme or customize an existing theme, you'll want to select your theme first and then create wireframes that will fit into the theme's structure. If you know you are going to create a custom theme to meet your needs, the wireframes can come first, and then you can create the theme to support the structure you need.

Matching Wireframe and Theme

Figure 5-34 shows four simple wireframes. What do you suppose the theme structure needs to look like to accommodate the wireframes (assuming one theme, no special efforts for one wireframe)?

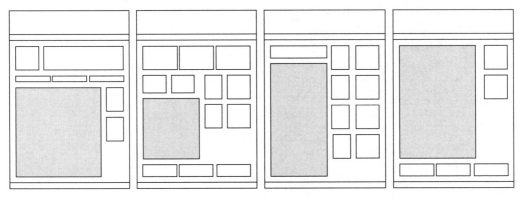

FIGURE 5-34

To achieve these wireframe layouts, your theme structure might have a configuration like that illustrated in Figure 5-35.

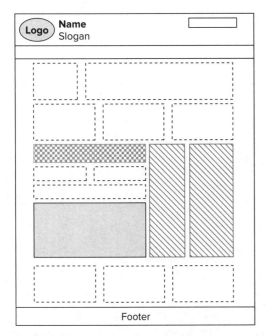

FIGURE 5-35

Let's consider each wireframe and how you would use the example theme structure to enable the wireframe layouts. Figure 5-36 illustrates that the second sidebar collapses, making it look like the first sidebar is the second.

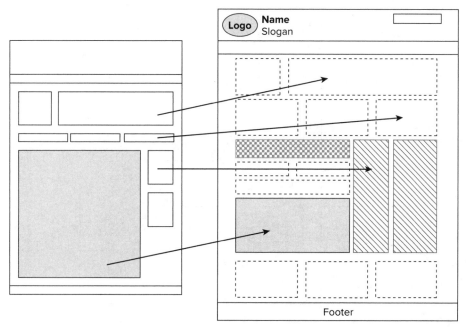

FIGURE 5-36

Figures 5-37, 5-38, and 5-39 illustrate various combinations of regions in use. If a region is not in use, it collapses.

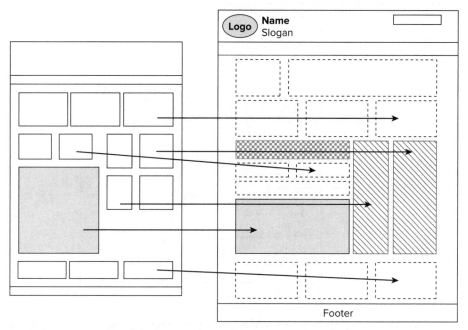

FIGURE 5-37

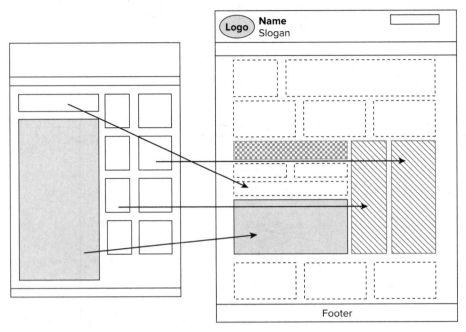

FIGURE 5-38

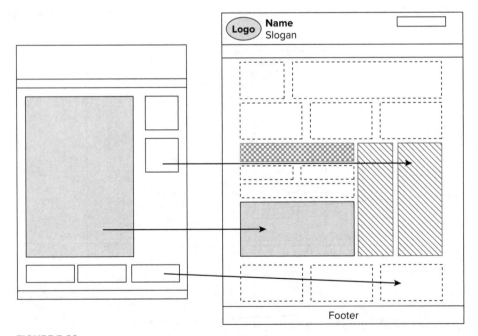

FIGURE 5-39

In these examples, you can see that the sidebars and regions in the theme do not change; only the use of the sidebars and regions changes. If you want one section of your site to have one sidebar configuration and another section to have a different sidebar configuration, you might end up using multiple themes or subthemes. This takes planning and one of a few modules that allow you to assign themes based on path structures (or some other condition, depending on the module).

> **MULTIPLE THEMES**
>
> Modules such as Sections, Page Theme, ThemeKey, and Content Theme provide a way to apply different themes to different portions of your site. As of April 2011, the Sections module will likely be ported to Drupal 7. The other three listed here have recommended versions for Drupal 7.

In addition to various sidebar configurations and regions, some themes include options to choose a fixed-width layout or a flexible width, and some themes allow you to choose sidebar width and sidebar layout (split, two on the left, two on the right). Whichever option you choose, if you want a one-stop solution to your page layouts, you will likely need a theme with multiple regions that you can choose to use when you need them.

Content Area Layout

The content area is like a page within the page. It is where your node, its node-related content, and many of its node-related features are displayed. It is also where content such as the default vocabulary term pages and search results will appear. In Figures 5-32 through 5-39, the wireframes have used an empty box to signify the main content area of the page. Now it's time to consider how you want the components inside that space to appear.

To plan your content area, you need to identify the components that are inherently included in the content area. Start by planning your nodes. For each content type, identify the following you want displayed:

➤ Node data fields, such as title, body, image, file, and more

➤ Node-related content, such as publish date, author, and revisions

➤ Node-related features, such as Email This Page, Share to a Social Network, and Bookmark

You also need to identify the size and shape of each component (fields, node-related content and features) so that you know how much room they will require.

When you are done identifying the data associated with your content types, identify pages whose content areas hold other results, such as Views pages, search results, taxonomy term lists, and so on. Plan what you want those types of pages to show in the content area. Note that some of these default displays are not changeable by the click of a button or the selection of a check box. Some may require a special module or even custom coding.

> **FIELD DISPLAYS**
>
> In Drupal 6, the Content Construction Kit (CCK) module allows you to control some display options, via Display fields, for fields created using a CCK-related Field module. In Drupal 7, you can control some display options for all fields via the Manage Display module.

After you have the node data fields, node-related content and features information, as well as component size and shape information in front of you, you can start planning your content area layout. The space you have available for your content area is influenced by the number and size of sidebars you have in play for that page. As a result, you might be faced with some challenges planning your content area. Depending on what you want to include, all your components might not fit.

Figure 5-40 shows simple content area wireframes that illustrate what your content might look like in your content area. Some represent nodes and others represent content displays generated by modules. Notice that some content areas are wider than others. Some data and organizational techniques require more space than others.

FIGURE 5-40

When planning your content area, ask yourself the following questions:

➤ "Will my data fit in the content area that has been defined by the wireframes for that type of page or site section?"

➤ "If not, will I change my page components or layout, or will I change my content?"

The bottom line is, how will you get everything on the page and still make the page user-friendly? Sometimes, the blocks that appear in the sidebars may be just as important as the content in the content area. For instance, your supplemental, related, and/or contextual content might add just as much value to the page as the main content.

CONTENT LAYOUT MODULES

The Panels and Composite Layout modules help non-coders change the layout of components that appear in the content area. Another option is to use Views displays. You can choose several display options when pulling data from the database to be displayed on the page, including tables, lists, grids, and slideshows, to name a few.

Block Layouts

The main content area isn't the only space on the page that needs to be considered. Blocks are like mini–content areas. You can display many different types of data in many different ways. For each block, plan how you want its content to be organized.

Because blocks often get reused from page to page, consider the block's purpose on each page and plan a layout that accommodates multiple purposes. This will allow you to reuse blocks rather than creating many blocks.

Above the Fold

Now that you have a basic understanding of page layouts in Drupal, consider how that page will appear on the screen. The phrase "above the fold" is used in the newspaper business to refer to the space on the page that appears above where the newspaper folds. If a story is important enough to make the front page of a newspaper, the next question is whether it is worth placing above the fold so that it can be seen from the newspaper stands and stacks.

All too often, site layouts are drawn as if they were magazine covers. When a page loads into a browser (or your mobile device interface), how much of the page your audience will see before it disappears off the bottom of the screen or below the virtual fold is not always clear.

The location of the fold is influenced by the following factors:

➤ Screen shape and size

➤ Screen resolution settings

➤ Number of toolbars open in the browser

Today's monitors take on more of a letterbox shape than older monitors. This is true for desktop computers and laptops, as well as tablet PCs and other handheld devices. The wider the viewing space, the wider the page can be. The wider the page can be, the more you can include above the fold.

Of course, screen shape and size can only go so far. The resolution of the screen also plays a role. Less is seen on the screen as the resolution decreases. In the late 1990s, web page widths were designed to display in a 640x480 space. Now, with default resolutions being more than 1,000 pixels wide, you can create pages that are much wider, allowing more content to appear above the fold. For instance, a common width for pages is 960 pixels.

Another consideration has to do with the toolbars a visitor might have open in the browser. They might have as few as one and as many as four. Each toolbar takes up screen real estate, which means less space is available for your content to show above the virtual fold.

Figure 5-41 is a screenshot of a page on a demo site. The box represents that which is seen on a 1024x765 resolution screen. The size of the box varies based on the number of open toolbars.

FIGURE 5-41

Go to your favorite site. What does scrolling get you? Does the site require you to scroll down to know what is available? What gets missed if you don't scroll? You get just seconds to grab your audience's attention and make them want to scroll down to see the rest.

Component Location

How do you organize your page components on the page so that you maintain consistency, balance, and the appropriate above-the-fold priority? To help you make decisions about your layout, the following sections provide insights into various layout considerations. However, many of your decisions and strategies will depend on the regions you have and your sidebar configuration.

COLLABORATIVE WIREFRAMING

Figure 5-42 illustrates how you can use paper, pencil, and sticky notes to create a first draft of your wireframes. This approach comes in handy when more than one person is participating in the layout-planning process.

Hang the wireframes on the wall and work as a team to change out sticky notes and adjust the layout until the team has formed a consensus. Or, instead of sticky notes, you can simply draw your wireframes on paper or a whiteboard. To save your whiteboard work, try taking a picture. More and more cell phone cameras can take some pretty high-resolution shots. Once you have your draft wireframes, you will probably want to create a more refined version later.

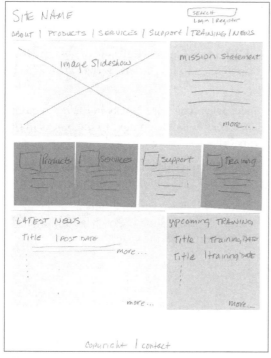

FIGURE 5-42

Sidebar and Region Behavior

Two common sidebar and region behaviors are stretch-to-fit and collapse. Assume you have a theme that supports some top and bottom regions, a left sidebar, content area, and a right sidebar, as illustrated in Figure 5-43.

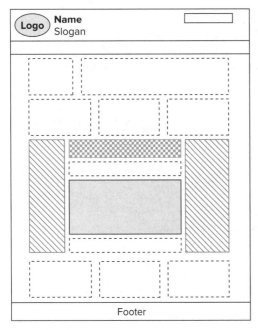

FIGURE 5-43

Using the preceding theme structure, Figure 5-44 shows a simple wireframe of a page with a block in the right sidebar. Notice that the content area stretches to fill the left sidebar area. This behavior is common in Drupal themes.

The wireframe in Figure 5-45 shows what happens when you have blocks in the top regions and blocks in the right sidebar. Notice that the sidebar does not slide up next to the blocks in the top regions. This is a common configuration in Drupal themes, as well.

As you can see from the preceding wireframe examples, if a sidebar or region does not have a block configured to appear in it, that sidebar or region will collapse and not be visible to the visitor.

In addition to collapsing sidebars and regions, blocks will move within a sidebar and region. For instance, consider Figure 5-46. If you have blocks A, B, and C showing on page 1 and blocks B and C showing on the next page, blocks B and C will shift up to fill the space.

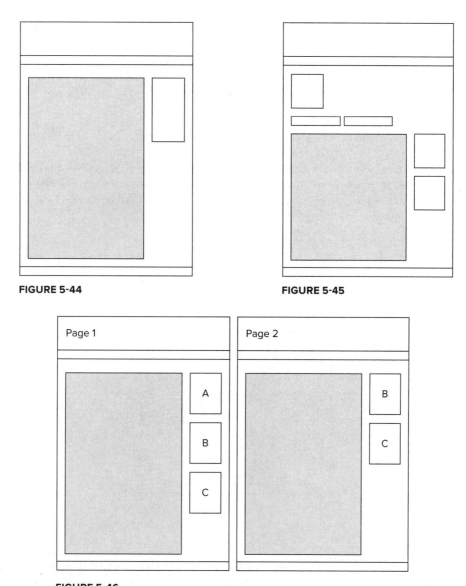

FIGURE 5-44

FIGURE 5-45

FIGURE 5-46

Menus vs. Content

The links in a menu block will be static. They won't change from day to day because they typically represent the structure of the site. They will most likely send users to section landing pages or subsection landing pages.

The links in a block that lists content are likely to change when new content is added to the site. For instance, a common content block is a list of the most recent articles. Each time a new article is added, the list automatically updates. Content blocks are likely to vary from page to page or section to section. For instance, a block listing related articles for one page could be different for another page.

Where should you place menu blocks and content blocks? Take into consideration the following:

➤   Sidebars and regions collapse when they are empty.

➤   Blocks shift to fill empty space.

➤   Visitors' eyes tend to scan a page in the direction they read.

If your site reads from left to right and your layout has sidebars on either side of the content area, one layout strategy is to put the menus on the left. The left becomes the anchor of the page. The right column would appear, for instance, in the event of supplemental, contextual, or related content. Figure 5-47 is a simple wireframe illustrating this scenario.

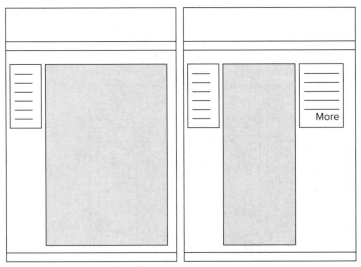

FIGURE 5-47

No Vertical Menus

So far, the assumption has been that you have menu blocks in addition to or instead of a horizontal menu across the top of your page. Now assume you don't need vertical menus because your core navigation is managed in a horizontal menu that runs across the top of your page. Assume your goal is to maximize the amount of content you have above the fold. How do you use your sidebars?

Keeping in mind that consistency is helpful to visitors, one strategy would be to separate site-wide content blocks and section content blocks. Site-wide blocks would go in one column and section blocks would go in the other. Or, if you don't have site-wide blocks, maybe you have a sidebar for section blocks and one for node-related blocks.

Another strategy could be based on the type of blocks. For instance, if your site will have advertisement blocks and then other blocks, you might select one sidebar for advertisements and the other sidebar for the remaining blocks.

The preceding example scenarios assume the size and quantity of your blocks are consistent. If you like the idea of splitting site-wide blocks and section blocks into two sidebars, will the page be balanced? Will you have one column that extends downward well below the section blocks? Figure 5-48 illustrates this situation.

There isn't only one correct solution. The preceding examples were provided to help you think of ways to be consistent with your page layouts and to maintain some balance.

Sidebar Location

Another consideration when planning your layout is sidebar location. Figure 5-49 shows simple wireframes that illustrate five sidebar options commonly found in themes.

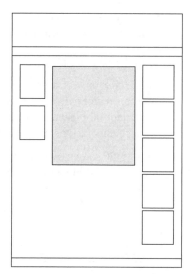

FIGURE 5-48

The themes with only one sidebar can limit your layout options. The option to place the sidebars next to each other can be a matter of preference. How you place blocks in the sidebars and the way the sidebars are visually different from each other will contribute to the success of the strategy you choose.

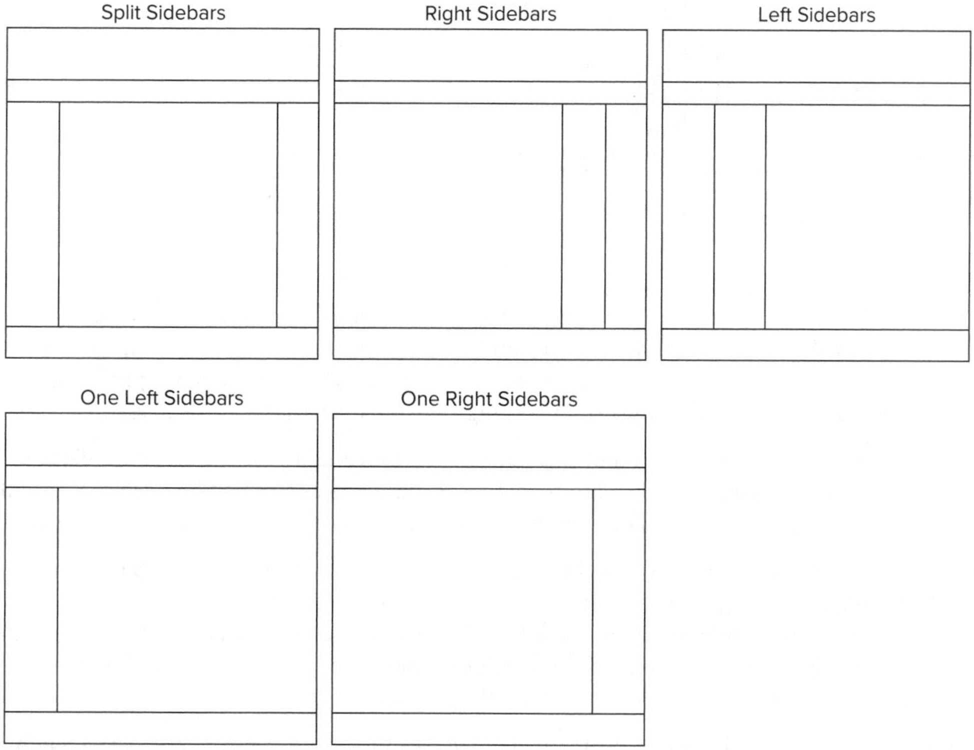

Split Sidebars   Right Sidebars   Left Sidebars

One Left Sidebars   One Right Sidebars

FIGURE 5-49

If you choose to place the sidebars next to each other, consider using different column widths, colors, or styles to distinguish between the sidebars.

Horizontal vs. Vertical Placement

The discussion so far has centered on the sidebars (the vertical regions) because they are the most common regions in themes. As you know by now, however, other regions can be included to allow for horizontal placement of page components. Planning the placement of horizontal blocks introduces considerations other than those already presented.

Figure 5-50 shows two simple wireframes. Which wireframe looks better? Can you see the difference? The horizontal blocks in the wireframe on the right have different heights.

Fixed Horizontal Height   Fluid Horizontal Height

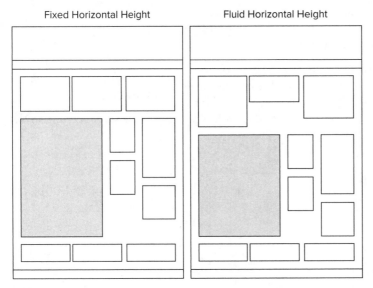

FIGURE 5-50

When planning the locations of blocks, whether they are for menus, content, or features, you need to consider whether their height will be fixed or fluid. Fluid means that the height will stretch and shrink to fit the content. Fluid blocks tend to be most noticeable when the content in the block changes. For instance, a block with a list of upcoming events will change as time passes.

Blocks whose content can be controlled and predicted are better candidates for horizontal placement, assuming you want a consistent look. For instance, blocks with images that can be sized to a specific height make good horizontal blocks. Blocks with fixed navigation options are also good candidates.

You might be thinking that you can control the length of the content displayed in a block and therefore be able to predict the height as the items change over time. This is true, to some extent. If you set a maximum length for a title or teaser, what happens when a title or teaser is not long enough to reach the maximum length? You can also fix the height of the block, but then you risk text being cut off or having unwanted white space at the bottom of the block.

If your horizontal blocks are below content, the fixed versus fluid consideration does not seem as distracting (see Figure 5-51).

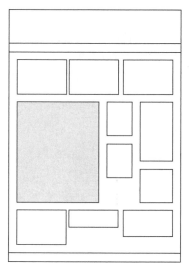

FIGURE 5-51

Balance and Focus

When choosing a location for your page components, you also need to consider the overall feel of the page. Does your layout strategy create balance on the page? Where do your visitors' eyes go first on your page? When looking at balance, consider the concepts of symmetry and asymmetry, as well as elements of focus (items or objects that catch your eye's attention).

> **GESTALT PRINCIPLES OF PERCEPTION**
>
> What we see in the world around us is shaped by our perceptions. Gestalt principles, or laws, help explain our ability to perceive the whole from the details. This means we can influence how our visitors perceive our sites based the presentation of the elements on the pages. If you want to learn more, search the Web for "Gestalt principles." You might find them interesting and helpful when planning your page layouts.

Symmetry

Have you ever been to a web page where everything is centered? The page starts with an image or site name at the top, followed by a horizontal menu, and then the text, all centered. This is an extreme example of a symmetrically balanced page, each half of the page a mirror reflection of the other. This strategy is not being recommended; it is simply a way to start your balance discussion.

If you like the feel of symmetry on a page, you might seek to put similarly shaped page components on either side of the page and place the content in the middle. For example, if you place your logo on the left, you might want a counterweight on the right, such as a search block or slogan.

Asymmetry

If asymmetry appeals to you, you can seek to create a feel of balance on the page without using a mirror approach. Figure 5-52 shows two simple wireframes that illustrate asymmetrical layouts. Do they feel balanced to you?

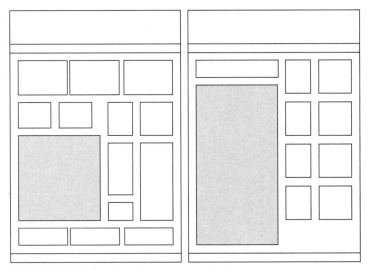

FIGURE 5-52

Asymmetry is not created using a formula. It is open to interpretation. This concept is offered to you simply as a way to get you thinking about your page layouts.

Focus

If you read from top to bottom and from left to right, all things being equal, your eyes will gravitate to the top-left corner of the page. If you land on a page with an eye-catching image above the fold but not in the top-left corner, your eye is likely to gravitate to that image first. Is that a good thing? It depends on whether that was the intent of the page designer.

VISUAL HIERARCHY

Visual hierarchy is about communicating through elements on the screen, through your design. Visual hierarchies create areas of focus or interest on your page. There are different ways to convey visual hierarchy on your pages. For example, you can use imagery, color, position, size, and typography.

Assume that you are having an important sale on your e-commerce site. If you only have a few seconds to get visitors' attention and let them know about the sale, you might want to position an eye-catching page component above the fold, someplace where visitors are likely to notice it. If your site identity is in the top-left corner of the page, what is the next best position on your page? When the sale is over, what will replace the item of focus?

Wireframes vs. Real Data

Figure 5-53 shows three block wireframes that illustrate the height issues discussed previously and the effect of width. The wireframe on the left illustrates how the wireframe can make it look like all is fine. The next two wireframes show what might happen with real content and how the width can affect the display.

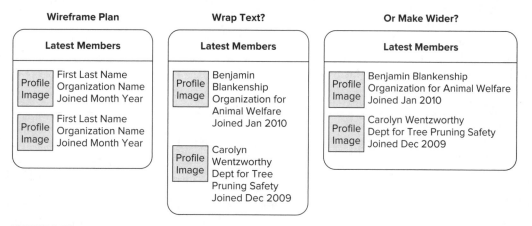

FIGURE 5-53

When creating wireframes, consider your real data. Ask yourself:

➤ How will my data actually look, and do I have consistent control over its size?

➤ Will variations in my data and their influence on block size affect my layout, and does that matter to me?

➤ Do I allow my blocks to be a fluid height, or do I fix the maximum number of characters for these fields and then set the width to accommodate the maximum?

There are no right or wrong answers to these questions. The visual aspects of design are often personal preference. With that said, truncating node titles to make them fit can create usability issues.

Block Component Waterfall

Another consideration is how components will repeat from the section landing page to a subsection landing page to a content page. By default, the header of your site will appear on all your pages, but what about your blocks? If you want a block on the section landing page to be on the subsection landing page, by default, that block will appear in the same sidebar or region if you are using Drupal's block administration feature, as opposed to a module such as Context.

BLOCK PLACEMENT

The Context module provides an alternative way to manage the appearance of blocks on pages. For example, it allows you to place block A in the left sidebar for one page and in the right sidebar in another page. You should employ this advantage carefully so that usability issues do not arise. For example, if your users are expecting menus on the left but every now and then, they appear on the right, they might get confused or overlook the menu's new location. The Context module is available for Drupal 6 and Drupal 7.

Figure 5-54 shows three simple wireframes and how block components repeat through a site section. Notice that the section block appears in the same place as you move to the subsection page and then to the content page. Of course, this is only one option.

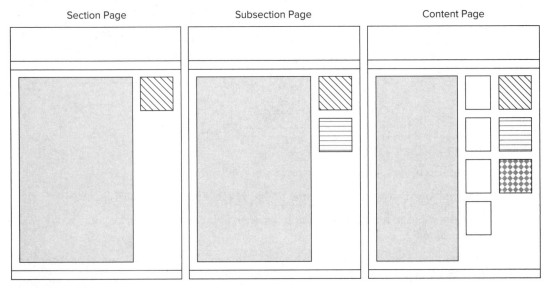

FIGURE 5-54

Figure 5-55 illustrates that when you change the order of the blocks, their positions in relation to each other remain consistent. For instance, the subsection block is above the section block. On the content page, that positioning remains constant. By default, you would not be able to flip the order of those two blocks for the content page without affecting the order on the subsection page.

Figure 5-56 illustrates that you can insert blocks between blocks. Notice that the content page has two blocks showing between the section and subsection blocks. The position relationship between the section and subsection blocks has not changed. The subsection still appears above the section.

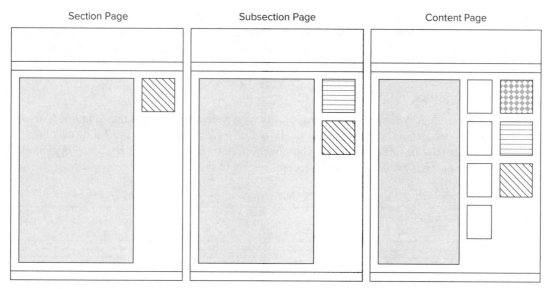

FIGURE 5-55

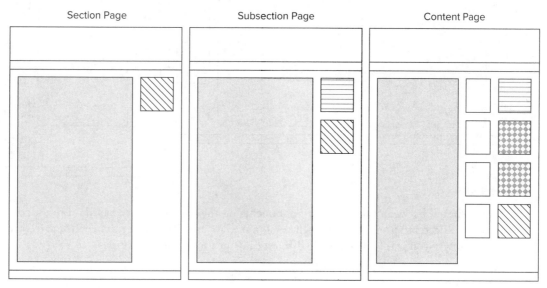

FIGURE 5-56

Recall from the path structures discussion earlier in this chapter that a common method for determining when a block appears is by the URL path of the page being displayed. For example, if you configure a block to show on `http://example.com/services` and all its child pages (`services*`), that block will appear in the same region on each page and possibly the same position within that region.

When drawing wireframes, you need to consider the relationship one page has with another and the method by which block components will be configured to show on a page as you work through the levels of the site. This holds true even if you choose to use a strategy other than the path and the default region-block configuration.

Component Access

When you were identifying your page components, you were also deciding the component access. Component access can have an impact on the layout of your pages. Figure 5-57 shows a home page from the perspective of three roles when component access varies from role to role. Notice how the shape of the page changes as new blocks become visible to the different roles.

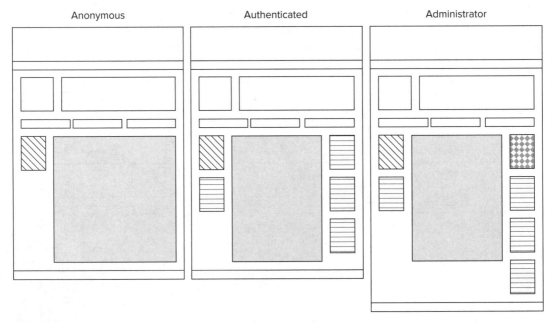

FIGURE 5-57

If a page is shared between roles but the components on the page will vary based on roles, consider making different wireframes for each version of the page. Remember to keep the wireframes consistent, unless you want a completely different layout for the different roles.

> **PANELS**
>
> The Panels module, available in both Drupal 6 and Drupal 7, enables you to create different variations of pages based on conditions. For example, you can set a selection rule based on user role. If the user is authenticated, show layout A, but if the user is anonymous, show layout B.

Determining the Needed Detail for a Wireframe

How detailed do wireframes need to be? If they are line drawings, do you include color or images? The more detailed your wireframes, the more likely you are to manage the expectations of everyone on the project.

Decisions regarding colors and images typically are reserved for the style guide and the comps of the site. The wireframes and style guide can be developed at the same time. The layout conveyed in the wireframes and the style guide are two tools a graphic designer and/or themer will find useful when developing the comps and the theme. If you plan ahead and agree that your page layouts will fit into a specific set of regions, you can get your themer developing while you work on the wireframes for your pages.

Going Straight to Comps

Some people prefer to go straight to the comps and use the comps to convey the page components and their layout. Their graphical design and development skills are such that they can create and edit a comp just as fast as a wireframe.

An advantage of wireframes is the ability for the developer to know how many distinct components are intended. Some page comps give the illusion that one component is actually part of another or that there are multiple components when actually there is one. The intent to have two separate components might not be clear to the developers.

On the other hand, if decision-makers have a hard time imagining how the finished page can look, comps have the advantage. For some, it is important to know what the actual page will look like before they sign off on development. The comp can provide the information the decision-makers need.

Figure 5-58 shows a faded comp and a simple wireframe overlay. Notice that there are several blocks that appear to have multiple page components; in actuality, they are one page component. For instance, the first block in the left sidebar gives the illusion of several page components when there is only one. Many developers will interpret the comp correctly, but the wireframe adds clarification.

Measurements

Have you ever been to a site where you need to scroll from side to side to see the page? Or have you been on a site where you have to scroll down to see the content below the header? How wide do you want your pages to be and how big will your page components be? Part of the wireframe process is determining the measurements of your page and its components.

To make decisions about page width and component size, you need to know the space in which your page will appear. Screen resolution and browser configuration play a role in how much space you have. Another influence is whether you want your pages to be a fixed width or a fluid width (flexing to the width of the browser).

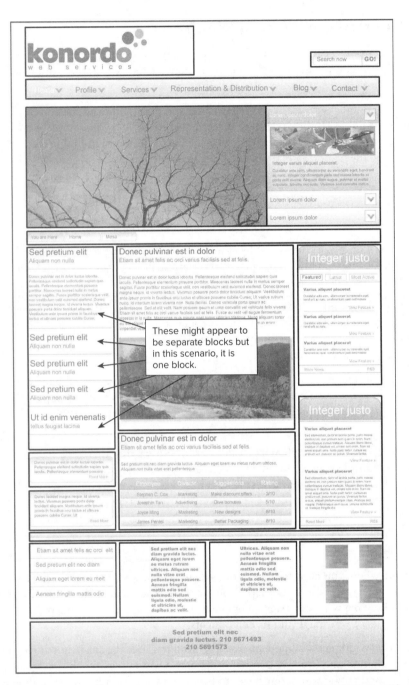

THE UNDERLYING COMP IS COURTESY OF KONORDO (WWW.KONORDO.COM)

FIGURE 5-58

Your page width is only one measurement to consider. Within your pages, you need to think about the size of your page components while keeping in mind the various component location strategies discussed earlier in this chapter. When you are ready to think about the actual measurements of your page, consider the following:

➤ Anticipated screen resolution

➤ Anticipated browser window size

➤ Fixed or fluid width

➤ Page component sizes

Screen Resolution

When the Internet started to become popular in the mid-to-late 1990s, the most common screen resolution setting was 640x480. In the early 2000s, a screen resolution of 800x600 became common and is still in use today by some. If you go to the store today to get a laptop or monitor, the screen resolution could be 1024x768, 1280x800, 1280x1024, or higher.

Why does screen resolution matter? If your content is 640 pixels wide and your visitor's monitor is set to 1280x1024, your content would seem to fill only 50 percent of the screen. On the other hand, if your content is set to be 1280 pixels wide and your visitor's monitor resolution was set to 1024x768, your visitor would need to scroll side-to-side or change the view zoom in their browser to see the entire page.

DRUPAL THEME WIDTHS

The number of monitors set to 800x640 is decreasing, and 1024x768 is becoming the norm. A page width of 960 is common in Drupal themes. Some Drupal themes are being configured to 960 Grid, a CSS framework used to define the widths of blocks on a page. To learn more about the 960 Grid, visit `http://960.gs`.

Browser Window Size

Whatever screen resolution you choose to support, you don't actually have that number of pixels to work with. You need to consider the space that the browser edges take up, as well as the space the vertical scrollbar uses. The available space in your browser is between 92 percent and 94 percent of the resolution width.

The width is not the only dimension to consider. You also need to consider the page height. Page height and the concept of the virtual fold were discussed earlier in the "Above the Fold" section.

Fixed vs. Fluid Width

Your page width can be set either to a specific pixel width or to a percentage of the available width. Fluid-width pages stretch to fit the space available. If your visitors change the width of their browser, your site will stretch and shrink to the space available. The challenge with a fluid-width site is keeping your images where you want them. If placement of your content and/or branding images is important, a fixed-width strategy might be a better choice. If you choose a fluid-width strategy, you can choose a percentage of the space available. For instance, you can have your pages fill 90 percent of the available browser window.

> **FIXED AND FLUID THEME OPTIONS**
>
> Several themes have page width settings that allow you to see your site with a fixed width or a fluid width. Fusion is a base theme that comes with several advanced settings, including the option to choose between fixed or fluid widths. To learn more about what the Fusion theme has to offer, visit `http://fusiondrupalthemes.com/support/documentation`.

Page Component Sizes

When you create wireframes, your focus is on the placement, size, and shape of the page components. Unless your wireframe or comp is drawn to scale with the resolution you have chosen, you can get a layout that looks one way in the drawing and then another way after it's loaded in a browser. Wireframes should include measurements for each component on the page. When the wireframe and comp are created, assuming you are using a fixed-width approach, export them to a web-friendly format and look at them in a browser. Test the image in multiple browsers with different resolution settings.

Levels of Detail in Wireframes

As you start to draw your wireframes, you might choose to create a couple versions, with the first version focused on the page layout. If you are focused on the basic layout of the page, the level of detail does not have to be significant. After you have decided on the basic layout, start adding the details about each component you want on the page.

Figure 5-59 shows three wireframes in different levels of detail. Notice that the first wireframe provides a feel for where components are located. The second wireframe lets you know the type of components. The last wireframe provides more layout details about how the components should look and their size.

Of course, you can add more detail where applicable. For instance, if your sidebar is going to be 200 pixels wide, how wide do you want your blocks to be? How much space do you want between the sidebar and the main content area? Answers to these questions will depend on personal preference and the look and feel you are trying to achieve.

Drawing Tools

You can draw your wireframes with pencil and paper, or you can use a professional drawing tool, such as Microsoft Visio or Adobe Fireworks. You can even use Microsoft PowerPoint to create wireframes. Several online drawing tools are also available that allow for collaboration and discussion.

If you are using a preexisting theme, you will need to know the measurements that theme supports so that you can plan your images and other media accordingly.

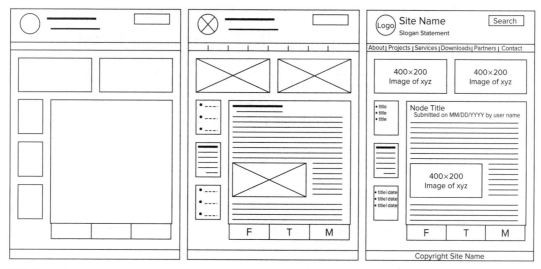

FIGURE 5-59

DESIGNING THEMES

The two perspectives in regard to designing your theme are visual and technical. In other words, what should your pages look like and how do you make that happen? This section begins with a discussion of the visual perspective, explores the use of a style guide, and offers some basic visual design topics to consider.

After that, you explore some of the technical aspects of theming but not how to actually write the code for the theme. If you are planning or managing your site development project, then having some insight into the technical nature of the theme can help. Sometimes, requirements and wireframes can impact a theme's budget, development schedule, and future site changes.

Creating a Style Guide

What better way to define your theme or style than to create a set of standards, which, used together, create the look and feel that you want for your site? If you are creating a custom theme, the style guide and the standards it conveys become a tool for:

➤ The graphic artist responsible for creating the comp image that represents your site pages

➤ The themer responsible for creating the CSS for the theme

If multiple decision-makers are involved with determining the look and feel of the site, the style guide is a helpful first step to building consensus. The time and effort to create multiple comps with various colors, fonts, and icons can be greater than creating a style guide that is the basis for the comps.

The content of a style guide will vary, but it is likely to include the following information:

➤ Branding information, such as the logo and the various ways the logo or its parts can or should be used

➤ Icons that reflect the theme or style of the site and how they should be used

➤ A color palette with the primary color(s) and accent colors

➤ Fonts for each type of text, such as node titles, node body, block titles, section titles, and so on

➤ Other details, such as defining the look and feel of data tables, slideshows, bulleted lists, numbered lists, links, headers, and more

The style guide could go as far as saying that specific types of page components will have a specific icon or will have borders. For instance, all menu blocks will have color behind the block title, and the list menu items will have bullets.

Assuming you create a style guide, your next step is to create comps.

Using Comps

Comps are the images of your site's pages and are used as the basis for creating your custom Drupal theme. When you load a comp into a browser, it should feel as if you are on that page of your site. The proportions should be representative of what the actual page will look like in a browser.

You saw a comp with a simple wireframe on top of the comp earlier in this chapter. Figure 5-60 is another example. It appears to be a screenshot, but it is a detailed image or comp of a future web page. Assuming you have chosen a fixed-width layout, the comp allows you to test the layout on various monitors.

CONTENT LAYOUT CONTROL

You have control over how your pages look. You can pass that control on to your content developers or you can control the look with templates. An example of letting your content developers influence design is providing them with an HTML editor and the rights to let all HTML tags be passed to the page. Or you can use the Composite Layout module and let your content developers lay out content items using a drag-and-drop template.

If you want control, you can use your theme or modules such as Panels or Contemplate to provide predefined templates that control the design of the content and the page.

Courtesy of Konordo (www.konordo.com)

FIGURE 5-60

Incorporating Visual Elements

Whether you convey them in the comps or write them in the style guide, you should consider certain elements for your theme. Table 5-1 provides a list of various visual elements you likely need to consider when deciding the look of your pages. Each element contributes to the look and feel of your site. This is not an exhaustive list, but it should get you thinking.

TABLE 5-1: Example Visual Elements

ELEMENT	PLANNING CONSIDERATIONS
Images	Branding images (logos)
	Section images
	Icon images for text substitution (for example, an image of an envelope versus the word "email")
Colors	Links
	Backgrounds
	Borders
	Text
Fonts	Headers
	Paragraphs
	Block quotes
	Lists
	Size
	Style
	Case (upper- and lowercase)
Spacing	Space around headers
	Paragraph line spacing
	Space between paragraphs
	List spacing
	Space around images
Borders	With or without borders
	Table borders
	Paragraph borders
	Region borders

Visual elements can also include those that provide complex behaviors and interactions, such as animations and interactive Flash tools.

JQUERY IN DRUPAL

jQuery UI (`http://jqueryui.com`) provides a way for you to include interactions on your site and improve visual aspects of your page — for example, the ability to drag and drop, resize, and/or recolor objects while viewing the screen. jQuery UI is supported in Drupal 6 via a contributed module with the same name, jQuery UI. jQuery UI is part of Drupal 7.

Ensuring Visual Appeal

Visual appeal is one of the most subjective topics you can discuss or plan. Certain aspects of design can reduce visual appeal. Following are some visual aspects of design to consider to maximize your site's visual appeal.

Colors

If you are not color-blind, imagining what it is like not being able to see colors as they were intended is hard. This might not seem like a big deal, but what happens when you put two colors together and not all visitors can see the images or text as you intended? For instance, some people can't distinguish between red and green or blue and yellow. Personal taste aside, not all colors go well together. Give some thought to your choice of color backgrounds and text combinations and ensure significant contrast.

Text Over Images

Not everyone can easily read text that has lines, multiple colors, and possibly other text behind it. Imagine a government seal with an image with a ring of text around it. Now put a paragraph of text over it. What happens to the letters in the paragraph? If the logo has the color black and the letters in the paragraph are on top of the black portion of the image, the letters are likely to disappear.

Believe it or not, even if the seal is a faded watermark, it doesn't matter. It might help a little but it is still a distraction.

Fonts

Some font families are more appealing than others. For instance, some fonts, such as Times New Roman, can make the words on the page appear slightly blurred if the size is less than 12 point. Verdana is considered a web-friendly font in all sizes.

PIXELS AND SERIFS

Monitors are made up of pixels — tiny blocks of light that form shapes on your screen. Pixels are typically square, although round-pixel monitors exist. When you try to present a curved edge with a series of square blocks, the edges of the curve can appear jagged or blurred.

Serifs are the little stems that get added to letters in some fonts (see Figure 5-61). Serifs have curved edges. The serifs can cause text to appear slightly blurred compared to sans-serif fonts like Arial. This can affect onscreen readability.

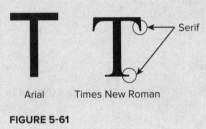

Arial   Times New Roman

FIGURE 5-61

Another consideration with fonts is their availability. When you install software on your computer, sometimes it comes with its own fonts, giving you font options that others don't necessarily have. If you choose to use a unique font as a way of branding your site, a chance exists that your visitors won't see the page the way you do. Fonts that are most available across operating systems include:

➤ Arial / Helvetica

➤ Times New Roman / Times

➤ Courier New / Courier

In addition, fonts such as Palatino and Verdana are available on many computers.

In addition to the font family, font size plays a role in visual appeal. Have you ever been on a page where you couldn't change the size of the font? You can prevent your visitors from changing the size of the text on your page and therefore potentially changing the page's look and feel. This practice is not recommended, and with the push for accessible pages, you don't see this issue much anymore. To help ensure your site is readable by the broadest possible audience, let your visitors change the font size if they need to.

Screen Clutter

A cluttered page can be distracting and overwhelming and can drive your visitors away. How can you tell whether your page is cluttered?

Ask yourself whether there is sufficient white space. Are the components on the page distinguishable? Next, do some user testing. User testing can tell you whether your target audience finds your page too busy and why. Remember, different audiences like different page layouts and styles.

Your audience might like a screen full of things to do or they might be minimalists and find a page with a lot of white space more visually appealing.

Consider the simple wireframes in Figure 5-62. Do either of the wireframes appear cluttered to you?

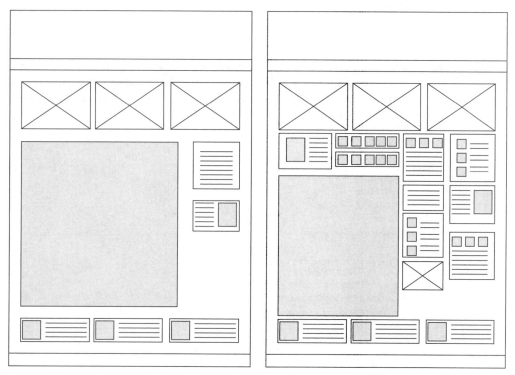

FIGURE 5-62

For some, a screen full of information is just what your audience wants; for others, it will be a turnoff. If you want to know whether your design is "appealing" and potentially usable, consider performing a paper usability test with a sample from your target audience.

Exploring the Theme

Do you need to know how a car engine works in order to drive a car? No. Do you need to know how all the code associated with a theme works in order to plan your design? No. Although the answer to both these questions is no, that doesn't mean a conversation with your car mechanic wouldn't be easier if you knew a little about how your engine works. The same logic applies to themes.

This section briefly explores the files in the theme that are used to create the pages you planned in your site structure and wireframes:

➤   .info — The .info file provides information about the theme, such as its name, the Drupal version it works on, setting features, and regions.

➤   template.php — This is where you place snippets of PHP code when you want to override a theme function or give the theme instructions.

➤ `.css` — Files that end in `.css` contain your styling, the Cascading Style Sheet (CSS) code that provides direction on layout, colors, fonts, and more.

➤ `.tpl.php` — Files that end in `.tpl.php` provide the HTML markup that produces what you see in your browser.

.info File

When you are looking at a theme on Drupal.org, it is not always easy to determine what regions it might have. If the theme description leaves you wondering, you can download and unpack the theme and locate the `.info` file. For example, Figure 5-32 illustrates the regions in the Zero Point theme. The `zeropoint.info` file defines those regions with the following code:

```
regions[left] = Left sidebar
regions[right] = Right sidebar
regions[above] = Above
regions[banner] = Banner
regions[header] = Header
regions[user1] = User 1
regions[user2] = User 2
regions[user3] = User 3
regions[user4] = User 4
regions[content_top] = Top content
regions[node_middle] = Middle node
regions[node_bottom] = Bottom node
regions[content_bottom] = Bottom content
regions[user5] = User 5
regions[user6] = User 6
regions[user7] = User 7
regions[user8] = User 8
regions[below] = Below
```

The names of the regions, such as `left`, `banner`, `user1`, and `below`, are decided by the developer of the theme. Some names are common, such as: `left`, `right` (also known as `first` and `last`), `content_top`, and `content_bottom`.

Template.php

Some themes provide options for managing the display of various page components. If you are not sure what a theme includes and you don't have time to install the theme and look at it, you can get a little insight by opening the `template.php` file and looking for a list of settings like the following:

```
$defaults = array(
    'style' => 'grey',
    'layout-width'    => 0,
    'sidebarslayout'  => 0,
    'themedblocks'    => 0,
    'blockicons'      => 2,
    'pageicons'       => 1,
    'menutype'        => 0,
    'navpos'          => 0,
```

```
    'roundcorners'      => 1,
    'headerimg'         => 1,
    'cssPreload'        => 0,
    'loginlinks'        => 1,
    'user_notverified_display'          => 1,
    'breadcrumb_display'                => 1,
    'search_snippet'                    => 1,
    'search_info_type'                  => 0,
    'search_info_user'                  => 1,
    'search_info_date'                  => 1,
    'search_info_comment'               => 1,
    'search_info_upload'                => 1,
    'mission_statement_pages'           => 'home',
    'front_page_title_display'          => 'title_slogan',
    'page_title_display_custom'         => '',
    'other_page_title_display'          => 'ptitle_stitle',
    'other_page_title_display_custom'   => '',
    'configurable_separator'            => ' | ',
    'meta_keywords'                     => '',
    'meta_description'                  => '',
    'taxonomy_display_default'          => 'only',
    'taxonomy_format_default'           => 'list',
    'taxonomy_enable_content_type'      => 0,
    'submitted_by_author_default'       => 1,
    'submitted_by_date_default'         => 1,
    'submitted_by_enable_content_type'  => 0,
    'siteid'                            => '',
    'fix_css_limit'                     => 0,
    'rebuild_registry'                  => 0,
);
```

Notice the `layout_width`, `sidebarslayout`, `breadcrumb_display`, `taxonomy_display_default`, `taxonomy_format_default`, `meta_descriptions`, and so on. This is a quick glimpse into some of the advanced theme setting options this theme provides. Some themes don't offer these features, whereas others offer more features.

.css Files

CSS can be stored in one or more `.css` files. The `.css` files can be found with all the other files or stored separately in a `css` directory. Although your theme has `.css` files, that doesn't mean that all the components on your page are being styled by the CSS in your theme. A module that creates a display such as a page or a block might have its own CSS file. To change how a module styles its display, you copy the module's CSS into your theme and edit the style. This is referred to as an *override*. It is not good practice to edit a module's files directly.

.tpl.php Files

The HTML markup for each page on your site is produced using template files that end in `.tpl` `.php`. There are many `.tpl.php` files, but the most common are those that define the page, node, block, and comment. Similar to CSS, modules that create a display will likely have a `.tpl.php` file.

Page

The code in `page.tpl.php` and the theme info file, combined with the CSS, defines the structure of the page (regions, main content area, sidebars, headers, footers, and so on).

If your wireframes have pages whose structure needs to vary from the rest of the site, you can create a page template file and the applicable CSS for that page. For instance, your theme can include a file called `page-blog.tpl.php`. With a little PHP in the `template.php` file, this template would render the layout for a node created with the blog content type. You can also create a template for a single node by using `page-node-2.tpl.php` (assuming the node ID is 2).

This might seem a little technical, especially if you aren't the one creating the theme, but understanding your options is important. The decisions you make now about the method by which a page layout will be rendered can influence update and maintenance processes later. For instance, if you know that the layout of your pages will likely need to change and you don't have the budget to hire a themer to make the changes you might need to consider using one of the content layout modules. Learning to configure a module is sometimes easier than learning how to theme.

CONTENT LAYOUT MODULES

The Panels module helps you override how the theme's `page.tpl.php` and CSS render the page without requiring you to know PHP, HTML, or CSS.

Node

The node shows in the content area of the page by default. The node has its own default template file, called `node.tpl.php`, which loads when the page loads. The node template is similar to the page template in that you can create different node templates for different types of content or specific nodes.

Figure 5-63 shows simple wireframes for three content types: page, event, and media. Notice that each content type has its own set of fields, which, in turn, have their own unique layout.

You can produce the page content type and media content type layouts using Drupal's configuration options because their fields are presented one after the other. The field arrangement in the event content type has fields next to each other, a layout requiring some additional effort. One option is to create a node template for the event content type.

NODE CONTENT LAYOUT MODULES

The Panels and Composite Layout modules allow you to arrange the fields of a node by placing the fields into preexisting panes or zones (similar to regions). For a more precise layout, you can edit your theme or you can use the Contemplate module. If you want to arrange the fields on the create/edit form for a content type or a web form, you could try the Arrange Fields module. Panels, Contemplate, and Arrange Fields each had recommended versions for Drupal 7. As of April 2011, work to port the Composite module to Drupal 7 has not started yet, but interest is there.

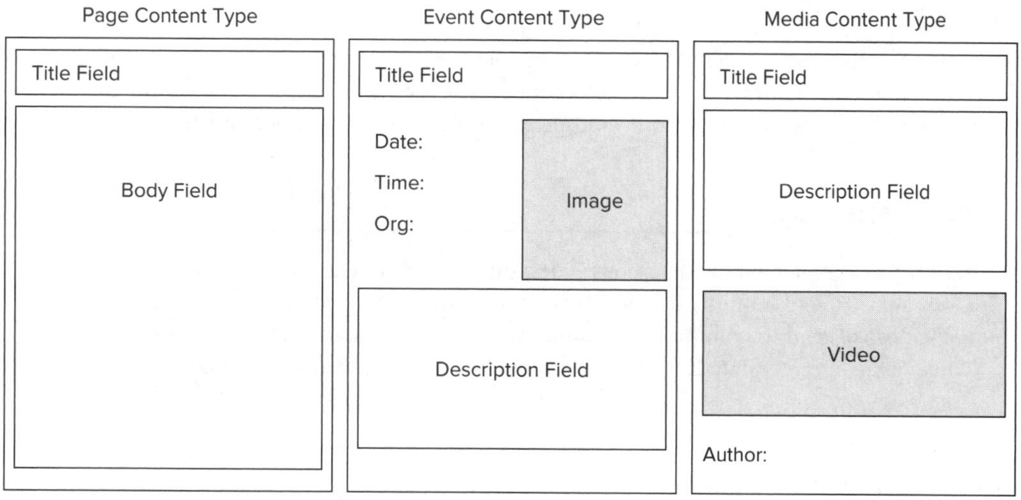

Page Content Type · Event Content Type · Media Content Type

FIGURE 5-63

Block

Just as with pages and nodes, code in a template file controls blocks — in this case, the `block.tpl`.`php` file. This template also loads when the page loads.

> **VIEWS BLOCKS**
>
> One of the most common ways to create blocks is via the Views module. When a block is generated by Views, one of Views' templates is used to create the layout of the block. If you want to theme a Views display, Views will give you file-naming conventions and the code you need to customize the layout of the display you want to change. In many cases, however, you need only create some CSS to customize your Views display.

When planning the look and feel of your blocks, you don't necessarily need to theme each block separately. This is where some planning can save time and resources. For instance, if you know that you will have a series of blocks across multiple pages that list nodes and you want that list to look a certain way, you can create theme code that applies to all blocks from that module. The cost associated with theming a site with a lot of custom blocks can be quite high if each block is themed separately.

> **BLOCK THEMING**
>
> The Skinr module enables the themer to define a set of reusable theme settings for your blocks — for example, create a block and select a block theme that will apply to that block. One block theme could have color behind the block title while another doesn't. Of course, you can make more significant differences.

Comment

Comments have their own template as well — `comment.tpl.php`. Similar to node templates, if you want comments to appear one way for the event content type and another way for the media content type (and so on), you can create unique comment templates for those content types.

> ### COMMENT FIELDS
>
> In Drupal 6, you need to use modules designed for comments, such as the Comment Upload module, to add fields to comments. In Drupal 7, you can add the same type of field to comments as you do nodes. For the same reasons you might create a custom template for a node, you might do the same for a comment.

Module Templates

As mentioned previously, modules can generate blocks and pages. For instance, the Search module will create a page with search results. The search results are not a node, but the content appears in the main content area of the theme. If you want your search results to appear in a specific way, you can override the `search-results.php.tpl` file.

> ### VIEWS PAGES
>
> A page is another type of display that you can create with the Views module. You can theme a Views page display the same way you can theme a Views block display.

With some pages, such as those created by the Views module, you get some help selecting the file-name of your template. Figure 5-64 is a screenshot from a view called story_menu. This information appears on the interface where you set up your view. If you edit a view and click on the Theme: Information link under Basic settings, you get the information shown in Figure 5-64.

The theme information provides a list of filenames that you can use when creating a template for your view page. If you wanted the story_menu page display to look different from the default layout provided by `views-view.tpl.php`, you could use a theme file called `views-view--story-menu--page.tpl.php`, place your custom markup in that file, and place that file in your theme directory. If you wanted to override all your view page displays, you could use `views-view--page.tpl.php`. This information and strategy is available for each view display, such as block.

> ### DEFAULT TEMPLATE THEME
>
> Drupal 7 ships with a theme called Stark that has been specifically designed to show you what your site would look like if you were using the core theme template files and any contributed module themes.

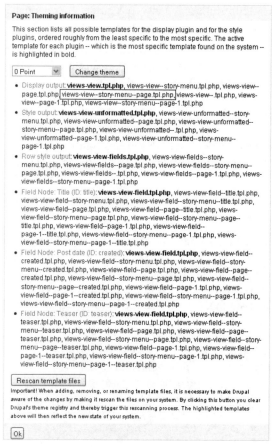

FIGURE 5-64

Drupal core and its contributed modules come with default templates, but you need to have a theme enabled to interact with the system. Drupal themes override the core templates (at a minimum, the page template). Depending on what you want your site to look like, you could end up overriding all the theming templates that come with Drupal and its modules. The amount of work to create a basic theme that relies on existing templates is less than the work required to customize each template. More work means more cost and time.

ACCESSIBILITY IN DRUPAL

Accessibility means that "people with disabilities can perceive, understand, navigate, and interact with the Web, and that they can contribute to the Web."[3] The Web Accessibility Initiative (WAI), at www.w3.org/WAI, provides guidelines widely regarded as the international standard for web accessibility. "In 1998, Congress amended the Rehabilitation Act of 1973 (29 U.S.C. 794d) as amended by

---

[3] Introduction to Web Accessibility: www.w3.org/WAI/intro/accessibility.php

the Workforce Investment Act of 1998 (P.L. 105 - 220), August 7, 1998 to require Federal agencies to make their electronic and information technology (EIT) accessible to people with disabilities."[4]

With that said, what does accessibility have to do with your theme and how does Drupal stand up against accessibility standards? First, your theme produces the HTML markup and CSS that creates accessible pages. For instance, Section 508 states "A text equivalent for every non-text element shall be provided (e.g., via "alt," "longdesc," or in element content)."[5] This means that your theme files (from your theme or from a module) need to be able to render the attributes that provide the text equivalent. Another 508 requirement states that "markup shall be used to associate data cells and header cells for data tables that have two or more logical levels of row or column headers." Simply put, this means your theme files need to create tables with header cells. These and many other requirements are associated with the HTML and CSS your theme produces.

How does Drupal stand up to being 508-compliant? It depends on the theme you choose, the modules you use, and the content that content developers insert into nodes.

If accessibility is a requirement for your site, you need to evaluate the theme and modules you select to ensure that the markup they generate is compliant. You also need to establish a review process to ensure that the content entered into a node is compliant. For instance, did the content developer copy and paste formatted content from a Microsoft Word document into a field with an editor? Depending on the editor, you can paste a lot of non-standard code into the body of a node.

 In each version of Drupal, the ability to create accessible pages has improved. In June of 2010, the Drupal Accessibility Statement was posted at `http://drupal.org/about/accessibility`*. For tips on how to ensure your site is accessible, review the article "Accessibility and Drupal" at* `http://drupal.org/node/394094`*. To find a 508-compliant theme, try* `http://drupal.org/project/themes?text=508`*. For an 11-point 508 checklist, check out* `http://drupal.org/node/465106`*.*

Testing for accessibility is going to be the key to ensuring your site is and remains compliant. If testing produces issues, you will need to determine the source of the issue. You might need to override a core or module theme template to remedy the situation.

MOBILE WEB

The statistics are staggering in regard to mobile web usage. The number of handheld devices being used to surf the Web is growing faster than you might imagine. The technical strategies for getting on the Web vary. What you want to do on the mobile Web will influence your options and the strategy you choose. For instance, do you want to provide quick and easy mobile-style access to content on your site? Maybe your goal is to provide an app that gives your audience quick and easy access to podcasts housed on your site. Plan now so that you can make informed decisions regarding the resources needed to go mobile.

---

[4] Standards: `www.section508.gov/index.cfm?fuseAction=stds`

[5] 1194.22 Web-based intranet and Internet information and applications: `www.section508.gov/index.cfm?fuseAction=stdsdoc#Web`

For additional information on mobile web development, consider Professional Mobile Web Development with WordPress, Joomla! and Drupal, *by James Pearce (Wrox, 2011).*

The most basic decision you need to make is whether you need a different version of your site for mobile devices. Most handheld devices come with the ability to view the Web the same way it is viewed via a laptop or desktop computer. Depending on your site's purpose and design, this might be all you need.

If you want a specific mobile presence, you need to plan. Depending on what you want for your mobile presence, you might need to walk through the requirements and design processes again. Following are some basic questions that will help you decide how much planning you need to do:

➤ Is the goal for the mobile presence different from that of the full site?

➤ Will your visitors need to log in?

➤ Will any of your site features need to be available, such as e-commerce, file download, animation interaction, and so on?

➤ Will the features run in a mobile environment?

➤ What content and components will you want to reuse or will you need a different set of components?

➤ What layout do you want to use?

➤ Will you want to use a separate domain for your mobile site?

➤ What strategy do you want to use for detecting mobile users so that you can redirect them to the mobile version of your site?

➤ Will you want mobile users to have the option to view the full site?

➤ Will you need to create different versions of your mobile site to accommodate different devices?

MOBILE DRUPAL

Modules and themes designed to support a mobile Drupal site are available. For instance, the Mobile Tools module provides features such as mobile user detection, redirection, and theme switching, as well as several other useful features. The Mobile Theme module enables you to choose a mobile theme. Each module is available in Drupal 6 and being ported to Drupal 7.

Several mobile themes are available as well. For instance, Mobile has a version for Drupal 6 and a -dev version for Drupal 7. Mobile Basic is new on the scene with a Drupal 7 -dev version. Or you can start with a base like Fusion Mobile and build your own mobile theme. Fusion Mobile also has a -dev release available for Drupal 7.

SUMMARY

Design involves more than colors and graphics; it also includes the structure of the site, the content layout, and the various interactions you want your visitors to experience.

When creating a design plan, remember that your site is comprised of many pages, each of which needs to be planned. Choose a strategy that allows you to plan in bulk. That is, create reusable patterns and designs for your components to help keep site and page development efficient and to maximize usability.

Although you can run multiple themes in your site, a good practice is to have one theme that can support most if not all of your page layouts. For those pages that need a layout other than what the theme supports, you can create custom theme templates and CSS or use a module designed to help you change your layout. The most common page that deviates from the norm is the home page.

And now, with your requirements and design in hand, you are ready for development.

PART II
Building and Sustaining Your Website

▶ **CHAPTER 6:** Planning Development

▶ **CHAPTER 7:** Coordinating Implementation

▶ **CHAPTER 8:** Sustaining the Site

Planning Development

The chapters in this book are presented using a waterfall methodology, proceeding from one phase of the project to the next. So, if you are following the chapters of this book on a real project, you have not started developing your site. In real life, the chances of that being true are slim. Many in the Drupal community prefer an agile or rapid application development (RAD) approach to development. Drupal's preexisting modules and flexibility provide a platform for rapid development as requirements are identified.

 If you are just diving into this book and are not familiar with development methodologies, you can get a brief introduction in Chapter 2, "Managing Open Source Projects."

Rapid development, no matter what strategy you embrace, assumes that you understand the modules being implemented and their ability to be flexible (or not) as additional requirements are identified. This chapter provides some insights that will help you gauge how far down the development path you want to go before all your requirements and design decisions have been made.

By the end of this chapter, you should be able to:

➤   Identify tasks that will help manage the development process

➤   Critique modules before installing them

➤   Distinguish between development and production environments

➤   Consider development sequences

➤   Pick a documentation strategy

➤   Facilitate a testing process

➤   Choose a method for populating a site

PLANNING A DEVELOPMENT PROCESS

No single way exists to develop a site or even plan the development of a site. However, common tasks get performed, either formally or informally. For instance, when a developer learns you want to insert images into your nodes, he or she will consider the available techniques for inserting images, choose one, and configure it. In short, the steps are as follows:

1. Identify the requirement.
2. Identify options to meet the requirement.
3. Evaluate the options in context with other requirements.
4. Choose an option.
5. Implement the chosen option.

Depending on the complexity of your site, this might be the process your developer uses. But many sites aren't that simple. The following tasks walk you through a process for planning your development:

1. Create requirements inventory.
2. Create a build recipe.
3. Identify development sequences.
4. Set up your environments.
5. Build your site.
6. Test your build.
7. Populate the site.
8. Go live.

In the long run, the development method you choose (waterfall, agile, RAD, and so on) will influence whether you will perform these tasks in part or in full as you develop your site. These tasks provide a way to:

➤ Manage expectations in regard to meeting requirements.

➤ Coordinate team talent.

➤ Document development decisions that can be referenced during maintenance and site enhancements.

Until you have made your decision regarding development methodologies, reviewing the tasks in this chapter will give you insight into basic development decisions that get made when configuring a Drupal site.

CREATING A REQUIREMENTS INVENTORY

This section kicks off the requirements inventory topic with an analogy. Imagine that you have a bunch of stuff to store, so you go to the store and buy storage containers. While packing your stuff, you realize you didn't buy containers that could hold all your stuff. If you had created an inventory of your stuff, assessed the nature of your stuff, and evaluated your container options before buying, you might have made the right container decisions.

The same idea applies to development. By inventorying the components you need to develop, you can assess the nature of the components and how they relate to each other. Having a view of the big picture will help you make decisions that integrate well with each other.

In Drupal, as with many other content management systems, the development process is not necessarily performed page by page. Many functions and features in Drupal interconnect with each other or get shared from one feature to the next. To determine which modules and configuration settings are best for your site, knowing as much as possible about what will be required can help.

To help illustrate this point, consider the simple site flowchart and wireframe shown in Figure 6-1.

From this simple chart, you know that you need some blocks, content, and navigation, at a minimum. But is this enough to know how to develop the site? No. If all you had to go on was that flowchart, you might need to ask the following questions. If a detailed set of requirements and wireframes accompanied the flowchart, the answers to these questions should be available.

➤ How many content types will you need?

- ➤ Will any of the content types hold content that will be categorized?
- ➤ Will any of the content types have unique fields, or will all the fields be the same?
- ➤ Will any of the content types be used by one user role?

➤ How many blocks are there?

- ➤ Will any of the blocks repeat from one section to another?
- ➤ Will repeating blocks from one section to another remain in the same place?
- ➤ Will any of the blocks appear in the content area?
- ➤ Will any of the blocks' appearance and/or content be subject to conditions that are present when a page loads?

➤ How many landing pages will there be?

- ➤ Will section landing pages need breadcrumbs?
- ➤ Will all section landing pages look the same?
- ➤ Will section landing page layouts be different from the theme structure?

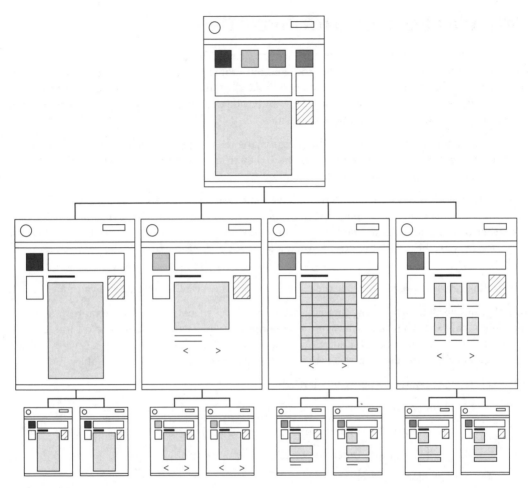

FIGURE 6-1

➤ How many different navigational strategies will be used?

    ➤ Will you use menus?

    ➤ Will you use dynamic lists?

    ➤ Will you use node outlines?

    ➤ Will you use breadcrumbs?

- ➤ Are breadcrumbs required?
  - ➤ Will each section of the site have breadcrumbs?
  - ➤ Will breadcrumbs be based on a menu, outline, vocabulary term hierarchy, or something else?
- ➤ Will SEO-friendly URLs be used?
  - ➤ Will the paths be generated automatically or manually?
  - ➤ Will all types of content have their paths defined the same way?
- ➤ Will content access need to be restricted?
  - ➤ Will the restrictions be based on site sections?
  - ➤ Will the restrictions be based on roles?
  - ➤ Will the restrictions be based on content types?
- ➤ Will there be a need to categorize content?
  - ➤ Will those terms be available to the end user?
  - ➤ Will the terms be used in prepackaged queries?

Obviously, these are not all the possible questions but probably enough to make a point. The answers to some questions won't necessarily impact the development process, but others will. Although wireframes are a great place to start, documented requirements complete the picture.

 Chapter 10, "Example Build Recipes," has a sample requirements inventory for the site defined in Chapter 9, "An Example Plan."

CREATING A BUILD RECIPE

A *build recipe* is just another way of referring to the combination of modules and module configurations needed to build the inventory you just created. Following is a review of decisions you want to make in order to create your build recipe.

Selecting a Drupal Profile

If you are new to Drupal, you might not know you can choose from different Drupal distributions (also known as installations). They are still Drupal but they come with preinstalled contributed modules and sometimes custom modules that make the profile support a certain type of site. Some commonly known profiles include:

➤ Acquia Drupal, from Acquia

➤ Drupal Commons, from Acquia

➤ Open Atrium, originally developed by Development Seed and currently owned and maintained by Phase2 Technology

➤ Open Publish, from Phase2 Technology

➤ Open Public, from Phase2 Technology

➤ Pressflow, from Four Kitchens

For a list of other profiles, see "Installation Profiles," at `http://drupal.org/project/installation+profiles`.

Before you make a decision, perform the next task of selecting modules that will support your requirements and design. If you find that the module and configuration strategies used in one of the distributions match the solution you would use, then that profile might be a quick way to get the development ball rolling and be a way to save you time and money.

But quick is not always best. Before you commit to a profile, look at the package. Are you wedded to that profile after you have it? That is, is it customized such that using the default version of Drupal to update your site would create issues with the customization provided in the installation? Will the customization in these profiles continue to be supported? The issue of continued support will always be a consideration, whether you are using a distribution or any contributed module. Answering this question won't be easy in all cases. Investigate who developed the distribution. Ask questions of the developer. Research the issue queue on Drupal.org to see how the developer is managing bugs, support requests, and feature requests. Evaluating a distribution is similar to evaluating modules, which is discussed the following section.

Selecting Modules

Assume that you are going to use the basic Drupal installation found on Drupal.org. Your next step is to identify the module combinations that you will use to build your site. As discussed in the following sections, you should consider several evaluation points when selecting a module.

Supporting the Requirement

The first evaluation point, of course, is the module's ability to meet your requirements. Drupal's modular approach to development means you might need more than one module to build one feature. Some developers prefer assembling multiple modules to create a feature, as opposed to seeking out one module that does it all. A challenge with seeking out a do-it-all module is whose definition of do-it-all it supports.

Avoiding Module Conflicts

When selecting a combination of modules to support different features or a group of modules to create one feature, you need to consider module conflict. Sometimes, one or more modules may conflict with other modules. Known conflicts are sometimes posted on the module's project page on Drupal .org. Sometimes, you can learn about them in the module's issue queue. The module developer probably won't know about a conflict until someone reports it.

Some conflicts are fixable, whereas others are not. It depends on:

➤ Which APIs the module relies on

➤ Whether the module is changing or overriding a core function

➤ Whether the module is contrary to what the other module is doing

If the conflict is fixable, the module developer still might not be able to fix it. Hearing, "It doesn't break when I do that" from the module developer may mean that your development team needs to fix the problem, given that you have the environment where the conflict is occurring.

> **MODULE PATCHES**
>
> If you find a conflict, a chance exists that someone else found the conflict and has submitted a patch. The patch might need review or you might find that the patch has been accepted into the -dev version of the module but is not ready to be in the recommended version. If you patch the module, the practice is to contribute the patch back to the module developer in the event others have a similar issue. But before you do, be sure you have permission to contribute the patch.

Selecting Active and Supported Modules

Over time, developers of modules get busy on other tasks and don't have time to continue development on the module they donated. As core updates and contributed module updates occur, the probability that other modules will need to be updated as well increases. You will know whether a module needs to be updated if you perform an update to one or more modules or to core and you suddenly get an error on the site. If you select a module that is not actively supported and the new bug is related to that module, you might have to remedy the situation yourself or pay the module developer to do it.

You might be wondering how to know whether the module is actively supported. Several clues indicate a module's support. The following sections explore the project page for an active and popular contributed module called Views, located at `http://drupal.org/project/views`.

Project Information

Figure 6-2 shows the Project Information section of the Views module's page at Drupal.org (as of January 2011).

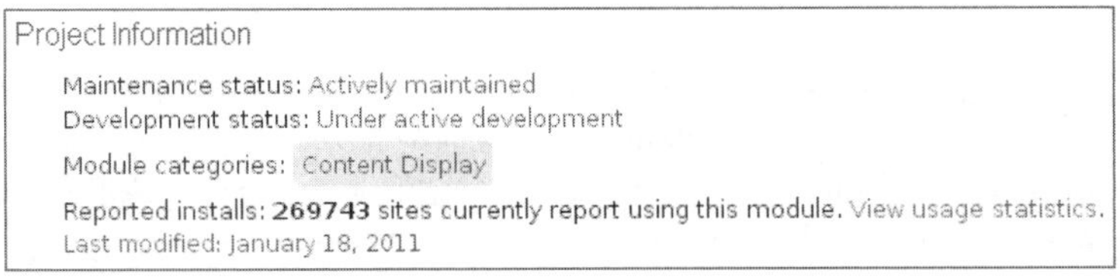

Project Information

Maintenance status: Actively maintained
Development status: Under active development

Module categories: Content Display

Reported installs: **269743** sites currently report using this module. View usage statistics.
Last modified: January 18, 2011

FIGURE 6-2

Does the development status indicate that the module is under active development? If the maintenance status says unknown or inactive, you risk not getting any support if an issue arises. A high number of reported installations is another indication of the module's popularity. The more popular the module, the greater probability the module will be supported, if not by the module developer, then by others in the community. Not all modules need to be modified frequently, but if open issues exist and the last modified date is recent, the module developer is working to support the module.

Version Dates

Another way to assess the activity level of a module is to look at the version dates. Figure 6-3 shows the version dates for the Views module (as of May 2011).

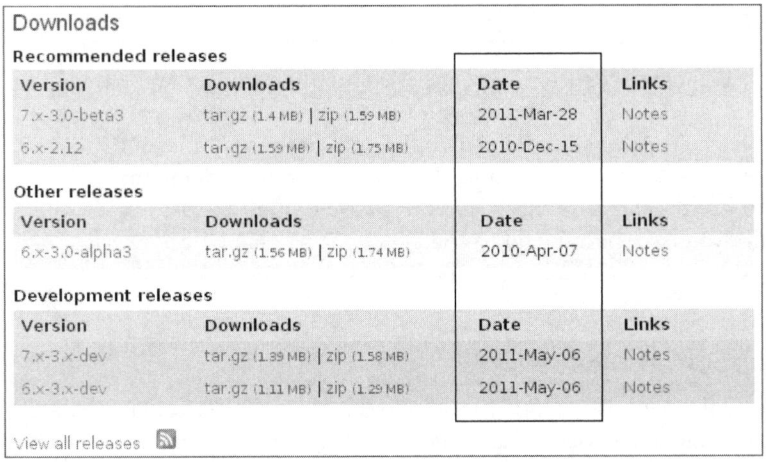

Downloads

Recommended releases

Version	Downloads	Date	Links
7.x-3.0-beta3	tar.gz (1.4 MB) | zip (1.59 MB)	2011-Mar-28	Notes
6.x-2.12	tar.gz (1.59 MB) | zip (1.75 MB)	2010-Dec-15	Notes

Other releases

Version	Downloads	Date	Links
6.x-3.0-alpha3	tar.gz (1.56 MB) | zip (1.74 MB)	2010-Apr-07	Notes

Development releases

Version	Downloads	Date	Links
7.x-3.x-dev	tar.gz (1.39 MB) | zip (1.58 MB)	2011-May-06	Notes
6.x-3.x-dev	tar.gz (1.11 MB) | zip (1.29 MB)	2011-May-06	Notes

View all releases

FIGURE 6-3

Dates are not necessarily an indicator that the module is not supported, but if a version date for both the recommended and development releases is more than a year old, you should look further to see whether the dates are old because there haven't been any issues to address.

Open Issues

Figure 6-4 shows issue information (from January 2011) about the Views module. If you are new to Drupal and don't know better, you might think you should avoid this module because it has 865 open issues and 304 bugs. Although issue statistics are an indication of the health of a module, they can be misleading.

The first thing to understand about these statistics is that the open issues include feature requests and support requests, as well as bugs that are in various states of being addressed. Also, the bugs may or may not be actual bugs in the module; they could be unusual issues unique to the user of the module, or they could be associated with a version of the module still in development. Sometimes, bugs are reported but not enough information exists to provide support. When using these statistics to evaluate modules, scanning the issues and seeing what people are talking about is best. Look at how many of them apply to the version you will be using.

FIGURE 6-4

Dependencies

Several modules depend on the Views module, and until recently, Views did not depend on another module. Figure 6-5 shows a statement indicating that the Views module for Drupal 7 has a dependency on the Chaos Tool Suite (CTools).

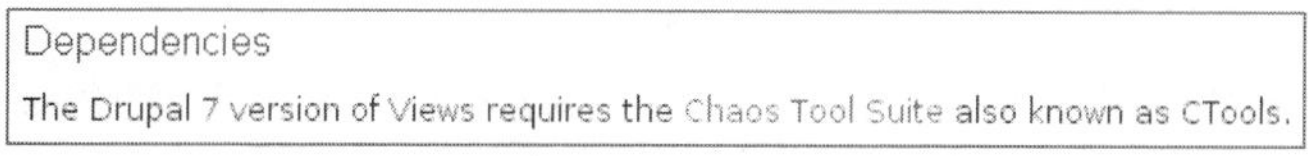

Dependencies

The Drupal 7 version of Views requires the Chaos Tool Suite also known as CTools.

FIGURE 6-5

Why consider dependencies? Assume module A has a dependency on module B. One can assume that the developer of module A has a vested interest in the success of module B because without module B, module A won't work. Sometimes, the developer of module A might help support module B to ensure module A can continue to exist. This assessment criterion is not perfect but it might be an indicator that more than one person is interested in supporting a module.

Consider the dependency of Views for Drupal 7 on CTools. On the surface, the appearance is that the developer of Views would have a vested interest in making sure the developer of CTools continues to support CTools. In this case, it just so happens that the developer of CTools and Views is the same person, so the CTools module will likely be supported.

There are other types of dependencies to note. For instance, there are modules that depend on third-party applications. The Wysiwyg module allows HTML editors to be used on a Drupal site. In this case, the editors are not Drupal modules but applications, such as CKEditor (http://ckeditor.com/) and TinyMCE (http://tinymce.moxiecode.com/). The files for each editor are placed within your Drupal site directories.

Another type of dependency is between a module and an application you need running on your server. For instance, the ImageCache module requires either ImageMagick (www.imagemagick .org) or the GD2 library (http://libgd.org or https://bitbucket.org/pierrejoye/ gd-libgd/overview). These applications are not installed in your Drupal directory. For installation information, see www.php.net/manual/en/refs.utilspec.image.php.

Sponsors

A module with one or more Drupal vendors as its sponsor has a better chance of being maintained than one supported by only one person. It is implied, but not assumed, that Drupal vendors have multiple resources that can provide support. Figure 6-6 shows that the Views module is sponsored. It should be noted that Earl Miles (aka, merlonofchaos) dedicated three weeks to the initial development of the Views module in 2005. Since then, Views has been instrumental in Drupal's continued growth.

Sponsorship

- This project is sponsored by IO1. We provide specialist consulting services in Enterprise Drupal, Views & Panels. Visit us at www.io1.biz or Contact us.

FIGURE 6-6

Assessing Module Quality

Just because a module can do what you need it to do, that doesn't mean its code is well written. To some extent, coding is like writing. You might see someone else's writing and think, "I would have written that sentence differently." That doesn't mean the sentence is wrong; it just means that it could be different or better, depending on your own style.

Assessing code quality is somewhat of a subjective process, but you can use objective measures to get you past code style differences. The following sections provide five perspectives you can consider when assessing the quality of contributed modules and custom modules developed for your site as well.

Defects

Defects are imperfects in code that cause inadequate performance or failure in the functionality of the module. Obviously, you don't want defects in your module code. Defects are not always easy to detect. For instance, if you do not have your site set to show errors on the page or log them, you might not know there is an issue. On the surface, your site might appear fine, but in the background, you could have problems.

While developing, you can either show errors or log your errors. When using logs to track issues, you need to understand that Drupal has logs and the server has logs, and they don't always match. Server logs will provide details that your service provider will need in order to investigate what might be going wrong. What you might think is a defect in your code could be conflict with a setting on your server.

> ### DRUPAL AND SERVER ISSUES
>
> Apache, the open source application that provides web services to your server, will likely have ModSecurity running. Depending on how your server is configured, you might need to adjust the settings for the mod_security module, as some of its rules may disrupt Drupal's normal operation. For more information, visit `http://drupal.org/node/695902`.

With new code, don't be surprised if you think it is working and then suddenly it is not. Each time you add another module to your site, you increase the risk of a code conflict. If you haven't added a module but you have made other changes, such as adding content or changing module configurations, these tasks can trigger an issue as well.

For instance, assume your module code defines a field called Email. Your code assumes it is going to get an email address. Unless you remember to verify that the data entered is formatted correctly, your module could stop working. Users are great at doing the unexpected — that's why testing is important.

CODE REVIEW

Drupal includes a number of modules to aid you in reviewing your code. For example, the Coder module (available for Drupal 6 and Drupal 7) provides two modules: Coder Review (for code review) and Coder Upgrade (for code manipulation).

Another module that aids in code development is Grammar Parser, available for Drupal 7. It helps you analyze and modify a source code file.

The Secure Code Review module provides additional review services associated with writing secure code. As of May 2011, there was a -dev release for Drupal 7.

Variable-Based Coding

Variables are containers that store data. If you are new to this concept, imagine the following equation: 3 + 4 = 7. This can also be written a + b = c, where a, b, and c are variables. If you create a form and collect values for a and b, you can write a function that computes c and returns that value to your user. The practice of including data in your code is referred to as *hard-coding*.

In a dynamic system, hard-coding data into code is not a great practice. If you need to change the data used by the module, you shouldn't have to change the code. Also, if you plan on contributing the module to the community, you will need a way for others to insert the data they need. So, a good coding practice is to use variables. If the data associated with variables needs to be stored for reuse on a regular basis, you could create a specific database table for the data or you can use Drupal's default Variables table, located in the database.

Standards

Does the code meet Drupal's standards for coding? With so many developers creating and sharing code, following Drupal's coding standards is a good practice for every developer. You can find more information about coding standards at `http://drupal.org/coding-standards`.

Even if you, the developer, are not going to share your custom module with the community, you might not be the only developer to work on the site. You will help future developers follow what you have done and not have to redo your work later if you follow Drupal's coding standards.

Security

In order to understand some basic secure coding practices, you need to understand a little about how data gets:

➤ Entered and stored

➤ Retrieved and displayed

Figure 6-7 is a conceptual illustration of how data is entered and stored.

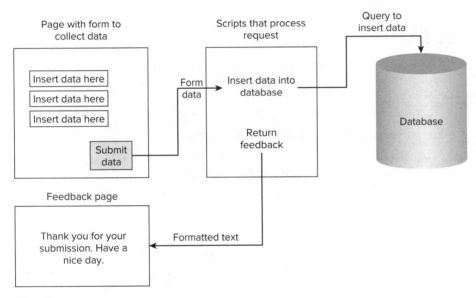

FIGURE 6-7

Figure 6-8 is a conceptual illustration of how data is retrieved and displayed.

If you are using one of Drupal's many features to create your forms, collect and store data, query the data, and display it, you are already using Drupal's secure coding practices. If you are creating a module that performs these types of processes, you need to make sure your code also uses Drupal's secure coding practices.

Following are some common practices to check for when assessing a module's secure coding practices:

➤ Ensure users should have access to the form to enter data and/or to retrieve data.

➤ Check the status of the data being retrieved to see if it should be retrieved (e.g., is it published?).

➤ Check that data entered into the form meets formatting requirements.

➤ Use POST and GET appropriately.

➤ Use placeholders in the database queries to prevent SQL injection attacks.

➤ Sanitize the output from the query so that any inappropriate formatting or code that was stored on input is not executed on output.

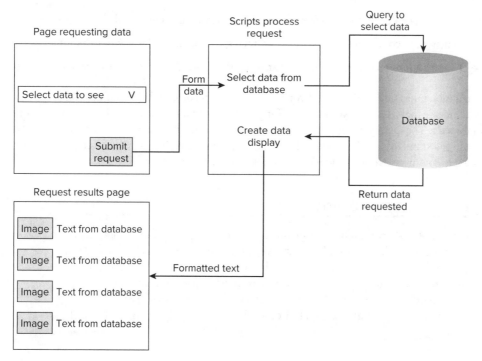

FIGURE 6-8

Contributed modules from Drupal.org likely have been tested by several community members, including those looking for security-related issues. When you develop your own modules, just you and your team are doing the testing. Take extra care to evaluate the new code you have developed.

Security issues are reported to the Drupal Security Team, which provides a list of advisories at http://Drupal.org/security. The advisories describe the issue and any available solutions. You can subscribe to the security announcements newsletter if you want to monitor security updates.

A review of a specific module's issue queue can also reveal whether someone has reported a security issue and the solution. Drupal's community of seasoned developers has a vested interest in using secure code, so a strong chance exists that any initial issues will be caught before the module gets too far along in its distribution.

 Cracking Drupal (Wiley, 2009) provides valuable information about vulnerabilities and security-related issues that you can use to evaluate your site and modules.

Code Documentation

Another way to assess the quality of the module is by the documentation included within the code. This might be a personal preference, but well-commented code is a sign that a developer recognizes the following:

➤ Others might need to edit the code and comments will help them edit the correct portion.

➤ Commenting the code is more efficient than trying to remember later what the intent was.

➤ The Drupal community uses comments for more than just documenting the developer's intent.

Code documentation takes time and effort. If you want well-commented code in your custom modules or custom theme, include that as part of your request for proposal so that the developer knows to accommodate the requirement. The quality of the comments can be somewhat subjective, so if code comments are important, include a standard by which you will evaluate the comments. If you are a developer, consider submitting sample comments from past work as examples of what you are proposing.

CODE COMMENT STANDARDS

The purpose of code comments can be more than just to provide explanations of what a snippet of code is doing. For instance, they can provide information about functions and variables that are supported by the module or theme but are not enabled by default. The Doxygen and comment-formatting conventions are located at `http://drupal.org/node/1354`. Doxygen is a documentation generator for various programming languages, including PHP.

Assessing Module Accessibility

Chapter 5, "Creating a Design Plan," briefly addressed the Web Accessibility Initiative and the need for accessibility compliance. Although the theme is used to produce the markup that becomes the page in the browser, you still need to ensure the output the module produces is compliant.

For example, assume you have a module that allows you to add an image. The module should provide a way to allow the user to add a value to the ALT attribute so that value can be read by automated screen readers. Or assume the module produces a data table. The cells in the first row of the table should be table headers.

If you need to ensure accessibility, allow time in your development schedule to evaluate the modules accordingly.

Vetting Module Combinations

One way to vet a module combination is to read the modules' documentation to determine if there are any known conflicts or coding deficiencies that would prevent two or more modules from working with each other. Unfortunately, the quality of documentation can vary from module to module, so reviewing the docs might not yield everything you need to know.

Another step you can take, assuming you don't already have experience with the modules being considered, is to install and test the module combination to see whether or how it will work. You might have to do this for each solution you identify to see whether it is the right solution for you. For instance, assume you have a requirement to moderate content before it goes live. You can do this in several ways, and each way has its own processes. Until you try them out, you might not know which processes are needed and supportable or which options might conflict with other site requirements.

Identifying Module Compromises

As you identify module combinations and development strategies, the following scenarios might surface:

➤ You might come across requirements that are not perfectly supported.

➤ You might need to use a -dev version of a module if you want that functionality.

➤ Times may occur when meeting requirements entails customization outside the budget.

When any of the preceding scenarios is the case, you might need to revisit your requirements and design to decide whether the requirement or design component is worth the additional effort or potential risk of using -dev code.

Getting Module Feedback

Who seeks feedback from whom? If you are a site owner working with a developer and want to maintain and enhance your site on your own after it is launched, you need to understand why certain modules are being selected over others. You might want to require that the developer provide a development plan with the modules to be used and how those modules will support the requirements and design.

Another time when module feedback might be needed is if the requirements aren't clear. As a developer, you might see several solutions to a requirement, depending on how that requirement is interpreted. If you choose a solution without first discussing your decision with the site owner, you might not deliver a solution the owner anticipated. Seeking clarification saves time and effort in the long run.

The idea of feedback may be obvious, but is mentioned here as a reminder that benefits are associated with keeping all parties informed. Seeking feedback takes time, so be sure to plan accordingly.

Planning Custom Modules

Depending on the site you are creating, you might know from the start that you will need one or more custom modules. Or you might come to this understanding after reviewing existing modules only to find that none exist that do exactly what you need. When developing your own modules, you should consider a few things:

➤ Determine module scope

➤ Test modules

➤ Contribute modules

➤ Maintain modules

➤ Choose module developers

➤ Choose between modules and themes

Determining Module Scope

As discussed in the following sections, scope is not only about what you want a feature to do but also how it is packaged.

Module Functionality

When you describe the functionality you need in a module, a strong chance exists that after you have the module, you will notice that something is missing. Or you might notice that the new functionality has had a ripple effect on other modules or even Drupal's core — in other words, a conflict.

Is it scope creep to add the functionality you forgot? Maybe. Is it scope creep to address the conflicts? Some developers will see it as such, and others won't. As a developer, you benefit by understanding which modules are in play on the site so that you can avoid conflicts. As a site owner, discuss with your developer the possibility of module conflicts and agree up front how to rectify the situation. That way, both parties have managed expectations before a potential issue arises.

Packaging Modules

A module is a bundle of code. The bundle of code can do many things. For instance, the scope of the module might be one feature or several features bundled together.

One way to decide whether multiple features should be bundled into one module is to consider whether you might need to disable one of the features in the future. If several features are bundled in one module and you disable the module, you not only lose the feature you are trying to disable but also other features you didn't want to disable.

The challenges associated with bundling multiple features into one module might sound obvious, but sometimes, a developer will create a module called "Site name" and place in it a series of small features or feature enhancements to support several requirements. Bundling might make sense at times. For instance, the module could include a feature of overrides to several modules, each override making small tweaks in the other module's labeling, format, and so on. It is not necessarily bad practice, but you do need to understand and plan for it. If you bundle several features, be sure the code is documented so that you know which function performs which task. That way, if you ever need to break the module into separate modules, you can.

Testing Modules

As a module is being built, the developer should perform unit testing on the various functions or methods included in the module. "Unit testing is the art and practice of taking a small portion of code, a unit, and subjecting it to programmatic tests to prove its correctness."[1] The developer will

---

[1] Douglass, Robert, An Introduction to Unit Testing in Drupal: www.lullabot.com/articles/introduction-unit-testing

likely perform basic use case testing to confirm that the module performs to the specifics presented in the module requirements.

But developer testing might not be enough. As mentioned in the earlier section on assessing module quality, one of several aspects to evaluate is a module's potential for defects.

AUTOMATED TESTING

The SimpleTest module provides a framework for automated unit testing in Drupal. It provides test scenarios and allows you to create your own. The documentation for SimpleTest is located at http://drupal.org/simpletest.

In order to plan your module testing process, you need to identify what is expected of the module. This not only includes the functionality of the module but also how the module's quality will be assessed. You might need to perform a complete assessment prior to the end of the project if you are using an iterative and/or incremental development methodology and the module is a milestone deliverable (versus end-of-project deliverable).

Testing processes and methods can vary. A testing process might include the following:

➤ Requirements that define how the module should perform

➤ A unit testing tool and applicable test case

➤ A way to provide an independent assessment of the module's performance in accordance with requirements, standards, use cases, and various controls that influence how a task or step is performed

➤ End users who can perform the tasks and then document the tasks they were performing when the module experienced an issue

➤ A way to collect issues and manage their resolution

➤ A code evaluator who understands the quality standards the module needs to meet

➤ A schedule for testing and repair

It is one thing to imagine the task the module needs to perform; it's another to actually do it. Your testing process might reveal deficiencies in the initial requirements and/or design of the module. The identification of requirement deficiencies is an opening for scope creep. It is important to know this is a possibility. Agreements between site owner and developer should help manage expectations associated with refining the functionality of a module.

Contributing Modules

One reason so many modules exist to choose from in the community is that people contribute their custom modules. Before code can be shared with the community, the rightful owner of the code needs to agree to share it. Who is the rightful owner of the code — the site owner or the developer? This topic should be addressed in the contract between site owner and developer before development takes place.

Maintaining Modules

Are you going to keep your module or share it? Either way, the module needs to be maintained. Before you commit to a custom module, are you ready to maintain it? All modules are susceptible to breakage when core or contributed modules are updated, whether the module was developed in-house or by the community. The process of maintenance is different for modules you contribute to the community and modules you keep in-house.

In-house module maintenance focuses on ensuring that your custom module continues to work on your site. This means you need to have the resources on hand to update the module when other updates are performed.

If you contribute your module and want to maintain it in the community, you will be responsible for responding to issues that are submitted by members of the community who try to use your module. Your module will be evaluated the same way the contributed modules on your site are evaluated.

If you do not have the resources to maintain the module either in-house or in the community, you could contribute it to the community and announce that you are looking for a maintainer. If others find your contribution useful, you might get a taker. You won't have control over this person unless you negotiate that kind of relationship, but at the least, you have potentially helped others in the community succeed with their sites.

Choosing Module Developers

The hiring process for a Drupal developer is not different from hiring any other individual or vendor. You define the work, advertise, evaluate those interested, and make a decision. This process has a greater chance of succeeding if the description of the work is accurate and you know what to look for in the candidates. Because the topic is module development, following are a few tips to help you screen your candidates:

- ➤ **Module quantity matters** — The skills required to build one module are not necessarily the skills needed to build multiple modules that need to integrate with each other and the rest of your site. A module developer can be a person with PHP skills and knowledge of how to develop for Drupal. For more complex sites, you are likely to need a software architect and maybe one or more developers.

- ➤ **It's more than just PHP** — Yes, Drupal is developed with PHP, but not all PHP web development practices are going to integrate well with Drupal. For instance, if you pick up a book on learning PHP for the Web, you will likely learn how to create a form, capture data with that form, and store the data in a database. The process you would use in that scenario is different from what you would use when creating a form and storing data in Drupal. Drupal has an extensive set of APIs (functions) that developers need to use in order for their modules to work with Drupal.

- ➤ **Use Drupal tools** — There are several modules and/or applications designed specifically to support best practices in Drupal development. A Drupal developer should know what they are and how to use them. Three examples are Drush, Devel, and SimpleTest.

- ➤ **Configure before coding** — In addition to knowing how to use Drupal's APIs, a developer also needs insights into how the modules they are developing will integrate into the configuration of the site. Therefore, a module developer should be able to configure a Drupal site using existing core and contributed modules. For instance, if you need a module that adds a feature to a node, the developer needs to understand how nodes are created (in other words, the role of the content type).

➤ **It is more than code** — Developing is more than writing code. There are Drupal coding practices to be followed as well as testing to be performed. Drupal development practices (`http://drupal.org/contributors-guide`) and books (`http:/drupal.org/books`) are available on the topic of developing for Drupal. A developer should be familiar with Drupal development practices.

The point is to make sure that your developer knows Drupal. That the developer has worked with other PHP-based systems doesn't mean he or she can use those practices when developing a Drupal site.

 If you are going to develop for Drupal, you need to become familiar with the Drupal APIs, located at `http://api.drupal.org`. *The first page presents a list of Drupal components, and reading about these first is recommended.*

Planning Theme Development

When creating a build recipe for your site, don't forget about the theme. In Part I, "Planning Your Website," you learned the following about themes:

➤ A theme is a bundle of code and images used to create what you see in the browser.

➤ You can use a preexisting theme or create your own.

➤ You use the theme's regions, sidebars, and main content area to display your page components.

➤ You can configure the placement of the regions, sidebars, and main content area to support many different layouts.

➤ Your theme pages are made up of several template files (page, node, block, and so on) joined together to form the page.

➤ Drupal's core modules and contributed modules contain theming instructions in the event your theme does not have instructions for that type of page component.

➤ You can override the default layout of the theme by adding new template files and/or using content layout modules.

The preceding information was provided to help you design page layouts that could be supported in a theme as well as predict when your design might deviate from your theme's default structure. Page layouts that deviate from your theme's configuration will require additional development effort in order to reach your layout goals.

As you might guess, not all themes need to be created equal. When planning the development of your theme, you need to decide whether you want to:

➤ Start from scratch or use a preexisting theme base

➤ Provide basic configuration settings or advanced theme settings

To make these decisions, you need to be aware of your options.

Creating Themes from Scratch

What does it mean to create a theme from scratch? Some might say it means you start with a blank file and manually create all the code for the template files and CSS yourself. Others would say you make copies of the `.tpl` files that come with Drupal and its modules, override them where necessary, and create your own CSS.

If you want to build your theme from scratch, several theming books are available that can help you get exactly what you want. Although it is possible to create a Drupal theme starting with nothing, you might not want to. The time and effort to reinvent the wheel might not be worth it.

Before you commit to coding everything on your own, take a look at the base themes (also known as starter themes) that are already available. Base themes enable you to kick-start your theming process, while at the same time helping you use good Drupal theming practices. The following sections focus on using base themes or starter themes to reduce your time and effort and to increase the chances that your theme includes all the features you need and not have defects.

> **BASE THEMES**
>
> Several base or starter themes are available at Drupal.org. Themes such as Zen, AdaptiveTheme, Fusion, Basic, NineSixty, LayoutStudio, and others provide varying degrees of preexisting functionality and documentation to help you create the theme you need.

Using a Base Theme

To make an informed decision regarding the use of a base theme, you need to understand the concept of subthemes. Most, if not all, base themes assume you will use a subtheme when using the base theme.

Consider this analogy. Drupal is the core to the content management system (CMS), and you can add different modules to the core and come up with different types of sites. Well, base themes and subthemes are similar. You install the base theme and then use a subtheme to enhance or modify the base into what you want. The base theme provides the "core" of the theme. You can override as much of the base theme as you want using the subtheme, just as you can override Drupal's core functionality using modules.

Subthemes are useful when your site needs multiple looks depending on the section of the site. For instance, assume you are creating a business site and each department wants its own color scheme. One way to manage this is to create a series of subthemes that are then assigned to each department's site section.

GUI THEMING TOOL

The Sweaver module, available for both Drupal 6 and Drupal 7, provides a graphical user interface that helps you change the CSS in your theme without having to open the CSS files and edit them.

Choosing a Base Theme

Themes are projects on Drupal.org, just as modules are projects. The criteria you use to evaluate modules are similar to the criteria you would use to evaluate a theme, whether it is a base theme or not. The theme should:

➤ Support your design

➤ Work with the modules in use

➤ Be actively supported

➤ Produce accessible markup

After you have narrowed down the base themes that meet these criteria, your next step is determining whether the theme provides the configuration settings you need.

Basic Configuration Settings

When you install Drupal, your site already has a theme enabled, ready to be configured. In Drupal 6, the Garland theme is enabled; in Drupal 7, the Bartik theme is enabled. You can configure the global settings and theme-specific settings.

Figure 6-9 shows the global settings in Drupal 6. Notice that you can choose to show features such as the mission statement, slogan, search, and so on. You also can upload your own logo.

Figure 6-10 shows the theme-specific settings for the Garland theme in Drupal 6. Notice that the settings page does not include "Display post information on," which is included in the global settings. Also note that Garland has a theme-specific setting for color. The color wheel is not a standard theme option in contributed themes.

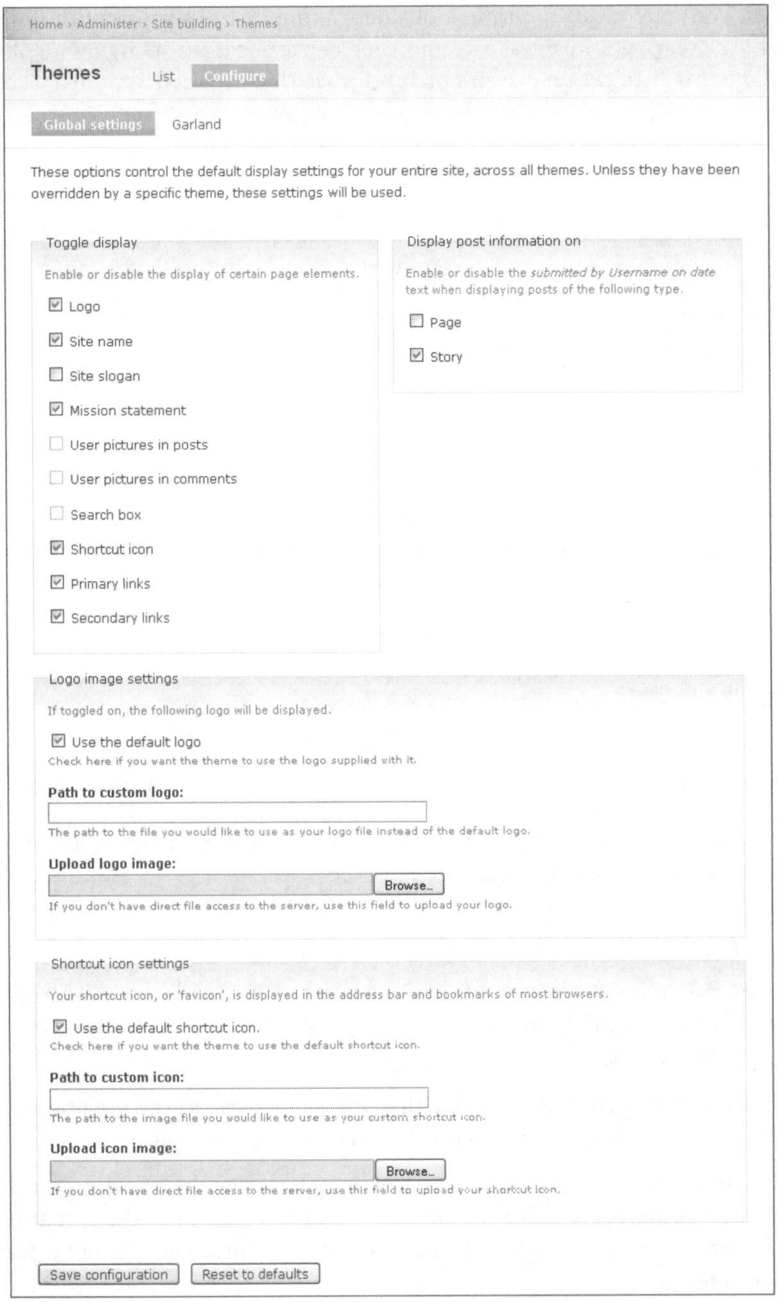

Home > Administer > Site building > Themes

Themes   List   Configure

Global settings   Garland

These options control the default display settings for your entire site, across all themes. Unless they have been overridden by a specific theme, these settings will be used.

Toggle display

Enable or disable the display of certain page elements.

☑ Logo

☑ Site name

☐ Site slogan

☑ Mission statement

☐ User pictures in posts

☐ User pictures in comments

☐ Search box

☑ Shortcut icon

☑ Primary links

☑ Secondary links

Display post information on

Enable or disable the *submitted by Username on date* text when displaying posts of the following type.

☐ Page

☑ Story

Logo image settings

If toggled on, the following logo will be displayed.

☑ Use the default logo

Check here if you want the theme to use the logo supplied with it.

Path to custom logo:

[   ]

The path to the file you would like to use as your logo file instead of the default logo.

Upload logo image:

[   ] [Browse...]

If you don't have direct file access to the server, use this field to upload your logo.

Shortcut icon settings

Your shortcut icon, or 'favicon', is displayed in the address bar and bookmarks of most browsers.

☑ Use the default shortcut icon.

Check here if you want the theme to use the default shortcut icon.

Path to custom icon:

[   ]

The path to the image file you would like to use as your custom shortcut icon.

Upload icon image:

[   ] [Browse...]

If you don't have direct file access to the server, use this field to upload your shortcut icon.

[Save configuration] [Reset to defaults]

FIGURE 6-9

FIGURE 6-10

Figure 6-11 shows the global settings for Drupal 7. Notice that the "Display post information on" setting is not available. These display settings are now managed on the content type configuration page under Display settings.

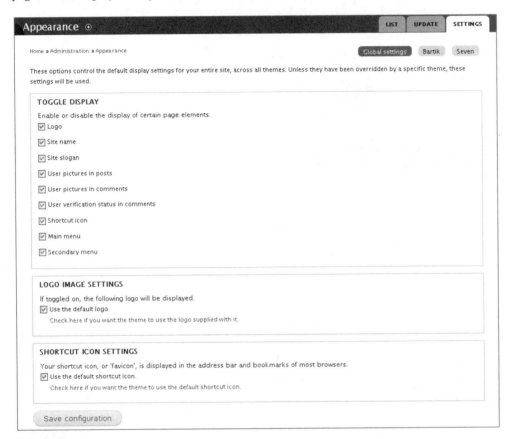

FIGURE 6-11

Figure 6-12 shows the option to upload your own logo. If you deselect "Use the default logo," you get the option to upload your own logo. The same applies for the shortcut icon (favicon).

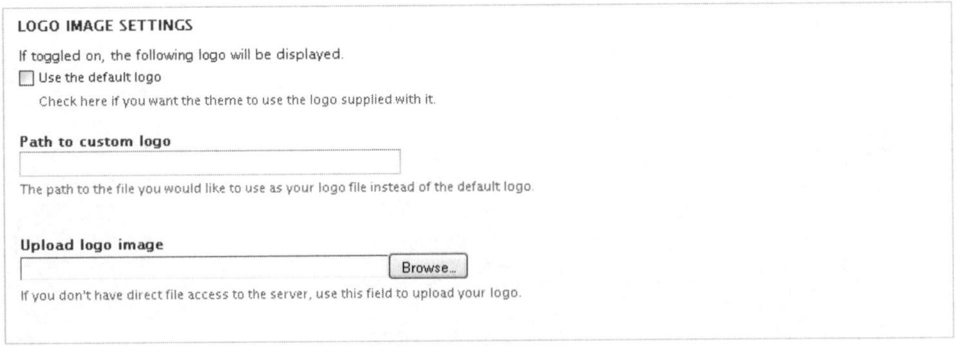

LOGO IMAGE SETTINGS

If toggled on, the following logo will be displayed.

☐ Use the default logo

  Check here if you want the theme to use the logo supplied with it.

Path to custom logo

The path to the file you would like to use as your logo file instead of the default logo.

Upload logo image

[Browse...]

If you don't have direct file access to the server, use this field to upload your logo.

FIGURE 6-12

Figure 6-13 shows the settings for the Bartik theme in Drupal 7. Notice that Bartik has the color settings; otherwise, the theme-specific and global settings are the same as Garland.

FIGURE 6-13

Advanced Configuration Settings

So far, the theme settings have been fairly basic. With the exception of the color selection feature in the default themes, you aren't left with a lot of settings that affect the layout and design of your pages.

You might recall from Chapter 5 the three perspectives of design:

➤ **Page structure** — The page structure refers to the placement and size of the sidebars, regions, main content area, and the various other components that appear on the page, such as the mission statement, site name, site slogan, menus, and footer.

➤ **Components on the page** — The page components include blocks, data fields, node author, and more.

➤ **Visual elements** — The visual elements refer to the colors, fonts, images, and so on.

How would you like to be able to install your theme via a settings form, and make layout decisions and visual element decisions on the fly? Table 6-1 shows a sampling of advanced configuration settings taken from three themes: Fusion Core, AdaptiveTheme, and Zero Point.

Fusion Core and AdaptiveTheme are base themes that you can use to create your custom theme. Zero Point, however, is a theme that is ready to use but also provides advanced settings so that you can make some structural and style changes without having to change the theme code.

Each of these themes includes many of the settings listed in Table 6-1. Decide what is important for your theme to have and choose accordingly, or you could build your own configuration-rich theme.

TABLE 6-1: A Sampling of Advanced Theme Configuration Settings

PAGE STRUCTURE	PAGE COMPONENTS	VISUAL ELEMENTS
Page width	Node author	Color scheme
Page grid layout	Node publish date	Block styling
Sidebar location	Taxonomy vocabulary terms	Page icons
Sidebar width	Menu expansion	Block icons
Sidebar height	Header image rotator	Search form text
Block height	Node links	Font family
	Skip navigation	Font size
	Mission statement	
	Breadcrumbs	
	Search results	
	Horizontal login block	

In addition to settings that help you create the look and feel you want, some themes come with administrative and development support settings, such as:

➤ Hide help messages

➤ Show block editing and configuration links

➤ Enable grid overlay mask for administrators

➤ Rebuild theme registry for every page

➤ Avoid IE stylesheet limit

➤ Add/remove CSS classes

For the most part, the advanced settings deal with theming configurations that apply site-wide. For instance, you can have breadcrumbs or no breadcrumbs. Of course, without the breadcrumb setting, you would have to manually change your theme code to either show or hide the breadcrumb.

But some settings are more granular. Figure 6-14 is a screenshot of a simple node with the username and publish date showing at the top.

FIGURE 6-14

Figure 6-15 is a screenshot from Drupal 7 showing the content-type configuration settings. It shows you have the option to either show or not show both bits of data. In Drupal 6, this setting is on the theme's global settings administration page.

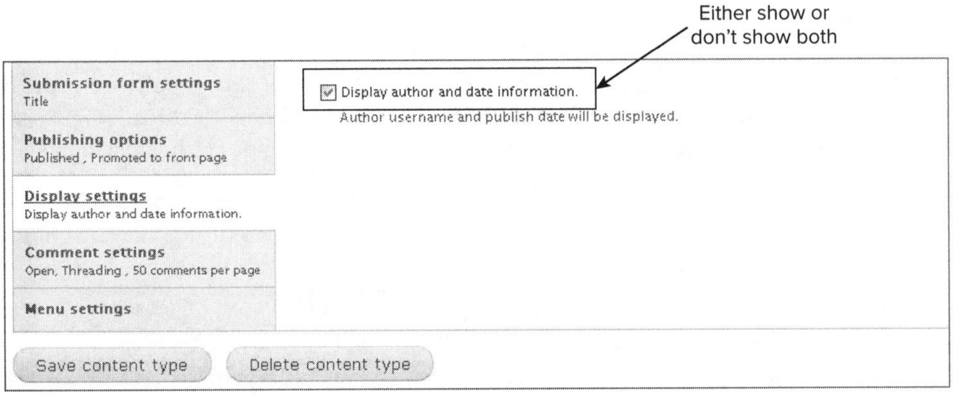

FIGURE 6-15

Figure 6-16 shows advanced settings in the Zero Point theme. Notice the settings allow you one more level of granularity. You can override the default for each type of content and choose what you want to display.

Granularity is not limited to which components appear on a page. Some themes have a block style setting. This allows you to define multiple block styles and then apply a style on a block-by-block basis.

> **BLOCK THEMING**
>
> As mentioned in Chapter 5, the Skinr module enables the themer to define a set of reusable theme settings for your blocks.

Theme or Module?

A time may come when you need some custom functionality but it doesn't become a module; instead, your developer puts the custom code in one of the theme's template files. The developer's experience and the purpose of the functionality will influence this decision. But sometimes, there are options.

The theme defines the structural layout of your page and how the components, which are placed in that layout, are styled. Modules help you define the page components your theme will display. Most of the time, it is fairly straightforward what the theme code will do and what module code will do. However, consider the Log in | Register component, as shown in Figure 6-17.

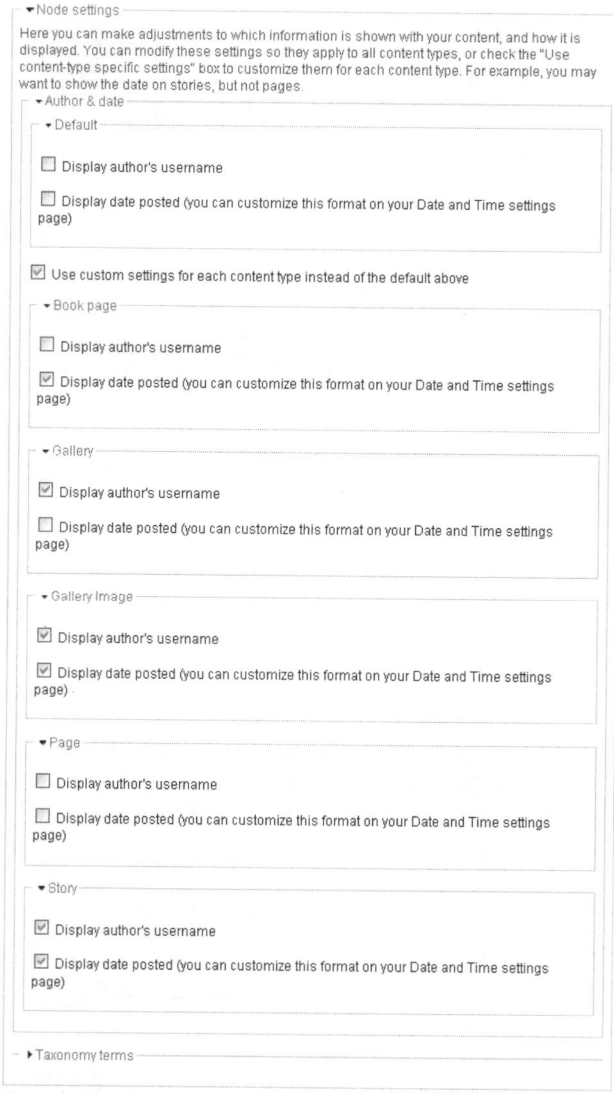

FIGURE 6-16

It is not uncommon to find this in the theme. This component is created via a function defined in the theme `template.php` file. The `page.tpl.php` (or any other `*.tpl.php`) file includes a call to this function in order to output the results (the links), styled as defined within this function (e.g., presented as table, (un)ordered list, etc). The exact placement of the links is defined by the position of the call in the `.tpl` file and influenced by styles as written in the theme's CSS file. If you change your theme, this component will go away unless you add its code to your next theme.

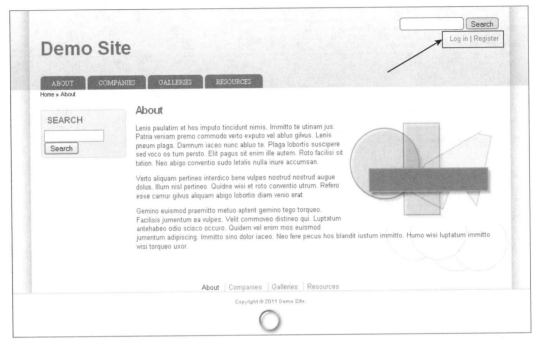

FIGURE 6-17

Page components like these are often created in the theme, but there might be a time when it makes sense to enable a component like this to a module so that you can have more control over if, when, or where they appear. Following are criteria you can use to decide which development approach to use (assuming you have the option to create a page component in a module versus in a theme).

➤ **The page component needs to be movable** — That is, it should show in one place on one page and another place on another page.

➤ **The page component needs to be removable** — That is, it should be visible under some conditions but not under other conditions.

You need to be aware of how each page and its components are assembled and whether custom features are embedded in the theme or a module. Development decisions like these can influence the effort required to make updates and changes later.

 If you are not familiar with Groups.Drupal.org, consider checking it out. You will find Drupal-related discussions on many topics. For instance, what does a theme do versus what does a module do? Want to hear what others think? Check out `http://groups.drupal.org/node/114809`.

IDENTIFYING DEVELOPMENT SEQUENCES

What gets developed when? The answer to this question is shaped by your build recipe and development method, as well as the availability of your development team.

Build Recipe

There is a prerequisite nature to developing Drupal sites. In other words, you cannot configure some site features until you have configured other features or until you have installed all the modules. This is rather obvious. What is not always obvious is the sequence.

The sequence you use depends on what your site requires and the build recipe you are using to accommodate the requirements. Following are a few scenarios that describe some common sequences. Identifying your recipe prerequisites will help you plan who is doing what and when.

Build and Theme

You can start to build your site and develop your theme at the same time. A common build sequence includes, but is not limited to, the following steps:

1. Set up the development environment.
2. Install your chosen Drupal installation.
3. Enable and configure the modules you are going to use.
4. Configure content-related items, such as content types and vocabularies.
5. Set up custom menus to be ready for links.
6. Create test data.
7. Create views displays (such as blocks and pages).

Your next step, after creating your blocks, might be to start configuring your blocks to show on the appropriate pages. You might recall from the Chapter 5 discussion on themes that blocks are placed in theme regions and sidebars. While your custom theme is being developed, you might get the urge to use a default or contributed theme temporarily, just to get the page-configuration process rolling while you wait for your theme.

The potential problem with this strategy is that the regions in the default theme might not have the same names as those in your custom theme. When you switch over to your custom theme, it is likely that most, if not all, of your block-to-region assignments will not get assigned to the correct region in your custom theme. This means starting over.

When you are ready to start assembling your pages, having a version of your theme installed is best. It doesn't have to be perfect but should at least have the sidebars and regions defined. With the theme in place, you can start configuring page components to appear in the appropriate sidebar and region at the appropriate time.

At some point in your theme-development process, your themer might need access to your site and the page components that need to be themed in order to finish the theming process. This will occur when you have page components whose default theme needs to be different or overridden. For instance, if you have a view that needs a display that is different from the default display, your themer might ask for access to the views to retrieve the view's theme information.

Custom Module Development

The preceding sample sequence does not take into consideration any custom modules that you might need. Your developer is going to favor development strategies that work for him or her, so coordination up front is important. With that said, one strategy would be to divide and conquer — that is:

➤ Have part of your team perform the tasks described earlier (building and theming).

➤ Have another part of your team develop and test your custom module(s).

Remember that you will need to test your custom module(s) in more detail than you would modules that have been vetted by many users in the community. Don't misunderstand: you need to test your entire site build, but new code needs to be debugged before it is introduced to your site. If it works in its development and testing environment, you can install it on a test instance of your site and test its ability to integrate with the other modules.

Development Integration

Imagine that you are creating a series of related sites. Each site has its own set of requirements, but, for the most part, the sites have the same functionality. Because the sites are related, you need to provide shared user profiles. A shared user profile, in this scenario, means that no matter which site the user is in, his or her profile is the same. Each site-specific activity is captured in one profile.

The sequence question is, do you create and launch the sites, and then add the shared user profile feature, or do you configure the sites from the start with this custom feature? If you are up against the clock to get the sites launched in a hurry, you might consider the former — build them and then integrate them.

This approach could have a cost. For instance, if your audience is using the sites you launched, chances are that each site will have user accounts before you integrate them. If that is the case, your integration effort now has one more requirement — to develop a way to merge all the user accounts together to form one user account and thus one profile.

If you have this situation or something similar, ask yourself whether the extra effort and cost tomorrow is worth the schedule today. Or consider whether integration of a feature is even possible later.

Development Methodologies

Chapter 2 briefly introduced you to the waterfall, RAD, spiral, phased, and agile development methodologies. With the exception of the waterfall methodology, the methodologies support some form of non-linear development — that is, development starts before all requirements and designs have been decided. Following are three tips that can help you be successful with any of the methodologies:

➤ **Manage expectations** — Define up front how and to what extent your requirements and design are going to be defined and documented within the structure of the methodology.

➤ **Correct implementation** — Use the chosen methodology correctly. Some methodologies come with manuals and require training.

➤ **Facilitate** — For some clients, the activities associated with the development methodology might vary from how the organization typically operates. Changes to organization traditions can be hard to accept at times. Before implementing a methodology, check to see if all parties are comfortable with what the methodology requires.

If you are the site owner, work closely with your development team from the start. Map out the process and identify whether it meets your responsibilities to your organization. Can you or your organization adjust to a methodology typically used by your developer? If not, can your developer use a methodology you are comfortable using?

If a methodology is important to you, state so in your request for proposal. You don't want to sign a contract with a development shop that has only one way to do development if that way doesn't fit with your organization.

Project Team Availability

In a perfect world, all the resources you need would be ready when you need them. But what if they aren't? Your build recipe and development methodology will influence when you need your resources onboard. For instance, if you are using a waterfall methodology, you don't need your full development team onboard until after you have planned your site. Although having a representative of the development team at your requirements and design meetings to clarify issues in real time helps, and can save potential confusion later, it is not required.

You also have options regarding when you need your themer onboard or when you can start your custom module development. Your schedule will determine whether you choose a linear approach to development (one development task at a time) or whether you have multiple tasks being performed at the same time.

If you are the person orchestrating the development team, make a list of roles you need on the project. Compare their schedules with your estimated development schedule, which is based on the development sequence you have identified. Are your resources going to be available? How flexible can you be?

SETTING UP YOUR ENVIRONMENTS

Environment refers to the computers and/or servers upon which you will build and launch your site. The following decisions surface when planning and setting up your environments:

➤ Development versus production

➤ Servers and hosting

➤ Version control

➤ Access control

Development vs. Production

Sometimes, it is easier to understand something if you can see an example first. Figure 6-18 illustrates one project's use of development and production environments.

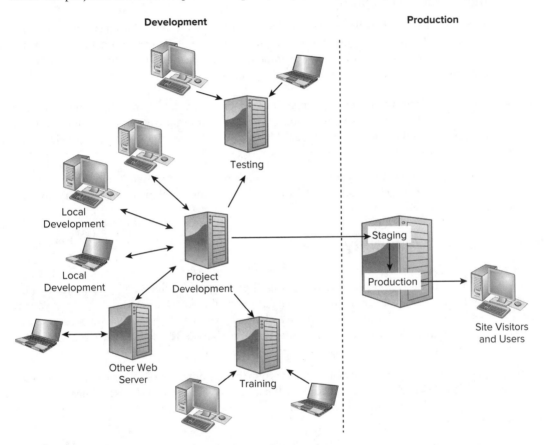

FIGURE 6-18

Several servers are being used in the development of a site. This project has one central development server to host the development version of the site and to perform version control. Some developers interact with this version of the site directly and some work offline on local servers before submitting their work to the central development server.

On this project, there is a training team and a testing team. When a version of the site is ready to be used to create training materials or to conduct training, a copy of that site version is placed on the training server. When there is a version of the site ready for testing, that version is placed on the testing server. Work proceeds on the development server, adding new features, addressing issues discovered during testing and/or training.

On this project, content development will not be done in the development environment. When enough of the site is ready so that actual content can be uploaded to the site, that version of the site is placed on the production server as a staging site. The assumption is that once the remaining features of the site have been ported to staging, the staging version will become the production (or live) version of the site.

This project illustrates the potential complexity of site development and production environments. There are numerous scenarios and environment combinations that a project can use to manage the development of a site.

Table 6-2 provides a list of common activities and the environment in which they might be performed. The activities in the table, like those in the previous project scenario, are only one way to define your environments. Not all projects need to be managed at this level. This sample is provided to help you explore your options.

TABLE 6-2: Sample Environments

TASK	DESCRIPTION	WEB SERVER	DOMAIN
Coding	To develop custom modules or themes.	Can be the coder's private web server. Can be a laptop or a dedicated CPU for local development environment.	`http://localhost` is the likely domain for the local development environment. The domain on a private server will depend on how the developer has the server configured.
Site Code Assembly	To integrate and configure core, contributed, and custom modules and themes.	Can be a project dedicated web server. Should be configured to match the server that will host the live version of the site. The server often restricts access so that the development version of the site is not accessible by search engines or the general public but is accessible by the project team.	`http://devprojectname .developershop.com` might be the domain if a development shop is developing the site. The objective is to not use the actual domain of the site.
Unit, Integration, and Regression Testing	To verify the code doesn't break the site and that it will hold up if someone inputs unexpected data.	Both local and project web servers could be used for testing. Local development environments are not always configured as the actual site server is configured, so after the initial local testing is performed, testing should move to the project server.	Can be performed on `http://localhost` and/or `http://devprojectname .developershop.com`. Depending on the size of the project, integration and/or regression testing might be performed on a separate version of the site. For example, the domain might be `http://ittestprojectname .developershop.com.`

continues

TABLE 6-2 *(continued)*

TASK	DESCRIPTION	WEB SERVER	DOMAIN
User and Load Testing	To confirm the site and/or the network it is on performs as designed, is usable, and can handle the traffic that is anticipated.	A separate testing environment provides a controlled environment so that development can continue, if necessary.	A testing domain such as `http://testprojectname.developershopc.com` might be used to mimic a live experience without opening the actual site to search engines and the general public.
Content Population	To add real content to the site. Development/sample content is added throughout the build process for purposes of testing and to see the pages come to life as they are configured and themed.	Content can be entered as part of development on the development server. It can also be entered in a staging environment or straight into the production environment.	If on development, it might be `http://devprojectname.developershop.com`. Staging might by `http://staging.sitedomain.com`. The production site would be `http://sitedomain.com`.
Live Site Launch	To flip the switch and take the public version of the site live.	The server for the live site will have the actual domain associated with the site.	The production site would be `http://sitedomain.com`.

Every project is different. The workflow between decision-makers, site developers, content developers, testers, and so on varies from project to project. Your objective should be to define what you need (or what you can manage). If you can't have the perfect setup, at the least, you should ensure:

➤ The site is built to meet your requirements.

➤ The site has been tested.

➤ The public sees the site you want it to see.

DEVELOPMENT PLATFORMS

You don't have to set up development and production servers on your own if you don't want to. There are service providers that will do it for you. One example is Pantheon, The Drupal Platform for Developers.

Pantheon is a hosted development, testing, and production (live) solution. Developed by seasoned Drupal developers, Pantheon provides a hosting solution configured for Drupal. It provides automated development and testing services, uses Git to manage code versioning, and provides Apache Solr, Varnish, and Memcached as integrated services that enhance your site's performance. Pantheon offers free development and testing environments.

To learn more about production environments, visit `http://getpantheon.com`.

Servers and Hosting

Development and production environments require web servers. Web servers require some type of hosting service, either a purchased service or one provided by in-house resources. Whether you purchase a service or provide your own, note that not all servers are configured the same. If you are purchasing your server space, note that not all hosting plans are the same, either.

Before shopping for a hosting service, thinking about what Drupal needs and what your site needs regarding services and performance helps.

Server Requirements

Drupal will run on different server platforms. A detailed set of system requirements is located at `http://drupal.org/requirements`. The following is a short summary:

➤ **Operating system** — You can use Linux, Unix, or Microsoft Windows.

➤ **Web server** — Apache is recommended, but Microsoft IIS will work.

➤ **Database server** — Your options vary depending on the version of Drupal you use. Drupal 6 supports MySQL and PostgreSQL. Drupal 7 also supports SQLite as well as other databases.

➤ **Language** — Drupal is a PHP-based system.

➤ **Disk space** — Before you start adding data to the database and media files to your server, your disk space requirements range from 3 MB to 40 MB or more, depending on the modules you add.

> **SERVER CONFIGURATION CHANGES**
>
> Drupal 7 has a vendor-neutral abstraction layer for accessing database servers. This means you need the PDO (PHP Data Objects) database extension installed on your server. To learn more about Drupal 7's abstraction layer, visit `http://drupal.org/developing/api/database`.

The server is one thing; what you can do on the server is another. Following are some basic web-hosting plan evaluation criteria. At a minimum, you need a plan that allows you to:

➤ Create databases

➤ Access your databases via a tool like phpMyAdmin

➤ Choose the PHP version you want

➤ Allocate additional PHP memory

➤ Manage PHP module settings

➤ Modify ModSecurity settings

➤ Run PDO database extensions (assuming a Drupal 7 installation)

➤ Choose the MySQL version you want or other database if required

➤ Host multiple sites with or without subdomains

➤ Add applications (ImageMagick, Drush, and others)

➤ Use a control panel (for those who are not command-line savvy)

➤ Access server files via FTP

Plans that offer this level of service are not hard to find. Just be cautious with plans that offer unlimited space for $9.95 a month. Space isn't the only thing you need.

Server Configuration

If you have more than one physical server box, you might have more than one server configuration. For instance, just because a server has a LAMP (Linux, Apache, MySQL, and PHP) stack doesn't mean it will process your site code the same. Did you know that different versions of Linux are available, depending on the type of environment you are using: desktop, laptop, enterprise, and more? For instance, there is Ubuntu, Fedora, OpenSUSE, CentOS, and more.

Not unlike your personal computer, servers can have different configurations but still provide the same services. But the devil is in the details. A feature that works on one server might not work the same way if that site is on another server. Of course, the odds of this happening are slim, but they do happen, so it is worth noting.

 Drupal.org has many resources regarding server configurations. See "Server Tuning Considerations," at http://drupal.org/node/2601, *for more details. You can search Drupal.org for other tips.*

Why do you need to be aware of server configurations? If you set up your development and production environments such that they are on different platforms, you will want to run tests in both platforms. This is where having a staging site on the production server is helpful. If you can, configure the development and production servers the same way.

> **PROVIDER CONFIGURATIONS**
>
> Even if you open multiple accounts with a hosting provider, you still might get different server configurations.

Web-Hosting Plans

When choosing a web-hosting plan, you not only need to consider how it is configured and what you want to be able to do (as previously discussed), but you also need to consider the traffic to your site. Processing capability, load capacity, and security management are three factors that can influence your choices.

Following are four common types of plans, each providing various levels of processing capacity, load capacity, and security management:

➤ Shared hosting

➤ Virtual private server (VPS) hosting

➤ Dedicated or managed server hosting

➤ Cloud hosting

If you need more than what plans like these can offer, consider adding a content distribution network (CDN) service to your overall plan. Instead of requiring your server to manage every request from your visitors, a CDN can manage the requests for you, allowing requests through to your server as needed.

> *Check out Drupal.org's Marketplace for hosting options* (`http://drupal.org/hosting`). *Not all providers are listed; that a service provider is not on the list doesn't mean it can't support a Drupal-friendly environment.*

Shared Hosting

On a shared hosting plan, your sites are on a server with many other people's sites — hence, the name "shared." Shared hosting is the least flexible of the four types being discussed here. Figure 6-19 is a simple conceptual illustration of shared hosting.

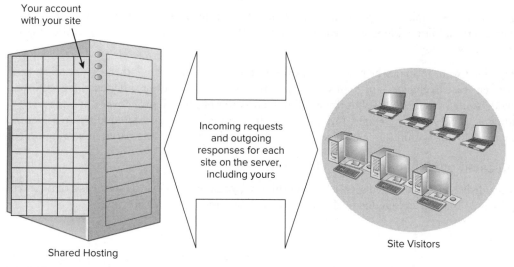

Your account
with your site

Incoming requests
and outgoing
responses for each
site on the server,
including yours

Shared Hosting

Site Visitors

FIGURE 6-19

Of course, not all shared plans are the same; some plans offer more than others. For instance, you might have unlimited space but limitations in other areas, such as:

➤ Little or no permissions to change server settings

➤ Limited PHP memory allocation

➤ Limited control of PHP and MySQL versions

Each limitation can affect whether your site will work on that shared hosting plan. For instance, as you increase the number of modules you have in play, the more PHP memory you are likely to need. So, if your plan limits the amount of PHP memory your site can use on the server, you might need a different plan.

DRUPAL PHP MEMORY

Although Drupal's core requires little PHP memory (16 MB for Drupal 6 and 32 MB for Drupal 7), you likely will need more than this. A Drupal 6 site running the CCK and Views modules might need as much as 64 MB. Add the ImageCache module, and you might need as much as 96 MB. The functionality of the CCK and ImageCache modules is included in Drupal 7, but that doesn't mean you won't need more than 32 MB when you add Views and other modules.

Virtual Private Server Hosting

The virtual private server (VPS) is a space on a server that acts like a private server. This means your virtual space is on the same box with other virtual spaces (or customers). This is similar to shared hosting in that the hosting provider can have more than one customer on a physical server box, but you have more flexibility with your server settings and added security.

Figure 6-20 is a simple conceptual illustration of VPS hosting. The separation between each account illustrates the additional flexibility you have with a VPS. The number of accounts on the physical box can vary.

If you don't want to share the processing power of the server with many other virtual private servers, often you can change your plan so that you are on a box with fewer other customers. Not all providers offer this flexibility, but if you think your server needs will grow over time, consider finding a provider that is flexible. Buy small now if your budget is limited and move up as demand requires. Moving within the same hosting provider is easier than moving between hosting providers.

Dedicated or Managed Server Hosting?

With a dedicated or managed server hosting solution, you are the only account using that server. Figure 6-21 is a conceptual illustration of dedicated or managed server hosting.

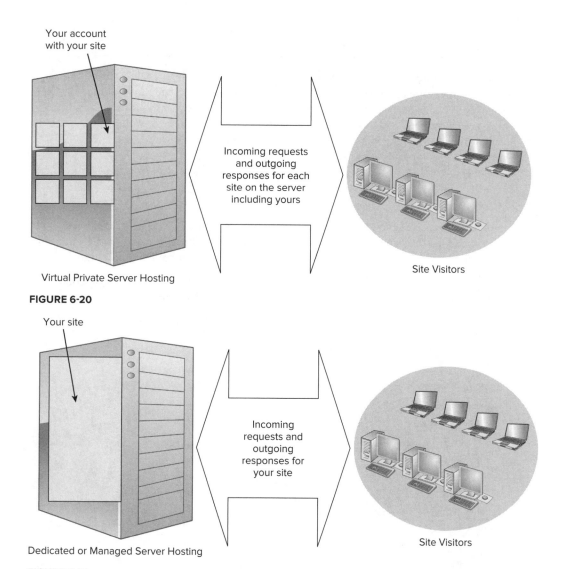

Your account
with your site

Incoming requests
and outgoing
responses for each
site on the server
including yours

Site Visitors

Virtual Private Server Hosting

FIGURE 6-20

Your site

Incoming
requests and
outgoing
responses for
your site

Site Visitors

Dedicated or Managed Server Hosting

FIGURE 6-21

The difference between dedicated and managed is that in many cases, you are responsible for managing the configuration of a dedicated server, whereas the service provider manages the dedicated server for you. The degree to which you manage the configuration of a dedicated server will vary from one provider to the next. Of course, your costs are higher than shared and VPS hosting. Just remember that not all boxes are the same.

MANAGED SERVER HOSTING

If you want to know that your service provider is familiar with Drupal, involved in the community, and can provide an environment tweaked for Drupal, you might consider a managed service provider such as BlackMesh. BlackMesh maintains and optimizes the entire LAMP stack, especially Apache and MySQL, as well as the entire Drupal stack of Drupal, Varnish, SOLR, and memcache. See `http://blackmesh.com` for more details.

Cloud Hosting

Add more processing power and load capacity with a cloud solution. Cloud hosting allows you to lease virtual, scalable infrastructure on an as-needed basis. Cloud hosting uses cloud-computing technologies, which, in turn, allow multiple servers to manage your incoming and outgoing traffic.

If you are used to the idea of a hard drive on a server that stores your files, the idea of cloud hosting might be hard to image. Figure 6-22 is a simple conceptual illustration of cloud hosting.

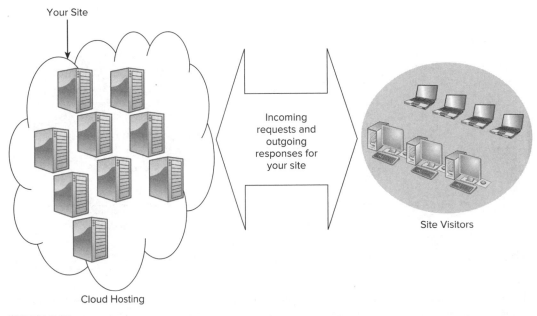

FIGURE 6-22

 The video at `www.webhostingsecretrevealed.com/web-hosting-knowledge/a-brief-on-cloud-hosting/` *provides a clever animation that illustrates how cloud hosting works.*

The advantages of cloud hosting include:

➤ Processing power of multiple servers

➤ Options to pay as you use

➤ Increased bandwidth to manage high-traffic loads

➤ Expands to fit your needs

➤ High availability because you are not relying on one server

---

CLOUD HOSTING AND DRUPAL

Acquia Cloud provides a managed hosting platform as a service designed for Drupal performance. It provides a scalable environment preconfigured with advanced performance technologies, such as Varnish, Nginx, APC, and Memcache. You can choose either a stand-alone server installation or a multi-server, clustered, highly available configuration. For more information, visit `http://acquia.com/products-services/managed-cloud`.

Content Delivery Networks

If cloud hosting is not enough, a content distribution network (CDN) might be what you need. A CDN helps you distribute your content by bringing the content closer to your visitors via caching and redundancy. It increases the bandwidth available to your content, reducing the download time of your content, and saves your hosting environment from having to respond to every request for content. Figure 6-23 is a simple conceptual illustration of a CDN, with the assumption that the site is hosted on a cloud (which is not required).

CONTENT DELIVERY NETWORK OPTIONS

Several CDN options are available. For example, Amazon offers two CDN solutions: Amazon CloudFront (`http://aws.amazon.com/cloudfront/`) and Amazon Elastic Compute Cloud (`http://aws.amazon.com/ec2/`). Akamai (`http://www.akamai.com/`) is another CDN option. It offers tens of thousands of servers around the world that help the Internet withstand the daily requests for rich, dynamic, and interactive content, transactions, and applications.

Version Control

If you have ever collaboratively created a presentation document, you probably know that you need a way for everyone to contribute edits to the document while maintaining one master document. This can be done in several ways. For instance, those collaborating can submit edits for the document, but to keep individual edits from being overwritten, one person needs to filter the edits and apply them to the master. This is a form of version control.

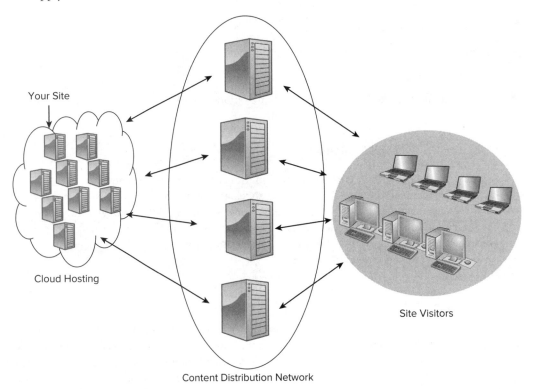

FIGURE 6-23

When you have environments such as those described in Table 6-2, you need a form of version control to manage multiple development and production sites. In these environments, you need to manage multiple types of data:

➤ Code (core, modules, themes)

➤ Configuration settings

➤ Content data

➤ Various types of media content

Code Version Control

Discussions about version control often focus on code updates. If several developers are building a custom module or theme, you need to keep track of the different bits of code they submit to the module or theme files. The objective is for each developer to update the same file(s) on the development server without overriding updates from others inappropriately. Fortunately, several version-control tools are available to assist with the process. For instance, Git, Subversion, and Concurrent Versions System (CVS) are just a few. Drupal core and its contributed modules are managed with Git.

To understand better how version control works, you can find some good resources at http://drupal.org/node/299067. *If you are new to version control, you might find the resource called "A Visual Guide to Version Control"* (http://betterexplained.com/articles/a-visual-guide-to-version-control/) *helpful. The visual aids make the discussion easy to follow.*

If you are not building any custom modules or themes, times will still occur when you need to change the code on your site and therefore track the versions of your site. For instance, if an issue with a module or with Drupal's core is discovered, often a patch to remedy the issue is posted to Drupal.org's issue queue. Until the patch is integrated into the next release of the module or core, you might need to use the patch if you are experiencing issues. Tracking patches helps all the developers on your team know what has changed.

Drupal, contributed modules, and contributed themes all have updates on occasion. Using a version-control tool helps your developers update the site code while at the same time keeping each other aware of the update.

Technically, you don't have to use a version-control tool to update your code. You could use traditional file-management techniques, such as creating backups of your files. It is likely you have used this technique in your everyday file-management processes. For instance, the first version of a presentation might be saved as "draft." In the next iteration of your presentation, you add some topics and address some comments. Instead of saving over draft, you create a new version called "draft2," thus creating a backup of draft in the event you need it. The process continues, saving each new version with a different name.

When it comes to module files, the process is a little different. The names of the files in your modules need to be the same. So, before you create the next version of a module file, you would save the existing file with a new name, as a backup. You might find that you have several backups, depending on how many times you add new functionality to your module.

Imagining the manual version-control processes described could already have you thinking about some of the inefficiencies associated with traditional, manual version control. For instance, how do you allow more than one developer to edit a module file at the same time and not save over each other's work? Two people open the file; the first person saves but the second person doesn't have the edits. The second person saves and all the edits from the first person are overridden.

The objective for a version-control process is the same: to track code changes and updates on your site and ensure you have backups in the event you need to revert to a previous state.

DRUPAL VERSION CONTROL

Drupal's core and its contributed modules and themes are stored in a Git version-control repository at http://git.drupal.org. Git is a version-control tool. You can find a Git reference guide for module maintainers at http://drupal.org/node/711070, and the start of a Git reference guide for site builders at http://drupal.org/node/803746, as well as many other version-control resources on Drupal.org.

Configuration Version Control

Due to Drupal's extensive module collection, you'll spend much of your site-building and/or mainte-nance time on configuring modules. Configuration settings are stored in the database. How do you manage version control on the database, especially if you have multiple developers?

The following sections describe some configuration version-control techniques, each of which has its pros and cons, depending on your project and development team. As you review each practice, keep in mind that each project and each developer will have his or her own preferred practice of dealing with configuration version control. If you are planning on maintaining the site yourself after launch, you need to understand the version-control practices of the development team so that you can either use the same practices or come up with a plan to convert to another version-control process.

Backing Up the Database

During the site-build process and as part of site maintenance, a simple database backup process might be all you need. For instance, if you are building your site incrementally and have the first two features working on your site, you might want to make a backup of your database before starting to build your third feature. That way, if anything goes wrong with the installation and configuration of the next feature, you can restore.

The same practice applies when making updates to your site, as well. When you update core or a module, you sometimes need to run the update process (`http://example.com/update.php`). This script will make any applicable changes to the database and its data. When you run `update .php`, you are reminded to make a backup of your database in the event an issue occurs and you need to restore your site to its previous state.

> **DATABASE BACKUPS**
>
> The Backup and Migrate module, available for both Drupal 6 and Drupal 7, pro-vides an administrative interface in your Drupal site for creating a backup of your site's database.

Using a Version-Control Tool

When you export your database as a backup, you are provided with a file with data and the database schema (table and field structures). They can be together or separate, depending on what you are trying to version. Some version-control tools can treat the export file like any other file that has code in it, saving the differences between the new export and the previous. Because databases can be quite large, they can take up a lot of space in a version-control database. You will want to plan your backup practices if you use a version-control tool to maintain your data-base versions.

Updating with Module Code

If the changes are simple, some developers will write commands in the module that insert data into the database when they submit a change to the module. Ask yourself whether coding the configuration or simply doing it by hand is more efficient. If you are sending the update to several sites, using code to implement the configuration updates might be more efficient. Or, if the configuration updates are going to be a regular part of the module updates, including them in the code of the module might also be appropriate.

FEATURES MODULE FOR CONFIGURATION MANAGEMENT

The Features module was developed so that site configurations created in a development environment could be ported to one or more production environments quickly and efficiently. The idea is similar to the module code concept, except the Features module writes the code for you and creates a separate module that you can install just like any other module. Also, the Features module approach is not restricted to one module. It is about a site feature, one that is created through a series of module installations and configurations. Each time the feature is updated in development, you can update the Features module and then export it to production when you are ready. The Features module is available in Drupal 6 and 7.

Exporting and Importing Modules

Another way to manage configuration versions is to export the settings associated with a module or what that module creates. For instance, the Content Construction Kit (CCK) provides a way to export the configuration information associated with a content type and its fields. The script can be saved as a backup or used to create the same content type and fields in another site (assuming the other site has the appropriate modules enabled).

The Views module is another example. You can export a view you have created and save the export script as a backup, or you can use it to create the same view in another site (assuming the other site has the data architecture the view references).

With respect to version control, each time you decide to change a content type or view or something similar, it is a good idea to create a backup version first so that you can restore the original setting if your changes are not successful.

MODULES THAT EXPORT/IMPORT

In Drupal 6, CCK provides a content copy feature that allows you to export and import a content type and its fields from one site to another via a simple text form. As of May 2011, the CCK project page reports that content copy has not been ported to Drupal 7, but the Drupal 7 version of the Features module has the option to export and import content type and fields with the result being a feature module that you enable like another module.

The Views and Panels module provides an export/import feature. Of course, these assume that the site to which the view or panel is being transferred has the same basic setup so that the fields referenced in the view or panel are available.

Content Version Control

Content comes in the form of data that is stored in your database and can include files that you have attached (images, video, and documents). How do you manage content versions in your site? It depends on the context of the version — that is, whether it is pre-production content or post-production content.

Managing Pre-Production Content

When you go from development to production for the first time, you copy the entire development site (code, database, and files) to the production environment because the production site doesn't exist yet. If you use the development environment to continue developing content, the process of updating the production site with content from the development site will likely be in the form of exports and imports.

The export/import modules associated with nodes can help with the process of creating nodes in the production site using exported content from the development site. Because not all content types are the same, you might find that you need to customize your own export/import tool to support this process.

EXPORTING AND IMPORTING NODES

You can export and import nodes in a couple of ways. The Node export module provides several ways you can manage your node export requirements. It also has a feature that helps export and import attached images and files.

Another perspective is to create nodes with data. The Feeds module enables you to create nodes from imported data, the source of which can be in various forms. The module also provides a way to map the data fields in your site to the data fields in your source file.

An alternative would be to continue content development on the production site but use a moderation process to prevent unedited content from being made public. The next section considers this idea.

Managing Post-Development Content

Assume that your site is on your production server. The site might be live or it might be in maintenance mode so that the public can't see it. You are actively adding content such as articles, blogs, or even new products. With Drupal's revision feature (part of the content type workflow settings), you have the option of keeping a copy of the previous version of your node when you are done with your edits. That way, you can revert to an earlier version if you find your edits are no longer accurate.

But what if you want to create content actively but keep it hidden until it has been edited and approved? Different techniques are available for moderating content and content revisions. You can use Drupal's publishing options and simply deselect Published until the node is ready. Or, you can use one of several contributed modules, each offering varying degrees of control of workflow and revision tracking.

> **REVISION OPTIONS**
>
> The Revisioning module helps you manage content workflow and revisions. One of its features allows content authors to revise an existing node but keep that revision unpublished until it has been reviewed. While it is being reviewed, the previously approved version of the node is live. The Revisioning module is available in Drupal 6 and Drupal 7.

Access Control

As discussed in Chapter 4, "Collecting Requirements," part of your analysis was to determine who should be able to access your site and server. At that time, you might not have known exactly how you would be configuring your development and production environments, but at least you had a starting point. Use that information as part of your decision criteria when selecting a hosting plan.

Many ways exist to access a server remotely, and each hosting plan will have its options. Each plan has its pros and cons and not all hosting services support these options:

➤ Version-control tool, such as Git

➤ Control panel via a web browser

➤ Command-line application running from your computer

➤ FTP application running from your computer

Design your development plan and identify who should access what on the server. Identify what these users will be doing and, therefore, the type of access that is required. Talk to hosting providers to see what they support before you purchase, and to your development team about what access they feel is best.

DOCUMENTING YOUR DEVELOPMENT PLAN

The people who plan a site are not always the same people who plan the development of the site. The requirements and design plans enable planners, designers, and decision-makers to communicate what the site needs to be with the development team. The development plan enables the development team to communicate how the requirements and design can be met. Together, these documents provide a foundation for managing expectations in both directions. As the project proceeds, there is a chance that something will change. By updating the requirements, design, and development plans to reflect the changes, you continue to provide a means of managing expectations.

The development plan is more than a way to communicate with planners, designers, and decision-makers; it is also a tool to manage the development process. It helps you identify whom you need, what they need to do, and when you need them to do it. Basically, it is a project management tool. Documentation can also help you:

➤   Define contractual obligations

➤   Manage negotiations

➤   Create budget and schedule adjustments

➤   Contribute to the preparation of test plans

➤   Validate that requirements will be met

➤   Support client training

➤   Plan future site enhancements or updates

Seeing development push forward without documentation is not uncommon. The modularity of Drupal enables developers to assemble a site quickly, even before development plans are considered. For relatively basic sites, justifying the time to document may be hard, so some people rely on their memory. Why does documentation seem so hard for some? Common reasons that people avoid documentation include:

➤   Not knowing what to document

➤   Not knowing where to store the documentation

➤   The continuous updates required as changes are made

➤   The interruptions caused by stopping to document

➤   The time it takes

The strategy you use to document your requirements, design, and development plans is up to you. Again, your development methodology is going to influence your strategy to some extent. Following are a couple of documentation strategies to consider.

Project Lifecycle Site

You might choose to install a preconfigured management site or create a simple site where decision-makers can go online and define the need for the site. They can input their requirements and come to a consensus as a team by coauthoring the requirements. The designers and developers can review the requirements and comment on whether and how the requirements can be met. If any requirements require customization, that feedback can be provided so that decision-makers can approve it or decide to change the requirement. As development progresses, if issues arise, comments can be submitted to the decision-makers and/or development team so that resolution can be obtained.

An advantage to this approach is that it creates a living document that connects requirements, design, and development in one resource. With all pieces connected, you can manage expectations from start to finish.

A challenge with this approach is the overlap between requirements and development solutions. For instance, you could create three requirement entries for three content types. To create each content type, the developers will need the same modules. This can become repetitive for the development team, entering the same development solution over and over. If you use this approach, you will need a strategy to address redundancy. For instance, you might want to categorize requirements so that they can be bundled into development tasks.

MANAGEMENT SITE TOOLS

Several applications are available that you can use to document. For example, you can try a Drupal distribution called Open Atrium (`http://openatrium.com`), a platform designed to build team portals, or you can look at systems such as BaseCamphq (`http://basecamphq.com`) or ActiveCollab (`www.activecollab.com`). The structure of your team will influence which tool is best for you.

Development Management Site

An alternative to a full lifecycle site is one used to manage just the development plan. After reviewing the requirements and design, the development team enters the tasks associated with development into the site. From there, communications can be tracked and managed.

To ensure that the development plan addresses all the requirements, each development task should include a copy of the requirement or design element. This could mean copying the data into the development task or attaching the applicable portion of the requirement or design.

An advantage to this approach is the same as that mentioned in the preceding "Project Lifecycle Site" section: it creates a living document that connects requirements, design, and development in one resource. It just does it differently.

A disadvantage to this approach is the duplication of requirements and therefore having to manage two versions of requirements (the original requirements and the requirements that were copied). To address this challenge, you might choose to use the development management site to manage requirement changes and retire the original requirements documentation.

Combining Documentation Strategies

When you have a client team defining requirements, a designer creating the design, and a development team planning development, you often end up with multiple documents and possibly multiple documentation tools. If your team (planning, design, and development) is fully integrated from the start, you can create one solution. The development methodology you choose will influence your circumstances. The goal is to recognize potential challenges and be prepared to design a solution that meets your needs before you get too far into the project.

BUILDING YOUR SITE

Recall that there are several development methodologies that you can use to manage your development project. It is possible that you could have Drupal installed, modules loaded, and some configuration complete before all your requirements, design, and development plans have been created.

If you have walked through all the steps discussed so far in this book, however, now it's time to execute the development plan you have created. The legwork you have done up front should make development an efficient process.

Depending on how complicated your site is, you might find that issues arise, you forgot something, or maybe what was once thought to be a great idea isn't anymore. The foundation you built by planning your site will help you manage these occurrences.

So, what do you do first? The previous section, "Identifying Development Sequences," provided insights into the tasks you would perform while building your site. You could have chosen a development sequence like the following:

1. Install Drupal.
2. Start developing the theme (if applicable).
3. Start developing custom modules (if applicable).
4. Start developing content offline.
5. Download all the modules identified in the development plan.
6. Enable the modules.
7. Configure the modules (create all the content types, fields, vocabularies, views, path structures, image presets, and so on).
8. Install and test custom modules.
9. Install and test the custom theme.
10. Build each section of the site with sample content.
11. Create a staging version of the site.
12. Clear sample content, where appropriate.
13. Upload content.
14. Continue developing, if necessary.
15. Merge new development into the staging version.
16. Create the production (live) site.
17. Maintain the site.

This book does not provide the actual click-by-click instructions for building a Drupal site. You can find numerous books and videos about implementing various modules and features. Part III of this book provides an example site and development plans and explores various strategies for creating a specific site.

TESTING YOUR BUILD

Although this task is being presented after the "build-your-site" step, the planning for testing your build started long before the build. When you identified the requirements, you were making a list of items that need to be tested. When you identified your audience, you were identifying potential testers. When you identified the processes and tasks that your users need to be able to perform on your site, you were creating test scenarios. When you created use cases, you were creating testing procedures. You can use all this information to facilitate testing.

Testing is more than determining whether your site works. Tests occur during development, as well. If you are planning a development schedule, you need to allow time for unit, integration, and regression testing before testers begin user acceptance and usability testing. If you have a lot of Drupal development experience, you can easily forget that each time you download a new version of a module, technically, you are downloading a module you have not used. Yes, the functionality is the same, but the code has changed. You might need to do a little testing or at least review the issue queue to see whether you need to watch for anything.

If you have hired a developer to help build your site, you might participate in the testing process during development. For instance, if you have a custom feature being developed and that custom feature has several components, your developer might seek feedback and testing help from you to assess whether progress is going in the right direction. Partially completed features can trigger thoughts and questions that need to be addressed sooner rather than later in the development process. Agile development methodologies recognize this issue and provide flexibility in the development process.

Following are some testing insights to help you plan your testing.

Integration Testing

Figure 6-24 is a conceptual illustration of integration, the bringing together or combining of parts to make a whole.

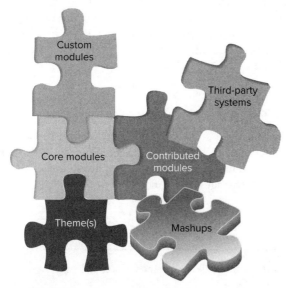

FIGURE 6-24

The process of building a Drupal site is based on module integration. Install and configure modules, and you get some type of functionality. However, not all modules play nice with each other, as you are probably aware. Integration testing reveals module conflicts.

Hypothetically, each time a module is enabled and configured, the developer would test whether it works. Then, the developer would add another module, test whether it works, and then test whether previous modules still work. Some Drupal sites can have 5 contributed modules or 100 contributed modules. Performing integration testing on every module can be a lengthy process and is often not performed for each module installed.

Decisions on whether to test are based on the following:

➤   **The nature of the module** — for example, whether it changes the behavior of a core functionality or another module already installed

➤   **Developer experience with the modules** — for example, whether the modules have been used together in the past without issue

Integration testing is performed by the development team.

Regression Testing

"My site is working great; if I change a setting, will it cause something to break?" Regression testing tests changes. For instance, suppose you have a page that displays a grid of images. Each image is 125 pixels wide. The width of the image is set using a preset created with the ImageCache module. The page is created with the Views module. You decide to edit the preset from 125 pixels to 120 pixels. If you don't test your change (check to see how it looks), you won't see that the view no longer references the preset. The change broke the view configuration. This is easily fixed: just assign the preset to the view again and save.

The preceding example is fairly basic. When software developers think of regression testing, they are more likely to think about changes in the code than changes in a configuration setting. For instance, assume you have a custom module and it works. Then, during user acceptance testing, someone notices that a requirement was overlooked. You agree to make the changes to the custom module. You do another unit test and it looks like the addition will be fine. When you add the module to the site, you rerun the user testing to see:

➤   If the new functionality works

➤   If the old functionality still works as expected

With unit testing or user testing, you could experience an issue that wasn't there before, due to the change you made in the module. This scenario doesn't have to be about a custom module. You could have a similar situation where you patch a contributed module and that patch causes other issues to arise. Remember, just because it was working before, that doesn't mean it will continue to work after you change code.

> **REGRESSION TESTING ON DRUPAL**
>
> Drupal has automated patch testing to ensure that the development version of Drupal remains as stable as possible. Learn more at http://drupal.org/node/332678.

Site Security Testing

Security issues can surface from multiple sources, such as:

➤ Coding practices

➤ Site configuration settings

➤ Environments in which the site or system operates

➤ Connections made between systems

➤ Third-party applications

➤ Business practices and policies

Site security testing assesses your site's vulnerabilities and, if necessary, tests those vulnerabilities with penetration testing. A vulnerability assessment process often includes the following activities:

➤ Identify the resources that make up your system, such as features, data, and processes.

➤ Identify and prioritize vulnerabilities associated with the resources.

➤ Identify how to mitigate the risk of the vulnerability.

The earlier section, "Assessing Module Quality," lists common coding practices that can reduce a module's vulnerability to attacks. A vulnerability assessment on coding practices can be performed on the entire site or just on select modules.

Vulnerabilities associated with site configuration can include but are not limited to the following:

➤ Untrusted users are allowed to create unfiltered posts, thus enabling them to enter dangerous code.

➤ Untrusted roles have access to administrative interfaces.

➤ Files with unsafe file extensions can be uploaded.

In addition to coding and configuration, security testing can also include assessments, such as evaluating:

➤ Server access vulnerabilities

➤ Directories on the server are writable when they shouldn't be

➤ Possible encryption weaknesses

➤ Weaknesses in the connections between systems

Not all vulnerabilities come from the hardware and software associated with the system. There is also the human factor to consider. Business practices and policies can create opportunities for security vulnerabilities. For instance, is there a policy that prohibits the printing or copying of sensitive information? If so, how is the policy enforced?

Even if you have checked and double-checked your work, it doesn't hurt to get a second opinion. If security is of extreme importance, consider hiring a consultant to review your policies, configurations, code, and maybe even the physical space where your site resides.

SECURITY REVIEW

The Security Review module offers a quick way to assess whether you have any basic Drupal configurations that create security issues.

User Acceptance Testing

Does your site do what it is supposed to do? Does it meet the requirements and design agreed upon? To answer these questions, you need to know what the site was supposed to do to begin with; you need the requirements and design plan. The requirements and design plan include:

➤ The processes and tasks that need to be supported in the site

➤ The use cases describing the behavior of the site

➤ The layout of the pages and the components required for each interface

If you don't have use cases for each requirement and you want to perform user acceptance testing, you will need to write test scenarios that test users will perform on the site.

Test scenarios are more than "Create an event node." They typically include the steps that users are expected to follow. A test user follows the steps and reports what happens. If no issues surface, the feature passes. Note that the test isn't about whether a test user can figure out what to do; that is usability testing (discussed next).

When the site meets the requirements and design, it is ready to be used. This means populating the site with real content (assuming you haven't already done this).

Usability Testing

Depending on what you want your users to be able to do, you might want to test your site or at least certain sections of your site to see whether your target audience can perform the tasks you need them to perform.

Usability testing on a completed site can be nerve-racking because nobody wants to redo work. This is where a cost/benefit analysis can be helpful. Does it cost more to perform the test and learn you might need to redo a couple of things than it costs to lose opportunities to meet your goals? If your goals are monetary, missing them might cost you more in the long run.

Technically, you don't have to wait until the site is done to conduct usability testing. You might consider an incremental approach to development and test the site as features become available. Of course, you will still want to assess the site as a whole, but at least you have minimized the potential of usability issues on specific site features. If you find usability issues, you can redesign the feature, the interface, the workflow, etc., taking into consideration the results of the usability test.

Accessibility Testing

Not everyone can use a mouse, nor can everyone see or hear. An increasing number of organizations, institutions, and agencies require their sites to be accessible to people with disabilities.

A number of tools for testing your pages are available online. For example, a popular tool is WAVE, by WebAIM (`http://wave.webaim.org/`). Regardless of which tool you choose, if you use the same code over and over to produce your pages, you don't have to test every page on your site. For instance, your theme will render your story page the same way each time. As long as you use proper HTML coding practices consistently in the body of your nodes, you should be able to test a sampling of pages to determine whether they have any issues.

To learn more about accessibility testing, check out the W3C Web Accessibility Initiative Evaluation Overview at `www.w3.org/WAI/eval/`. You can also search the Web for "Section 508" to find resources that can help you meet the government's standard for accessibility.

POPULATING YOUR SITE

When developing a site, you typically don't use real content; you use test or sample content. After you know the site works with the test content, you clear the test content and enter real content. So, what do you need to consider when loading real content? To answer this question, consider three additional questions:

- ➤ How much content do you want on the site prior to launch?
- ➤ Where will you load the real content — on the development site or a staging site?
- ➤ How will you load the content to your site?

> **TEST CONTENT**
>
> The Devel module provides several development helper tools. One of the tools generates test data for nodes, vocabulary terms, users, comments, and some fields.

Separating Pre- and Post-Launch Data

Rule number one: no test data on a live site. Okay, that one is obvious.

Rule number two is to be sure to load enough content that demonstrates the site is open for visitors. If you plan to launch your live site with a press release and announcements to your intended audience, you should have content loaded that gives your visitors a reason to be there, and a reason to come back. What your site needs to show upon launch is up to you.

Using a Development vs. Staging Site

Depending on the complexity of the site, some people load their content in their development site. There isn't anything wrong with this practice, although some potential issues exist.

If active development is going on in the development site, you run the risk that a development task will cause a problem and the developers might need to revert to a previous version of the site. You could lose content. If you use a staging site, where iterative development is not occurring, you might be better off. But in either case, don't load real content until you know that the content type configuration is done. Changes to content types after you load your content can cause rework.

If your content is being developed and edited offline while your site is being developed, you can load your content when you have a stable environment. You don't have to wait for the site to be ready to start developing content.

Loading Content

Two processes commonly are used for loading content:

➤ Data entry

➤ Data migration

Data Entry

Data entry refers to the process of manually entering data or content into the various content-oriented fields in your site. Following are some tips to help you manage data entry.

HTML Editors

HTML editors provide an easy way to format the content of the body of a node. Following are some tips that can save you time and effort when using HTML editors. With minimal training, your content editors will be well on their way to troubleshooting formatting issues and creating trouble-free content.

Source Button

Turning on the Source button is helpful, assuming, of course, the editor you have installed has one. This button enables your content editors to view the HTML that is being generated. You might be thinking, "I thought using an editor meant I don't have to know HTML." Yes, that is true, but occasionally, formatting can get a little messed up and being able to look at the source to assess the situation helps.

For example, Figure 6-25 shows a sample node body in development, and Figure 6-26 shows the source of the node body. Notice that the first paragraph appears to wrap automatically when the text reaches the image.

Notice how the lines
stop at the image

Body:

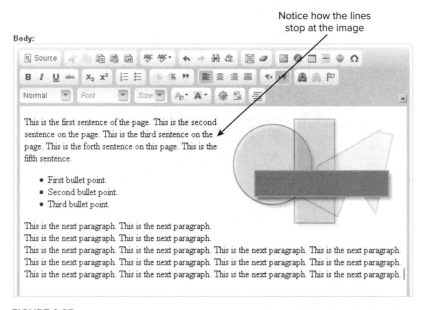

FIGURE 6-25

Body:

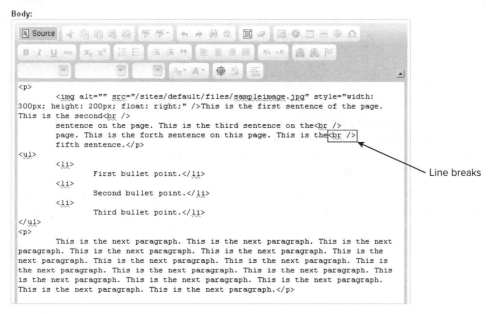

Line breaks

FIGURE 6-26

Looking at the source helps when your content does not appear to lay out as you would like. Notice the <br /> tag in Figure 6-26. Someone hit Shift+Enter each time the text got close to the image. When the node is saved, the text does not remain close to the image, as shown in Figure 6-27.

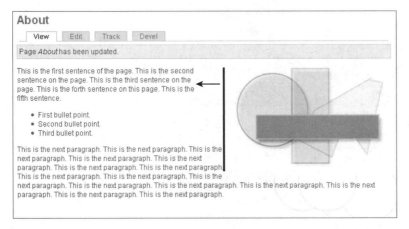

FIGURE 6-27

Image Source

You can embed an image in the body of your node in several ways. Assume you have uploaded an image using an image field and inserted the image into the body with an insert button. If you click on the image in the body (see Figure 6-28) and then click on the image editor icon, you see options that let you manipulate the image size, add ALT text, and change the image source. The image source is the focus right now. You likely will see what is referred to as an *absolute path* to your image, which might look as follows:

```
http://dev.sitename.com/sites/default/files/images/picture.jpg
```

If you are developing your content on a development server, technically, you are providing an absolute link to the development site. When you transfer your site to your production server, your production site will have links back to images on your development server, because the path to your image includes the domain. If you shut down your development site for some reason, your images won't be there anymore.

Solutions are available. One is to update the database with the proper path. For instance, perform a find/replace on the node revisions table and replace dev.sitename.com with the correct URL, or you could turn the absolute URL into a virtual URL, such as the following:

```
/sites/default/files/images/picture.jpg
```

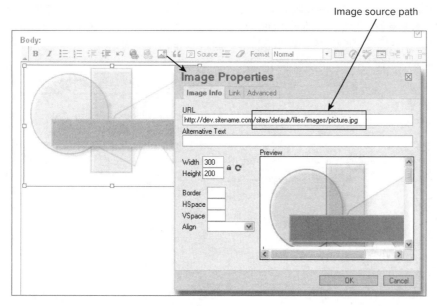

Image source path

FIGURE 6-28

Copy/Paste

If you prepare your content offline in a Microsoft Word document, then copy/paste the content into a body field, a chance exists that your HTML editor will capture formatting instructions from Word. You don't want Word's styling embedded in your node content. It can interfere with your CSS and can prevent you from applying further editing with the HTML editor.

Figure 6-29 shows text copied from a Word document into a node with an HTML editor.

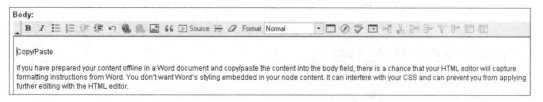

FIGURE 6-29

Figure 6-30 shows the source of the same node. Notice the difference between the source code shown in Figure 6-30 and Figure 6-26. What you see in Figure 6-30 is only half of the Microsoft styling being inserted into the node with the basic Paste command. To see the rest, you would have to scroll down.

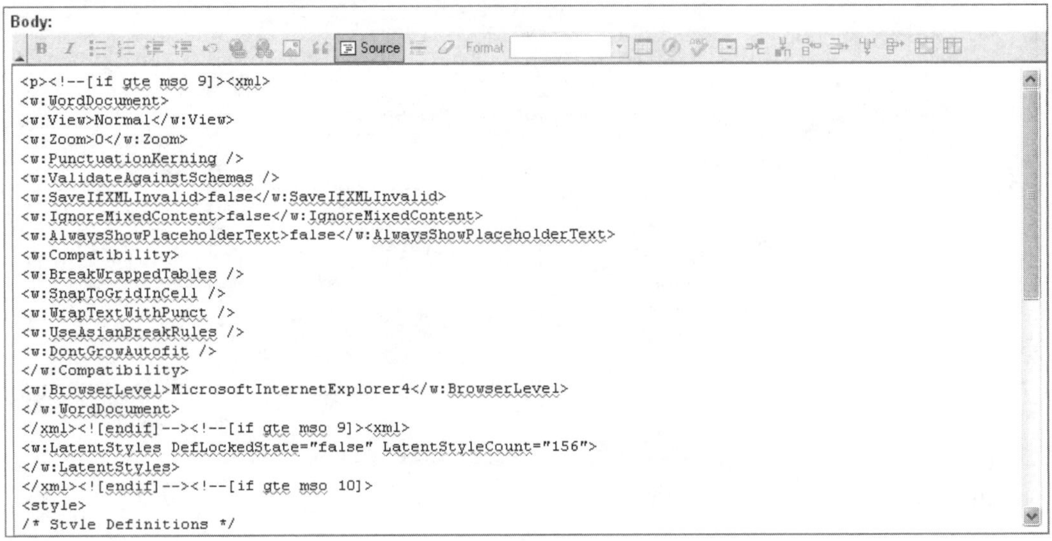

FIGURE 6-30

Some editors enable you to choose "Paste from Word," but that option does not always work to clear all Word formatting. The manual process is to copy from Word, paste into Notepad (or the Mac equivalent), copy from Notepad into the body of the node, and then start your formatting.

If you copy/paste from another site, you could run into similar issues. For example, you might inadvertently grab a `<div>` tag. The possibility exists that the `<div>` tag that you embed in the body of your node could interfere with the display of a page that includes a teaser of that node.

> **MANAGING INTERNAL LINKS**
>
> The Linkit module provides an easy interface for internal linking. Linkit links to nodes, users, views, and terms by default, using an autocomplete field. It provides a link button, similar to the ordinary link button in most editors. The module is available for Drupal 6 and Drupal 7.

Input Filter Permissions

When you enter content into a node and save it, that which you enter gets saved in the database. This includes the text and any code that you enter. When others view the node, they see what you entered minus any HTML tags you, the content developer, don't have permission to use. For instance, just because you have an image editor button and use it to embed an image doesn't mean that image will appear when the node is viewed.

If you have permission, you can select an input format that allows your images to show when the node is viewed. Configuring your site with the input formats you need is part of development, so make sure you have requirements that address the type of editing you need to perform. Knowing which format to use (assuming your permissions give you an option) is part of training.

Media Preparation

Do you remember dial-up Internet? If you never experienced it, you are lucky. If you did, you learned that some pages would take a long time to load. It was frequently due to the images weighing a lot. Back then, a page that contained a 2 MB image was not appreciated.

Although many people today have high-speed connections, that doesn't mean that loading one or more 2 MB or 3 MB images in your pages is okay. Some of your visitors might not have a great connection. So, what do you do?

In addition to configuring your content types to limit the size of file your content developers upload, you can also ask them to make the images smaller before uploading them. So, instead of uploading a 2 MB image, they upload, for instance, a 75 KB image.

RESIZING IMAGES

Another solution to image weight issues is the Image Resize Filter module. This module allows you to resize a large image that has been embedded in the body node. The module creates another image based on the resizing directions provided, and a copy of the resized image is saved. When visitors view the page, the smaller image is loaded.

Media is not limited to images. If you have video or audio planned for your site, you will want to consider its size (weight and shape) before loading it to your site. For instance, will you be displaying a video in the content area? How wide is your content area? How wide is your video? Other considerations include server space and the server's ability to manage the delivery of potentially large files to your site visitors. If you have a busy site, make sure your server can manage the load.

Data Migration

Data migration is the process of moving content from one place to another. The topic of moving content from one site to another was discussed earlier in this chapter under the topic of version control. But data migration in the context of loading content to your site is only one step before going from development to production.

Assume you have another site that has numerous pages of content and you want that content to be moved to your new Drupal site. How do you do it without re-creating the content manually? Migrate the data.

Depending on the source of your data, this task might be easier said than done, but it can be worth it. You do not want someone to say, "Hey, all we have to do is insert some records in the database and we are set to go." There is more to data migration than that. Why? For starters, node data is stored in more than one table in the database, and each node has a unique identification number that gets generated by Drupal. You need Drupal's APIs in order to generate the Drupal data associated with the nodes. Several migration tools are available at Drupal.org that can either perform your migration or provide a model for the custom migration scripts you will need.

MIGRATING YOUR CONTENT TO DRUPAL

Not surprisingly, many people have migrated to Drupal. Fortunately, many have shared their experiences on Drupal.org. The "Migrating to Drupal" post at `http://drupal.org/documentation/migrate` provides insight into the resources available to get you started with your migration. The Feeds module is another way to migrate content from one source to another.

If you need help migrating data, there are services available as well. For example, Cyrve (`http://cyrve.com/`) specializes in migrating into Drupal sites.

If your migration is from a legacy site to your new site, you might need to migrate the following:

➤ **URLs** — Move the URL for the source page, assuming you are migrating from a legacy site to a new site. Migrating URLs helps users find the pages they have bookmarked.

➤ **Files** — Move files that are attached to legacy pages and stored on a different server. The process you used to associate your files to your data can influence your file-migration process.

➤ **Code** — Remove embedded code in the legacy pages that will no longer be required on the new site.

➤ **Images** — Moving images is similar to moving files and depends on the method you used to associate your images with your content.

➤ **Dates** — The publish date associated with the legacy pages provides identification information and is useful for content validation.

➤ **Author** — The author in Drupal is the username. If you need to migrate author information, you might need to associate the migrated content with a user account.

➤ **Tags** — Move existing tags used for categorization. If you are going to keep the same data architecture, you will need a way to migrate the tags and associate the tags with the content.

The more complicated the migration, the more time and resources you may need, which could affect your schedule and budget. You might find that the existing tools won't do what you need, so you may have to create your own migration tool.

SUMMARY

This chapter presented a series of tasks that you can use to plan your site's development. Development can be an expensive process, and without a plan up front, you could waste valuable resources.

The planning process starts with creating a requirements inventory, to take the site description and turn it into a list of things that need to be created. With a big-picture look at the site and what is required in hand, your next step is to design a development solution or build recipe. What modules are needed and why? With all this information in front of you, start sequencing the development tasks so that you can create a schedule and manage your team's workload.

You can't do anything without a space to do it in. This chapter explored various development and production server options and how not all servers are created equal.

With your development plan in place and your environments ready to go, the build process is primed for success. While you are off building and developing the site, others can be preparing for testing. Fortunately, the requirements collected will have most, if not all, of the data needed to test the site.

And then there is content — the reason people come to your site. Depending on the process you choose to load content to your site, content development could occur in a development environment, in a production environment, or both. Migrating content from one source to another to populate your site takes careful planning and adequate resources.

While your site is being developed, you can be planning its implementation. Depending on the role of your site, you might have a lot to do. Chapter 7, "Coordinating Implementation," explores various tasks that you might need to perform to ensure a successful implementation.

7

Coordinating Implementation

That this chapter is presented after development does not mean that all planning for implementation occurs after development. As a verb, *implement* means "to carry out; to put into action; perform."[1] Based on this definition, you could say you started implementing your site when you started planning your site. Or you could say that you started implementing your site when you started developing it.

This chapter describes taking your site live by considering implementation from three perspectives: technical, organizational, and human.

From a technical perspective, implementation tasks could range from making the site public to integrating the site into an existing system.

From an organizational perspective, implementation could be as simple as modifying your personal schedule to update your site. Or your site could represent a new online division in your organization and require you to:

➤ Hire new staff

➤ Update your organization's financial procedures to accommodate revenues and taxes

➤ Update your marketing campaigns and strategies

➤ Modify business processes

➤ And so on

From a human perspective, implementation could mean you need some training on how your site works. Or it could mean that you need to:

➤ Gain approval from management

➤ Facilitate buy-in from employees

➤ Train employees to use the site

---

[1] Dictionary.com: `http://dictionary.reference.com/browse/implement`

➤ Develop and train employees in new business processes

➤ Modify employee responsibilities

➤ And so on

By the end of this chapter, you should be able to:

➤ Assess the impact your site might have on your organization and staff

➤ Assess your training needs and identify a potential strategy

➤ Identify basic site-configuration settings common on live sites

CHANGE MANAGEMENT

When you decided to build or rebuild your site, you recognized and accepted the need for change. By engaging others in your organization, you took your first steps toward building a commitment for change. As you collected requirements and decided what your site should or should not do, you helped others to acknowledge that change was coming. Although you might have experienced resistance to this change, coming to a consensus with your team before taking your site from planning to development is important.

When you were planning your site, if you included those who will use the site, as well as those who will sponsor the site, you have already taken steps toward managing change. Now, it is time to assimilate the new into the existing. In order to assimilate, you need:

➤ To know how your current state will be different in the future due to your new site

➤ A plan to get from the current state to the future state

Assessing Current and Future States

To assess current and future states, start by asking the following questions:

➤ How are things done now and how will they be done later?

➤ Who is doing what now and who will be doing it later?

➤ Is anything not being done now that will need to be done later?

➤ Do you have the resources for the new tasking?

Chances are, you already have a lot of this information, especially for the future state. Information about the future state should be in your requirements. When you created your requirements, you likely also assessed your current state.

The easy way to start your assessment of current and future states is to work backward from the future state to the current state. Locate the site process and task requirements and ask how the process- and task-related requirements differ from what you do today. Then ask what you aren't doing today but will be doing after your site is operational. Answers to these two questions will get you a list of differences between the current and future states of your organization (be it an organization of one or thousands).

To accommodate these differences, make a list of the resources you will need — for instance:

- ➤ New operating procedures
- ➤ Updated user guides
- ➤ Training on new procedures
- ➤ Staffing changes
- ➤ And so on

To help illustrate this type of assessment, consider the following example scenarios.

Changes to Current State

If you have never had a site or if your new site is different from your current site, there likely will be changes to accommodate. Consider the following scenario.

Current

Assume you have an event-management process that requires attendees to send an email request in order to register for an event. A list of registrants is maintained in a spreadsheet based on email requests. Confirmation is sent to the registrant after the name is added to the list in the spreadsheet. The current process requires you to have access to your email and the spreadsheet.

Future

The future state uses a registration form on your site. The data collected via the form is stored in your site database. Your site has a report that lists those who have registered. Registrants are sent an email confirming their registration when they save the form. You monitor registration by looking at the online report. You have the option to export the report for offline use.

Changes

Other than the process steps, what else changes? For starters, your event-registration acceptance task changes. You no longer have to go to your email to see whether any registration emails have come in; instead, you can go to your site. You no longer have to manually create and maintain a spreadsheet with registrant information. You no longer have to manually send a confirmation email.

What resources do you need in order to change your process? It depends. If you were the type of person to monitor your email registration requests on your phone and now you need to be logged in to a site to monitor event registrations, you might want a different device for accessing your site. You might also need some training on how to access the registration information.

Plus, don't forget your customers. If your customers are familiar with your existing process, how will you tell them about the new process? Perhaps you just have to change your ads from an email address to a URL. But don't underestimate the potential for your customers to resist change. If they are used to emailing you when they want to register for an event, they may continue to do so and ignore your new site.

Initially, you might need to support two processes: the current method and the new method. To support the current method of accepting emails, it will be you who uses the online form versus your customer. You will take the information emailed to you and enter it into the form for your customer.

In time, with continued strategic communications, your customers will likely switch to the new process. It will be your choice as to how long you support both methods before you send the polite message that you can no longer complete the registration process for them and they need to use the form.

This is just one example, and not all change will require this much planning. If you have been part of the project from the beginning, you may have difficulty imagining that your changes will be difficult to implement. Try to imagine being the person who is just hearing about the change for the first time.

Additions to Current State

Change isn't always about something today being different tomorrow. It can be about something more, something in addition to what is happening now. This next scenario provides an example of adding something new to your current state.

Current

Assume that your organization does not have a website. Your current methods of communication consist of newsletters and emails. You have designed and developed a new site that will provide several new communication opportunities for your association including the newsletter and emails.

Future

The processes you used to manage your newsletters and emails have changed, but that is not all. You now have a site, whereas you didn't have one before. You also have new communication opportunities, such as online discussions and a feature called "Ask the Expert."

Changes

With a new site and services come new responsibilities that require specific skills and time. New skills and time might mean new staff or changes in existing staff responsibilities. New responsibilities can require training and changes in compensation. Training will likely be a one-time cost, but additional compensation will continue.

These types of changes can have ripple effects in your organization. For instance, simply adding new tasks to an existing staff member might not be possible without shifting workloads for multiple staff members. These changes might require training and compensation as well.

As for your customers, those currently getting your newsletter and emails, your new site might mean you need new outreach efforts to let them know you are online as well as letting them know you are offering more. If your customers are not used to online discussions, you will need a strategy that encourages them to participate online.

Each scenario is different, of course, so no single solution exists. Your goal is to assess change from all perspectives.

Other Potential Changes

If this is your first site and you are wondering which post-launch processes you might have over-looked when you were collecting requirements, here are a few items to consider.

Customer Service

Assume your business sells products in a brick-and-mortar store and has a customer service department to support your products. You decide to create a website so that your customers can purchase your products online.

➤ What happens if your customer has a technical problem?

➤ Who will provide assistance?

➤ When will assistance be available?

➤ What skills must your customer service representatives possess?

For your online presence, you'll need to determine whether to use your current customer service representatives or add different staff trained specifically for the site. Will you distinguish between support for the products you sell and support for the online environment in which you sell your products?

Site Maintenance

If you have never had a site before, a new process to add to your organization is site maintenance. That site maintenance can be overlooked is hard to imagine, but it happens. Maintenance efforts can vary, depending on the content in your site, how user account requests are configured, and the technology in use on the site.

Chapter 8, "Sustaining the Site," provides additional insight into site-maintenance tasks. For now, here are three categories of site maintenance to consider when identifying potential change:

➤ **Content** — What are your plans to maintain the content on your site? A frequently over-looked content-maintenance task is link validation (ensuring links to other sites remain valid). You might also have time-sensitive content that changes on a regular basis.

➤ **Users** — User-maintenance tasks can include cleaning out user accounts for fictitious users, blocking users who misuse the site, and helping users gain or regain access to the site.

➤ **Technology** — Technology maintenance includes analyzing the available updates before implementing them. You will need a plan and a schedule for performing technology updates.

Site Content Growth

In addition to content maintenance, you might have content growth. If you are building a Drupal site, content growth likely is expected. Why else would you choose a content management system (CMS)? The effort you expend to populate your site before it is launched is likely a temporary effort. Tasks that people normally perform might be set aside so that content can be written in anticipation of the big day. What about after launch?

If the purpose of your site is to grow content, what processes and resources do you need to put into place to ensure new content is generated? Will you need a writing team, a marketing team, or both?

If your content is generated internally, you likely will need internal resources to continue the development of content. If your site's content is generated externally, you will need strategies to engage the external resources and motivate them to contribute to your site.

Strategies for Managing Change

Numerous resources are available that cover change management in more detail than what is presented in this chapter, so please seek out change-management expertise if the following insights do not address your change requirements.

Any time you change what is done today with something new, you may encounter questions, concerns, doubts, and even resistance. The goal of change management is to manage the questions and concerns and to create a process that provides a structured transition from old to new. The following sections provide some insights to get you thinking about what you might need in your organization before your new site goes live.

Awareness and Buy-In

Just because someone is aware that a change is going to occur does not mean he or she has bought into the change. People who have bought into a change don't have to like the change; they simply have agreed to change their behavior to accommodate the change. Managing change is easier when those who are about to experience the change are aware of it and have bought into it.

Circumstances exist when awareness and buy-in cannot be obtained from all those affected by the change. Business strategies might require secrecy. Management by consensus is not always a good strategy, either. So, what do you do? No one right answer to this question exists, as you can imagine. A good option is a collaborative solution, in which decision-makers work with process owners to define, build, and implement the solution that meets the need and is within the boundaries that can be supported.

Following are some insights to help you consider awareness and buy-in in your organization:

➤ **Sponsorship** — The people responsible for sponsoring the resources need to be aware and provide buy-in. This one is easy to imagine. Unless you have buy-in from those who control the resources that you need for building and maintaining the site, the site likely won't get built.

➤ **Process owners** — All sites create and/or support one or more processes for an organization. Who will own the process? Who will perform the process? Who will support the process? For instance, it might seem obvious, but you limit your chances of success if department A builds a site for department B without asking department B whether it needs a new site and/or what that new site should do.

➤ **Process users** — Looking from the other direction, the people who will use the new site will need to be aware and provide buy-in to what is planned for the site. For instance, if you have a strong following on your current site and don't want to lose that following, reach out to your followers and ask them what they like and don't like about the site. Ask them how they would feel if you changed the site. You might get some great ideas.

Process Design Collaboration

When offline processes are moved online, chances are they will change. Assuming your process team and your site-development team worked collaboratively to convert the offline processes into online processes while collecting requirements, you are more than halfway to managing the process change.

If you are just starting out and want to increase your chances that the online version of the process will be accepted by all the process users, one strategy is to get the right people in the planning sessions. For instance, consider including the people:

➤ Who perform critical steps in the process (the linchpin)

➤ Who say, "If it ain't broke, don't fix it" (the squeaky wheel)

➤ Whom the team trusts to provide guidance (the subject matter expert)

While designing the new online processes, be sure to plan how the old processes will be retired or integrated into the new processes. When you get to implementation, most of your work is done. Assuming you have documented your new processes, you can use that information when developing the applicable training.

Change Support

Depending on the complexity of your site and the amount of change it brings, you might need temporary change support. Chances are that not everyone is going to catch on the first time they learn about the changes. Change support is the point of contact(s) where process users can go to ask questions, surface issues, or even make suggestions for improvement.

The duration of the change support needs to be coordinated with decisions regarding when the new process will be in full swing. If process users are reluctant to change and the old process continues to work, you could end up with a long transition. Identify and plan how and when to turn on the new process and turn off the old. Make those decisions known and provide the necessary support to ensure everyone makes the move.

TRAINING

Training is a component of or tool for change management. You can approach Drupal training from several perspectives. In context with site implementation, training goals can range from "I need to be able to add content to the site" to "I need to be able to add new functionality to the site." Where do you draw the line? Do you need to manage content, administer users, monitor performance, reconfigure module settings, add features, and so on?

Although training often occurs after the site has been developed, you need to plan for training before the implementation phase begins so that training can be executed in a timely manner. When you created use cases, and when you were analyzing your audience and defining roles for your site, you were defining potential training requirements and learners. If you assessed your current state and future state as a way of managing change, you were identifying gaps that might need to be supported with training.

Planning your training is similar to planning your site:

➤ Analyze your needs

➤ Define your objectives

➤ Design a solution

➤ Develop the solution

➤ Deliver the solution

The following sections provide insights into the instructional design process. The insights are provided to help you start planning your training design, development, and delivery.

Analyzing Your Needs

Because Drupal training is such a broad topic and spans many options, the first step is to analyze your training needs. To do this, start by asking the following questions:

➤ Which tasks associated with your site need to be performed?

➤ When do the tasks need to be performed?

➤ How often should the tasks be performed?

➤ Who should perform the tasks?

Tasks

After you launch your site, workloads change. Figure 7-1 illustrates the potential workload shift you might experience when going from production to operations (or post-launch).

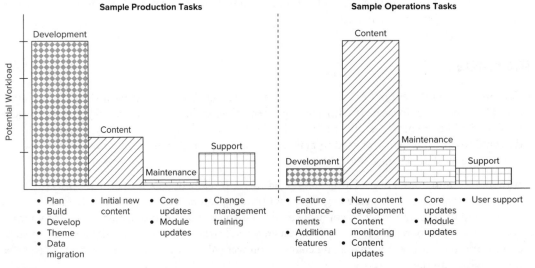

FIGURE 7-1

This example assumes that you have plans to grow the content of your site, that you might need to do some additional development, and that you need to perform maintenance on both the code and the content.

As you can see, there are several types of tasks that will need to be performed, and it is likely the same people won't perform them all. When you identify and analyze the tasks that need to be performed, you have a better sense of which organizational role should perform the tasks and the skills they will need.

The people who fill these organizational roles will be your learners. The learners' preexisting skills will influence how many tasks need to be trained, and the learners' learning styles will influence your instructional strategies. Also, the learners' availability will influence your delivery strategy.

Content-Related Tasks

As with other types of tasks, the learning objectives for content-related tasks will vary. Answers to the following questions can help you identify learning objectives associated with content-related tasks:

➤ What is the difference between the content types?

➤ Will you use an HTML editor or will you create your HTML offline with an application?

➤ Will you need to know how to add content to menus or will your navigation update automatically?

➤ Will different roles have access to different content types and/or data fields?

➤ Is there a content-moderation process?

➤ Will media be edited prior to being uploaded to the site?

Many, if not all, of the site-related content tasks that you need to perform are listed in your requirements. For instance, when you performed your process and task analyses while collecting requirements, you probably identified the processes and described tasks associated with content development. That information can provide the basis for the training you might need.

Defining the tasks is the first step in defining the click-by-click steps you need to include in your training materials.

Development- and Maintenance-Related Tasks

Depending on the complexity of your site, development- and maintenance-related tasks are often performed by a trained Drupal builder/developer or by the same team that developed the site. When defining the objectives and topics for your future development and maintenance tasks, you will likely answer the following questions:

➤ Will your team add and configure modules?

➤ Will your team create database queries and displays?

➤ Will your team update the site code?

➤ Will your team monitor site and system logs?

➤ Will your team be responsible for addressing any issues in the logs?

The quantity and scope of post-launch development and maintenance tasks can be large, especially if you have a complex site with a lot of customization. If you are the site owner and have been working with a vendor to build your site, are you ready to build Drupal development capacity in-house or do you want to establish a maintenance relationship with your vendor? Before deciding to build in-house capacity for development and maintenance, consider whether you have the work to justify such resources. In other words, will you have enough work to keep the in-house staff busy and justify the long-term investment?

The answer does not have to be all or nothing. You could work with your development team to identify the types of development and maintenance tasks you can perform in-house and then establish a vendor relationship for the other types of tasks.

Before committing to a list of training topics, consider reviewing Chapter 8, which provides insights into maintenance tasks you might need to perform.

Support-Related Tasks

Support-related tasks tend to focus on user management. You might need both internal and external user training, depending on the types of tasks users will perform. Support-related tasks are influenced by several factors, including:

➤ The type of user accounts

➤ The permissions users have

➤ The tasks users are expected to perform

➤ Whether anyone can create an account or accounts are restricted

In order to provide support to users, your support staff will need to be trained to:

➤ Create/approve/block an account

➤ Help users configure their profiles

➤ Instruct users how to perform common tasks, such as creating content

➤ Troubleshoot problems

➤ Know when to elevate an issue

Timing

Sometimes, the old saying, "It's all in the timing" is true. Two perspectives are associated with timing and training.

Of the tasks you need to perform, when do you need to know how to perform them? For instance, will you schedule training just in time or will you make training part of the site delivery? If you choose a just-in-time strategy, you will need a training strategy that can deliver the training when you need it.

Another aspect of timing has to do with when the site will be ready versus when you can start developing the training documents. If you are documenting procedures for training but decisions regarding how the procedures will be configured in the site are still being defined, you need to decide if it is it worth the effort to create documentation before all decisions are made and then spend time redoing the documentation when decisions have been finalized or simply wait until the site is ready.

Frequency

Another consideration when analyzing your training needs is associated with return on investment. For tasks that you will perform on a regular basis, it makes sense to provide training. If you need a task performed once or twice, you can either train staff to perform those tasks or contract out the tasks. If the task is simple, the cost of training might be justified. But if the task is more complicated and requires additional skills other than knowing where to click, the cost might not be justified.

For instance, site enhancements are likely to be performed infrequently and require skills beyond what basic training can provide. If your plan is to build an in-house development team, will you do it via training or will you hire people who already possess the requisite skills? Or will you rely on a vendor to help you add enhancements on an as-needed basis and skip training at this level?

Quantity

The number of people who need to be trained and the number of different organizational roles those people fit into will influence the number of courses that need to be developed and the number of learning events to be scheduled.

If you break your tasks into the three categories discussed previously (content, users, and technology), you might need three (or more) courses, depending on the complexity of your site and the different tasks performed within each category.

Regarding scheduling, if you have many people who need to be trained, group training (online or classroom) would be an efficient strategy. An advantage to group training is the opportunity for the participants to hear each other's questions and discuss the tasks they are learning. A challenge for group training is scheduling. Finding a time when all participants are available and can afford to be away from their normal duties can be difficult. Self-paced learning might be your only solution.

Defining Your Objectives

Your task analysis should provide a list of post-launch tasks for which training is required and a list of who needs to be trained. Depending on how granularly you defined your tasks, there still might be some room for interpretation. To help clarify and manage expectations, learning objectives can come in handy.

When defining objectives, sometimes you need to break your tasks into steps or activities so that a more precise understanding of what is expected can be defined. For instance, assume the task is to manage the growth of the content on the site. Your learning objectives might be that, at the end of the training, the learner should be able to:

➤ Create a node

➤ Edit a node

➤ Add a node to a menu

➤ Add terms to a vocabulary

➤ Edit the number of items listed in a view block

➤ Create a view block listing content titles

➤ Add a block to a page

Notice that each action that a learner needs to be able to perform is described with a verb that can be assessed. For instance, if the learner needs to be able to create a node, the learning activity should provide them the opportunity to create a node, and the assessment should test that behavior.

Objectives that use verbs like "understand," "know," and "do" are open to interpretation, and therefore, activities and/or assessments aren't easily defined. These types of verbs can also limit your ability to manage expectations; one person's definition of "understand" might not be the same as another person's definition.

You might need help from the development team to make a complete list of objectives after you have defined the scope of the task. Don't forget, the use cases you created when collecting requirements will provide a great starting point.

Designing a Solution

Designing a training solution means defining an instructional and delivery strategy that meets the objectives and addresses the various constraints identified during the training needs analysis.

Not all subject matter experts can, on their own, take their vast knowledge and skills and express them in a way that others without their background can understand. This is when a technology-savvy instructional designer can help.

Instructional Strategies

Instructional strategies define how the instructional materials are presented, which activities are needed to enable learning, and the order in which the instruction and activities are offered. This section is not intended to discuss everything you might need to design your instructional strategies, but the following sections provide some insights to help you get started.

ACTIVE LEARNING CREDO

"When I hear, I forget.

When I hear and see, I remember a little.

When I hear, see, and ask questions or discuss with someone else, I begin to understand.

When I hear, see, discuss, and do, I acquire knowledge and skill.

When I teach to another, I master."[2]

Content Structures

To enable learners to perform a specific task and meet the learning objective associated with the task, identify the facts, concepts, rules, and procedures the instruction will need to include. Then identify when and how each should be presented to the learner in order to maximize learning and retention.

When identifying the right mix of each content structure, remember that the learner potentially is processing new facts, concepts, rules, and procedures all at once. Cognitive overload is going to be your challenge. The upcoming "Teaching Strategies" section provides some ideas on how to avoid this issue.

Facts

Facts include terms and definitions that learners need to know in order to learn a concept, rule, or procedure. In Drupal, terminology is probably one of the first hurdles your learners will need to jump. Consistent and contextual use of facts will be important for long-term retention. Determine if:

➤ There is terminology that will be used in the instruction.

➤ The term has more than one meaning.

➤ The learners need to be able to define the term in order to understand the concept, principle, rule, or procedure.

These determinations contribute to decisions regarding the sequence of the instruction.

Concepts

Concepts can reference both the abstract (e.g., freedom) and the concrete (e.g., trees). Initially, the concept of HTML pages being generated dynamically can be difficult for some to envision, especially if they are used to traditional HTML site development, where files sitting on the server are

---

[2] Silberman, Mel. *Active Training: A Handbook of Techniques, Designs, Case Examples, and Tips, Second Edition*. Pfeiffer, 1998.

sent to the browser. Determine if there are topics that require the learners to imagine something happening. Identify how and when they should be presented.

Rules

Rules define how something will work. With Drupal, there are many ways to accomplish something but there are also underlying "rules" that govern your options. For instance, to extend Drupal, you need to implement a hook (or API). The hook acts as a rule, the way Drupal works. For each task the learner needs to perform, are there any underlying rules that will help them understand that they do, or do not have options to perform the task differently from what is being taught?

Procedures

Procedures are established or correct methods of doing something and are often believed to be the easiest content structure to teach. Procedures are typically the click-by-click steps one performs when executing a task on a Drupal site. Assumptions that procedures are easy to teach, especially with technology, can create problems with the learner.

For instance, many instructors believe that you can teach a procedure using the "just do it this way" approach. However, without an understanding of the facts, rules, and/or concepts associated with the procedure, learners just know the steps and can't deviate from them or troubleshoot if something goes wrong. Also, when learners know why a procedure should be performed a certain way, they are more likely to remember it later.

On the other side of this coin is the problem of providing too much information. For instance, when you teach someone how to create a node, you don't have to give a technical review of the node module and how it works. You might just need to explain what the term "nodes" refers to and that they are created with content types. The learning objective and audience will influence the level of detail you need to include.

Teaching Strategies

One way to avoid or limit cognitive overload is to use a teaching strategy that helps the learner reuse existing knowledge. For example, use analogies as a teaching strategy. This helps the learners put new facts, concepts, rules, and procedures in context with what they already know, thereby reducing the amount of new information they actually need to learn.

You can create your own teaching strategy, but here are a few examples to get you thinking:

➤ **Experiential learning** — Provides real-world experiences that take into consideration the student's prior knowledge

➤ **Problem-based learning** — Provides learners with a problem and facilitates the acquisition of the appropriate knowledge and skills to solve the problem

➤ **Direct instruction** — Provides structured information supported by activities that reinforce learning

Many other teaching strategies are available. You can create your own or you can combine the best aspects of multiple strategies. For example, you might use a direct instruction strategy that presents the information in a contextual scenario, providing learners with a real-world experience to which they can relate. In addition, you might use analogies to help the learner connect with new information and provide them with problem-solving activities to apply what they are learning.

Delivery Strategies

Part of designing a solution is choosing a delivery strategy. The following sections describe a few delivery strategies to help you start planning your training solution.

An Instructor-Led Strategy

Instructor-led training comes in two forms: classroom and at-a-distance. At-a-distance training typically implies online, but it could mean other forms of correspondence.

In both situations, the instructor leads the class by presenting information, demonstrating procedures, coordinating activities, answering questions, and facilitating the overall learning experience. When delivering classroom training, it is important to have multiple instructors to help learners through challenges they might have with activities. Although well-documented activities should be a given in technology training, they can help to reduce the ratio between learners and instructors.

A Self-Paced Strategy

Not everyone has time to go to training classes. Add to this the need for just-in-time learning, and you can justify using a self-paced approach to training. A self-paced strategy can have an instructor on call to answer questions, but the instructor is not facilitating the learning process. Or, the learning experience can be offered without support.

Self-paced instruction should be well documented to compensate for the information typically presented by an instructor. A self-paced strategy can use text-based tutorials, user guides, videos, and animations.

The length of self-paced learning experiences tends to be short and focused on one or two learning objectives. This gives learners flexibility when shaping their curriculum, allowing them to focus only on what they need to learn and when they need to learn it.

An Internship Strategy

If you want to be able to enhance existing features or add new ones after the site is delivered, you might need to have an in-house site builder on your staff. You could hire a person who is trained in Drupal or you could train someone. One way to train is via an internship.

With cooperation from and coordination with the development team, you can include a person from your staff on the development team and turn him or her into a Drupal intern. This might mean that you take an existing staff member and send him or her to sit with the development team to learn how to build Drupal sites. Or you could hire someone specifically to be an intern.

Declaring someone a Drupal intern does not ensure he will learn what you need him to learn. This is where coordination with the development team will help ensure that the intern can meet the learning objectives identified when planning your training requirements.

The advantage to this approach is that the intern learns Drupal and the specific development strategies used for your site. If you think this approach is worth pursuing and are going to hire a vendor, be sure to include it as a requirement when requesting quotes. Not all vendors can accommodate interns and the work required to facilitate their learning process.

Developing the Solution

Once you have a solution designed, develop the necessary materials. Depending on your strategy, you could have different types of materials to develop. It takes time to develop instructional materials, but, as suggested previously, you can save time and effort by referencing and possibly reusing documented processes, tasks, and their applicable use cases. You increase the chances that your training will be remembered if you provide learners with materials that can be useful references later.

Table 7-1 provides four components of training (information delivery, activities, facilitation, and assessment) and the types of materials or actions that will likely need to be developed or planned for each delivery strategy discussed previously.

TABLE 7-1: Sample Instructional Materials

	INSTRUCTOR-LED	SELF-PACED	INTERNSHIP
Information delivery	Live presentations and/or demonstrations. Classroom discussions. Assigned or suggested readings.	Recorded and/or scripted presentations and/or demonstrations. Online discussions. Suggested readings.	Informal discussions with mentor, supervisor and colleagues. Assigned or suggested readings.
Activities	User guide with instructions for hands-on, scripted activities.	User guide with instructions for hands-on, scripted activities. Can also include references to additional resources for clarification.	Hands-on work assignments on real-world projects. Detailed written instructions might not be provided.
Facilitation	Instructor guide with instructions for course structure, schedule, and other administrative information.	A syllabus or suggested course of study.	Coordination of work assignments performed by supervisor or mentor. Work assignment decisions influenced by agreed-upon learning objectives.
Assessment	Options include successful completion of an activity, instructor-to-student inquiries, and quizzes.	Can include successful completion of an activity and/or quizzes that offer immediate feedback (automated grading).	Supervisor and/or mentor evaluates work performed.

Delivering the Solution

Delivery of training depends on the solution you designed. If the following questions have not been answered already, this is the time to do it.

➤ Where will training be hosted, in a classroom or online?

➤ When will training be offered?

➤ If instructors are provided, who will they be?

Where Will Training Be Hosted?

If you are going to use a traditional classroom setting, there are some logistics to consider:

➤ **Geography** — Where is the room located and is it easily accessible? When selecting a space, take into consideration travel to and from, parking, building access, and room access.

➤ **Cost** — Is there a cost for the space? If you need to rent a room, you will have a rental cost and you might need a deposit. If you cancel the training, you might lose the deposit. Some rentals charge additional fees for projectors and other equipment.

➤ **Equipment** — Who will provide what equipment? Technology courses typically mean computers. If learners don't have laptops, you might need to provide them. You will also need a projector for the instructor. Whiteboards and/or flipcharts are useful as well, and don't forget the right kinds of pens. (Whiteboard pens run out of ink fast when used on paper.)

➤ **Learner space** — How much elbow room do learners need? Unless the room is preconfigured as a computer lab, you might not be able to fit as many people as you normally would. For instance, if a room typically holds 20 people for a meeting, it is likely that it will fit only 12 to 16 comfortably when computers are added. Remember that the computers and course materials take up space.

➤ **Food** — Can you concentrate when you are hungry? Events that last longer than three hours will likely need some form of refreshment. If the session runs over lunch, consider bringing in lunch. Once learners leave the room, other aspects of their lives can take over, causing you to lose up to an hour of teaching time waiting for people to return and get settled in.

If you using at-a-distance training, will you use a learning-management system or will your create your own method of providing the instructional materials and activities online? In either situation, following are a few logistics to consider:

➤ **Access** — Will access to the course need to be restricted? If you don't want outsiders finding and using your course materials while they are online, your solution will need access control.

➤ **Cost** — Will you "rent" a virtual space or build your own? It costs money to host training online, whether the money comes in the form of a usage fee or labor to develop a solution.

➤ **Tracking** — Will you or your learners need "proof" they received the training? If the answer is yes, the technology you choose will need a way to track the learners' attendance and/or access, depending on whether you are tracking an instructor-led or self-paced learning experience.

When Will Training Be Offered?

If the training is self-paced, "when" refers to when the online training will be available and for how long. But just because training is available doesn't mean learners will take advantage unless motivated to do so. Motivation can come from within or from external influences, such as encouragement from a supervisor.

Attendance is often easier to ensure when training is instructor-led and in a classroom. Removing learners from their day-to-day responsibilities can help them focus on learning. With the potential for conflicting schedules, scheduling training can be a challenge. Following are a few considerations when planning a training schedule:

➤ **Length** — If you have the time, a series of short sessions can help people accommodate not being away from responsibilities for too long. Or you can get it all over with at once with one or more back-to-back days of training. Some learning objectives lend themselves to short increments, while others are better served all at once.

➤ **Project schedule** — If learners need to hit the ground running as soon as the site is launched, your training schedule will be influenced by the launch date and by when a training version of the site will be ready. This situation might necessitate a non-incremental approach to delivery.

Who Will Conduct the Training?

If an instructor is part of your training solution, who will it be? You might use a developer from the development team or a trainer with experience on the subject being taught. Or you might create trainers with a train-the-trainer approach. Following are a few factors that can influence your decision:

➤ **Learning objectives** — If the objective is advanced or very unique to the site, a member of the development team might be your best choice. Because so many processes and tasks performed in a Drupal site are not unique, you might be able to use an experienced trainer for some site-specific learning objectives.

➤ **Training experience** — It helps if the instructor has experience delivering training. Instructors need to be able to adjust with the classroom dynamics by answering questions, managing issues that come up, and so on. An experienced trainer can be a developer on the development team or an external training vendor.

Remember, the instructor or trainer is not necessarily the person who should design or develop the instruction. The skills used to design and develop instruction are not the same used to deliver instruction. With that said, technology trainers are often trained to design, develop, and deliver training.

MARKETING

A goal of marketing is to reach your target audience and let them know you are open for business. Another goal is to get them to interact with your site as you intended. That could mean reading content, commenting, posting content, buying products, and more.

Marketing is like change management and training in that strategies are made before implementation starts. For instance, when you were collecting requirements, you made decisions regarding search engine optimization (SEO). You considered metadata, keywords, and SEO-friendly URLs. At this point, you have a rocking new SEO-friendly, content-rich site ready to appeal to your target audience and you want them to find it.

You can go all out and hire a marketing professional to help you design and execute a marketing plan, or you can do some research and develop and implement your own plan. Many free and low-cost resources are available that provide ideas and strategies to help you get the attention of your target audience and encourage them to visit and interact with your site.

If you are not ready to hire a marketing consultant familiar with website marketing strategies, the following strategies can help you start analyzing your options. Keep in mind, however, that the success of these strategies depends greatly on the purpose of your site, your audience, your competition, your resources, and your ability to execute the strategies appropriately.

SEO Strategies

If your audience is the type who will use a search engine to find what they need, you will want to be number one (or at least top 10) in their search results. Unless your site offers something very unique, you are likely to have some competition for the first 10 places in a search result. The art of reaching a top slot in a search engine has changed over the years and will continue to change as technology evolves. Your site can reach the top of the search result in several ways, as you can imagine, and numerous online and book resources are available to help you get there.

Following are three basic strategies that can help you increase your chances of being found in a search engine. The options you have regarding how to execute the strategies are numerous and can be found in several SEO resources.

Search Engine Optimization (SEO) Secrets *(Wiley, 2011) offers insights into advanced SEO strategies that can help your site move up in the search engine rankings.*

When you are ready to configure your site to be SEO-friendly, Drupal 6 Search Engine Optimization *(Packt Publishing, 2009) provides hands-on actions you can take to implement SEO in your Drupal site.*

Keyword Content

Optimize your site with content rich in the specific keywords your users will be searching. This is above and beyond any metadata strategies you might have planned. This strategy focuses on including the keywords directly in the text of your pages as content.

One way to do this is to blog. Publish useful and interesting information geared toward the interests of your target audience. Include words that your target audience will search for. Give them a reason to visit your site, such as to become clients, community members, supporters, and so on.

Inbound Links

Increase the number of inbound links from other reputable sites, which can improve your search engine rankings. You can create links from others site to yours in several ways, but be careful; some strategies would be considered as spam, which could reflect negatively on your site. The goal is to have reputable sites linking to your site.

For instance, you can use a traditional strategy and prepare a press release and demonstrate to an online editor or reporter that your story is newsworthy. If it is, that editor or reporter (neutral party) might write an article and share the news with his or her audience.

The article isn't necessarily going to be, "Hey, look who just launched a great website!" It will be about the newsworthy information you are offering. Because news stories quote sources, you (and your business or site) will likely be mentioned as the source, thus getting your name out there. The readers of the article might look you up. If you choose this route, choose reporters associated with news venues that you know can reach your audience.

Another option is to guest blog for someone else in addition to blogging on your own site. If your target audience visits an online resource on a regular basis, and that resource accepts interesting and useful articles from external resources, then try to negotiate for a "Brought to you by..." or "Written by..." link back to your site. You both win. They get content to keep their site going and you get to reach the audience they already have.

Online Advertising

You have seen online advertising — those banners and blocks that hold ads and appear above, beside, below, and even within the content you're interested in viewing. There are different methods for displaying these types of ads. Before you make any decisions about online ads, you need to plan.

Identifying keywords and terms that describe your content is one step in the process of planning your online ads. Another consideration is the design and cost of your ads, as well as the return you hope to make. You might find that the money you spend on this type of advertising does not gain you the site interactions (usually sales) you need.

 Peter Kent's Pay Per Click Search Engine Marketing for Dummies *(Wiley, 2006) provides useful insights into making decisions about online advertising.*

Traditional Ad Placement

Until recently, people paid to have their ads posted on a site, similar to how they would pay to place ads in a newspaper or magazine. These types of ads were purchased based on the timing or number of displays. You could pay to have ads on a site for a week, month, year, or whatever increment of time you negotiate. Or you could buy a predetermined number of times your ad would be loaded into a browser.

With this type of online advertising, you don't know if your ads are being seen. Your ads could be online at a time your target audience isn't. Or they could be placed "below the fold," such that unless the person viewing the page scrolls down, your ads don't get seen. The low click-through rates (the number of ads that were clicked) for traditional ad placements prompted new ideas in online advertising.

Pay-Per-Click Ads on Search Engines

One way to increase the chances that your ad will be seen by your target audience is to present your ad when your target audience says they are interested. For instance, each time your audience uses a search engine, they are looking for something. If you can let them know you have what they are looking for, when they are looking for it, you increase your chances that your ad will be seen by your target audience.

Of course, that doesn't mean the ad will lead to a visit to your site or even a desired interaction with your site (purchase, comment, post, search, browse), but it is a start. Given the number of people who use search engines, it would be cost-prohibitive to pay each time your ad is displayed in conjunction with a search that is consistent with what your ad offers. Instead, you pay an ad service if someone clicks on the ad.

The space available for such ads is limited, so you have to compete with everyone else who wants their ads to show. This is where bidding comes in. The more you are willing to pay per click, the higher the chances are that your ad will get displayed to the person performing the search. Figure 7-2 illustrates where Google places pay-per-click ads.

FIGURE 7-2

Google, Yahoo!, Microsoft, and others offer pay-per-click advertising options. It is worth looking into your different options before committing.

Pay-Per-Click Ads on Content Pages

Pay-per-click advertising is not limited to search engines. For instance, Google's AdSense and Yahoo!'s Content Match programs allow you to deliver contextual ads — ads on pages where content matches the keywords associated with your ad. The owner of the site that hosts the content pages agrees to show the ads.

Social Networking Strategies

Tell a friend or colleague. Tell the community. Tell them in person or online. The concept of networking or meeting people in a business or social context isn't new, but the Internet has taken networking to a whole new level over the past few years, with Twitter, Facebook, LinkedIn, and other similar online community sites. You don't have to physically go to a networking event to tell your audience you have new site; you can tell them online.

However, before you start posting announcements on community or networking discussion boards, take the time to listen to the conversations to get a sense of the rules and community etiquette. More and more online communities are cracking down on people posting promotional ads in places that are intended for discussion. You don't want negative publicity when you are trying to get positive publicity.

Traditional Strategies

Print and media advertising is a traditional way of reaching out to your target audience and letting them know that you are in business. Different platforms are available for advertising. Newspapers, magazines, brochures, flyers, conference booths, radio, and television have been around for quite a while and still have a role to play in getting the word out. They work for brick-and-mortar products and services, why not for Internet-based products and services? You've probably seen or heard ads that promote a dot-com site on television or the radio.

A challenge associated with traditional strategies is ensuring you get a return on your advertising dollar investment. If you go this route, do your homework and consider consulting with a professional.

CONFIGURING YOUR SITE TO GO LIVE

The day has arrived; your site is ready to go live. It has been transferred to the production server, where it will be accessed via your domain. It is in maintenance mode, waiting to be released. However, before you take your site out of maintenance mode so that others can see it, you might still need to do a few tasks.

When you are developing a site, you can enable certain settings and features to help development run smoothly. When a development site is transferred to the production environment, the development-oriented settings go with it. So, before you make your site live, make sure the following settings are configured for your live site.

Configuring Performance Settings

At a minimum, consider the following types of default performance settings for your live site: caching and bandwidth optimization:

➤ **Caching** — When building a site, you need to see your work come to life as it happens, which means you don't want your pages cached. Caching refers to the temporary storage of data in such a way that the data can be delivered by the web server efficiently. As a result of caching, changes made to your content are not available to your visitors until the cache has been cleared and rebuilt. While developing, both Drupal's caching functionality and the developer's browser caching are typically disabled.

When your site is ready to go live, you might want to enable caching on your site. Drupal can store and compress pages and blocks and send the compressed pages to your visitors upon their request.

➤ **Bandwidth optimization** — Another way to improve your site's performance is to limit the number of requests your server needs to process. For instance, depending on the modules you have selected for your site, you could have more than 30 Cascading Style Sheet (CSS) files, each responsible for a visual element on your site. One step toward bandwidth optimization is CSS aggregation and compression into one file, thus reducing the number of files that need to be processed and sent to your visitor.

Drupal also has the option to aggregate (but not compress) JavaScript files used on your site, potentially improving the responsiveness of your site. If JavaScript files run on your site, you might consider this option as well.

CSS AGGREGATION

Internet Explorer limits the number of CSS files it can process. If you exceed the number, your site is rendered without your CSS. Drupal's Performance setting "Optimize CSS files" aggregates and compresses the CSS files into one file, thus allowing you to overcome the issue.

Configuring Cron

Drupal comes with a file called `cron.php`, which contains code that performs maintenance tasks on your site. For instance, `cron.php` updates your search index and aggregator feeds and manages the size of your database logs. You can run it manually or you can configure your server to run it for you on a regular basis.

 In Drupal 6, you set up cron manually. Drupal 7 has a built-in cron feature. To learn more about cron, visit `http://drupal.org/getting-started/6/install/cron`.

Configuring Log Reporting

In order to support routine maintenance and troubleshooting, you should configure two log-reporting settings:

➤ **Error reporting** — Error reports during development are often sent to the screen so that errors appear as they occur. This is an important component of the build and test process. When your site goes live, you might not want your site visitors to see errors on the screen if they happen to occur. Part of maintenance is the routine review of the error logs to determine whether any issues arise.

➤ **Logging and alerts** — By default, the only setting is the maximum number of log records you want to store in the database. The number is your choice. If you have concerns about server space and database size, a lower number might be appropriate.

> **SYSLOG MODULE**
>
> The Syslog module, available for both Drupal 6 and Drupal 7, logs events by sending messages to the logging facility on your server. To learn more about the Syslog module, visit `http://drupal.org/documentation/modules/syslog`.

Checking Security

If your site requires a certain level of security, you should already have met those requirements and have testing procedures in place. This check is to ensure you don't have any settings in place that are convenient for development but not production. Following are some examples:

➤ **Permissions** — Make sure the authenticated users don't have any admin permissions.

➤ **User accounts** — Make sure account-creation settings are configured to meet your needs.

➤ **Default input format** — Make sure the filtered HTML input format is set as the default.

➤ **PHP filter** — If you have the PHP filter enabled, make sure only trusted administrators have access to that filter.

➤ **Settings.php properties** — Make sure the server properties for `settings.php` file are not set to write.

For more information about security, check out Greg Knaddison's book Cracking Drupal *(Wiley, 2009). Don't forget that the Security review module offers a quick way to check for many of the configuration settings that can lead to an unsecure site.*

Updating Theme Settings

There are two theme settings you might want to change on your live site:

- ➤ Administration theme for content editing
- ➤ The option to have the theme registry rebuilt on every page

Drupal comes with the option to show users a different theme when they are on the administration pages. This configuration is helpful when you want to show blocks that are for administration pages only. You also have the option to show the administration theme when adding or editing content.

If your development approach is to load real content during development, your development team might prefer to use the administration theme versus the public-facing theme. After the site is launched, content management will likely change to other roles. To maintain a consistent experience for people adding and editing content, you might want them to see the add/edit forms in the public-facing theme.

Depending on the theme you are using, your theme might have an option to rebuild the theme registry on every page. This setting is useful to enable when developing your theme. However, constantly rebuilding the theme registry will hinder your site performance; therefore, you should disable it on a production site.

ADMINISTRATION MENU

The Administration menu provides the option to clear the theme registry and the site's caches manually.

Disabling Modules

There is no need for unused modules to be enabled on the live site. Modules can get enabled during development but later be identified as not needed. Sometimes, those modules don't get disabled and uninstalled. If you want all aspects of unused modules removed from the site, you not only need to disable and uninstall the module, you might also want to remove the module from the server and clear records from the certain database tables. Why? Not all uninstall processes clear all the data associated with a module that was once enabled. Are legacy records in the database a big deal? They shouldn't be. It's up to you how "tidy" you want your database to be.

Other modules play an important role in development and troubleshooting. They should be disabled until they are needed for minor troubleshooting. For instance, the Devel module provides several tools for developers but is not used by your site visitors. Before your site is live, you should disable modules that provide development support and therefore are not required to run the production site.

MAINTENANCE PLANS

Going live often means your relationship with your development team is coming to an end, especially if they are from an external vendor. Before you flip the switch, do you have everything you need from your developers? Are you ready for the following tasks?

➤   Routine maintenance

➤   Planned maintenance

➤   Site management

Chapter 8 provides insights into each of these tasks so that you can plan accordingly. Given the types of tasks that you can do in-house and the types of tasks needed to sustain your site, you need to decide whether you want your development team to help you maintain your site.

SUMMARY

This chapter explored several types of tasks you might need to perform before your site goes live. Note that you need to start planning for these tasks before you reach implementation.

When you planned your site, you made decisions that can influence change in your organization, training requirements, marketing strategies, and maintenance. When planning your site, consider including representatives from those who will use the site, train users, plan and conduct marketing campaigns, and provide maintenance after the site is launched.

Sustaining the Site

Congratulations! Your site is live. Initially, activity will probably be low until your promotional efforts reach your target audience. During this time, you might get some feedback (beyond the feedback collected during testing), and you might make some minor changes to fine-tune certain aspects of the site.

With some luck, your site will start to grow. You will add new content; your community interactions will increase; perhaps you will start to sell your products. After a while, your site could become a virtual landmark. Your audience visits on a regular basis and fresh quality content or products are loaded on a regular basis. While all this is happening, you are conducting maintenance and management tasks to sustain your site.

By the end of this chapter, you should be able to:

➤ Distinguish between routine and planned maintenance

➤ Identify multiple site-management tasks performed after site launch

PERFORMING ROUTINE MAINTENANCE

Routine maintenance involves various monitoring and backup tasks performed periodically in an effort to identify issues, updates, and opportunities in a timely manner. The following sections describe some common routine maintenance tasks that you might want to schedule as a means of sustaining your site.

 Chapter 7, "Coordinating Implementation," provides insights into cron jobs.

Monitoring-Related Tasks

Drupal comes with several reports that display site status, logs, performance data, and feedback, depending on how you have configured your site. These reports are your tools for monitoring the activity on your site. You can monitor your site daily or weekly, whichever supports your needs.

Monitoring, however, is not limited to the regular intervals you define. There might be times when you want to increase your monitoring. For instance, assume your site supports events and as part of those events, users will visit your site and perform a task during a specific range of dates. As a result, you might need to monitor your site's performance continuously during that time to ensure that your site performs as needed under the additional load. Monitoring helps you detect issues and address them in a timely manner. Of course, the assumption at this time is that you have planned a production environment that can handle load spikes.

 Chapter 6, "Planning Development," discusses different types of hosting plans. Recall that cloud hosting offers the ability to adjust to fluctuations in server loads.

This section discusses the following basic tasks:

➤ Monitoring logs

➤ Monitoring updates

➤ Monitoring performance

➤ Monitoring feedback

Monitoring Logs

Logs are records of system events. Your system is made up of your Drupal site and the environment in which it runs. System event logs are records of various actions performed by Drupal and/or your server. There are two sets of logs you can monitor: Drupal logs and your server logs.

Drupal Logs

The following are Drupal's three default logs:

➤ **Recent log entries (Drupal 6) or Recent log messages (Drupal 7)** — Data on site usage, performance, issues (errors, warnings, etc.), and more.

➤ **Top "access denied" errors** — A list of URL paths where visitors received the "Access denied" message when they tried to access a path they do not have permission to access.

➤ **Top "page not found" errors** — A list of URL paths where visitors received a "Page not found" message when they tried to access a page or path that does not exist.

The Recent log entries or messages report runs a list of system events. Figure 8-1 shows the Recent log messages report in Drupal 7.

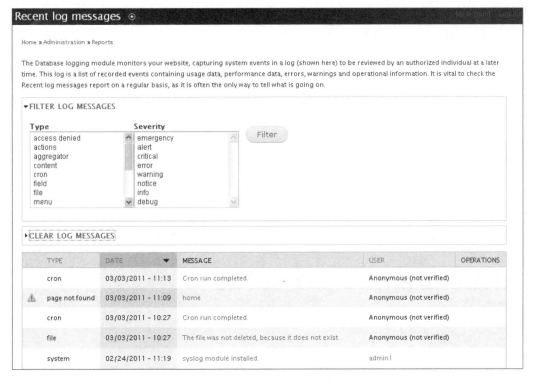

FIGURE 8-1

As you can see from the list of filters, different types and levels of severity of events get logged. Figure 8-1 illustrates a few examples of the types of events you will see — for instance, the notice that the regularly scheduled cron job has run. Another commonly logged event, not shown in Figure 8-1, is when someone has logged in.

The *page not found* event is a repeat of what gets listed in the Top "page not found" errors report, but the event log provides additional data. Figure 8-2 shows the data you get when you view a *page not found* event.

Not all events are what they appear to be. The *file* event shown in Figure 8-1 might appear routine because it is a notice. If you didn't know better, you might assume that the anonymous user has permission to edit a node and thus delete a file. But anonymous users can't edit nodes on this sample site, so who is trying to delete a file, and which file? Figure 8-3 shows the details for this event. As you can see, not much is there to go on. A search on Drupal.org reveals that the event is associated with a bug, and a patch is available for it.

These are just a sampling of the types of events that get recorded. Other types of events include notices that a node has been updated, a PHP error has occurred, a search has been performed, or an email has been sent, to name a few. Monitoring the log can help you detect issues, resolve the issues, and prevent them in the future.

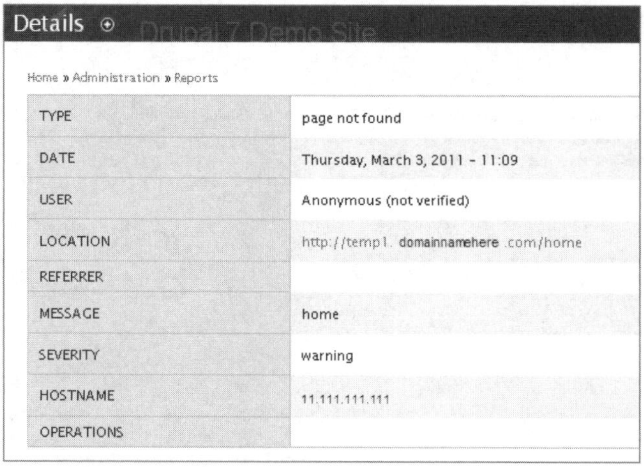

FIGURE 8-2

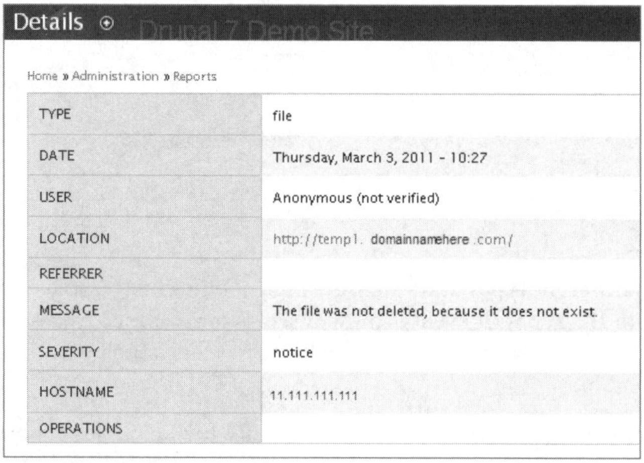

FIGURE 8-3

Server Logs

Although the Drupal logs are helpful, they might not show everything. That's when your server logs (also known as *system logs*) will come in handy. Depending on your hosting plan, you might not have access to the system logs for your site. If you do, two logs provide detailed information about your site's activity: the access log and the error log.

Access Log

The access log shows the requests processed by the server. You will see when various search bots and spiders access your site, but for the most part, you see the requests the server is processing. Each time a path is requested by your visitor or by Drupal on behalf of your visitor, the request is logged. Following are several sample log entries.

➤ 11.11.111.111 - - [15/May/2011:13:57:04 -0400] "GET /robots.txt HTTP/1.1" 200 1540 "-" "Mozilla/5.0 (compatible; YandexBot/3.0; +http://yandex.com/bots)"

➤ 11.11.111.111 - - [15/May/2011:14:16:43 -0400] "GET /misc/ui/jquery.ui.theme.css?lkf19c HTTP/1.1" 200 19215 "http://domainnamehere.com/" "Mozilla/5.0 (Windows; U; Windows NT 5.1; en-US; rv:1.9.2.17) Gecko/20110420 Firefox/3.6.17 (.NET CLR 3.5.30729)"

➤ HTTP/1.1" 200 5186 "http://domainnamehere.com/admin/appearance?render=overlay" "Mozilla/5.0 (Windows; U; Windows NT 5.1; en-US; rv:1.9.2.17) Gecko/20110420 Firefox/3.6.17 (.NET CLR 3.5.30729)"

➤ 11.11.111.111 - - [17/May/2011:08:29:24 -0400] "GET /node/4 HTTP/1.1" 200 22992 "http://domainnamehere.com/" "Mozilla/5.0 (Windows; U; Windows NT 5.1; en-US; rv:1.9.2.17) Gecko/20110420 Firefox/3.6.17 (.NET CLR 3.5.30729)"

➤ 11.11.111.111 - - [17/May/2011:08:29:25 -0400] "GET /favicon.ico HTTP/1.1" 404 45 "-" "Mozilla/5.0 (Windows; U; Windows NT 5.1; en-US; rv:1.9.2.17) Gecko/20110420 Firefox/3.6.17 (.NET CLR 3.5.30729)"

In addition to monitoring expected requests, the access log comes in handy when investigating whether your server or site might have been hacked. The log provides the server administrator with information regarding the source of the hack and therefore, hopefully, means of correcting the situation.

Error Log

The server's error log shows errors the server encountered when processing requests. Sometimes, the issue recorded is not something you will address right way. For instance, the following error indicates that the favicon.ico file does not exist in the path noted. This may or may not concern you.

[Mon May 16 14:17:27 2011] [error] [client 11.11.111.111] File does not exist: /home/ dbusername/domainnamehere.com/html/favicon.ico

Sometimes, the log indirectly reveals a defect in the code. Mod_security is good at letting you know you might have a coding issue. Mod_security is an open source application that protects your server from various types of attacks. It has a series of rules that can be configured to safeguard against what requests it deems inappropriate. Depending on the how the rules are configured in your environment, you might get an error when others do not. If a code remedy is not readily available, an adjustment to a rule can resolve the issue temporarily.

Figure 8-4 is a screenshot of an error that was occurring at one time in the Drupal community.

In this instance, this issue was accompanied by the following error when trying to save the node:

Forbidden: You don't have permission to access /node/73/edit on this server. Apache/2.0.51 (Fedora) Server at domainnamehere.com Port 80

FIGURE 8-4

The server error log recorded the issue. Following is an excerpt from the log:

"POST /book/js/form HTTP/1.1" 403 301 "http://website.com/node/add/page"

Handler: redirect-handler

mod_security-action: 403

mod_security-message: Access denied with code 403. Pattern match "!(^application/x-www-form-urlencoded$|^multipart/form-data;)" at HEADER("Content-Type") [id "9001"] [severity "EMERGENCY"]

The scenarios in which this error occurred varied and the issue appears to have been resolved. However, a temporary workaround to this particular issue was to adjust a mod_security rule. In this scenario, the configuration file called `modsecurity-carp.conf` was modified. This solution assumes you have a hosting plan that gives you access to your mod_security rules.

```
<Location /book/>
SecFilterRemove 9001
</Location>
```

Your error logs also report suspicious activity. Following are four errors where it appears someone might have been trying to find a weakness in the site. Notice how the attempts occur in rapid succession and the requests varied the path when trying to access `setup.php` (`//db/scripts/setup.php`, `//dbadmin/scripts/setup.php`, `//myadmin/scripts/setup.php`, and `//mysql/scripts/setup.php`).

➤ [Wed Apr 20 00:35:10 2011] [error] [client 11.11.111.111] mod_security: Access denied with code 403. Pattern match "^$" at HEADER("USER-AGENT") [id "1002"] [severity "EMERGENCY"] [hostname "domainnamehere.com"] [uri "//db/scripts/setup.php"] [unique_id "Jmo-@n8AAAEAAG8HpnIAAAAI"]

➤ [Wed Apr 20 00:35:11 2011] [error] [client 11.11.111.111] mod_security: Access denied with code 403. Pattern match "^$" at HEADER("USER-AGENT") [id "1002"] [severity "EMERGENCY"] [hostname "domainnamehere.com"] [uri "//dbadmin/scripts/setup.php"] [unique_id "Jm56UX8AAAEAAHTWE4QAAAAO"]

➤ [Wed Apr 20 00:35:11 2011] [error] [client 11.11.111.111] (13)Permission denied: access to //myadmin/scripts/setup.php denied

➤ [Wed Apr 20 00:35:11 2011] [error] [client 11.11.111.111] mod_security: Access denied with code 403. Pattern match "^$" at HEADER("USER-AGENT") [id "1002"] [severity

"EMERGENCY"] [hostname "domainnamehere.com"] [uri "//mysql/scripts/setup.php"] [unique_id "JndVCn8AAAEAAHUoZFAAAAAh"]

With the aid of an online IP address (changed in the preceding examples) lookup service, you can learn more about the server that submitted the requests recorded in your error log. If you suspect errors reflect inappropriate attempts to access your site, you can try to report the behavior to the server administrators associated with the IP address.

If you see an issue in your Drupal logs, look at your server logs to see whether additional information is available. That information can be helpful to your server administrators and/or module developers when they help you investigate the problem.

Monitoring Updates

Drupal and its contributed modules are updated to resolve issues and provide enhancements. Instead of making you research each module on your own, Drupal provides an *available updates* setting that lets you manage if you want to know when updates are available. Figure 8-5 is a screenshot from Drupal 7 illustrating that you have the option to check for updates daily or weekly. You can configure an email message to be sent when updates are available, as well as limit notifications to show only security updates. The *available updates* setting is available in Drupal 6 but is limited. In Drupal 7, you get a new feature that allows you to check for module updates that are currently disabled on your site.

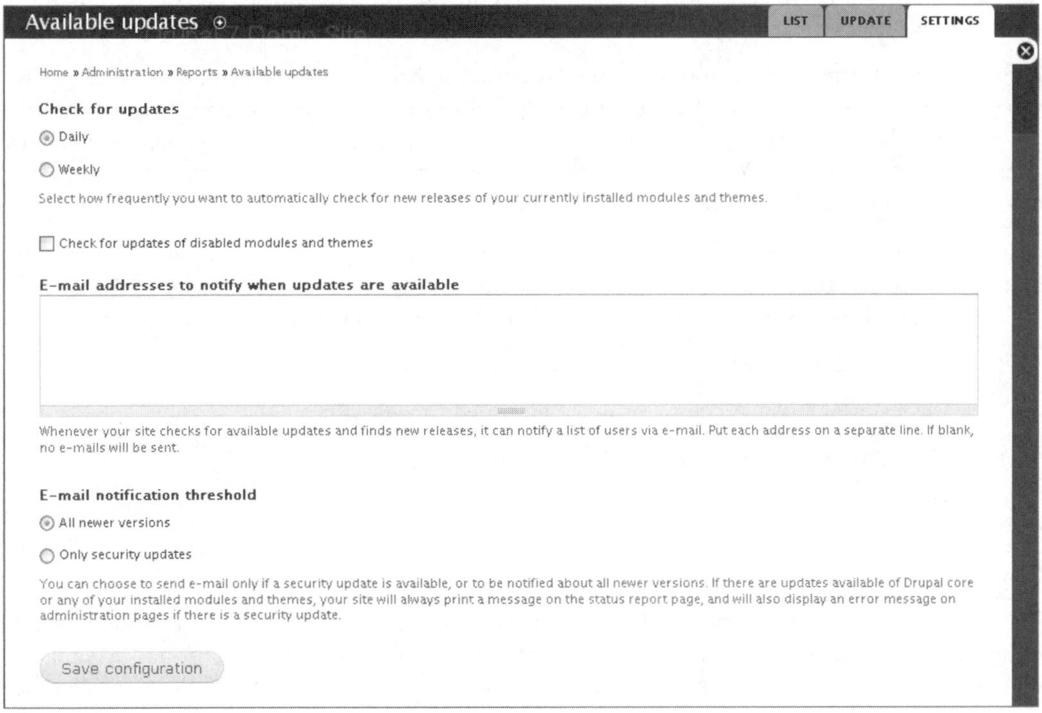

FIGURE 8-5

Monitoring for updates is not the same as actually performing updates. You should not apply updates to sites without planning.

Monitoring Performance

As discussed in Chapter 4, "Collecting Requirements," the process of defining your site's requirements includes making plans to monitor your site's performance. Now that your site is launched, you need to implement your plans for tracking your site's performance, including its response time, popularity, usability, and defects.

DRIES BLOGS ABOUT NEW RELIC

In his post "Playing with New Relic on Acquia Hosting," Dries Buytaert describes his experiences so far with New Relic, a performance-management tool. Based on the screenshots he provides, the reporting features appear to be quite useful. Read more at `http://buytaert.net/playing-with-new-relic-on-acquia-hosting`.

Response Time

During development, you might have conducted performance testing to determine how many requests your server can process and how fast those requests can be delivered. Assuming these initial tests demonstrate that your site will perform as you intend, you might not be inclined to monitor response time unless your site has undergone changes.

However, monitoring performance on a regular basis can help you identify unexpected response time issues. For instance, if you have multiple applications and/or sessions competing for the same processing resources on your server, your response time might increase as each application or session waits to be processed. You might see this only on occasion, but knowing that it is happening can be useful when trying to prevent response time issues.

Also, the load you anticipated at the beginning could change over time, as you add more resources, gain more visitors, and increase site interactions. Monitoring response time for changes can alert you to changes in your site or server's activity. The changes might be anticipated due to:

➤ A recent advertisement that pushes people to your site

➤ The result of a new process/feature being added to your site

➤ An unexpected problem needing further investigation

➤ Abuse on your system

Popularity

A site's popularity often is measured by the number of hits it receives. That is not the only measure of how active your site is, of course, but you know this if you've read the "Performance Analysis" section in Chapter 4. If you haven't had time to think about measuring your site's popularity, here is one more remainder.

Figure 8-6 is a screenshot from Google Analytics (performance monitoring tool) that shows a sampling of the various performance-related measures you can collect.

For instance, a search engine optimization (SEO) strategy is to have other sites link to yours. In this example, 31 percent of the hits come from referring sites. Another example is the average time on site measure. Are your visitors hitting your site and then quickly bouncing off, or are they sticking around? A lot of hits with only seconds on the site might not be an indication that your site is popular; rather, it could be an indication that the site or search engine referring your site is doing a good job at getting visitors to click your site link.

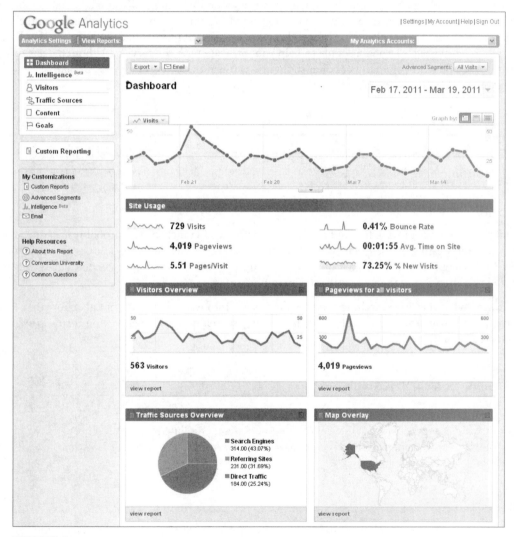

FIGURE 8-6

The process you use to monitor your site's popularity will depend on how you defined your performance-tracking requirements and on how the performance requirements were met. Drupal comes with several reports that provide basic popularity-oriented analytics:

➤ **Recent Hits** — Shows which pages have been viewed recently, including when they were viewed, the IP address of the visitor, and, if the user is logged in, his or her name.

➤ **Top Pages** — Shows which pages on your site receive the most traffic.

➤ **Top Visitors** — Shows who (by username or IP address) is coming to the site, and enables you to ban them from logging in again.

➤ **Top Referrers** — Shows the URL used by your user to find your site, the number of times that URL is used, and the last time the URL was used.

The default Drupal reports are not necessarily in a user-friendly format, so you might choose to connect to one of several external web services to provide additional analytics services, to make increasing the data that is collected easier and to improve your ability to analyze it. For some of the services, you will need a Drupal module to help you integrate with the service. Although decisions regarding the collection of analytical data should be planned before development, in many cases, you can make these decisions after the site has launched.

ANALYTICS

The Google Analytics module, available for Drupal 6 and Drupal 7, allows the Google Analytics service (`http://google.com/analytics`) to track statistics on your site.

Usability

Assuming you tested for usability and all was well before you launched, you probably don't need to repeat usability testing on a regular basis. With that said, if you see that your visitors are searching for content using terms that are part of your navigation structure, you might wonder why they feel the need to search rather than using the navigation features.

Monitoring what they are searching for provides insight into what they want but also how they behave on your site. You might need to learn why they search versus navigate. Monitoring will give you that heads-up.

SEARCH ANALYTICS

Drupal comes with a report called Top search phrases that you can use to monitor your visitors searches. The Search Engine Referers module provides a report of which search engines your visitors used to find your site. As of May 2011, this module is available in Drupal 6.

Defects

As you can imagine, you don't want to launch a site that has defects or errors. Assuming you caught all the issues before your site launched, what can you monitor regarding defects?

When you monitor the logs on your site, you are looking for not only expected activity but also unexpected activity. You might have tested your site and found no defects, but were you able to test every scenario? If the content on your site changes on a regular basis, you need to be able to guarantee that the new content won't cause an unexpected issue.

Monitoring Feedback

This task assumes you have a way for your visitors to provide feedback, including the following:

➤ At a minimum, you might have a contact form with an option to send a message to the webmaster conveying an issue on the site.

➤ You could set up a feedback form on your site to collect input.

➤ You could receive feedback via node comments.

Each of these examples could require a different monitoring process. The contact form might be configured with different email subjects that send email messages to different email accounts (sales, support, feedback, etc.). If you use a feedback form, you might access the feedback form data via an online report. The comments might trigger email messages to be sent, but you still might need to log in and review them with the node.

Configuring your forms (contact, feedback, and/or comments) so that visitors need to be logged in to post a comment or provide feedback reduces the probability that you will get inappropriate posts, but it doesn't eliminate them. If you have your forms open to anonymous visitors, you will want to monitor your feedback posts closely, particularly if the posts are shown on the site. In both scenarios, anonymous or authenticated access, the use of a spam blocker such as Captcha or Mollom adds another way to limit abuse in forms.

FEEDBACK OPTIONS

The Feedback module enables visitors to provide feedback for the page they are currently viewing. You can expand the Feedback module by adding the Unfuddle Feedback module (`http://unfuddle.com`). This module provides integration between Feedback and Unfuddle ticketing system. As of May 2011, these modules are available for Drupal 6 and have a -dev version for Drupal 7.

Backing Up Your Site

Unless you have an automated process or service for creating file and database backups for your site, you might want to consider a routine for creating the backups manually, which means someone needs to have access to your site and/or server. The strategy you choose could be influenced by the size of your site and/or your resources. Storing backups of very large databases takes space.

BACKUP OPTION

The Backup and Migrate module provides a handy tool for creating database backups without your having to log in to an application like MyPHPAdmin. You can perform the backup from your site's admin interface. This module is available for Drupal 6 and Drupal 7.

Typically, you make backups in the event something happens to the server that causes you to lose data. For this reason, when establishing a backup process, consider storing your backups someplace other than your server, such as a local drive or other offline storage device. If the worst thing happens, you don't want to lose your site and the backups at the same time.

HOSTING BACKUPS

Most, if not all, hosting plans run backups so that they can restore client information in the event of a problem. Check with your provider regarding their support for restoring your site files and database.

PERFORMING PLANNED MAINTENANCE

While you are monitoring your site, you might find that the data you collect points to the need to update your site. The most common updates will be core and module updates. Drupal is not unlike many other software applications in that it has patches and updates that address various issues that you might or might not be experiencing.

The process of updating isn't necessarily hard, but if you are having your site built for you and you aren't planning on signing up for a maintenance agreement, you will need to have someone in your organization who is trained to perform updates.

Planning the Update Process

The nature of open source is such that updates can become available frequently and at irregular intervals. Updates can include, but are not limited to, the following:

➤ Code patches for bugs

➤ Functionality enhancements

➤ New functionality

➤ Code restructuring

➤ Changes in the way the module output appears

➤ Security improvements

Each of these changes to the code has the potential to conflict with modules you have in use before and after you perform an update; therefore, you need to plan for regression testing. The more modules you have installed, the higher the likelihood that you need to update some of them and test.

The complexity and purpose of your site influences the process you use to update the core and your contributed and custom modules. It could be as simple as follows, or it could be more complicated if you have multiple modules with interdependencies and the core to update at the same time.

1. Investigate what the update provides.

2. Assess the impact of the update.

3. Make a backup of your site.

4. Put your site into maintenance mode.

5. Install the update (according to the applicable update instructions).

6. Test the update.

7. Take your site out of maintenance mode.

Another perspective regarding complexity has to do with active sites. If you have an active community site whose content is updated on a regular and frequent basis, you will need to create a plan that tests the updates in a development environment before porting them to the live site. In a way, you are performing the update twice. This strategy allows your site to continue being available while you ensure the updates will not negatively affect your site.

Scheduling Updates

You can choose to update your site each time a new version of Drupal core or a contributed module is made available, or you can plan your updates to be done all together, after several updates have become available. Your update process, the purpose of the update, and your available resources will influence how often you schedule updates.

Updating Custom Modules

You might need to update custom modules, just as with any other modules. If your custom module has a dependency on another module and that other module gets updated, you might find that your custom module needs an update as well. If you hired a contractor to create your custom module, you might need to retain or hire a contractor to maintain your module, assuming you don't have an internal development team by that time.

Upgrading Your Site

Going from Drupal version 6.19 to version 6.20 is one thing. A step up like this typically is viewed as routine. Upgrading from Drupal 6 to Drupal 7 is quite another thing.

Full-version upgrades for Drupal's core require planning. Not only do you change the core, but you also change each contributed and custom module you are using. You must update the theme as well. Basically, the site becomes a new site. It might look the same when you are done, but the code won't be.

The planning doesn't have to be what you did when you first planned your site. At a minimum, it is a development plan where the current configuration is compared to what the new version offers. Each aspect of the current site is mapped to its new version. Features on the current site that are no longer supported on the new site likely will need a new strategy if they are to be continued into the new version.

Although one can argue that performing a core upgrade is part of site maintenance, it is not a process typically performed quickly and easily.

SITE MANAGEMENT

While your tech-savvy folks are off monitoring logs and ensuring the technology is functioning properly, your content- and user-savvy folks will be busy with site management, making sure the site has fresh content and users are happy.

Site management can encompass different tasks. In this section, it is assumed to include tasks associated with content and user management. However, some might include routine maintenance tasks discussed previously as well.

Many, if not all, of the tasks you need to perform after your site is launched were defined when you collected your requirements, created a design plan, and planned your site implementation. The tasks described in the following sections are sometimes overlooked when a site is launched.

Managing Content

What else can be said about content that hasn't already been said in the previous chapters? Honestly, not a lot. You know what your content is, how it should be displayed, how it should be created, and so on. However, you might have overlooked a few processes as you breathed a sigh of relief when your site went live.

Adding New Content

Hopefully, the post-launch task of adding new content has been well planned and you are ready to go. Of course, not all sites have new content on a regular basis. Assuming yours does, do you know where you will get new content topics? Monitoring the search phrases that get entered on your site might provide some ideas.

When visitors search your site, they are hoping to find what they need. If you provide what they need, they might come back. Tracking search phrases submitted on your site is one way to learn what your audience needs. If your site does not provide content that matches the search phrases, you might consider adding content on those topics if they are applicable to your site.

TOP SEARCH PHRASES

Both Drupal 6 and Drupal 7 come with a report called Top search phrases that lists the top search phrases on the site. This list is pulled from the watchdog table in the database. This table gets refreshed on a regular basis. If you want to use this default feature in Drupal, you will want to schedule regular reviews of the phrases.

Finding something to write about is only part of adding new content; you also need to get the content written. Following are a couple more reminders regarding new content:

➤ **Schedule new content development** — How often do you need new content?

➤ **Coordinate content authors** — Can your content authors meet your schedule? Do you have enough authors to meet your needs?

➤ **Engage your editors** — Are you going to moderate content development and provide editing services? Do you have the resources to manage the volume of content you need developed?

➤ **Train content authors and moderators** — Will you add new authors and moderators and, if so, will they need to be trained? Did your training strategy take this into consideration?

Updating Content

Change happens, whether we want to admit it or not. That means the content on your site, although accurate today, might need to change in the future as your organization, processes, tasks, and so on change. Consider scheduling periodic content reviews to assess whether your content needs to be updated or archived (unpublished).

Another potential content update has to do with the search phrases mentioned previously. Are you providing content that matches the search request? If so, do the search phrases being used match the terms in your content? If your content does not match the search requests, is there anything you can do to update your existing content so that it is easier to find?

Verifying Links

Have you ever visited a site and found a link that sounds exactly like what you need, but the link doesn't work? If you are going to link to other sites, a chance exists that these links will break. You can't control pages on other sites, so consider scheduling periodic link checks to ensure your site doesn't have broken links.

LINK CHECKER

The Link checker module periodically checks links in your content and reports broken links in a log. The module is currently available for Drupal 6, and work is being done to port it to Drupal 7.

Monitoring Comments

If you allow visitors to comment on your site's content, you will want to monitor what is being said. Even if you set up your site to allow only registered users to post comments, you can still get unwanted or inappropriate comments, more commonly known as *spam*. So, monitoring is still a good idea.

Another reason to monitor comments is to engage with your users, to hear what they are saying, or even to answer questions. By responding to questions quickly, you increase your chances for return visits. Remember to review comments on a regular basis.

 Visit Comment Notifications at http://groups.drupal.org/node/15928 *for a comparison of five modules that support some form of comment monitoring.*

Monitoring Search Engine Optimization

If someone goes to a search engine and types in a keyword or keyword phrase, will she find your site on the first page of the search results? One day, you might find your site in the top 10 and then a month later, it isn't. The strategies that you initially implemented might no longer be working for a couple reasons:

➤ Search engines change their ranking algorithms.

➤ Your competition might have improved their SEO strategies and become more relevant.

The topic of SEO is not specific to Drupal, but it is an important part of site management. If you find that your initial strategies aren't working, reassess them.

Providing User Support

The purpose of your site will influence the type of user support you need to provide. For instance, if you have an e-commerce site, you will need to provide a way for customers who have technical or usability issues when processing payments or finding items to purchase. This isn't something you want to assume will happen, but in the event it does, you want to ensure that your customers receive the best support possible. Furthermore, if it turns out to be a repeatable issue, you will want to investigate and fix it before it becomes a larger issue (such as losing site visitors or customers).

AN EXAMPLE SUPPORT SCENARIO

A class reunion site was set up to collect reunion payments. Someone logged in to the site daily to see whether any orders were placed. On occasion, users would show up, start the order process but never finish. These users were contacted and assistance was provided. The problem appeared to be a usability issue in that the users didn't notice the option to pay by credit card when they got to the PayPal payment page. By monitoring the order queue, the site administrator could help facilitate the sale of reunion tickets. If this site were going to be used for an extended period of time, the site developer would want to revisit the purchase process to make it easier to use.

You likely already have your user support processes planned, but the following sections offer a few reminders, just in case.

Account Support

If you require visitors to create an account before posting to your site, you might need account support. For instance, assume you've set up your site so that users need to verify their account via a link sent in an email. Sometimes, the email doesn't get to the users; two common reasons why this might happen include:

➤ Your server is having an issue and can't send email.

➤ The email recipient has an enthusiastic spam blocker.

Who should the user contact for assistance? How should the user request assistance? Depending on their reasons for creating an account, some users won't take the time to request assistance. If you monitor the user accounts on a regular basis, you will be able to see the accounts that have been activated and those that haven't. You can follow up with the users and proactively provide assistance and increase the probability that your users will have a positive experience while interacting with your site.

Monitoring your user accounts also lets you find fake accounts — those created for the purpose of spamming your site. Of course, by requiring email verification, you reduce the probability that a spambot will successfully create an account.

IMPORTING USERS

After your site launches, a time might come when you need to help a group of future users access the site. The User Import module can help you import multiple users using a comma-delimited file, saving you time and effort. As of May 2011, this module is available for Drupal 6 and a Drupal 7 patch is being reviewed.

Support Access

Assume you have assigned someone to monitor user support requests and proactively monitor user activity.

➤ How will users request assistance?

➤ When will support be available?

A user can use several methods to request support. For instance, you can provide synchronous chat, phone, email, and/or an online form. If you missed providing a way for user support communication while planning your site processes, you can easily add a contact form or node that provides instructions for contacting you.

The world has gotten a lot smaller and anyone at any time can be interacting with your site on the Internet. If you haven't done so already, consider planning when support services will be available. Depending on the purpose of your site, you might need to provide live support 24/7 (for example, for an e-commerce site).

Support Tracking

Similar to tracking change requests and test results during development, tracking customer requests can help you manage and coordinate service. It can also provide you with a running list of issues that can reveal performance trends and opportunities to improve. Tracking support requests can also provide contact information from your users, enabling you to offer your customers special opportunities. For instance, if you have customers who experience issues when trying to make a purchase on your site, you might decide to send them a "We thank you for your patience" reward and offer them a discount on their next order.

TICKET TRACKING

The Support Ticketing System module provides a basic ticketing system with features such as email integration, ticket activity charts, ticket assignments, and more. As of May 2011, this module was available for Drupal 6 and a -dev version was available for Drupal 7.

If you just need a simple method, you can build your own with a content type and fields, an access control module, views displays, and rules for email notifications. Assuming each module used to create your ticketing process is supported by the Features module, you could use the Features module to export your ticketing "feature" into a module that you can install on other sites.

SUMMARY

This chapter presented a sampling of the types of tasks you need to perform after your site has launched. Here are few things to remember:

➤ A difference exists between routine monitoring/troubleshooting and planned updates.

➤ A difference exists between updating within a version (Drupal 6.19 to 6.20) and upgrading to the next version (Drupal 6 to Drupal 7).

➤ Different organizational roles might need to perform the different monitoring tasks.

➤ Remember to back up your site and your database or use an automated feature to do it for you.

➤ As your site grows, your site's performance can diminish, so you need to monitor and make adjustments, as necessary.

➤ Be proactive when monitoring the interaction with users on your site.

➤ Maintain your content for accuracy and consistency.

➤ Track your user support so that you can identify trends to address in future enhancements.

Chances are that one day, something will change and you or your audience will go in different directions. Your site will either fade into history or you will return to the beginning to determine a new purpose and new requirements for your redesigned site. If that is the case, you will start the project lifecycle over again.

PART III
An Example Site

- ▶ **CHAPTER 9:** An Example Plan

- ▶ **CHAPTER 10:** Example Build Recipes

An Example Plan

Chapters 3 through 8 focus on the activities associated with planning a site, creating a development plan for that site, implementing the site, and preparing to sustain the site. Reading about the processes, tasks, and analyses presented in those chapters isn't always the easiest way to understand what is being suggested. Sometimes, an example makes it easier to understand. Each of the preceding chapters presented isolated examples, but that might not be enough to understand the big picture.

This chapter presents a sample plan for a multipurpose, yet basic, site. The order in which the plan is presented matches the sequence of processes, tasks, and analyses presented in Chapters 3 through 5. The effort to create the plan was iterative and incremental:

➤ The process started with paper-and-pencil brainstorming of the site's purpose, processes, tasks, content, and so on.

➤ After the initial brainstorming notes were captured, the process was started again, this time adding more detail and making decisions about how to proceed.

➤ With each step forward in the planning process, additional requirements were uncovered and previous planning steps were updated accordingly.

This example plan is just one way to create and organize your project planning.

PROVISO

The site plan defined in this chapter is not based on a real project. The plan reflects only a sampling of what is possible. The decisions reflected in the example plan have been designed to demonstrate one of many ways to document your plan as well as to demonstrate some content management strategies.

THE CLIENT

The story begins with Gary, an avid cyclist who wants to learn more about cycling and to meet other cyclists in his community. He starts by buying some books on cycling and surfing the Web for how-to videos. He also talks with other cyclists whom he meets on various rides.

Gary finds a lot of resources in various places and thinks it would be nice if he had one place where he could organize the resources and share them with others. He decides that a website would be a good option but doesn't know where to start.

Even though Gary has some experience creating basic HTML web pages, he assumes that creating a website is an ambitious project and shares his vision with fellow cyclist and information architect, Claire. Claire indicates that building a site might not be too ambitious, given the open source systems that are available today. However, until they think through the idea, they won't know for sure what creating a site would take.

She explains that recently, most of her work is for sites being built in a system called Drupal. Her clients seem to think a lot of it. She has been meaning to learn more but hasn't taken the time. Maybe this project would be a good motivator.

They decide to make Gary's idea a learning opportunity for both of them. The following sections describe the requirements and design for the site they want to build.

THE PURPOSE

The purpose of the site is to help enable cyclists, at any level, to learn about cycling, improve their skills, interact with other cyclists, and find the resources they need. A multipurpose site like this one needs multiple site strategies. Gary and Claire choose the following three strategies:

➤ **Learning management** — The site needs learning opportunities that help cyclists learn from various trusted resources. The site would provide learning opportunities, as well as links to offsite opportunities. Learning materials would be designed to allow for self-guided and self-assessed learning.

➤ **Community** — The site needs a way for cyclists to meet online, share their personal lessons, and ask questions of the community.

➤ **Mini-brochures** — A large part of cycling is the equipment and the services associated with maintaining equipment. A frequent question is, "Where can I get a … for my bike?" The site would provide a way for vendors of cycling products and services to create a brochure page on the site.

Each strategy will support one or more purposes. Table 9-1 summarizes how the strategies will support the site's purpose.

TABLE 9-1: Supporting the Site's Purpose

PURPOSE	LEARNING MANAGEMENT	COMMUNITY	MINI-BROCHURE
Learn about cycling	Lessons and learning resources about cycling	Learn by asking questions and sharing cycling-related experiences	Learn about cycling by reviewing products and services
Improve cycling skills	Lessons and learning resources that focus on skills development	Improve by attending cycling-related events	Improve skills by locating and hiring a coach
Interact with other cyclists	NA	Interact via online discussions, sharing experiences, and attending events posted by the community	Interact by joining cycling clubs or teams
Find cycling resources	Find learning resources	Find resourceful information in the community	Find product and service providers (merchants)

THE COMPETITION

Gary and Claire search the Web for *cycling community* and get several hits. It seems that Gary's idea is not original, but he doesn't see a community site that looks exactly like what he has in mind. Some sites offer classes; a couple offer forums; most have cycling-related events, places to ride, and the occasional cycling photos section. Another common element he notices is geography; they all seem focused on a specific location. This makes sense given cycling isn't something you can experience online.

What he doesn't see offered by the communities he looks at are online how-to videos or quick guides that his audience could print and take with them on rides.

Another web search for *how-to cycling videos* yields several video resources. The most impressive cycling video source is found at Livestrong.com founded by Lance Armstrong. Gary has no plans to compete with such an organization; instead, he wants to help his audience find these resources and learn from them. Another search for *how-to cycling guides* yields several sites, such as About.com and PerformanceBike.com.

After Gary's initial investigation, it looks like his idea to combine online learning experiences (video and guides) with community interactions might be somewhat unique. He is not going to center his site on a geographic location, so he won't compete with cycling sites that cater to a specific location. His hopes are to include events, merchants, and clubs from all around the country and even overseas. His site is about being a hub that brings resources together.

Even if it turns out that his idea is not unique enough to compete with the community sites out there today, Gary and Claire have a personal goal: to learn Drupal.

THE REQUIREMENTS

With the purpose of the site identified and the general scope of the site defined, the next step for Gary and Claire is to define the site further. In the requirements phase of the project, Gary and Claire define what learning management, community, and mini-brochures will be and how they will enable cyclists to learn about cycling, improve their skills, interact with other cyclists, and find the resources they need. Their first step is to understand their audience better.

Audience

Although Gary and Claire have already agreed that cyclists are the primary audience for the site, they quickly realize that many types of cyclists exist, each with his or her own needs. They also recognize that the information and interaction they envision for the site might be of interest to others in the cycling community. Therefore, they decide to refine what they mean by *cyclists*.

Segments

One way to segment an audience is to recognize the goals associated with different members of an audience. In the case of cyclists, Gary and Claire identify the following categories:

➤ **Casual rider** — Individuals in this category are likely to ride only when the weather is nice. They are likely to combine cycling with another activity, such as a picnic or social gathering. They probably won't travel far for the ride or ride a long distance.

➤ **Noncompetitive cycling enthusiast** — Individuals in this category are likely to use cycling as a regular form of exercise. They seek to improve their abilities so that each ride can take them farther and maybe even faster than the last ride. They might join group rides that emphasize bike-handling skills. Some will travel long distances to ride on roads and trails they have never seen before.

➤ **Competitive cyclist** — Individuals in this category like to compete, but cycling is not their profession. They are likely to have full-time careers or to be full-time students. They take their riding beyond general fitness. They seek out the best equipment and services they can afford. They are likely to be on a cycling team. Some have a private coach to help them improve their skills and fitness.

➤ **Elite/professional racers** — Individuals in this category are either professional racers or racers working to become professional. Their job is to race and, therefore, they need to do it well. They are likely to be on a professional team or will be seeking a professional team. They, too, will seek the best equipment and services they can afford. Most will have a coach to help them improve.

➤ **Club/team leads** — Individuals in this category might be officers of an amateur cycling club or a professional cycling team. They make decisions about how the club or team is managed, and what rides and races are scheduled. They also obtain assistance or sponsorship from product/service providers and help members of the clubs or team find the resources they need.

➤ **Product/service providers** — Individuals in this category provide products and services to the individuals in the other categories, as well as to clubs and teams. They could be associated with a bike shop, product manufacturer, service provider, or consultant.

Personas

Gary and Claire decide to survey individuals in each category to learn more about their needs and interests. They visit local bike shops, attend races, go on group rides, and chat with cyclists in the park. After reviewing the information they gathered, they find that they could support individuals in each segment with their site. Trying to build a site that would meet the needs of such a diverse group, however, is more than they want to tackle. So, they decide to organize their audience into three groups, each playing a different role, in their strategy to build the site:

➤ Primary users

➤ Secondary users

➤ Administrators

To help them stay focused on defining what the site needs, Gary and Claire decide to create personas that represent the members of their target audience. For each user persona, the assumption is that they are web-savvy enough to create an account on a site and follow onscreen instructions for posting content to a site.

Primary Users

Because the purpose of the site is to help cyclists learn about cycling, improve their skills, interact with other cyclists, and find the resources they need, Gary and Claire decide to make the cyclists the primary users. Based on information they gathered about the different segments, they created four personas to represent their primary audience.

➤ **Casual rider persona** — Ralph rides a couple of times a month and wants to make the most of his ride. He wants to be comfortable and safe. He wants to be able to keep up with his younger colleagues who also like to ride. He doesn't have time to maintain his bike and has resources to pay a professional to provide those services. At the same time, he needs to be able to change a tire. Because he does not ride frequently, he would like to get quick refreshers on tire changing before he goes out on a ride.

➤ **Noncompetitive cycling enthusiast persona** — Carmen used to see herself as a casual rider but found that a couple times a month wasn't enough. She enjoys riding in groups but also likes the quiet of a solo ride. She is competitive in her profession and wants to see improvement with each ride. She has a limited budget and wants to refine her equipment over time, trading bike components with better components as she can afford them. She doesn't want a coach but instead would like to create her own fitness plan using ideas from others who have gone before her.

➤ **Competitive cyclist persona** — Gabe is a category 5 racer, just starting out. He used to be like Carmen but found that he enjoyed the group rides that got a little competitive, each rider pushing the other to go faster. He joined a local team and started learning how to race. Gabe is not the type to go halfhearted into a project. He has committed to racing and his goal is to move up a category a year. With such an aggressive goal, he wants to invest in the best equipment, hire a coach, and learn to race.

➤ **Elite/professional racer persona** — Cathy has been racing for years. She is a category 1 racer, one step from being a pro. She has the resources to make racing her focus. She has a coach, and equipment is more of a maintenance task than a new-purchase task. She replaces worn equipment with new, as needed. Her team has provided her with a budget for a coach. In the off-season, she enjoys the casual ride now and then with experienced group riders.

Secondary Users

Although these next personas are going to be important to the site's success, they are different from the primary users. These personas bring resources to the primary users. They might benefit from the site the same way the primary users do, but these personas have additional or different motivations for coming to the site and interacting.

➤ **Club/team lead persona** — Maggie is a racing club president. Cycling is an important part of her life and she has a knack for bringing people together and helping them achieve their goals. She gets satisfaction from seeing people improve. Raising money and bringing great racers into the club isn't easy. She could use some help from the cycling community.

➤ **Product/service provider persona** — Andy is a retired professional racer and part owner of a bike shop. He stays connected with the cycling community by riding on a regular basis, sponsoring a local team, coaching promising young riders, and providing quality equipment for various types of riders.

➤ **Subject matter expert persona** — Mary is a seasoned cyclist, racer, and coach. She has experience writing and presenting training online and in the classroom. Her passion is helping others succeed in their cycling efforts, and she has many years of experience to share. She is one of the experts who will be contributing learning materials to the site.

Administrators

Different types of administrators are needed for a site. The cycling site will have two types of administrators: site administrator and content administrator.

➤ **Site administrator persona** — Gary and Claire will be the site administrators (and maybe the site developers). At the end of the project, they will know what it takes to be the site administrators responsible for site configuration, monitoring, content management, and user support.

➤ **Content administrator persona** — Veronica will share the content-administration tasks with the site administrators. She is also one of several cycling subject matter experts who will be contributing learning materials to the site. Veronica has experience working with other subject matter experts (SMEs) to document what they know in an effort to create learning materials.

Use Cases

The next step for Gary and Claire is to identify how each persona would use the site. As Gary and Claire discuss the various tasks that the personas would perform on the site, a question surfaces: how much work would be performed offline, behind the scenes, and how much on the site? They decide to look beyond how the audience would use the site; they also consider the processes that encompass the tasks.

Learning Management

Based on interviews with the target audience, Gary and Claire learn that their target audience does not need managed learning. These people are more interested in self-guided, self-assessed learning experiences. The target audience wants the opportunity to learn what they need to learn, when they need to learn it. This feedback confirms the strategies chosen for the site.

Table 9-2 summarizes the tasks in the self-guided learning-management process and how the site will be used.

TABLE 9-2: Learning-Management Tasks

TASK	ALL PERSONAS	CONTENT ADMIN AND SME PERSONAS	SITE ADMIN PERSONA
Identify learning needs	Submit a suggestion or request specific learning materials be created	Review submissions forwarded from the Site Admin	Review submissions via an online report and receive email notices with requests Forward submissions to applicable SME and Content Admin
Design a learning experience	NA	Design learning experience offline	Review learning experience design offline
Develop the learning experience	NA	Develop learning experience offline	Review learning experience result offline
Organize the learning experiences	Use the categories to find learning experiences of interest	Categorize the learning experiences by topic and by hierarchy	Verify category assignment

continues

TABLE 9-2 *(continued)*

TASK	ALL PERSONAS	CONTENT ADMIN AND SME PERSONAS	SITE ADMIN PERSONA
Upload the learning experiences	NA	Upload different types of learning experiences in an unpublished state	Receive email notice when the new learning experience content has been saved
Review and publish the experience	NA	Respond to email comments from Administrator, if applicable	Access and review new unpublished learning materials, and if approved, publish them
Access and learn from the solution	Locate and access the learning experience via multiple navigational aids (search, lists, menu)	NA	Monitor search requests for topic ideas

In the future, assuming the site becomes popular and resources are available, Gary and Claire might add:

➤ The ability to develop learning content collaboratively online and publish it

➤ Blogs for featured cyclists

Community

The target audience indicates interest in hearing about and sharing cycling-related events in the community. Some are looking for a way to find other riders for group rides. They express an interest in asking questions and seeking lessons learned from more experienced riders.

Table 9-3 summarizes the tasks in a community process and how the site will be used.

TABLE 9-3: Community Tasks

TASK	ALL PERSONAS	CONTENT ADMIN AND SME PERSONAS	SITE ADMIN PERSONA
Request groups	Submit a suggestion or request a group be created	NA	Review submissions via an online report and receive email notices with requests
Set up groups	NA	NA	Create a space on the site for topic-specific discussion

TASK	ALL PERSONAS	CONTENT ADMIN AND SME PERSONAS	SITE ADMIN PERSONA
Facilitate group interaction	NA	Post compelling discussion topics that might interest the community	Post compelling discussion topics that might interest the community
Become a site member	Create a user account	NA	Monitor user accounts for inactive or spam-generating accounts
Join groups	Log in and join groups of interest	NA	Monitor group memberships
Post content	Post questions, provide tips, and place events on a calendar	Post questions, provide tips, and place events on a calendar	Monitor posts for inappropriate content Unpublish or delete inappropriate content
Comment on content	Comment on discussion, tips, and events	Comment on discussion, tips, and events	Monitor comments for inappropriate content Unpublish or delete inappropriate content
Connect with members of the site	Connect with another member of the site	Connect with another member of the site	NA
Access community content	Use multiple navigational aids to locate and access community posts	Use multiple navigational aids to locate and access community posts	Monitor popularity statistics

In the future, the site might offer private group spaces where cycling clubs or teams can hold private discussions and make announcements.

Mini-Brochure

When Gary and Claire interview various product and service providers, most express an interest in letting the cycling community know they are there to help. This does not come as a surprise. Not only are vendors interested, but clubs and teams are interested, as well.

Table 9-4 summarizes the tasks associated with a mini-brochure process and how the site will be used.

TABLE 9-4: Mini-Brochure Tasks

TASK	ALL PERSONAS	CLUB LEAD AND PROVIDER PERSONAS	SITE ADMIN PERSONA
Request a mini-brochure page	Submit a request to have a mini-brochure page	Submit a request to have a mini-brochure page	Review submissions via an online report and receive email notices with request
Upload content to mini-brochure page	NA	Upload contact information, provide a description, and categorize what is offered, and the post in an unpublished state	Create blank page and assign to the provider Receive email notice when brochure page has been saved
Review and publish the mini-brochure	NA	Respond to email comments from Admin, if applicable	Access and review new, unpublished mini-brochure pages, and, if approved, publish them
Access to mini-brochure	Locate and access mini-brochure pages via multiple navigational aids (search, lists, menu, and category terms)	NA	Monitor popularity statistics

In the future, this would be a great way to generate some revenue that could be used to support the site. If the site gets popular enough, the vendors with mini-brochure pages might want to pay for advertising displayed on pages other than their brochure page.

Content

By thinking about what the target audience will do on the site and noting those activities in simple use cases, Gary and Claire also identify the type of content they are going to have on the site.

 Chapter 4, "Collecting Requirements," discusses each part of the content analysis.

Learning Management

Learning experiences can be presented in different ways. The options to provide sequenced, multi-lesson learning experiences as well as single-page learning experiences are needed.

Each lesson will offer the option to provide quick facts or definitions to supplement the content on the page. This feature can help subject matter experts avoid redefining terms in the body of the lesson and help keep this type of content consistent throughout the lessons.

A way to provide links to learning experiences not on the site also needs to be available.

Table 9-5 provides a description of the lesson content associated with the learning-management process. Table 9-6 provides a description of quick fact or definition content.

TABLE 9-5: Lesson Content

ANALYSIS	DECISION
Type of content	Learning experience content.
Content purpose	Used to display one lesson.
User-content relationships	Written for and accessed by any persona or role.
Content data	Title — Text field.
	Lesson objectives — Multilined text field with HTML editor option.
	Narrative — Multilined text field with HTML editor option.
	Images — Allow up to three images embedded in the narrative. Limit size to 500 KB each. Allow JPEG, GIF, and PNG.
	Video display — Field to hold embedded link.
	Video link — Field to hold the link to the video source.
	Resource link — Option to provide a link to an online resource.
	Files — Allow one PDF file, limited to 1 MB.
Content sources	Images will be uploaded by content creator.
	Files will be uploaded by content creator.
	Videos will be stored on a video site and displayed in a field.
Data reuse	Title and lesson objectives — Need the option to display multilesson summary sheets.
	Images — Display lesson images in a gallery.
	Video link — Need the option to display list of videos linked in the site.

continues

TABLE 9-5 *(continued)*

ANALYSIS	DECISION
Content categories	Activity — Group lessons under the type of cycling activity. Topic — Group lessons based on lesson topic within a cycling activity. Lesson type — Group lessons by type of lesson.
Category terms	Activity (select one) — Maintenance, bike handling, strategy, fitness. Topic (free tag) — Create tags that describe the lesson further. Lesson type (select one) — Quick guides, short tutorials, resources.
Content relationships	Include option to create parent/child relationships and sibling relationships between lessons. Include option to relate the lesson to a community group discussing the same topic. Include option to relate the lesson to lesson's author profile.
Content metadata	Provide the option to include a unique `meta` keyword and description for each lesson.
Content language	The site will be in English. A multilingual site is not planned at this time.
Content access	Anonymous visitors and members can access the lessons. Subject matter experts should be able to create unpublished lessons. Site and content administrators should be able to publish, create, edit, and delete lessons.

TABLE 9-6: Fact Content

ANALYSIS	DECISION
Type of content	Supplemental content.
Content purpose	Provided to enhance the lesson content.
User-content relationships	Written for and accessed by any persona or role.
Content data	Title — Text field. Fact — Multilined text field with HTML editor option.
Content sources	Provided by the lesson author.
Data reuse	Available on each lesson that makes a reference to the fact. Multiple lessons can reference one fact without duplicating the fact.

ANALYSIS	DECISION
Content categories	Activity — Group facts under the type of cycling activity.
Category terms	Activity (select one) — Maintenance, bike handling, strategy, fitness.
Content relationships	Facts are related to lesson pages when the lesson page makes the connection.
Content metadata	NA
Content language	The site will be in English. A multilingual site is not planned at this time.
Content access	Anonymous visitors and members can access the fact.
	Subject matter experts should be able to create unpublished facts.
	Site and content administrators should be able to publish, create, edit, and delete facts.

Community

The community needs three types of content: discussions, tips, and events. Tables 9-7 through 9-9 provide a description of each type of content.

TABLE 9-7: Discussion Content

ANALYSIS	DECISION
Type of content	Discussion post.
Content purpose	Used to ask questions, solicit opinions, and simply facilitate online information exchange.
User-content relationships	Written for and accessed by any persona or role.
Content data	Title — Text field.
	Discussion — Multilined text field with HTML editor option.
	Images — Allow one image embedded in the narrative; limit size to 500 KB; allow JPEG, GIF, and PNG files.
Content sources	Images will be uploaded by the content creator.
Data reuse	Title and body teaser — Display list of discussion posts.
	Images — Display discussion images in a gallery.
Content categories	Activity — Group discussion under the type of cycling activity.
	Topic — Group discussion based on topic within a cycling activity.

continues

TABLE 9-7 *(continued)*

ANALYSIS	DECISION
Category terms	Activity (select one) — Maintenance, bike handling, strategy, fitness. Topic (free tag) — Create tags that describe the discussion further.
Content relationships	Associate a discussion post with one group. Make comments available for each discussion.
Content metadata	NA
Content language	The site will be in English. A multilingual site is not planned at this time.
Content access	Anonymous visitors and members can access the discussions. Members can start discussions and comment on posts. Site and content administrators can unpublish, create, edit, and delete discussion posts.

TABLE 9-8: Tip Content

ANALYSIS	DECISION
Type of content	Cycling tips.
Content purpose	Share lessons learned and helpful information about cycling.
User-content relationships	Written for and accessed by any persona or role.
Content data	Title — Text field. Tip — Multilined text field with HTML editor option. Images — Allow one image embedded in the narrative; limit size to 500 KB; allow JPEG, GIF, and PNG files.
Content sources	Images will be uploaded by the content creator.
Data reuse	Title and body teaser — Display list of tips posts. Images — Display tips images in a gallery.
Content categories	Activity — Group tips based on topic within a cycling activity. Topic — Group discussion based on topic within a cycling activity.
Category terms	Activity (select one) — Maintenance, bike handling, strategy, fitness. Topic (free tag) — Create tags that describe the tip further.

ANALYSIS	DECISION
Content relationships	Associate tip posts with one group. Make comments available for each tip.
Content metadata	NA
Content language	The site will be in English. A multilingual site is not planned at this time.
Content access	Anonymous visitors and members can access the tips. Members can post tips and comment on them. Site and content administrators can unpublish, create, edit, and delete tips.

TABLE 9-9: Event Content

ANALYSIS	DECISION
Type of content	Cycling-oriented events.
Content purpose	Let the community know about cycling-oriented events.
User-content relationships	Written for and accessed by any persona or role.
Content data	Title — Text field. Description — Multilined text field with HTML editor option. Start and End date and time — Date field for start and end date and time. Location — Place and address. Images — Allow one image but do not embed. Automatically resize the width to 400 pixels. Limit size to 500 KB. Allow JPEG, GIF, and PNG. File — Allow one PDF file, limited to 1 MB, to be uploaded.
Content sources	Images will be uploaded by the content creator. Files will be uploaded by the content creator.
Data reuse	Title and description teaser — Display a list of events. Title and dates — Display events on a site calendar. Images — Display events images in a gallery.
Content categories	Activity — Group events under the type of cycling activity. Topic — Group events based on topic within a cycling activity. Event type — Group types of events.

continues

TABLE 9-9 *(continued)*

ANALYSIS	DECISION
Category terms	Activity (select one) — Maintenance, bike handling, strategy, fitness. Topic (free tag) — Create tags that describe the tips further. Event type (select one) — Race, workshop, camp, group ride, sale.
Content relationships	Make comments available for each event.
Content metadata	NA
Content language	The site will be in English. A multilingual site is not planned at this time.
Content access	Anonymous visitors and members can access events. Members can post events and comment on them. Site and content administrators can unpublish, create, edit, and delete events.

Mini-Brochure

Tables 9-10 and 9-11 provide descriptions of two types of brochure content. Two segments (clubs and product/service providers) might be interested in letting the cycling community know they share their interests in cycling.

TABLE 9-10: Merchant Content

ANALYSIS	DECISION
Type of content	Information page about product or service providers or merchants.
Content purpose	To provide various merchants (shops, manufacturers, coaches, consultants, and more) a way to let the community know they exist and what they offer.
User-content relationships	Written for and accessed by any persona or role.
Content data	Title — Text field. Description — Multilined text field with HTML editor option. Location — Place and address. Email — Contact email address. Hours — Text field with HTML editor option (not applicable to all types of providers). URL — Field to hold the link to the merchant's site. Images — Allow one image but do not embed; automatically resize the width to 400 pixels; limit size to 500 KB; allow JPEG, GIF, and PNG files. File — Allow one PDF file, limited to 1 MB, to be uploaded.

ANALYSIS	DECISION
Content sources	Images will be uploaded by the content creator.
	Files will be uploaded by the content creator.
Data reuse	Title and description teaser — Display a list of merchants.
	Images — Display merchant images in a gallery.
Content categories	Merchant type — Group like providers.
Category terms	Merchant type (select multiple) — Shop, coaches and trainers, consultants, manufacturers, mechanics, and bike fit technicians. Other categories might be added.
Content relationships	NA
Content metadata	NA
Content language	The site will be in English. A multilingual site is not planned at this time.
Content access	Anonymous visitors and members can access merchant pages.
	Members with the appropriate role can edit/complete a merchant page enabled for them by the administrator.
	Site and content administrators can unpublish, create, edit, and delete merchant pages.

TABLE 9-11: Club Content

ANALYSIS	DECISION
Type of content	Information page about cycling clubs and teams.
Content purpose	To provide various clubs and teams a way to let the community know they exist and what they offer.
User-content relationships	Written for and accessed by any persona or role.
Content data	Title — Text field.
	Description — Multilined text field with HTML editor option.
	Email — Contact email address.
	URL — Field to hold the link to the club or team site.
	Images — Allow one image but do not embed; automatically resize the width to 400 pixels; limit size to 500 KB; allow JPEG, GIF, and PNG files.
	File — Allow one PDF file, limited to 1 MB, to be uploaded.

continues

TABLE 9-11 *(continued)*

ANALYSIS	DECISION
Content sources	Images will be uploaded by the content creator. Files will be uploaded by the content creator.
Data reuse	Title and description teaser — Display a list of clubs or teams. Images — Display club and team images in a gallery.
Content categories	Club type — Group like clubs/teams.
Category terms	Club type (select multiple) — Touring club, race club, professional team, amateur team. Other categories might be added.
Content relationships	NA
Content Metadata	NA
Content language	The site will be in English. A multilingual site is not planned at this time.
Content access	Anonymous visitors and members can access club pages. Members with entity permission can edit/complete a club page enabled for them by the administrator. Site and content administrators can unpublish, create, edit, and delete club pages.

User Profiles

After Gary and Claire identify the processes and tasks that the personas will perform on the site, they realize that the site is as much about the people (authors, members, merchants, and club leaders) as it is the content.

➤ Authors create the instruction.

➤ Members interact in the community.

➤ Merchant and club leaders post mini-brochures.

Gary and Claire have a list of tasks the personas would perform in context with the site content. Their next step is to identify tasks the personas would perform with respect to their site membership and their individual profiles. Gary and Claire identify the following user-centered tasks:

➤ View and edit their email addresses

➤ View and edit their usernames

➤ View a list of their posts to the site

➤ Process requests for member connections

➤ View a list of their groups

➤ View and delete their site bookmarks

➤ Enable and disable their content subscriptions

➤ Enable site members to send them private emails

➤ Tell visitors and members who they are

The next decision to make is how much privacy the users should have regarding the information associated with the tasks. Table 9-12 describes the content and features for the user profiles and who can see what.

TABLE 9-12: User Content and Features

DATA	USER OPTION	ANONYMOUS ACCESS	MEMBER ACCESS
User name	Self-selected and editable	Can access	Can access
Contact form	Option to enable	Cannot access	Can access
Picture or avatar	Option to choose an avatar or upload a picture	Can access	Can access
Member connections	List connections and connection requests	Cannot access	Can access
My posts	List posts and comments	Can access	Can access
My favorite pages	List bookmarked site pages	Cannot access	Cannot access
Site role(s)	Assigned by Admin	Can access	Can access
Notifications / subscriptions	Manage content subscriptions	Cannot access	Cannot access
Community groups	View groups where user is member	Cannot access	Cannot access
First name	Required for instructors, merchants, and club leaders Optional for members	Can access	Can access
Last name	Required for instructors, merchants, and club leaders Optional for members	Can access	Can access

continues

TABLE 9-12 *(continued)*

DATA	USER OPTION	ANONYMOUS ACCESS	MEMBER ACCESS
Location: city, state	Required for instructors, merchants, and club leaders Optional for members	Cannot access	Can access
Biography	Required for instructors Optional for members, merchants, and club leaders	Can access	Can access
Cycling role category	Required for instructors, merchants, and club leaders Optional for members	Can access	Can access

Communication

Communication is a two-way process. Gary and Claire want to hear from site visitors and members, and they want to be able to notify site members when new content is available. They also want to provide a way for members to send messages to other members. The following methods of communication are required:

➤ Contact forms

➤ Content notifications

➤ Request forms

➤ Comments

➤ Surveys

Contact Forms

Site visitors need a way to send private email messages to the site administrators and other members of the site. The site administrator message subjects will include:

➤ Report an issue

➤ Request information

In addition to a contact form for members to send messages to the site administrators, each member will have the option to include a contact form on their account so that other members can send them messages.

Content Notifications

Site members need to know when new content or comments have been added to the site. When site members join a community group, they will:

➤ Automatically be subscribed to content posted in that group

➤ Have the option to disable their subscriptions

➤ Have the option to subscribe to lessons, brochures, and authors

Request Forms

Visitors need a way to request lessons, brochure pages, and new groups. Data from the request form should be stored in the database and accessible via a report. The notification should be sent to the site administrators when a request has been submitted. The request form should be protected from malicious, automated spamming.

Comments

Site members need a way to interact with users who publish content on the site. One way to accomplish this is to let users comment on the content. Comments provide a way to foster discussions and idea exchange. Comments also provide an alternative way to post content on a site.

Surveys

The site administrators need a way to solicit information from visitors. The site administrators need to be able to conduct single-question surveys and multiquestion surveys. The surveys should be anonymous and managed on the site. Anonymous visitors should not be able to submit more than once. Survey results should be accessible on the site by the site administrators.

Search/Browse

Information about cycling is going to be located in many places on the site. Visitors will find information in lessons, discussions, tips, and maybe even brochure pages, but they also need to be able to search for content. Drupal's default search feature will be sufficient for this version of the site; however, in the future, Gary and Claire want to explore a more robust option (assuming the site gets busy).

In addition to a search feature, Gary and Claire will enable taxonomy terms and let the visitors use a menu of terms to find all pages that have been flagged with a specific term. This will bring each type of content together in a list. The users should be able to sort and filter the list.

Features

In addition to the preceding requirements, the site will provide the following features:

➤ Groups

➤ Aggregation

➤ Weather announcements

➤ Photo albums

➤ Subscriptions

➤ Bookmarks

➤ Friend connections

➤ Site abuse reporting

Groups

The site should include a space where visitors can have discussions and swap tips, a space where they can find others who share an interest in the topics being discussed. The site administrators need a tool that enables them to quickly configure a space that provides this type of organized interaction.

Aggregation

The site administrators need a tool to display news feeds from other sites. This is not a site for cycling news, but that doesn't mean the visitors won't be interested.

In addition to pulling feeds into the site, an option also needs to exist for pushing their own activities to others. Gary and Claire want to provide RSS feeds so that visitors or other sites can display their content as well.

Weather Announcements

Visitors to the site need a widget that provides weather-related data. The weather announcement initially will be for the region where Gary and Claire live. If the site grows and includes many members from other regions, the feature needs to be expanded to provide multiple weather announcements for select locations.

Photo Albums

Content administrators need a service that automatically reuses content images in a photo album. Images can tell a lot and entice someone to want to know more. Each time an image is added to the site, a thumbnail version needs to be displayed automatically on a page that groups images from sections of the site. The images should link to the page where they are included.

Subscriptions

Site members need a service that sends email notices when new content is added to the site. Busy schedules prevent many people from logging in to a community site to see whether anything new has been posted. Email notices are just one way to let members know the site offers something new to see.

Members of the site should be able to subscribe to different types of content and content authors. The option to subscribe should be convenient to the site members, preferably on the page with the content of interest. They also need a way to manage their subscriptions, turning them on and off as needed.

Bookmarks

Site members need a bookmark service that captures URLs for pages they want to be able to return to quickly. The bookmark feature needs to allow site members to click a link on the pages that can be bookmarked and then save that bookmark in the member profile. Members should be able to delete bookmarks at a later date from their profile.

Friend Connections

Site members need a service that enables them to connect with other site members. One way to do this is to include a "friends" option on the site. If one person recognizes another, he can get that person's attention by connecting as friends. No special privileges are associated with being friends. The other person should have the option to accept or reject the connection.

Site Abuse Reporting

Site visitors and members need a way to report to the site administrators that there is inappropriate content on the site. The method should not require the visitors or members to leave the page in question in order to submit a notification.

Roles

A lot of information about roles has already been indirectly referenced in the requirements so far. Table 9-13 summarizes this information by listing the system roles needed to support the planned processes and tasks.

TABLE 9-13: Roles and Permissions

ROLE	PERMISSION
Anonymous	Access all content
	Create an email-verified account
	Perform an advanced search
	Access some information on a user's account page
Authenticated	Join a group
	Create discussions, tips, and events
	Post a comment on any page that accepts comments
	Access additional information on a user's account page
Provider	Edit a product/service provider (merchant) page assigned to his or her user account
Club lead	Edit a club page assigned to his or her user account
Subject matter expert	Create a lesson page and associated facts

continues

TABLE 9-13 *(continued)*

ROLE	PERMISSION
Content administrator	Perform all tasks associated with content, including creating, editing, deleting, publishing, and unpublishing content
Site administrator	Perform all possible site-administration and site-configuration tasks

Performance

Although Gary and Claire's site is fairly basic, it could grow to be something much more. The following performance requirements will help Gary and Claire make decisions in the future:

➤   Response time

➤   Popularity

Response Time

The server environment needs to be able to accommodate the functionality of the site as well as the expected traffic. As traffic and, potentially, site functionality increase, the server environment needs to be expandable without interrupting service.

Popularity

In addition to traditional marketing strategies, the site will use metadata and SEO-friendly URLs to help search engines identify the content.

Gary and Claire chose Google Analytics to track the site's activity. The statistics collected by Google Analytics will help them determine whether they should add additional services to the site and whether paid advertising would benefit advertisers.

> **PERFORMANCE TIPS**
>
> Morningtime Digital Agency has published an article with 56 performance tips for Drupal 6 at `www.morningtime.com/Drupal-6x-Performance-Guide/513`. The agency does not claim that its tips are perfect, and it reminds you that all sites and their environments are different. However, if you are looking for ideas on how to improve your site's performance, this list might be useful.

Security

To limit common security issues, a minimum of the following is required at this time:

➤   **Code** — When the site is launched, all known security patches should be applied. No custom features are anticipated, but if they are needed, secure coding practices will be required.

➤   **Servers** — Only the site administrators will have access to the server, and each administrator will have his or her own login.

➤ **Content** — Users must be valid site members to add content to the site.

➤ **Files** — Files uploaded to the pages will be public. No restrictions are needed. Only web-friendly files will be permitted.

➤ **Abuse** — Forms will require a challenge and valid response before they can be submitted. Gary and Claire also want the site visitors to be able to flag content as offensive and have a message sent to the site and content administrators when such notices are sent.

➤ **HTML editor** — All posts, except those of the site administrator, will be filtered to prevent unauthorized HTML, CSS, or code.

➤ **User accounts** — User accounts will require email verification.

THE DESIGN

Now that Gary and Claire have identified how the site will be used and the content the site will include, they can create a design that accommodates these requirements. The following sections describe the process they use to plan the design of their first Drupal site.

Site Structure

The strategy for organizing the site is based on the type of content. Figure 9-1 shows a flowchart that illustrates the basic structure of the site. There is much more to the structure of the site than what is shown in Figure 9-1. The subsequent sections provide more structural information.

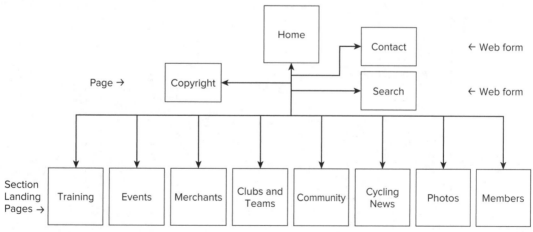

FIGURE 9-1

Although the intent is to place a copyright statement at the bottom of each page, the site still needs a copyright page that specifically states what can and cannot be used by others. Also, each page will contain a search field, but the search results need to be displayed, so that needs to be planned. Each page will also have a link to a contact form, which is another page that needs to be planned.

Training

The section that supports the learning-management aspect of the site will be called Training, which is assumed to be more inviting and easier to remember than Learning Management. The Training section will have two organizational strategies:

➤ Type of training opportunity (workshops, quick guides, resources, short tutorials)

➤ Topic (maintenance, bike handling, strategy, fitness)

If the format of the training is the first concern for the visitor, they can choose the type of training opportunity they prefer. If they don't care about format and only want to see what's available on, for instance, bike handling, they can look at all training opportunities that support bike handling.

Although this strategy provides flexibility for visitors and members, it is not the easiest strategy to put into a flowchart. The only reason Gary and Claire decided to create the flowchart in Figure 9-2 was to provide a way to communicate that the training materials would not be duplicated, that the content would be shared across the two strategies.

Training content is not the only content to be shared. The workshop content pages are actually event pages that are categorized as workshops and topic.

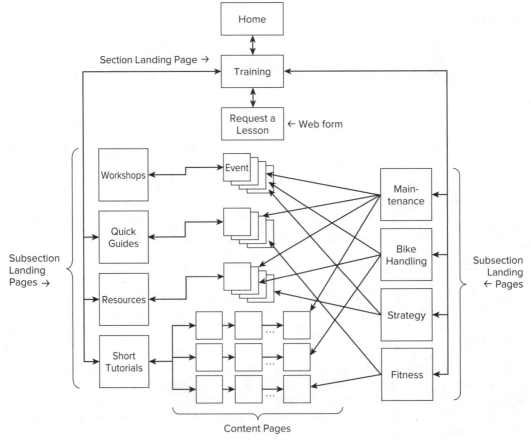

FIGURE 9-2

Events

The Events section of the site will provide a list of member-submitted events. The landing page will have a calendar, and type of event will have a page. Figure 9-3 shows the flowchart for the Events section of the site. The flowchart also shows that additional pages could be added if Gary and Claire identify more types of events.

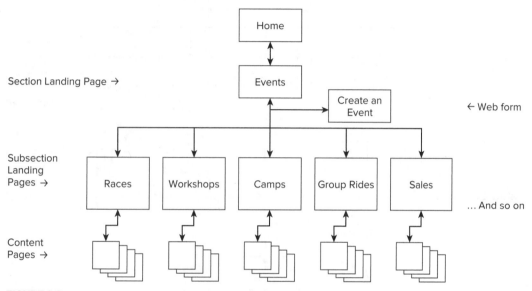

FIGURE 9-3

Training and Events share the same subsection called Workshops. The workshop event content pages will include navigation to Training and Events subsections.

Merchants

The Merchants section is similar to the Events section. A page will exist for each type of merchant. Figure 9-4 shows the flowchart for the Merchants section of the site. The flowchart also shows that additional pages could be added if Gary and Claire identify more types of merchants.

Clubs & Teams

The Clubs & Teams section is similar to the Events and Merchants sections. A page will exist for each type of club or team. Figure 9-5 shows the flowchart for the Clubs & Teams section of the site. The flowchart also shows that additional pages could be added if Gary and Claire identify more types of clubs or teams. The form to request a brochure page is the same form used by the Merchants section.

Community

Initially, the Community section will be divided into groups, one for each type of rider. Figure 9-6 shows the flowchart for the Community section of the site. Members of the site can join any group. Within each group, members can discuss topics of their choice and share cycling tips. The flowchart also shows that Gary and Claire could add additional pages to reflect additional groups, such as groups for clubs and teams.

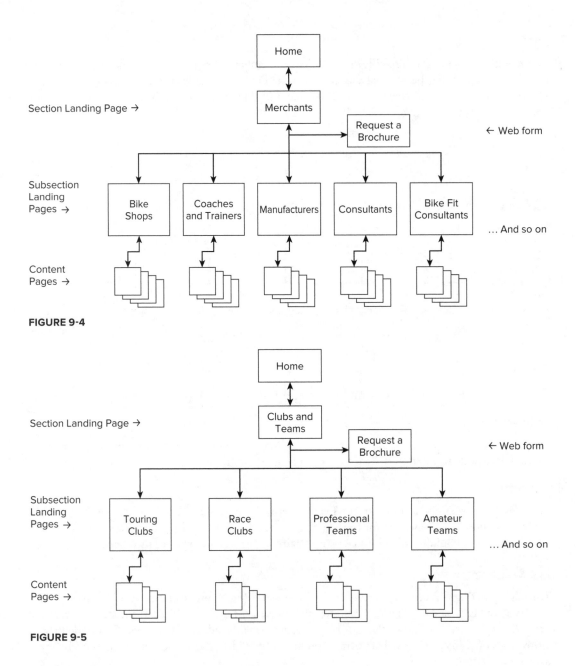

Section Landing Page →

← Web form

Subsection
Landing
Pages →

... And so on

Content
Pages →

FIGURE 9-4

Section Landing Page →

← Web form

Subsection
Landing
Pages →

... And so on

Content
Pages →

FIGURE 9-5

Cycling News

The Cycling News section of the site will aggregate news posts from other cycling-related sites. The plan is to have one or more teaser lists on the Cycling News landing page and then give visitors the option to see the full list from each RSS feed. Figure 9-7 shows the flowchart for the Cycling News section of the site. Notice that no pages are associated with the News Source pages. That's because the links on the News Source pages send visitors to the sites that host the articles.

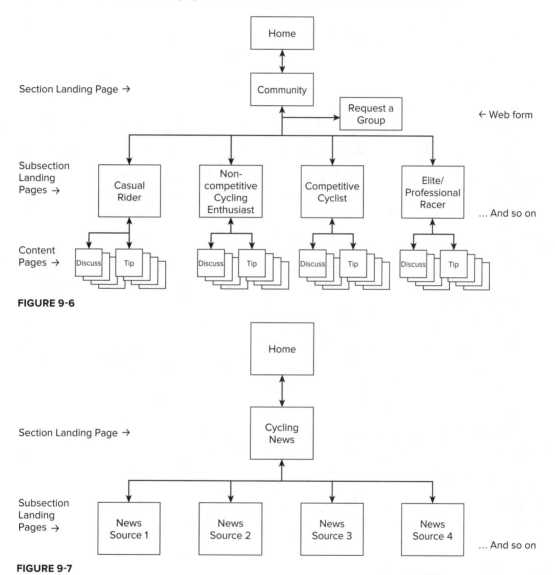

FIGURE 9-6

FIGURE 9-7

Photos

The Photos section of the site supports the photo album feature described in the requirements and its flowchart, as shown in Figure 9-8. The subsection landing pages will provide a photo album view of images that are shown on other pages. Clicking on an image will take the visitor to the page where the image is used. There are no image pages in this section.

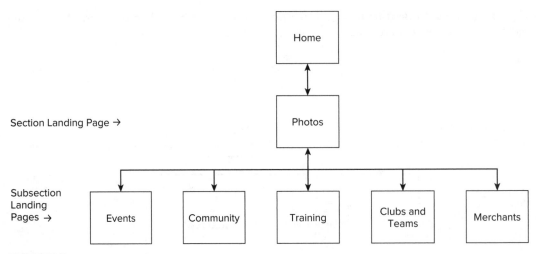

FIGURE 9-8

Members

The Members section of the site provides a list of site members and links to their profiles. Figure 9-9 shows the flowchart for the Members section. The landing page will have a sortable and filterable list of members.

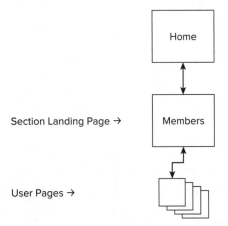

FIGURE 9-9

Page Components

Now that Gary and Claire have an inventory of the pages that need to be created, their next step is to plan what each page should include. They create a page component list for each type of page in each section. Each list is an organized narrative of what each page should include. They can use the lists to do some initial planning before moving on to the wireframes.

The following are sample page component lists from their plan. The complete list of pages is not provided, but the samples demonstrate the process they used.

Chapter 5, "Creating a Design Plan," provides a detailed explanation of the page components referenced in Tables 9-15 to 9-21.

Site-Wide Components

Table 9-14 describes the site-wide components for each page. The goal is to create consistency for the users.

TABLE 9-14: Site-Wide Page Components

COMPONENT	DESCRIPTION
Identification Information	Each page will have the site name and logo.
Path Structure	Each page will have a text-based URL, which means the URL for each page will not include special characters or reflect a database identifier.
	Each part of the URL will reflect a breadcrumb of pages. For instance, assume a page has the following URL:
	`http://example.com/merchants/shops/abc-bikes`
	If visitors remove part of the URL, they will land on a page. That means the following URLs will be valid pages:
	`http://example.com/merchants/shops`
	`http://example.com/merchants`
Core Navigation	Each page on the site will have a primary menu providing links to the landing page for each main section of the site:
	– Training
	– Events
	– Merchants
	– Clubs & Teams
	– Community
	– Cycling News
	– Photos
	– Members
	Each page will also have a link to the contact form and copyright page.
Features	Each page will provide access to the site's search form.

Home Page Components

The purpose of the home page is to provide a dashboard of site activity but, at the same time, not overwhelm visitors. Table 9-15 describes the components that should be included on the home page.

TABLE 9-15: Home Page Components

COMPONENT	DESCRIPTION
Unique Identification Information	NA.
Path Structure	`http://samplesitename.com.`
Unique Core Navigation	NA.
Supplemental Navigation	List of links to recent community posts. List of most recently added training posts. List of upcoming events. List of most recent news posts.
Contextual Navigation	At the end of each list of recent links will be a "read more" link that takes the site visitor to the applicable site section.
Core Content	Rotating slideshow with text and images that highlight the purpose of the site. Featured merchant, club or team, subject matter expert.
Supplemental Content	NA.
Related Content	NA.
Contextual Content	NA.
Unique Features	Weather announcement. Anonymous visitor — Message to join or log in. Authenticated user — Access to account-management options.

Training Section Components

The purpose of the Training section landing page is to provide visitors with a dashboard of training options. The Training section has the following types of pages:

➤ Section landing page

➤ Subsection landing pages

> ➤ Quick guide lesson pages

> ➤ Resource lesson pages

> ➤ Short tutorial lesson pages

> ➤ Fact pages

> ➤ Vocabulary term pages

Table 9-16 lists the components of the Training section landing page.

TABLE 9-16: Training Section Landing Page Components

COMPONENT	DESCRIPTION
Unique Identification Information	Training image.
Path Structure	`http://samplesitename.com/training.`
Unique Core Navigation	Links to the following subsection landing pages: – Quick guides – Resources – Short tutorials – Workshops
Supplemental Navigation	List terms from the Activity category that link to subsection landing pages listing the training pages flagged in that category. List of most recently added training posts. List of upcoming workshop events.
Contextual Navigation	At the end of each list of recent links will be a "read more" link that takes the site visitor to the applicable site section.
Core Content	A brief narrative describing the content found in the Training section.
Supplemental Content	NA.
Related Content	NA.
Contextual Content	NA.
Unique Features	Anonymous visitor — Message to join or log in. Authenticated user — Access to account-management options.

The purpose of the Training subsection landing pages is to provide an access point for lessons on a specific cycling activity and available workshops. Table 9-17 lists the components of the Training subsection landing pages.

TABLE 9-17: Training Subsection Landing Page Components

COMPONENT	DESCRIPTION
Unique Identification Information	Landing page training image.
Path Structure	`http:// samplesitename.com/training/subsection-title.`
Unique Core Navigation	Links to the following subsection landing pages: – Quick guides – Resources – Short tutorials – Workshops
Supplemental Navigation	List terms from the Activity category that link to subsection landing pages listing the training pages flagged in that category. List of most recently added training posts. List of upcoming workshop events.
Contextual Navigation	At the end of each list of recent links will be a "read more" link that takes the site visitor to a page listing all the applicable pages.
Core Content	A brief narrative describing the content found in the subsection. A list of lessons that match the subsection and that can be sorted.
Supplemental Content	NA.
Related Content	NA.
Contextual Content	NA.
Unique Features	Anonymous visitor — Message to join or log in. Authenticated user — Access to account-management options.

The three types of lessons are quick guides, resources, and short tutorials. The purpose of the quick guide and resource lesson pages is to display a single lesson or link to a single lesson. Table 9-18 lists the components of the pages for the quick guides and resources.

TABLE 9-18: Quick Guide and Resource Lesson Page Components

COMPONENT	DESCRIPTION
Unique Identification Information	NA
Path Structure	`http:// samplesitename.com/training/subsection-title/ title-of-lesson`
Unique Core Navigation	Links to the following subsection landing pages: – Quick guides – Resources – Short tutorials – Workshops
Supplemental Navigation	List of lesson titles sorted by title with the option to page through the titles List of upcoming workshops
Contextual Navigation	NA
Core Content	The lesson content
Supplemental Content	Definitions associated with terms in the text of the lesson
Related Content	Name, image, and biography teaser for the author of the lesson from the author's profile
Contextual Content	Icon or image that represents the activity associated with the lesson
Unique Features	Option to subscribe to this type of content Option to bookmark a lesson

The purpose of the short tutorial lesson pages is to present sequenced lessons that form the tutorial. Table 9-19 lists the components of the short tutorial lesson pages.

TABLE 9-19: Short Tutorial Lesson Page Components

COMPONENT	DESCRIPTION
Unique Identification Information	NA

Path Structure	First tutorial page:
	`http:// samplesitename.com/training/subsection-title/`
	`tutorial-title`
	Subsequent tutorial pages:
	`http://example.com/training/subsection-title/tutorial-title/`
	`title-of-lesson`

Unique Core Navigation	Links to the following subsection landing pages: – Quick guides – Resources – Short tutorials – Workshops
Supplemental Navigation	List of tutorial titles sorted by title with the option to page through the titles List of lesson titles in the current tutorial
Contextual Navigation	Links to the child lesson pages associated with a lesson Links to the previous and next lesson
Core Content	The lesson content
Supplemental Content	Definitions associated with terms in the text of the content
Related Content	Information about the author of the lesson from his or her user profile
Contextual Content	Icon or image that represents the activity associated with the lesson
Unique Features	Option to subscribe to this type of content Option to bookmark a lesson

The purpose of the fact pages is to provide short bits of text (quick facts) for terms or topics presented in a lesson. Quick facts are displayed via a block on a lesson page and, when accessed, pop up in a box over the lesson page (versus as a "normal" page in the site). Table 9-20 lists the components of the fact pages. Because these aren't regular pages in the site but, instead, a way to display a bit of text, the only component is the fact content and the URL required for all nodes.

TABLE 9-20: Fact Page Components

COMPONENT	DESCRIPTION
Unique Identification Information	NA
Path Structure	`http:// samplesitename.com/training/fact-title` (but is not visible)
Unique Core Navigation	NA
Supplemental Navigation	NA
Contextual Navigation	NA
Core Content	The fact content
Supplemental Content	NA
Related Content	NA
Contextual Content	NA
Unique Features	NA

The purpose of the vocabulary term pages is to list all content that has been flagged with a specific term. Table 9-21 lists the components of the vocabulary term pages.

TABLE 9-21: Vocabulary Term Page Components

COMPONENT	DESCRIPTION
Unique Identification Information	NA
Path Structure	`http:// samplesitename.com/category/vocabulary-name/term`
Unique Core Navigation	NA

continues

TABLE 9-21 *(continued)*

COMPONENT	DESCRIPTION
Supplemental Navigation	List of lesson titles sorted by title with the option to page through the titles
	List of upcoming events
	List of most recent news posts
Contextual Navigation	NA
Core Content	Teaser list of pages flagged with the term
Supplemental Content	NA
Related Content	NA
Contextual Content	NA
Unique Features	Anonymous visitor — Message to join or log in
	Authenticated user — Access to account-management options

Wireframes

Using the list of components for each page, Gary and Claire start strategizing what type of layout would accommodate the page components in each section of the site before they start drawing wireframes to illustrate the page-component placement on the page.

Their process starts with a list of sites they find visually appealing. They analyze the layout strategies for each site. Some sites were made with Drupal and others were not, but that didn't seem to matter. A pattern seems to emerge among the sites: Each has a main content area, areas on the page that were likely regions and sidebars, and a header and footer.

They discuss the layout of the sites and decide they want a two-column approach: the main content area being the first column on the page and the right sidebar being the second column. From the list of page components they initially drafted, it appears this strategy can provide:

➤ Sufficient space for the planned page components

➤ Sufficient space for large images and video

Figures 9-10 through 9-19 are wireframes that illustrate the layout of the home page and a sampling of the Training section pages.

Figures 9-10 and 9-11 are two versions of the home page. Figure 9-10 is what an anonymous visitor will see. Figure 9-11 is what an authenticated member will see. Notice the change in the right sidebar. Once an authenticated user logs in, the "Become a Member" block is replaced with a block title with the user's name.

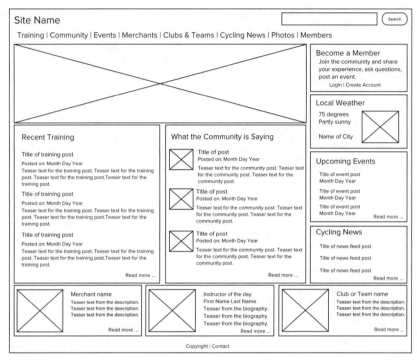

FIGURE 9-10

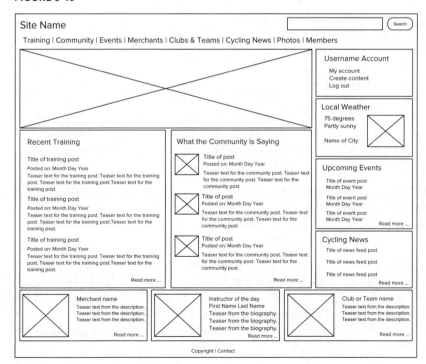

FIGURE 9-11

When visitors click on the Training link in the primary menu, they are taken to the Training section landing page. Figure 9-12 shows that the primary menu will have drop-down functionality, allowing users to gain quick access to subsection landing pages. Recall from the flowchart that the plan is to provide two ways to view training: type and topic. The "Lessons On:" block in the right sidebar is a menu (list of activity term links) that links to the topic subsection landing pages.

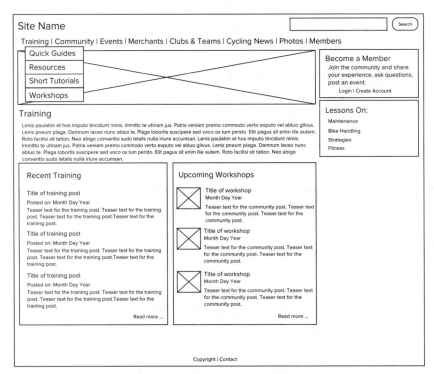

FIGURE 9-12

Notice that the "Become a Member" block is showing in this wireframe. If the member were logged in, the block with their username would be visible instead. This is true for the remaining wireframes.

If visitors click on a link from the drop-down menu under Training, they are taken to a subsection landing page — in this instance, Quick Guides, as shown in Figure 9-13. Notice that the list of lessons is limited to three per page but the visitor can page through the options. What is not seen, but is required, is the ability to sort on quick-guide-lesson title.

When visitors click on a quick-guide-lesson title, they are taken to the lesson page, as shown in Figure 9-14. Notice that the "Lessons On:" menu is not available at this level of the site; instead, a block listing other quick guides is provided. This is also the first time the fact "page" is available. The Definition block will appear only if there is a fact associated with the lesson. If there is more than one fact, the page appears under the fact teaser so other fact teasers can be viewed in the block.

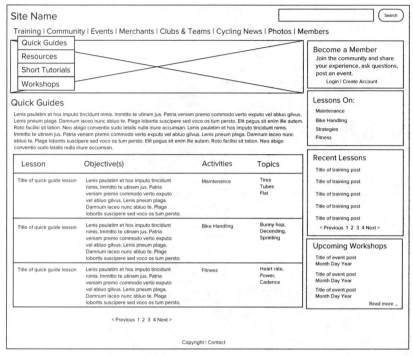

FIGURE 9-13

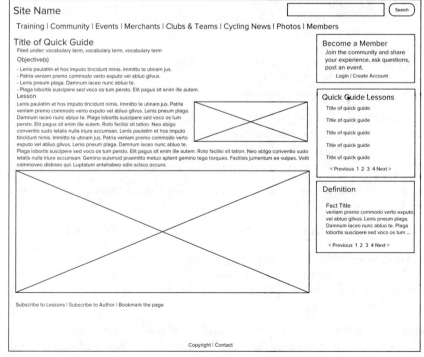

FIGURE 9-14

When visitors click on the title of the fact, a window pops up to show the full text of the fact. Figure 9-15 shows how the page behind the pop-up gets grayed out. The item being displayed is the node.

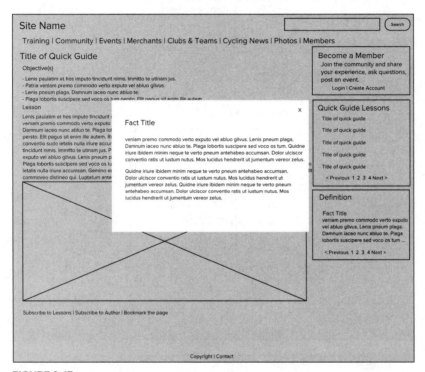

FIGURE 9-15

The subsection landing pages in the Training section will be similar. Figure 9-16 shows the Short Tutorials subsection. Notice the similarity to the Quick Guides subsection shown in Figure 9-13. The difference is what gets shown in the main content area.

When visitors click on a short tutorial lesson, they get a lesson page that is a little different from the quick guide or resource lesson pages. Notice the bulleted list of lessons under the text (shown in Figure 9-17), as well as the "next" navigation labeled "Lesson 1 >." Short tutorials are multipage lessons. The first page introduces the lesson and subsequent pages provide an organized learning experience.

When visitors click through to the next page of the short tutorial, the page changes a little. Figure 9-18 shows that the bulleted list disappears and the previous/next type of navigation is available.

Gary and Claire are using vocabulary terms to accomplish two forms of navigation on the site:

➤ **Site section navigation** — Similar to a menu, they are listing terms that link to subsection landing pages. Because they want the option to add terms in the future without having to create the landing page for that term and edit the menus, they are using a dynamic approach to managing their section navigation.

➤ **Content category navigation** — An alternative to traditional menu-oriented navigation, terms displayed with content will link to pages that list all content from across each section of the site that is flagged with that term.

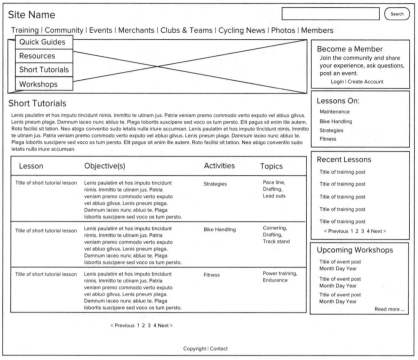

FIGURE 9-16

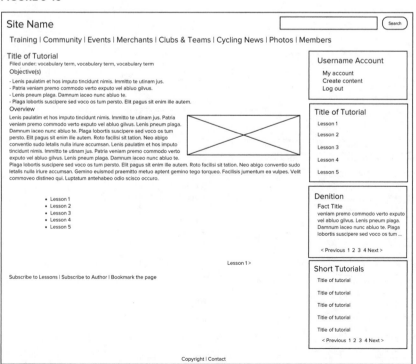

FIGURE 9-17

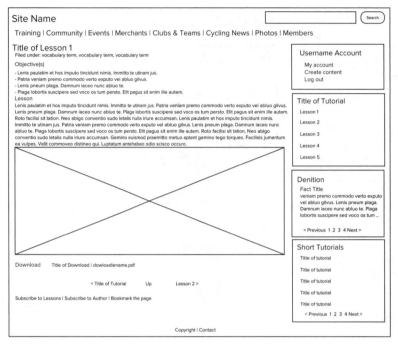

FIGURE 9-18

Figure 9-19 is a subsection landing page in the Training section. *Maintenance* is a vocabulary term listed in the block titled "Lessons on."

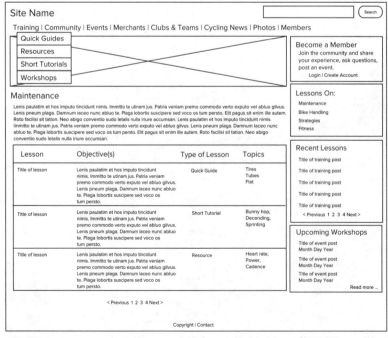

FIGURE 9-19

Figure 9-20 shows the page that appears when visitors click on the term *maintenance* (or any term) from a content page.

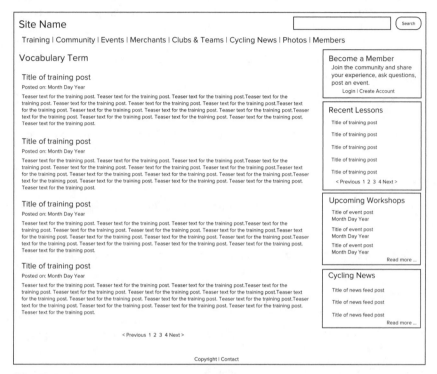

FIGURE 9-20

Style Guide and Theme

After looking at their budget and current skill set, Gary and Claire decide to try a contributed theme, one that is free for download from Drupal.org. This decision alters their strategy for creating a style guide and *comps* (graphic depictions of the various types of pages planned for the site). In this scenario, they don't need to create a comp. The sample screenshots from the contributed theme will be as close as they get to having a comp.

Style Guide

Because Gary and Claire are going to try a contributed theme, they decide against creating a traditional style guide and opt to identify a couple of styles to use as criteria when selecting themes:

➤ **Fonts** — The theme should use relative font size versus an absolute font size. This will allow a user to change the text size in the browser.

➤ **Colors** — Blue tones are preferred, but green is also an option.

They feel that if their style guide is too specific, they might not find a contributed theme that meets all their expectations.

Theme Decision Criteria

To help with their search for potential themes, they identified some theme-oriented selection criteria:

➤ **Advanced theme settings** — They prefer a theme with advanced settings and multiple regions.

➤ **Layout** — The theme should have sidebars on either side of the main content area (in case they want to add another sidebar to their layouts).

➤ **Regions** — The theme should have multiple regions to accommodate various page layouts.

➤ **Drop-down menu** — The theme needs to accommodate a drop-down feature for the primary menu.

➤ **Drupal version** — The theme needs a version that works in Drupal 6 and Drupal 7.

Gary and Claire searched through the themes on Drupal.org and found four themes that interested them. Figures 9-21 through 9-24 are screenshots (comp substitutes) of the four themes they found.

Figure 9-21 is a screenshot from the Danland theme (`http://drupal.org/project/danland`) demo site. The number of regions illustrated in the demo increases the number of possible page layouts.

Danland theme header image courtesy of Rodrigo Cunha (www.flickr.com/photos/rnbc/).

FIGURE 9-21

Figure 9-22 is a screenshot from the Simpler theme demo site (`http://drupal.org/project/ simpler`). The demo layouts suggest this theme might match the layouts in the wireframes.

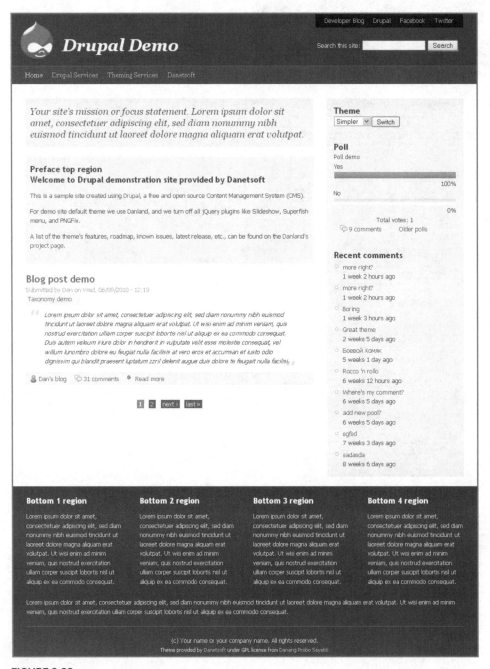

FIGURE 9-22

Figure 9-23 is a screenshot of a demo site using the Zero Point theme (`http://drupal.org/project/zeropoint`). The demo indicates the theme will support the layout of the site.

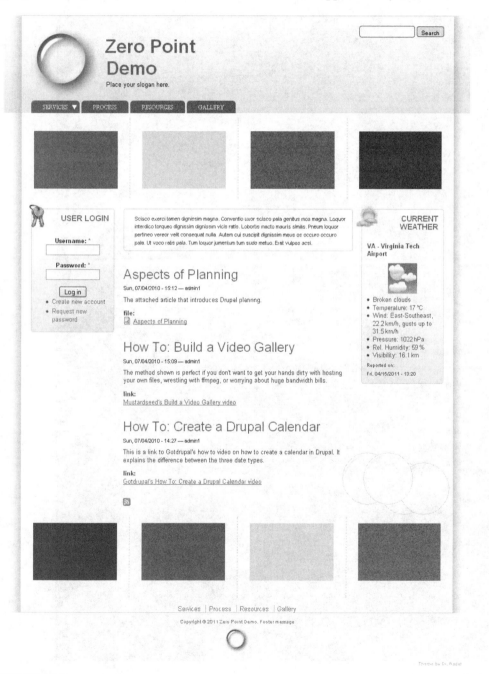

FIGURE 9-23

Figure 9-24 is a screenshot from the BlueMasters demo site (`http://drupal.org/project/bluemasters`). The demo site pages indicate this theme will also support the layout.

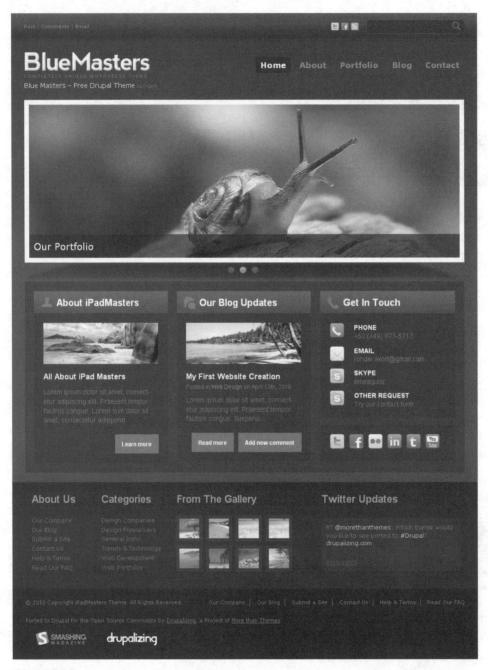

FIGURE 9-24

Theme Comparison

Initially, Gary and Claire select the preceding four themes based on their visual appeal. In other words, Gary and Claire like their look. The next step is to review the themes to ensure the themes meet their evaluation criteria.

Table 9-22 provides a comparison of the four themes based on the style guide and theme-oriented selection criteria Gary and Claire identified. The demo pages and screenshots suggest the regions will support their page layouts; however, Gary and Claire won't know for sure until they install the themes and take a look at the region configuration.

TABLE 9-22: Theme Comparison

CRITERIA	DANLAND	SIMPLER	ZERO POINT	BLUEMASTERS
Fonts	Relative	Absolute	Relative	Relative
Colors	Blue	Blue	Blue/Green	Blue
Advanced theme settings	No	No	Yes	No
Layout	Yes	Yes	Yes	Yes
Regions	To be confirmed	To be confirmed	To be confirmed	To be confirmed
Drop-down menu	Yes	No	Yes	Yes for Drupal 7
Drupal version	6 and 7	6 and 7	6 and 7	6 and 7

THEME EVALUATION

It was not clear from reading the project pages whether the fonts were relative or absolute. A review of the CSS would indicate which practice was used. One way to determine the font-sizing method is to download the theme and look at the CSS. Another is to look at the theme while it is in use. Three of the themes being considered have demo sites: Danland, Simpler, and BlueMasters. Gary and Claire evaluate the theme's font-size method by going to the demo sites and using Firefox's Firebug tool to view the CSS in use.

Many themes have multiple regions and strategies that are not conveyed on the theme project pages or in their screenshots. Sometimes, you have to install the theme to evaluate its potential and to know for sure whether the theme will work for you. A theme with a demo site is helpful.

Mobile Design

Cycling is a mobile event, so Gary and Claire assume that information about cycling should be available on mobile devices. Because many mobile devices have a web browser, people can access Gary and Claire's site while on the road.

But what will they see or not see? What should they be able to do? Who will be interested in the content of their site when they are out and about? As they consider these questions and others, Gary and Claire realize they are starting the requirements and design process over again, to some extent.

While planning the traditional version of their site, Gary and Claire realize they don't know which aspects of the site will appeal the most to their visitors. During the audience analysis, potential users of the site expressed an interest in each of the features they had planned. But until the site has actual activity, Gary and Claire can't be sure which features will be most popular. Should the mobile version of their site "do it all" or should it highlight specific features?

They decide to wait until their traditional site has been up and running for a few months. They will monitor the site activity and observe what areas or features the visitors frequent most. They will poll visitors to the site and ask them, "If you were accessing this site via a mobile device such as a smart-phone, what would you be looking for?"

DRUPAL AND MOBILE

Drupal creator Dries Buytaert, in his keynote address at DrupalCon Chicago, March 2011, said, "The future is being anywhere at any time, reaching any information or people needed at any device." He also stated that " ... multi-device publishing, or mobile, is going to be key ... " Learn more about the future of Drupal by watching his keynote speech at `www.archive.org/details/keynote_dries` (fast-forward to time stamp 37:30 to learn about the future).

SUMMARY

This chapter provides insights into the planning process by joining Gary and Claire while they walk through the steps to define their site. The process they follow is explained in detail in Chapters 3 through 5.

Here are a few things to remember when planning your site:

➤ You can organize your planning process by defining the purpose of the site first.

➤ Interviews with your potential audience can help you understand your audience's needs and, therefore, prioritize what you offer.

➤ Sometimes, you can use one content type for multiple types of content.

➤ Sometimes, you need a content type for content that will not be presented in the main content area.

➤ Site features add value to your site by increasing user interactions and services.

➤ A site flowchart doesn't always look like an organizational chart.

➤ Don't forget to think about supplemental and contextual navigation and content.

➤ Identify your page components and create wireframes for each type of page in each section of the site so that you can identify which blocks flow from one level of the site to the next.

➤ Using a contributed theme means you might not get exactly what your wireframes show.

➤ The requirements and design decisions made for a traditional site might not apply to users on small mobile devices such as smartphones.

10

Example Build Recipes

In Chapter 9, "An Example Plan," you joined Gary and Claire on their adventure to plan their first Drupal site. Now, you join them in a conference room where they have posted the flowcharts, wireframes, and various requirements documents on the walls. Luckily for them, Claire has a small conference room she seldom uses.

Gary and Claire discover that looking at one flowchart, one wireframe, and one requirement at a time doesn't provide the big-picture view of where they are going and how it is all connected. So, they decide to post the wireframes on a wall in the form of a flowchart. With each wireframe, they tack up the page component notes they had recorded. On another wall, they post their notes for the different types of content they had planned, along with the other requirements notes. They've done a lot of work but still have a way to go.

In this chapter, you will join Gary and Claire as they:

- ➤ Organize the requirements for their site
- ➤ Identify modules for their site
- ➤ Make decisions about their site's development sequence
- ➤ Make decisions about their site's environments
- ➤ Prepare to implement their site
- ➤ Agree on how to sustain their site

The information in this chapter exemplifies the topics discussed in Part II, "Building and Sustaining Your Website."

THE REQUIREMENTS INVENTORY

As Gary and Claire look at all the requirements notes, flowcharts, and wireframes for their site, they realize they need to create a lot of pages, content, vocabularies, and blocks. They need a way to organize their development efforts, so they create an inventory of the pages, content types and fields, vocabularies, and blocks to develop. They decide that the roles, search, features, performance, and security requirements already documented are organized sufficiently (see Chapter 9).

Pages

Gary and Claire review the flowcharts and the types of content they had defined and realize that a lot of pages weren't strictly content pages. Many were about showing one lesson, discussion, tip, event, merchant, or club. However, the other pages included:

➤ Section landing pages

➤ Subsection landing pages

➤ Request forms

➤ Create-a-page forms

➤ Search results

➤ Vocabulary term pages

While considering how they would create these pages, Gary and Claire ask the following questions:

➤ If these pages aren't your typical content (or node pages), what are they?

➤ Are the pages similar to each other such that we could use the same strategy over and over?

➤ Can we use one of the default content types that come with Drupal to make these pages?

To help them think through the process of identifying how to create these pages, Gary and Claire develop a set of decision criteria to assess each type of page and how best to create that type of page. The criteria include sample Drupal development strategies they learned from reading this book and from doing a little research on Drupal.org. The decision criteria provide sample page-development strategies based on:

➤ Main content area

➤ Main content area layout

➤ Navigation source

Gary and Claire create an inventory of the page types and identify the plans associated with each. The following sections present the decision criteria they created and their application to the pages.

Main Content Area Decision Criteria

The number of nodes that make up a page can influence the strategy used to generate the page. Table 10-1 provides decision criteria based on the object(s) shown in the main content area of a page. The strategies are just a sampling of what is possible.

TABLE 10-1: Page Development Strategies Based on Main Content Area

TYPE OF PAGE	MAIN CONTENT AREA OBJECTS	SAMPLE STRATEGIES
Single-node page	By default, a title is displayed. Displays content such as lesson, discussion, tip, event, and so on. Can include one or more blocks.	Generate the page using a node. Add blocks with a field or in a region located above or below the node content. Generate the page using Panel's node template page to show node content with blocks.
Multi-node page	Might have a title displayed. Content can be presented as a teaser list of nodes. Content can also be a series of full nodes. Can include one or more blocks.	Generate the page using a system default feature such as a vocabulary term page or search result page. Generate the page using a node in combination with the Composite module to show the objects. Generate the page using a Panel page to show the objects. Generate the page using a Views page to show the objects.
No-node page	Might have a title displayed. Content is typically displayed via different types of blocks. If a narrative exists, it could be data from a node field or a block.	Generate the page with a node without content and hide the title. Then use the theme regions above and below the main content to display the blocks. Generate the page with a node without content and hide the title. Then use the Composite module to display blocks. Generate the page using a Panel page. Generate the page using a Views page.

 Chapter 5, "Creating a Design Plan," talks about no-node, single-node, and multi-node content pages.

Main Content Layout Decision Criteria

If Gary and Claire are going to stick to a no-custom-code-development strategy, they need to think about how they can arrange content in the main content area. Table 10-2 provides decision criteria based on the desired layout of the objects shown in the main content area of a page. The strategies are just a sampling of what is possible.

TABLE 10-2: Page Development Strategies Based on Main Content Area Layout

LAYOUT	CONTENT AREA OBJECTS	SAMPLE STRATEGIES
Vertical placement	Objects (title, text, fields, nodes, or blocks) in the main content area of the page are stacked on top of each other.	Generate the page via a node. Add blocks with a field or in a region located above or below the main content. Generate the page via a node and use attached views. Generate the page via a node and use the Composite module to place the objects. Generate the page using the Panels module to lay out the content and blocks in a single Panel page or a node template panel. Generate the page using a Views page and include the text in the header or footer of the view.
Horizontal placement	One or more objects (title, text, fields, nodes, or blocks) in the main content area of the page are next to each other.	Generate the page via a node and use the Composite module to place the objects horizontally. Generate the page using the Panels module to lay out the content and blocks horizontally in a single Panel page or a node template panel.

 Chapter 5 describes block placement strategies and challenges.

Navigation Source Decision Criteria

Very few links on a Drupal page are generated manually. Gary and Claire notice their plan is to have visitors access most of the site pages using dynamically generated links found in dynamically generated lists. They realize that they need to understand the difference between how links are created on their pages and whether that could influence their page-development strategy.

Table 10-3 provides decision criteria based on how someone is navigating to the page. The strategies are just a sampling of what is possible.

TABLE 10-3: Page Development Strategies Based on Navigation Source

SOURCE	DESCRIPTION	SAMPLE STRATEGIES
Menu links	A link that has been manually added to a menu. The link that goes to a predefined path.	Use a predefined path for a node. Use a predefined path for a View page. Use a predefined path for a Panel page. Use a predefined path for a page generated by a module.
Taxonomy term links	Links from vocabulary terms to pages that display content flagged with that term.	Use the default path to go to the default content display. Override the default content displayed with the Panels module taxonomy term template. Enable and edit the Views module *taxonomy_term* page display and override the default display.
Views links	Links generated by the Views module that go to a predefined path based on the data being linked (for example, node title links to node); term links to default term display.	Use the default links provided by Views. Use Views' "Output this link field as a link" option and redirect the link to another view with a display that is different from the default.

Page Inventory Assessment

Armed with decision criteria and sample strategies, Gary and Claire start to assess what they planned for their pages. Their goal is to keep their Drupal learning curve manageable while using consistent development strategies across the site. Table 10-4 provides the following information:

➤ An inventory of the types of pages whose purpose is to do something more or different than displaying one node (lesson, discussion, tip, event, merchant, or club)

➤ Descriptive information in line with the decision criteria described earlier

➤ One or more page-development strategies for each type of page

At the end of their evaluation, when the option was available, they chose the node-based solution. This decision, however, depends on finding the right module(s), such as a module to hide the node titles.

Gary and Claire also note that they don't know enough about custom forms to identify options at this time. They will confirm their decisions and investigate the custom form requirement further when they start to identify, evaluate, and select their modules.

TABLE 10-4: Page Inventory

TYPE OF PAGE	MAIN CONTENT AREA	MAIN CONTENT AREA LAYOUT	NAVIGATION	SAMPLE OPTIONS
Home page	No-node Multiple blocks placed next to each other	Horizontal	Site URL	Panel page No-title node with Composite module
Section landing pages	Node-like content Text only Multiple blocks	Horizontal	Menu links	Panel page Page node with Composite module
Subsection landing pages, accessed via the main menu	Node-like content Text only Single block	Vertical	Menu links	Page node with view attached View page
Subsection landing pages, accessed via a dynamically generated block list	Node-like content Text only Single block	Vertical	Views links	Page node with view attached View page
Subsection landing pages, group home page	Single-node Single block	Vertical	Views links	Group node default Panel page
Module-based request forms	Contact form with text Search block form has no text	Vertical	Menu or plain HTML links to contact form Submit button to search	Default form display Other options to be determined during module selection

TYPE OF PAGE	MAIN CONTENT AREA	MAIN CONTENT AREA LAYOUT	NAVIGATION	SAMPLE OPTIONS
Custom request forms	"Request a lesson" and "request a brochure" have node-like content Text only	Vertical	Menu links or plain HTML links	To be determined during module selection
Create-a-page forms	Create event, create discussion, and create tip Node-like text instructions	Vertical	Menu links or plain HTML links	Default node-create form Panel node-create template
Search results page	Multi-node	Vertical	Search submit button	Default search result page Other options could be determined during module selection
Vocabulary term pages	Multi-node	Vertical	Taxonomy term links	Default term page display Modified term page via Views

Content Types and Fields

As Gary and Claire review the fields listed in the content type descriptions, they notice that several fields are being repeated from one content type to the next. They decide to make a list of fields for two reasons:

➤ To avoid creating duplicate fields as they both create content types

➤ To help them easily identify the modules they would need to create the fields

Although some fields appear to be the same, subtle differences exist. Gary and Claire are not sure whether those differences will require a new field to be created, so they list them separately. They also make an attempt to identify the type of field they will need, not knowing all the field options Drupal offers. For instance, they don't know yet whether Drupal has a special text field for emails.

The assumption during this process was that Gary and Claire would learn more about how fields work in Drupal and the different modules available to create fields that serve different purposes.

CONTENT CONFIGURATION TUTORIALS

Many tutorials cover the configuration of content types. The following tutorials are fairly comprehensive, nicely done, and free:

➤ Basics: Understanding Drupal's Content Types (CCK) [in Drupal 6] — `http://gotdrupal.com/videos/understanding-drupal-content-types-cck`

➤ Creating content types in Drupal 7 — `www.leveltendesign.com/blog/tom/creating-content-types-drupal-7`

➤ Introduction to fields in Drupal 7 — `www.leveltendesign.com/tutorial/video/introduction-fields-drupal-7`

➤ Adding fields in Drupal 7 — `www.leveltendesign.com/tutorial/video/adding-fields-drupal-7`

Table 10-5 lists the field label, description, content type using the field, and potential field type for each content-type field. Gary and Claire plan to investigate the field options in Drupal committing to a field type or, in some instances, identifying a field type.

TABLE 10-5: Content Fields

FIELD LABEL	DESCRIPTION	CONTENT TYPE	FIELD TYPE
Title	Node default	Lesson, Fact, Discussion, Tip, Event, Merchant, Club	Default title
Biography	Multilined text field with HTML editor option	User Profile	Default Body
Description	Multilined text field with HTML editor option	Event, Merchant, Club	Default Body
Discussion	Multilined text field with HTML editor option	Discussion	Default Body
Fact	Multilined text field with HTML editor option	Fact	Default Body
Narrative	Multilined text field with HTML editor option	Lesson	Default Body
Tip	Multilined text field with HTML editor option	Tip	Default Body
Email	Contact email address	Merchant, Club	Text

FIELD LABEL	DESCRIPTION	CONTENT TYPE	FIELD TYPE
File	Allow one PDF file to be uploaded and attached to the node Limit size to 1 MB	Lesson, Event, Merchant, Club	File
First name	Field to collect the first name of the user	User Profile	Text
Hours	Text field with HTML editor option (not applicable to all types of providers)	Merchant	Text
Images	Allow one image but do not embed Automatically resize the width to 400 pixels Limit size to 500 KB Allow JPEG, GIF, and PNG	Event, Merchant, Club	Image file
Images	Allow up to three images uploaded and embedded in the narrative Limit size to 500 KB each Allow JPEG, GIF, and PNG	Lesson, Discussion, Tip	Image file
Last name	Field to collect the last name of the user	User Profile	Text
Lesson Author	Field to create a relationship between the lesson and the lesson author profile	Lesson	TBD
Lesson Objectives	Multilined text field with HTML editor option	Lesson	Text
Location	Place and address	Event, Merchant, User profile	Location
Related Fact	Field to create a relationship between a lesson and a fact	Lesson	TBD
Related Group	Field to create a relationship between a lesson and a community group	Lesson	TBD
Resource Link	Option to provide a link to an online resource	Lesson	Text

continues

TABLE 10-5 *(continued)*

FIELD LABEL	DESCRIPTION	CONTENT TYPE	FIELD TYPE
Start and End Date and Time	Date field for start and end date and time	Event	Date
URL	Field to hold the link to the merchant site	Merchant, Club	Text
Video Display	Field to hold embedded link with HTML editor option	Lesson	Text
Video Link	Field to hold the link to the video source	Lesson	Text

Taxonomy Vocabularies

Although there aren't as many vocabularies as there are fields, some vocabularies repeat from one content type to another. To prevent duplication, Gary and Claire summarize the vocabularies the site needs, as shown in Table 10-6.

TABLE 10-6: Taxonomy Vocabularies

VOCABULARY	TERMS	CONTENT TYPE	SETTINGS
Activity	Maintenance, bike handling, strategy, fitness	Lesson, Discussion, Tip, Event, Fact	Select one
Topic	Create tags that describe the lesson further	Lesson, Discussion, Tip, Event	Free tag, multi-select
Club type	Touring club, race club, professional team, amateur team	Club	Multi-select
Event type	Race, workshop, camp, group ride, sale	Event	Select one
Lesson type	Quick guides, short tutorials, resources	Lesson	Select one
Merchant type	Shop, coaches and trainers, consultant, manufacturer, mechanics, bike fit technician	Merchant	Multi-select
Cycling role	Casual rider, non-competitive cycling enthusiast, competitive cyclist, elite or professional racer, club or team lead, product or service provider, subject matter expert	User profile	Multi-select

Blocks

As Gary and Claire look at all the blocks they need to create, several questions come to mind:

➤ How many blocks are duplicates (the same blocks appearing over and over)?

➤ How will they make the blocks?

➤ Do any of the blocks planned for one region appear in another region on a different page?

➤ How do they coordinate the development of all the blocks?

Gary and Claire decide to create a block development worksheet listing all the blocks, and are careful not to list the same block twice. Their worksheet summarizes information from the wireframe and the page component notes, and adds some additional information. The worksheet includes:

➤ The block title

➤ The page(s) and location on the page (left, center, right, top, bottom) where the block appears

➤ The data that should be displayed in the block

➤ The source of the block or block data

➤ The condition(s) that need to be met in order for the block to appear

Table 10-7 is an excerpt from their block development inventory worksheet. The actual worksheet is quite long, given the number of site sections, subsections, and content types planned for the site. The excerpt demonstrates the strategy they used. By organizing the blocks into a worksheet, Gary and Claire can:

➤ Divide and conquer, creating and configuring blocks at the same time

➤ Avoid duplicating blocks

➤ Complete the development of a block in one step (no need to go back and modify the block configuration each time the block appears on another page)

TABLE 10-7: Block Development Inventory Worksheet Excerpt

BLOCK	PAGE — LOCATION	DATA	SOURCE	CONDITIONS
Banner image	Home — Center	Rotating slideshow with text and images that highlight the purpose of the site	Images stored on the site	Path: Home page
Recent Training	Home — Center Training — Center	Lesson title, post date, teaser, link to Training section	DB query	Path: Home page Path: /training

continues

TABLE 10-7 *(continued)*

BLOCK	PAGE — LOCATION	DATA	SOURCE	CONDITIONS
What the Community Is Saying	Home — Center	Discussion or Tip title, post date, teaser, user image, link to Community section	DB query	Path: Home page
Merchant highlight	Home — Bottom	Merchant title, merchant image, teaser, link to merchant page	DB query	Path: Home page
Instructor of the Day	Home — Bottom	First name, last name, bio teaser, link to user page	DB query	Path: Home page
Club/Team highlight	Home — Bottom	Club title, teaser, link to club page	DB query	Path: Home page

Become a Member	Home — Right
	
	Section pages — Right
	
	Subsection pages — Right
		Text message, link to login, link to create an account	Manual	Path: Home page
				Path: `/training`
				Path: `/training/`
				`subsection-`
				`title`

Username Account Navigation Block	All pages	Links to tasks user can perform	Core navigation menu	User role: Authenticated users
Local Weather	Home — Right	Block with weather data: temperature, forecast, location, image of weather	Module	Path: Home page
Upcoming Events	Home — Right	Event title, event date, link to Events section	DB query	Path: Home page
Cycling News	Home — Right	Feed title, link to Cycling News section	DB query	Path: Home page

Banner image	Training — Center
	Training subsections — Center
		Image for training page	Image stored on the site	Path: `/training`
				Path: `/training/`
				`subsection-`
				`title`

BLOCK	PAGE — LOCATION	DATA	SOURCE	CONDITIONS
Upcoming Workshops	Training — Center	Event title for workshops, event date, teaser, event image, link to Workshop subsection	DB query	Path: `/training`
Lessons on:	Training — Right Training subsections — Right	List of terms from Activity vocabulary linked to subsection pages	DB query	Path: `/training` Path: `/training/subsection-title`
Recent Lessons	Training subsections — Right	Lesson title, pager	DB query	Path: `/training/subsection-title`
Upcoming Workshops	Training subsections — Right	Event title for workshops, workshop date link to Workshop subsection	DB query	Path: `/training/subsection-title`
Quick Guide Lessons	Quick Guide content page — Right	Lesson title for Quick Guides, pager	DB query	Path: `/training/subsection-title/lesson-title`
Definition	Lesson pages — Right	Fact title, teaser, link to fact pop-up, pager	DB query	If the lesson has a referenced fact

THE MODULE RECIPE

The next step for Gary and Claire is to identify the modules they need to build the content, configure site-communication strategies, manage users, create blocks, monitor performance, and help ensure security. They visit Drupal.org and see that more than 9,000 contributed modules are in various stages of development, supporting different versions of Drupal. They see a post on Drupal.org (`http://drupal.org/node/895314`) listing more than 60 Drupal 6 contributed modules that have been integrated into Drupal 7. They wonder:

➤ Which version of Drupal should we use — Drupal 6 or Drupal 7?

➤ How are we expected to know which modules we need?

TOP DRUPAL MODULES

Drupal.org provides a list of modules with their usage statistics. You can find this list at `http://drupal.org/project/usage`. For a quick introduction to 50 modules, check out Got Drupal's top Drupal modules video at `http://gotdrupal .com/videos/top-drupal-modules`. Although this video looks at modules based on the usage statistics from April 2010, the information is still valuable.

Gary and Claire perform a mini–cost-benefit analysis. They estimate the time and effort they would need to expend to:

➤ Review and learn the core functionality for Drupal 6 and 7 so that they could compare the two versions

➤ Research and identify the contributed modules they would need to extend Drupal's core to support their requirements

They compare their cost to the cost of hiring a Drupal consultant to advise them. They can only afford a few hours of the consultant's time, but because the cost associated with their time is greater than the cost of the consultant, they determine it would be money well spent.

Based on the analysis Gary and Claire had already performed and a three-hour session with the consultant, Gary and Claire have the following:

➤ A list of core modules in Drupal 6 and Drupal 7

➤ A list of core and contributed modules they would need to meet their requirements

The consultant advised that the modules identified might not be their only option. The following sections describe the results from the consultation.

Comparing Drupal Core Modules

The consultant hired explained that out-of-the-box Drupal 7 has more functionality than Drupal 6 and is primed to be more flexible than Drupal 6. It is likely the better choice, assuming Gary and Claire's site does not have any unique needs that only a Drupal 6 contributed module could meet.

Table 10-8 lists the core modules in Drupal 6 and 7. The description comes directly from the Drupal installation. The table reveals several new modules in Drupal 7 but not the 60+ modules referenced on Drupal.org (`http://drupal.org/node/895314`). Not all features and functionality are included in modules that you turn on and off. Although the table shows many modules as optional, many are recommended so that you can maximize your options. Drupal will install with several of the optional modules enabled.

Although you can gain insights into the functionality of Drupal by reviewing the list of core modules in Table 10-8, it does not tell you everything you need to know. No substitute exists for seeing Drupal in action. If you do not have the resources to install Drupal and work with it, consider watching some of the many free online video tutorials. Just watching can help you understand how Drupal works and can help you plan your development.

DRUPAL TUTORIALS

In addition to Drupal.org's tutorial list at `http://drupal.org/documentation/customization/tutorials`, you can find some great video tutorials online. The following list is a sampling of the sites that provide online Drupal video tutorials you can watch for free or for a small fee:

➤ Brian Stevenson.com — `www.brianstevenson.com/drupal/screencasts`

➤ Build a Module — `http://buildamodule.com`

➤ Drupal Dojo — `http://drupaldojo.com`

➤ Drupal Therapy — `www.drupaltherapy.com/screencasts`

➤ Got Drupal — `http://gotdrupal.com`

➤ Learn By The Drop — `http://learnbythedrop.com/archives`

➤ Level Ten Design — `www.leveltendesign.com/tutorial/course/getting-started-drupal-7`

➤ Lullabot — `http://lullabot.com`

➤ Lynda.com — `http://lynda.com`

➤ Mustardseed — `http://mustardseedmedia.com/podcast`

➤ Siteground — `www.siteground.com/tutorials/drupal-tutorial`

➤ Video Tutorial Zone — `www.videotutorialzone.com`

➤ YouTube — `www.youtube.com`

TABLE 10-8: Comparing Drupal 6 and Drupal 7

MODULE NAME	DESCRIPTION	DRUPAL 6	DRUPAL 7
Aggregator	Aggregates syndicated content (RSS, RDF, and Atom feeds)	Optional	Optional
Block	Controls the boxes that are displayed around the main content	Required	Optional
Blog	Enables keeping easily and regularly updated user web pages or blogs	Optional	Optional
Blog API	Allows users to post content using applications that support XML RPC blog APIs	Optional	NA
Book	Allows users to structure site pages in a hierarchy or outline	Optional	Optional

continues

TABLE 10-8 *(continued)*

MODULE NAME	DESCRIPTION	DRUPAL 6	DRUPAL 7
Color	Allows the user to change the color scheme of certain themes	Optional	Optional
Comment	Allows users to comment on and discuss published content	Optional	Optional
Contact	Enables the use of both personal and site-wide contact forms	Optional	Optional
Content translation	Allows content to be translated into different languages	Optional	Optional
Contextual links	Provides contextual links to perform actions related to elements on a page	NA	Optional
Dashboard	Provides a dashboard page in the administrative interface for organizing administrative tasks and tracking information within your site	NA	Optional
Database logging	Logs and records system events to the database	Optional	Optional
Field	Field API to add fields to entities like nodes and users	NA	Required
Field SQL storage	Stores field data in a SQL database	NA	Required
Field UI	User interface for the Field API	NA	Optional
File	Defines a file field type	NA	Optional
Filter	Handles the filtering of content in preparation for display	Required	Required
Forum	Enables threaded discussions about general topics	Optional	Optional
Help	Manages the display of online help	Optional	Optional
Image	Provides image-manipulation tools	NA	Optional
List	Defines list field types. Use with Options to create selection lists	NA	Optional
Locale	Adds language-handling functionality and enables the translation of the user interface to languages other than English	Optional	Optional
Menu	Allows administrators to customize the site navigation menu	Optional	Optional
Number	Defines numeric field types	NA	Optional

MODULE NAME	DESCRIPTION	DRUPAL 6	DRUPAL 7
Node	Allows content to be submitted to the site and displayed on pages	Required	Required
OpenID	Allows users to log in to your site using OpenID	Optional	Optional
Options	Defines selection, check box, and radio button widgets for text and numeric fields	NA	Optional
Overlay	Displays the Drupal administration interface in an overlay	NA	Optional
Path	Allows users to rename URLs	Optional	Optional
PHP filter	Allows embedded PHP code/snippets to be evaluated	Optional	Optional
Ping	Alerts other sites when your site has been updated	Optional	NA
Poll	Allows your site to capture votes on different topics in the form of multiple-choice questions	Optional	Optional
RDF	Enriches your content with metadata to let other applications (e.g., search engines, aggregators) better understand its relationships and attributes	NA	Optional
Profile	Supports configurable user profiles	Optional	NA
Search	Enables site-wide keyword searching	Optional	Optional
Shortcut	Allows users to manage customizable lists of shortcut links	NA	Optional
Statistics	Logs access statistics for your site	Optional	Optional
Syslog	Logs and records system events to syslog	Optional	Optional
System	Handles general site configuration for administrators	Required	Required
Taxonomy	Enables the categorization of content	Optional	Optional
Testing	Provides a framework for unit and functional testing	NA	Optional
Text	Defines simple text field types	NA	Required
Toolbar	Provides a toolbar that shows the top-level administration menu items and links from other modules	NA	Optional
Throttle	Handles the auto-throttling mechanism, to control site congestion	Optional	NA
Tracker	Enables tracking of recent posts for users	Optional	Optional

continues

TABLE 10-8 *(continued)*

MODULE NAME	DESCRIPTION	DRUPAL 6	DRUPAL 7
Trigger	Enables actions to be fired on certain system events, such as when new content is created	Optional	Optional
Update manager	Checks for available updates and can securely install or update modules and themes via a web interface	NA	Optional
Update status	Checks the status of available updates for Drupal and your installed modules and themes	Optional	NA
Upload	Allows users to upload and attach files to content	Optional	NA
User	Manages the user registration and login system	Required	Required

Site Modules

The consultant also provided Gary and Claire with a list of modules that could meet the requirements and design documented (see Chapter 9, "An Example Plan"). Because Gary and Claire weren't sure whether they could go with Drupal 7, they asked for a module recipe for both Drupal 6 and Drupal 7.

The module suggestions in the following tables are grouped into the following categories:

➤ **Content** — Modules that create the content requirements

➤ **Communication** — Modules that support the communication requirements

➤ **User** — Modules that provide user features called out in the requirements

➤ **Blocks** — Modules that create the blocks defined in the requirements

➤ **Performance and security** — Modules that support popularity and deter spam abuse

The module lists include both core and contributed modules. The status reflected in the following tables is as of April 2011. As of April 2011, some modules have not reached a recommended status on Drupal.org. The reasons vary from module to module. The few modules listed in the following tables that are not flagged as recommended are included because:

➤ The modules are close to completion and worth considering.

➤ No stronger alternative modules are ready to go.

➤ There is a temporary workaround.

A review of a module's project page will reveal the current status of a module. If a module is not ready now, it might be by the time Gary and Claire are ready to download and enable it.

The key used to signify the status of the module is as follows:

➤ **Available** — A recommended version of the module is available for that version of Drupal. The module might be an alpha, beta, or release candidate but is still being flagged as recommended by the module developer.

➤ **Required** — The module is part of the core and is required for Drupal to work.

➤ **Optional** — The module is part of the core and is available for use, but it is not required by the core. It could be required by another module.

➤ **NA** — The module is not required by that version of Drupal, or a different module is required to support that feature in that version of Drupal.

➤ **Dev version** — The module is available for download but is a development release. Development releases are not recommended for production sites.

➤ **In progress** — Discussions in the issue queue indicate work is being performed to develop the module for that version of Drupal.

➤ **Alpha version, not recommended yet** — An alpha version of the module exists but is flagged as "other releases" (refer to Figure 6-3, for example), which means the alpha version is not recommended yet.

Content

Table 10-9 lists, in alphabetical order, modules for meeting the site content and user profile content requirements. The modules provide many services. Some support content/data collection and storage; some support the display of content; and some are required to make Drupal work. For instance:

➤ **Comment** — The Comment module provides a way for users to post content and communicate with others.

➤ **Path and Pathauto** — These modules create SEO-friendly URLs, as well as provide a path condition used to manage block display.

➤ **Automatic Nodetitles** — This module helps you create a blank node and enables you to then use the blank node to create a page whose display is made up of blocks.

Gary and Claire were surprised when they reviewed the list of modules used to support the development of the site content. There seemed to be so many. The consultant reminded them that the nature of Drupal is modular. The modularity provides Drupal developers with the power to mix and match modules to create many different development solutions.

TABLE 10-9: Modules for Site Content

MODULE NAME	DESCRIPTION	SITE REQUIREMENT	DRUPAL 6	DRUPAL 7
Aggregator	Aggregates syndicated content (RSS, RDF, and Atom feeds).	Provide cycling newsfeeds.	Available	Available
Automatic Nodetitles	Allows hiding of the content title field.	Create landing pages with no-content node and hide the title.	Available	Available
Book	Used to connect the pages and create sequenced content.	Link multiple lesson pages into a short tutorial.	Available	Available
Calendar	Views plug-in to display views containing dates as Calendars.	Used in the events section landing page to show a calendar of events.	Available	Alpha version, not yet recommended
CCK	Content Construction Kit to add custom fields to content types.	Allow the addition of fields to lessons, events, and so on in a Drupal 6 site.	Available	NA
Comment	Allows users to comment on and discuss published content.	Provide commenting on discussions, tips, and events.	Available	Available
Content profile	Allows a content type to be associated with the user.	Requirement for a user profile node with content fields in Drupal 6.	Available	NA
Date	Defines a field to capture dates and times.	Add a date field to the event content type.	Available	Available
Date API	Comes with Date module.	Used by Calendar.	Available	Available
Email Field	Defines a field specifically for email addresses.	Add a field formatted for emails in merchant and club content types.	Available	Available
Entity	Extends the Entity API of Drupal's core.	Required by the Organic groups module.	NA	Available
Field	Adds custom fields to content types.	Allow the addition of fields to lessons, events, and so on in a Drupal 7 site.	NA	Required

MODULE NAME	DESCRIPTION	SITE REQUIREMENT	DRUPAL 6	DRUPAL 7
Field SQL storage	Stores field data in a SQL database.	Allow the addition of fields to lessons, events, and so on in a Drupal 7 site.	NA	Required
Field UI	Provides a user interface for the Field API.	Allow the addition of fields to lessons, events, and so on in a Drupal 7 site.	NA	Available
File	Defines a file field used to attach files to a node.	Used to upload and attach files to lessons, events, merchants, and clubs in Drupal 7.	NA	Required
FileField	Defines a file field used to attach files to a node Requires CCK.	Used to upload and attach files to lessons, events, merchants, and clubs in Drupal 6.	Available	NA
Image	Provides image-manipulation tools.	Used to upload and attach files to lessons, events, merchants, and clubs in Drupal 7.	NA	Available
ImageAPI	Provides an API used by the Drupal 6 ImageCache and ImageField modules. Comes with a choice of image toolkits, one of which needs to be enabled.	Used to support the modules that upload and resize images. Drupal 7 version extends what is included in Drupal's core.	Available	Dev version
ImageCache	Allows you to set up presets for image processing.	Used to resize images uploaded to merchants, clubs, and events, and image sizes in views.	Available	NA
ImageField	Defines a file field used to attach image files to a node. Requires CCK and FileField.	Used to upload and attach image files to lessons, discussions, tips, events, merchants, and clubs in Drupal 6.	Available	NA

continues

TABLE 10-9 *(continued)*

MODULE NAME	DESCRIPTION	SITE REQUIREMENT	DRUPAL 6	DRUPAL 7
Insert	Provides a utility that allows users to insert HTML references to images and files into the node body.	Used by the lesson, discussion, and tip content types for embedding images into the body of the text.	Available	Available
jQuery UI	Required by Calendar module.	Used by Calendar.	Available	NA
Link	Defines a field for link. Includes a title for the link and the option to open a new window.	Add link fields for video, resource, and merchant links.	Available	Available
Location	Provides several modules including a location field.	Used to show an event location and user's location.	Available	Dev version
Metatags	Allows you to add meta tags to Drupal pages in Drupal 7.	Add meta tags to lessons.	NA	In progress
Node	Allows content to be submitted to the site and displayed on pages.	Required to create and display all the site's content nodes.	Required	Required
NodeReference	Defines a field that allows you to connect one node to one or more other nodes. Comes with CCK.	Used to connect a lesson to a fact and lesson to lesson author user profile in Drupal 6.	Available	NA
Nodewords	Allows you to add meta tags to Drupal pages in Drupal 6.	Add meta tags to lessons.	Available	NA
Office Hours	Defines an "office hours" or "opening hours" field.	Used for merchant hours of operations field.	Available	Dev version
Option Widgets	Defines selection, check box, and radio button widgets for text and numeric fields.	Needed in Drupal 6 so you can select the image field option.	Available	NA

MODULE NAME	DESCRIPTION	SITE REQUIREMENT	DRUPAL 6	DRUPAL 7
Organic groups	Enables users to create and manage groups. Drupal 6 and Drupal 7 versions come with different modules that need to be enabled.	Used for community groups where discussions and tips are posted.	Available	Available
Path	Allows users to rename URLs.	Required by Pathauto.	Optional	Required
Pathauto	Automatically generates path aliases for various kinds of content.	Used to support SEO requirement to automatically generate friendly URLs.	Available	Available
References	Defines a field that allows you to connect one node to one or more other nodes.	Used to connect a lesson to a fact and lesson to lesson-author user in Drupal 7.	NA	Dev version
Taxonomy	Enables you to categorize content.	Each content type has one or more category requirements.	Available	Available
Text	Defines simple text field types. Comes with CCK.	Used to add text fields to content types and user profiles in Drupal 6.	Available	NA
Text	Defines simple text field types.	Used to add text fields to entities (nodes, user, terms, comment) in Drupal 7.	NA	Required
Trigger	Enables actions to be fired on certain system events, such as when new content is created.	Coupled with an action, this module would be used to send an email notice when a lesson is saved and needs to be published. An alternative is to use the Rules module.	Available	Available
Wysiwyg	Allows you add client-side editors to content fields. Requires the installation of an editor.	Provides user-friendly editing for text.	Available	Available

Communication

Table 10-10 lists the modules that support different types of communication on the site.

TABLE 10-10: Modules for Site Communication

MODULE NAME	DESCRIPTION	SITE REQUIREMENT	DRUPAL 6	DRUPAL 7
Poll	Allows your site to capture votes on different topics in the form of multiple-choice questions.	Used to meet the single-question survey requirement.	Available	Available
Webform	Adds a web form node to your Drupal site, which allows you to create web forms used to collect information from site visitors, including survey information.	Used to create the brochure, group, and lesson-request forms. Can also be used to create multi-question surveys.	Available	Available
Contact	Enables the use of both personal and site-wide contact forms.	Used to meet the site and user email contact requirement.	Available	Available
Notifications	Provides email notifications for various site events.	Used for sending emails and managing subscriptions. Needed for Organic Groups 6.	Available	Alpha version, not yet recommended
Messaging	The base module for the Messaging Framework used by the Notifications module.	Used in conjunction with Notifications to send template emails.	Available	Alpha version, not yet recommended
Token	Provides token-handling services for other modules.	Used by Notifications, Pathauto, and other modules.	Available	Available
Rules	Defines conditionally executed actions based on occurring events.	Used in combination with Organic Groups 7; Rules can be used to send email notices when content is posted to a group.	Available	Available

User

Table 10-11 lists the modules that support user-related features defined in the requirements.

TABLE 10-11: Modules for User-related Features

MODULE NAME	DESCRIPTION	SITE REQUIREMENT	DRUPAL 6	DRUPAL 7
Avatar Selection	Allows the user to pick an avatar image from a list already loaded by an administrative user.	User profile requirement for an avatar.	Available	In progress
Flag	Provides any number of flags for nodes, comments, or users.	The site page bookmark and flag-as-inappropriate requirements.	Available	Alpha version, not yet recommended
Tracker	Enables you to track recent posts by users.	View a list of users' posts to the site.	Available	Available
User Relationships	Enables you to create relationship types.	Friend connections requirement. Shows connections on user account.	Available	Available

Blocks

Table 10-12 provides a list of modules that support the development of site blocks defined in the design plan.

TABLE 10-12: Modules for Blocks

MODULE NAME	DESCRIPTION	SITE REQUIREMENT	DRUPAL 6	DRUPAL 7
Block	Controls the boxes that are displayed around the main content.	Build pages that show blocks of content and other features.	Required	Optional
Search	Enables site-wide keyword searching.	Provide a search option on each page.	Available	Available
Custom Search	Alters the default search box and results page.	Requirement under consideration.	Available	Available
Views	Tool for querying the database and displaying the results.	Use to create dynamically generated blocks and pages.	Available	Available
Weather	Displays current weather conditions from anywhere in the world.	Include a current weather block on the home page	Available	Available

Performance and Security

Table 10-13 provides a list of modules that support spam blocking and site analytics requirements. Note that two modules, Mollom and Captcha, help deter spam from being posted in site forms. The Mollom module requires you to sign up for the Mollom service (free and fee-based options), but the Captcha module does not. Gary and Claire will review each option and choose one.

TABLE 10-13: Modules for Performance and Security

MODULE NAME	DESCRIPTION	SITE REQUIREMENT	DRUPAL 6	DRUPAL 7
Mollom	An "intelligent" content-moderation web service that provides challenges similar to Captcha.	Forms will require a challenge and valid response before they can be submitted.	Available	Available
Captcha	Challenge-response test for web forms to determine whether the user is human.	Forms will require a challenge and valid response before they can be submitted.	Available	Alpha version, not yet recommended
Google Analytics	Allows you to integrate your site with the Google Analytics service.	To be used to track the site's activity.	Available	Available

Drupal Distribution

Gary and Claire discuss the option of using a Drupal distribution to kick-start their development process. They decide that because this is their first Drupal project and one of their personal goals is to learn, they will build their site from the ground up, starting with the default Drupal installation profile found at `http://drupal.org/project/drupal`.

Gary and Claire are leaning toward Drupal 7 but will need to assess their options for the bookmark and flag-as-inappropriate features since the Flag module does not have a recommended release at this time. Their options include:

➤ Removing the features from their requirements

➤ Trying what is available now and providing feedback to the module developer if something isn't working

➤ Waiting until the module has a recommended release before enabling those features

➤ Providing compensation to the module developer or another developer in hopes the module-development effort can be accelerated.

THE DEVELOPMENT SEQUENCE

Gary and Claire have never built a Drupal site, so they ask their consultant for a few tips to help them work efficiently. Their consultant explains that there is no single way to sequence development tasks but offers the following analogy to help them think about their overall strategy.

Imagine you need to bake three different types of cookies for a local bake sale. You could use the following process:

1. Go to the cupboards and pull out all the kitchen "tools" (pans, bowls, mixer, utensils, and so on) and ingredients needed to bake all three types of cookies, knowing that some of the tools and ingredients are the same for each type of cookie, and some are not.

2. Premeasure the ingredients for all three types of cookies and maybe even premix a few.

3. Assemble the ingredients for each cookie and dish out the cookie dough for each cookie while the oven preheats.

4. Bake all the cookies, assuming each cookie baked at the same temperature (and you had a big oven).

Another option would be to focus on one type of cookie at a time, repeating the baking process for each type of cookie. You would reuse the same tools and ingredients you already had on the counter, but you would add more tools and ingredients, as necessary.

With regard to developing your site, the process would be similar, using the following process:

1. Install Drupal.

2. Prepare all the modules, features, and components you will need to build all the pages on the site.

3. Create the pages of the site, using all the modules, features, and components you have configured.

Or you can install Drupal and prepare only those modules, features, and components you need for the first section of your site. Then move on to the next section, reusing what you have already created while adding additional modules, features, and components. Repeat the process until the site is complete.

Chapter 6, "Planning Development," covers three factors that influence your development sequencing: your build recipe, development method, and the availability of your development team members. Chapter 2, "Managing Open Source Projects," provides a brief introduction to development methodologies.

THE ENVIRONMENTS

Gary and Claire discuss the process they want to use to build their site. They want to work together, at the same time, on the same installation of the site. This means a site installed on their individual computers is not going to work for them; they need a hosting service.

They also decide to keep the development environment simple but secure. Neither Gary nor Claire is a software developer, so they don't have the skills to work in the various developer-oriented applications. For instance, they need to access and manage their web server using a graphical user interface (GUI) control panel, not a command-line interface.

Also, they want to be able to run multiple versions of the site in the same hosting environment (same server): development, training, and production (live). Therefore, the hosting service needs to be able to host multiple instances of the site under different domains.

In addition to allowing multiple sites, the hosting service needs to allow Gary and Claire to:

➤ Support multiple sites with multiple databases

➤ Provide domains and subdomains quickly and at a reasonable price

➤ Select the version of PHP and MySQL they want to use and provide support installing it

➤ Increase the PHP memory allocation above the default provided with the hosting plan, as needed

➤ Provide multiple user logins for the same account

➤ Provide Secure FTP access

➤ Provide technical support 24/7

➤ Maintain a regular backup service

After considering their list of environment requirements, Gary and Claire choose a virtual private server (VPS) plan — one whose processing capabilities can be expanded, if necessary.

THE IMPLEMENTATION

Site implementation is hard for Gary and Claire to start thinking about, given that they haven't yet built the site. Although they anticipate needing to update their implementation plan as they get closer to site launch, imagining the complete site and talking through what they need to do to implement the site helps them test their site plan and initiate some tasks that should not wait until the site is developed. The following sections describe their initial implementation notes.

 Chapter 7, "Coordinating Implementation," provides additional insights into training and marketing, as well as change management.

Expert Acquisition

From the start, Gary and Claire knew that they not only wanted to help people find learning resources, but they also wanted to provide their own learning resources. Because they aren't yet cycling experts, they knew they needed to partner with cycling experts to develop and sustain their site's content.

Their plan was to reach out to a local cycling coach with racing experience (in other words, a subject matter expert) to join their site team. They knew they needed to do this early in the development process so that the coach could start planning content development. The assumption was that Gary and Claire would work on developing the site while the content administrator and subject matter expert would start to:

➤ Identify lesson topics

➤ Draft lesson content

➤ Locate additional subject matter experts to write lessons

➤ Identify existing lessons they could let others know about

Gary and Claire suspected that if they waited to find their content administrator until after they developed the site, content for the site would not be ready when they wanted to launch. They did an Internet search and asked various cyclists whether they could recommend a coach. They got a couple of names and started the interview and screening process. They found the third partner, Rhys, in their venture.

Training Plan

Gary and Claire quickly realize that they are not ready to create training materials at this stage of the implementation planning process because the site isn't ready. However, they do have enough information to plan what training is needed. Creating a plan will enable their new content partner, Rhys, to help create the learning experiences when the site is further along. Until that time, they draft the following:

➤ A list of which personas will need site training

➤ A list of the tasks for which the personas will need training

➤ A strategy for delivering the training

Training Need

Gary and Claire review the personas associated with the site. The following personas could require training on how to use the site:

➤   Content administrator

➤   Subject matter experts

➤   Merchants and club leads

➤   Site members

Their primary focus is on the content administrator and the subject matter experts. Instruction developed for these roles could be reused in full or in part to create instruction for the other roles.

Training Objectives

The next step is to make a list of tasks each persona needs to be able to perform on the site. Most, if not all, of what they need was identified while they collected process and task requirements. However, a recap was a good test to see if they missed anything.

From this list, Gary and Claire can develop a series of training lessons. Not all tasks need documented training support. The site team can decide which tasks to document as they get closer to the end of the development process. The persona task lists are as follows:

The content administrator needs to be able to:

➤   Create, edit, publish, unpublish, delete, and format lessons, facts, merchant pages, club pages, and groups

➤   Locate and use the list of unpublished pages to review and publish appropriately

➤   Sequence and categorize lessons

➤   Troubleshoot basic HTML issues that might arise when formatting content with the HTML editor

➤   Help site members administer their content subscriptions

➤   Train subject matter experts and site members to perform their tasks

➤   Perform the tasks associated with being a site member

Subject matter experts need to be able to:

➤   Create and edit their unpublished lessons and facts

➤   Sequence and categorize lessons

➤   Troubleshoot basic HTML issues that might arise when formatting content with the HTML editor

➤   Help other subject matter experts post their lessons and facts

➤   Perform the tasks associated with being a site member

Merchants and club leads need to be able to:

> Edit their merchant or club pages

> Perform the tasks associated with being a site member

Site members need to be able to:

> Create a user account and profile

> Manage their user accounts and profile features

> Log in and join groups of interest

> Post questions, provide tips, and place events on a calendar

> Comment on discussions, tips, and events

> Connect with other members of the site

Training Strategy

After several discussions to review the audiences and topics to be trained, the site team comes up with two strategies:

> Live training

> Online videos

Live Training

Gary and Claire recognize that live training (in person or via webinar sessions) for their content administrator and key subject matter experts helps ensure important members of the site team are ready to execute their tasks. The one-hour sessions can be recorded so that they can be viewed multiple times.

Webinars provide a way to demonstrate the tasks as well as discuss various concepts, workflows, and site policies that need to be conveyed to users filling key roles on the site.

Online Videos

Gary and Claire spend some time watching existing Drupal training videos and like the short, to-the-point bits of instruction that they can access any time they want. They decide to do something similar to meet their site training needs.

They consider using the Organic Groups module to create a private group where they can post training videos via the tip content type. However, as they think about the process the various personas would use to access the group, they see a small flaw in their plan.

They realize some training videos in the private group should not be available to all roles. For instance, some videos for the content administrator tasks would not need to be accessed by subject matter experts, but others would. Gary and Claire decide to create a private group for each team role (content administrator, subject matter experts, and merchant/club leads). When they post a video that applies to more than one role, they can share that post across the applicable role groups.

This seems to be a reasonable approach, with the exception of the site members and visitors. Video tips must be available quickly and openly. Gary and Claire decide to house site member and visitor videos in a group that is viewable by the public (no group membership required).

Their next consideration is the content type. Can they post the video in a content type that is not designed to hold video? Their consultant reminds them that, as site administrators, they can enable full HTML access to the tip nodes they are creating and then embed the link to the video directly in the tip narrative. Using their existing strategy of storing their video on an external service, the embed strategy appears to be a good solution.

Marketing Plan

In addition to the already-planned SEO strategies (using `meta` tags and SEO-friendly URLs), Gary and Claire will also try a couple of social networking strategies, as well as a couple of traditional marketing strategies.

 Chapter 7 provides additional insights into marketing.

Social Networking Strategies

Gary and Claire want their site to be a resource that people from all over the country, and maybe overseas, would like to visit. So, what better way to reach beyond their back door than via online social networking?

They are going to start by creating the following:

➤ A Twitter account for the site

➤ A Facebook fan page

They plan to make announcements using practices acceptable to each social networking resource. They will also share links to their resources so that others can benefit from what they are doing.

They are going to participate in discussions on other sites, offering information appropriately. They will search cycling-oriented news sites for articles, and then donate blogs to those sites in the hope that their contributions will help others find their site.

Traditional Strategies

Although Gary and Claire are not focused on one location, they have a few ideas to help initiate some interest in their site. They plan to:

➤ Hand out flyers at local cycling events and bike shops

➤ Print T-shirts with their site's URL and logo, and wear them at local cycling events

➤ Print business cards with the site information so that they have a quick resource to hand to anyone who might be interested in learning more

THE SUSTAINMENT

Maintenance and site management are next on Gary and Claire's list of tasks to plan. They wonder whether their implementation planning doesn't already reflect the processes and tasks they need to perform after the site launches.

Their plan to add Rhys, the content administrator who is also subject matter expert (coaching and racing), addresses their need to keep fresh content on their site post-launch. They have a marketing plan that has repeatable tasks that carry forward post-launch. They even have a plan to provide training opportunities after the site is launched. What more do they need to do?

 Chapter 8, "Sustaining the Site," provides a list of maintenance and site management tasks performed post-launch.

Maintenance Tasks

Referencing the list of maintenance tasks in Chapter 8 of this book, Gary and Claire are able to create a schedule and a division of labor for monitoring their site. They agree to perform the following tasks:

➤ **Monitor logs** — Gary agrees to log in to the site and check the logs and update notices every other day.

➤ **Monitor performance** — Claire agrees to check Google Analytics every other day.

➤ **Create backups** — The hosting provider will make routine backups, but Gary agrees to back up the database weekly, to start with. They will discuss backup processes later, as the site grows.

➤ **Provide feedback** — Both Gary and Claire will be copied on the contact-form submissions, so they agree to check with each other before responding.

➤ **Monitor security updates** — Gary and Claire agree to monitor the updates for security issues and to create an update plan if updates are needed. They will not update the site automatically each time an update is released.

Site Management Tasks

Gary and Claire review the list of potential content and user management tasks listed in Chapter 8 and draft the following plans.

Content Management

In addition to the plans they have already made regarding new content development, Gary, Claire, and Rhys agree on how to address the following content management tasks:

➤ **Perform content updates** — Every six months, they will work with their subject matter experts and review the learning materials to ensure that they still reflect accurate practices in the cycling community.

➤ **Assess links in content** — Rhys agrees to make this task part of content maintenance and to use a free online broken links checker or to install the Link check module. Gary will add this module to the list.

➤ **Monitor comments** — Gary, Claire, and Rhys will subscribe to receive comments posted on all content types that have comments. They will also monitor reports from site visitors who flag content as offensive.

➤ **Monitor search engine recognition** — Rhys will periodically check search engine ranking for key topics covered in the site.

LINK CHECKER

The Link checker module extracts links from your content periodically and checks if they are still active. As of May 2011, there was a version for Drupal 6 and a -dev version for Drupal 7.

User Management

Several user-related tasks will need ongoing support after the site is launched. In addition to managing the general support requests submitted via the contact form, the content administrator (Rhys) will manage the following content requests:

➤ Request a group

➤ Request a brochure

➤ Request a lesson

The site team agrees to process each request within 24 hours of receiving the request, but they need a way to store all the requests and responses to requests in one place.

They discuss using a ticket-tracking system, but that seems like overkill right now. They decide to set up a shared email account that Gary, Claire, and Rhys can monitor. Replies to the emails will be stored in the same account for future reference. This seems reasonable, given that the group, brochure, and lesson requests are forwarded via email and stored in the site for future reference. The requests for support that come from the contact form are emailed as well, so this shared account will also get a copy of the contact form requests.

To limit duplicate support from being provided, they divide types of requests among themselves as follows:

➤ Rhys will handle content-related requests.

➤ Gary will handle technical issues (errors, problems).

➤ Claire will manage all other inquiries.

The site team agrees to revisit this process as the site becomes more popular. For example, they recognize they might want a ticket-tracking application after all.

SUMMARY

This chapter wraps up the book by describing several sample strategies for planning and organizing the site-development and site-sustainment processes.

Here are a few things to remember:

➤ Understand the clients (even if the client is you). Try to put yourself in their shoes. What they want and what they can afford in the long run might be two different solutions.

➤ Use the organizational worksheets provided by Gary and Claire or invent your own.

➤ Organize your development tasks, especially if you are working on a team. Duplication is wasted effort.

➤ Take a minute or two to think about your site-implementation and-sustainment plans. You could find that you missed a requirement.

INDEX

N